ALSO BY EDWARD HUMES

Buried Secrets
Murderer with a Badge
Mississippi Mud

EDWARD HUMES

no matter
how loud
I shout

A YEAR IN THE LIFE OF JUVENILE COURT

SIMON & SCHUSTER PAPERBACKS
New York London Toronto Sydney New Delhi

Simon & Schuster Paperbacks
A Division of Simon & Schuster, Inc.
1230 Avenue of the Americas
New York, NY 10020

This Simon & Schuster trade paperback edition March 2015

SIMON & SCHUSTER PAPERBACKS and colophon
are registered trademarks of Simon & Schuster, Inc.

For information about special discounts for bulk purchases,
please contact Simon & Schuster Special Sales at 1-866-506-1949
or business@simonandschuster.com.

The Simon & Schuster Speakers Bureau can bring authors to your live event.
For more information or to book an event, contact the Simon & Schuster
Speakers Bureau at 1-866-248-3049 or visit our website at www.simonspeakers.com.

Interior design by Jeanette Olender

Manufactured in the United States of America

10 9 8 7 6 5 4 3 2 1

Library of Congress Cataloging-in-Publication Data is available.

ISBN 978-1-5011-0293-6
ISBN 978-1-4767-9683-3 (ebook)

To Gabrielle and Donna

CONTENTS

FOREWORD

So little has changed.

Year after year, studies are unveiled with great fanfare and then shelved. Commissions are convened and then ignored, proposed reforms celebrated and then discarded. Today's juvenile justice system remains remarkably unchanged from the one I encountered when I first started *No Matter How Loud I Shout*. Juvenile court is still the unwanted stepchild of the justice system, still understaffed and underfunded, still struggling between the opposing poles of rehabilitation and punishment, still deeply misunderstood by public and policymakers alike. For better or worse, the stories of the boys and girls in these pages continue to resonate with relevance and timeliness. Their tragedies, crimes, losses, and fitful journeys toward redemption are mirrored all too faithfully by the experiences of the young people who inhabit today's juvenile court. So little has changed.

This is not as hopeless as it may sound. Even as the shortcomings of the system remain the same, so, too, do the occasional bits of magic that inhabit the halls of juvenile court: the child rescued, the family restored, the small victories that come just often enough to keep the judges, lawyers, and social workers from being crushed by despair, to allow them to return to fight another day.

The environment in which juvenile court operates, however, *has* changed. When I began this book, the nation's leading (or, at least, the nation's loudest) experts on crime statistics and juvenile delinquency were predicting an abrupt rise in violent juvenile crime. The already alarming statistical heights reached in the 1990s would be nothing compared to the following two decades, these experts from leading universities and think tanks predicted, basing their conclusions on the seemingly firm ground of demographics. The population of teens in America was about to explode. So, too, the experts said, would the population of young criminals, including a growing number of violent and remorseless teen offenders they branded the "super predators." Politicians picked up this idea and ran with it, making it a headline, making it a cause. And soon a majority of states had adopted new, more punitive laws that transferred more children to adult court and prison at ever-younger ages. Most of these policies remain in force today, with kids as young as thirteen automatically tried in adult court in some states, and eligible for life sentences without parole. Sixteen was the minimum age when I began this project.

Here's the problem with this course of events: the predictions that drove these "reforms" were wrong. Terribly, irreparably, inexcusably wrong. Juvenile crime has not increased since the mid-nineties. It has declined. The rise of the super predator was a myth. One of the leading experts who issued these warnings and helped popularize the term has admitted that he and his colleagues were wrong, realizing too late that "Demography is not fate."

Still, though the laws became more punitive, sanctioning life sentences for kids too young to shave, the juvenile justice system survived the super predator myth. When juvenile crime dropped, the drumbeat for dismantling juvenile court died away, along with the headlines and the confounded experts. The lower juvenile crime rates also bought time as budgets shrank and programs were cut. The lighter caseloads meant the court could hobble along through the years, with the same terrible flaws and the same unrealized opportunities as ever.

While haunting the halls of Los Angeles Juvenile Court for this project, I came to believe that the society we are, as well as the society we wish to be, is reflected in how we treat our young—including (perhaps especially) the young people in the care of the juvenile justice system, both the children in danger and, yes, the dangerous children. I do not think our efforts over the past twenty years do us much credit.

But don't take my word for it. Listen to Elias and George and Carla and Andre and Ronald and the others portrayed in this book, and decide for yourself. They are children on these pages, though their stories and insights and heartbreaks are often profound. Today, however, twenty years later, they are adults—at least those who are still alive, who survived those new, harsher laws that deemed them adults before their time. And think about this: today, each of them is somebody's neighbor or colleague or employee or cab driver or waitress. Maybe yours.

—Edward Humes
Los Angeles
July 2014

AUTHOR'S NOTE

AUTHOR'S NOTE

This book represents a year of observation of—and, at times, participation in—the juvenile justice system. It is the story of children, families, and professionals who inhabit the juvenile courthouses of Los Angeles, where the courses of young lives are profoundly altered every day, mostly in secret and only occasionally for the better. These are unvarnished accounts. No facts have been changed. There are no composite characters or fictionalized passages. Names of juveniles have been altered in accordance with state law and court order, but in all other respects, what follows is exactly what happened in the courthouses, probation offices, and juvenile halls—and in the lives of those who passed through them.

Two factors made this book possible. A court order by former Los Angeles Juvenile Court Presiding Judge Marcus O. Tucker granted me access to a system otherwise closed to the public. But a foot in the door is only a start; I also relied upon the courage, insight, and generosity of many people who labor within the system and who have come to believe that secrecy is harming, not protecting, their life's work. In particular, I wish to acknowledge and thank Peggy Beckstrand, James Hickey, Thomas Higgins, Paulette Paccione, Todd Rubenstein, Leah Karr, Wendy Derzaph and Kevin Yorn of the Los Angeles County District Attorney's Office; Sharon Stegall and Jane Martin of the Los Angeles County Probation Department; Sister Janet Harris, Catholic chaplain at Central Juvenile Hall; Michael Roussel and Sylvia Wells, delinquency court administrators; Leslie Stearns, Nancy Liebold, and Oksana Bihun of the Los Angeles County Public Defender's Office; attorney Sherry Gold; Judge Roosevelt Dorn, Judge Charles Scarlett, Judge Fumiko Wasserman, Judge John Henning, and Presiding Judge Richard Montes; and Commissioner Jewell Jones and Commissioner Gary Polinsky. Thanks also to David Bayles.

I received an unrivaled education about the inside of the juvenile justice system from Carla and George and the boys of the Unit K/L and M/N writing class: Geri, Elias, Chris, Louis, Juan, Ruben, Gabriel, Joseph, Ivan, Luis, Daniel, and James. Good luck and good lives to all of you.

A NOTE ABOUT NAMES

In accordance with state laws on confidentiality and the court order granting the author access to Juvenile Court, names of most juveniles (and their families) portrayed here have been altered. There are two exceptions: True names have been used for older juveniles convicted in adult court of major crimes such as murder; and for younger children tried and convicted in Juvenile Court for the same sort of violent felonies. In California, proceedings in such cases, whether in adult or juvenile forums, are open to the public, and the youths on trial enjoy no right to confidentiality. In cases in which juveniles were either acquitted of violent offenses, or were retained in Juvenile Court after attempts to transfer them to adult court failed, the author has voluntarily withheld their true names.

Intake

EXCEPT when earthquakes have rendered it unsafe for human habitation—temporarily, inmates are told—new arrivals at Central lockup are brought to the Old Wing. With its high walls of smog-blackened stone and filmy windows barred with flat, rust-colored strips of iron, the structure is ancient by Los Angeles standards, which is to say, it has been standing since before World War II. Its stone-block facade rears up unexpectedly, a grimy fortress in an otherwise desolate flatland of single-story industrial buildings, lumpy railroad crossings, and darkened, windowless warehouses stacked near a sprawling county hospital. Even hardened criminals gasp when they first see Central's medieval profile rising before them from the urban plain. The most observant of them, however, can take heart at their continued, valued place in society and commerce: A lone billboard overlooks the street leading to the lockup, a depiction of a man in a crown and royal red robes, flanked by a six-foot-tall pocket-paging device and a young woman squeezed into a transistor-sized red bikini. The man is the "King of Beepers," and his product is especially popular with the hundreds of drug dealers, gangbangers, and assorted other criminals who pass by his shrewdly placed advertisement in shackles each day, for whom beepers are both status symbols and necessary tools of the trade in this information age.

Past the billboard, at the terminus of Alcazar Street, there is a guard shack overlooking Central's drive-in entrance, but it is unmanned at night and the lot is poorly lit, the sort of place where people feel the need to hurry to their cars, locking the doors as soon as they get inside. At the end of this narrow and crowded parking lot, where the spots reserved for visitors are kept full by county employees, a towering brown metal door, big enough to admit a row of three semitrailers, creaks inward on oilless hinges every few minutes. Police cars and sheriff's vans pass in and out of this immense portal in a constant stream, making their night deposits, leaving behind people charged with every sort of crime imaginable, from shoplifters and drunks to carjackers and killers, linked together without distinction in long conga lines by those great equalizers, belly chains and handcuffs.

Newcomers arrive at Central mostly at night, emerging from squad cars and police vans to be herded inside the Old Wing, with its smeary walls and cracked linoleum floors, their nostrils assaulted by the universal jailhouse scent, a rat warren smell of urine and sweat masked by some sickly sweet cleaning agent vaguely reminiscent of pink bubblegum. There is a constant electronic buzzing in the air—an old airport metal detector that the lockup staff and visitors must pass through. Its alarm sounds nearly continuously, a piercing bleat no one monitors or heeds, notwithstanding the armed escape at the lockup a few months earlier. Flyspecked fluorescents buzz and flicker overhead, making the newcomers blink and squint as they walk in from the darkness. To some of the new arrivals, these surroundings are well known, bespeaking home, even comfort—as familiar as the aromas of morning coffee and frying bacon are to more fortunate folk. Others have never been in such a place, never seen it, smelled it, imagined it. Their eyes are wide with the ancient instinct to stampede.

The new arrivals are escorted one by one to a small room, where the Intake Officer conducts a brief interview, reviews the police reports, talks to the suspects' next of kin if they're around, then writes a two-page report with recommendations. Some of the intake officers have perfected a technique of quizzing newcomers that rarely, if ever, requires them to utter a complete sentence. They simply say, "Name? Date of birth? Address?" all the way down the form in front of them, like reading a shopping list, a complete interview done and only a few dozens words uttered in the process. This peremptory method belies the immense power the Intake Officer wields as a kind of pretrial judge, jury, and jailer rolled into one. He can recommend release or incarceration, prosecution or diversion to counseling, even dismissal of charges, and his calls carry great weight with the court. The recommendations tend to get more liberal as the lockup reaches its capacity each night—"You can only make so many of 'em sleep on mattresses on the floor before the ACLU shows up," the Intake Officer on duty this night confides to a cop escorting one of the newcomers.

The Intake Officer has already processed twenty-seven cases in a little over four hours—all manner of thieves, burglars, and gun-toting criminals, several probation violators, two carjackers, an arsonist, an armed robber, and a drive-by shooter. The Intake Officer is used to routine and rote, to offenders who fit the classic stereotypes, but of late the patterns had been changing, not so much because of the mix of crimes—that had remained fairly constant—but because of the type of people committing them. In recent days, he had referred for prosecution a stickup suspect who was rich, with a home in one of LA's most affluent neighborhoods and no need beyond sheer kicks for robbing anyone; a drive-by shooter who was female—still an oddity, even in an age of unprecedented violent crime; and a home invasion robber with one of the hardest-luck stories the Intake Officer had ever heard, having been raised by that ultimate dysfunctional parent, the state, only to be abandoned to a life of crime.

Tonight, he has an even more unusual newcomer, this one charged with murder—though that is not the strange part. Used to be murder cases were momentous exceptions to the plodding dullness of his job, but now they, too, had become almost routine. Dozens a month now. The "pop sheet" at the lockup is full of them. It is the circumstances of the case—and its probable outcome—that jump out at you. It is nothing short of bizarre.

The case involves a botched robbery at a freeway motel. Two armed suspects demanded money from the desk clerk, but another motel employee emerged from a back room with a gun of his own, blowing a fatal two-inch hole into the ringleader's chest. No one else was hurt. Still, the surviving robber—Geri Vance, who now stands before the Intake Officer—was arrested for murder in the death of his crime partner, the theory being that no one would have died had the robbery never taken place. It was a legal loophole in reverse, a murder charge for someone who had killed no one. The Intake Officer has heard of such cases, but has never actually seen one before.

"How can they charge me with murder? I never even fired my gun at anyone," Geri tells the Intake Officer, which is perfectly true—and, legally at least, completely irrelevant. "I was forced to take part in that robbery. I didn't want to do it, but I gave in. I know I have to do some time for that, I understand that. But I'm no killer."

There is an earnestness in Geri's manner and words that even the jaded Intake Officer can see. He almost feels sorry for the guy. "You'll have your day in court," the Intake Officer offers. Geri only winces.

Geri's case is in stark contrast to another murder case the Intake Officer handled just days before—a very ugly double homicide in which the suspect had already confessed to police that he killed his employers, a middle-aged married couple who owned a popular neighborhood ice cream shop in the View Park section of Los Angeles. Although they had long treated their counterman like a member of the family, the shop owners had recently chastised Ronald Duncan for chronically coming late to the shop. This so irritated Ronald that he decided to rob them, then blow their heads off with a shotgun while they drove him home from work. He boasted about it to a friend the next day, which was his downfall, as it is with a surprising number of criminals who would not otherwise be caught. The arresting officers in this case had handed him over at Central with obvious relief, as if he were contagious.

In both, the Intake Officer had to look through the thick rubber-banded packets of paper compiled by the police on each killing. Although they had both been brought in on murder charges, the two suspects couldn't have been more different. It seems clear that Geri the motel robber wasn't a killer at heart. The only reason he had been caught was because he brought his dying crime partner to a hospital emergency room after fleeing the Best Western they tried to rob. He could have gotten away clean, but chose to try to save a life instead. Then he had pretty much told the truth from the moment the police grabbed him at the hospital, immediately admitting to the robbery—not realizing he had signed his own murder warrant by doing so, his protests of coercion notwithstanding. He is bright and personable, with a sad history that began when he was abused and neglected as a child, left to roam the streets and to accumulate a record of minor crimes, none of them violent, at least until today. His fate had been sadly predictable, almost preordained, the Intake Officer figures.

But this other one, this shotgun-wielding killer, had come out of nowhere. Ronald Duncan had no criminal record, no known history of violence or abuse, no mental illness—just an unremarkable middle-class background, plodding and dull. He had cooked up a bogus alibi when the police caught up with him, then later confessed after a marathon session with detectives, without any apparent pangs of conscience or remorse. Once his initial fear at the unfamiliarity of the lockup faded, the Intake Officer saw a grin on Ronald's face, as if he had been brought to Central on a traffic offense, not a murder charge. He wondered aloud how much respect on the streets he'd earn for getting busted on such a serious rap. But when asked why he killed his employers, Ronald adamantly denied it—notwithstanding the police tape recording of him admitting to murder. Then he had the gall to ask, "Can I go home now?"

Both of these newcomers ended up on the same unit, the lockup's high-risk offender wing, joining the other murderers, rapists, and assorted other violent criminals awaiting trials or sentencing, stripped, searched, showered, and given orange jumpsuits to wear, their clothes and possessions boxed and tagged. After months, a year, possibly more, their cases will be resolved. The Intake Officer has no doubt which of the two murder defendants the system will end up treating more harshly.

Geri Vance, the would-be motel robber—the murder defendant who killed no one—faces life in prison without possibility of parole, and will almost certainly get it.

Ronald Duncan, the shotgun killer, can serve no more than eight years, and will probably do less. He can never see the inside of a state penitentiary. After his release, his record will be wiped clean, as if it never existed, the files sealed by state law, so that he can move freely, run for office, own a gun.

Even a man made cynical from running the intake desk too many nights has to marvel at this. But the Intake Officer doesn't dwell on such matters very long, nor does he try to manipulate some other result by injecting opinion into his reports. He gave up long ago trying to find sense in the workings of Juvenile Court.

There is just too much else to deal with—things were backing up in the Old Wing. Let some overworked juvenile judge worry about the rights and wrongs of it all. The Intake Officer still had to deal with two young car thieves, a twelve-year-old child molester, an assortment of warring gang-bangers, and a straight-A student who tried to hack her sister to death with a machete. There were papers to fill out and cells to fill up. It was a busy night behind the high stone walls of Los Angeles's Central Juvenile Hall.

Like always.

Elias is reading to my class, his dark eyes fixed on the paper quivering in his hands.

These are the things I learned when I was growing up:
I learned how to take a spray can of paint
and write my *nombre* on the wall.
I learned how to make a Walkman's motor into a tattoo machine,
so that I could get my barrio on my arms and my neck,
to show how much I love my homeboys.
I learned how to sell the weed and the rock.
These are the things I learned when I was growing up.

The seven other boys in the class nod as Elias reads. They are fourteen and fifteen and sixteen years old, and he is describing their lives as well as his own, lives that brought them to Central Juvenile Hall not as mere delinquents, like most of the 1,600 kids warehoused here, but as HROs— high-risk offenders. Geri Vance is in my class, and Ronald Duncan, part of a broad assortment of kids, some with futures, some without, most of them painfully aware which category they fall into. "We're the monsters they talk about on the news," sixteen-year-old Chris, a gentle-mannered robber of pizza deliverymen, told me matter-of-factly when I first started teaching the Monday-night writing class two months ago. "We're the ones you're sup- posed to be afraid of." I felt too guilty to tell him that I had, indeed, expected to find monsters when Sister Janet first led me to them. Hesitating outside the double-locked steel door to their unit, I had asked the Juvenile Hall chap- lain rather nervously why she had chosen these kids, rather than some less hardened, more salvageable boys or girls, and Janet had just smiled crypti- cally and said, "Because these boys need you more."

Elias has a stoic strength about him, quiet and shy, in the past too ner- vous to read his work aloud. At first, he always just folded his eloquent essays on life in the streets into tiny squares of paper, passing them to me in silence so I could read them privately. Tonight, though, his anger has boiled up from the page and into the classroom.

When I was growing up, I learned how to take
another person's car without a key,
how to drive it and sell it, or just leave it somewhere.
I learned how to sit down low
and look out the windows for the enemy,

to see them before they saw me.
And, finally, when I was growing up,
I learned how to load bullets into a gun.
I learned how to carry it and aim it,
and I learned how to shoot at the enemy,
to be there for my homeboys, no matter what.

"I hear you," James says, an obvious longing for the street in his voice. He has just penned an essay on how he'd like to drive a car over his ex-girlfriend, and it is not entirely clear that he is joking. The kids, in their severe jailhouse haircuts and the neon orange jumpsuits reserved for HROs, look pale and fragile beneath the hall's harsh lights, a few of them nursing adolescent wisps of mustache hair that only make them look younger. Yet, most of the boys in this room are on trial for thoroughly adult crimes—murder or attempted murder or armed robbery. They have witnessed and done terrible things. At the same time, these kids who could pull a trigger without a blink remain painfully timid about reading their work aloud, blushing, breathing hard, breaking a sweat just at the thought of standing before the class and baring themselves. Silence can claim the room like an advancing tide. Tonight, though, Elias, with his angry diatribe, is my unexpected hero. He has broken the ice.

And then this seemingly hardened gangbanger, this kid with the huge tattoo on his arm announcing his gang allegiance, "Sureño 13," surprises everyone. His voice drops nearly to a whisper, hoarse and urgent, his words taking a new direction.

These are the things I learned when I was growing up.
But this is what I want to know:
I want to know, who is going to teach me
how to pick out the right baby carriage for my little girl?
Who is going to teach me how to make up a bottle,
or to change a diaper, or to buy baby food?
Who is going to teach me how to be a father?
How to take care of my family?
How to live a life—a normal life?
These are the things I never learned growing up.
Who will teach me now?

When he finishes, the room is silent, not a cough, not a mutter, not a rustle of clothing, just the sound of Elias setting his paper down on the old Formica tabletop and, filtered through the room's walls of metal, cinder block, and safety glass with wire mesh embedded within, the muffled jailhouse sounds of feet shuffling, toilets flushing, young voices competing with the television bolted to the wall of the common room. Elias's eyes stay locked on his piece of paper. The sorrow and regret in his voice was so naked that the bravado and machismo that normally inhabit this room have evaporated like dew in the desert. Several boys are blinking hard.

None of them speak the answer to Elias's yearnings, though all know it well. The answer is: no one.

Elias has been in the system for years, without benefit or effect. "Probation isn't worth shit," he says. For him, it was token supervision, a monthly call to his PO, who had two hundred other kids to watch over. Elias never left his gang, as the judge had ordered, and no one noticed. On probation, he carried a gun. He did drugs. He skipped school. "Camp was a joke, too," he says of the county-run boot camps for delinquent youth. The gangs were recruiting there, inside a place where the kids were supposed to get away from the street life. There were race riots, drug use. It was ridiculous, he says, the system with its puny arsenal up against something far bigger and far deadlier. Elias's best friend had died in his arms, shot in a drive-by. His uncles had all gone to prison. His beloved grandmother was murdered. It was natural for him, his birthright: He just kept committing crimes. Nothing made Elias want to change—until, three days after his arrest as an accomplice to murder, he learned he was to be a father. Then he craved responsibility, normalcy, a future. But by then it was too late.

Now Elias keeps tucked in his right sock a color snapshot of his daughter, his most treasured possession. His baby was born while he sat in Juvenile Hall, and she has reached the age of eight months without ever being held by her father. They are likely to remain apart a good deal longer. Because of the seriousness of his case, Elias will almost certainly be tried as an adult, with a lengthy sentence, possibly a life term, ahead of him. This is what it has come down to in Los Angeles's juvenile justice system: life in prison for sixteen-year-old boys. Not just one or two or three like Elias, but hundreds of them.

"There's no one you can bring in to talk to someone and make them change, to make them not do crimes," Elias says, when I ask him what the Juvenile Court could have done to keep him straight. "I honestly don't think anything the system does is going to work. People have to change themselves. Nothing can make them change. Like for me, it wasn't until I had my baby girl that I realized I wanted to change, to settle down and get an apartment and a job and take care of her. No speech from a judge could make me give a damn. I had to have a baby before I could change. And now it's too late."

The words tumble out of Elias in a rush. In the space of fifteen minutes, he has spoken more than in ten previous classes, as if he was saving up his despair.

"God made me so that I could learn how to commit crimes," he finishes. "What's some judge or some probation officer gonna do?" I see he is looking directly at me now with those dark eyes, an old man's eyes in a sixteen-year-old's face, and I think at the time, as I do now, that there is nothing more sad than the sight of hopelessness in one so young. It is a look that seems, for the moment, to be reflected in every boy's face in the room.

"God made me so I could do terrible things," Elias says. "Why couldn't God help me learn how to be a father?"

PART ONE

We're Drowning

Take a trip in my mind
see all that I've seen,
and you'd be called a
beast, not a human being. . . .

Fuck it, cause there's
not much I can do,
there's no way out, my
screams have no voice no
matter how loud I shout. . . .

I could be called a
low life, but life ain't
as low as me. I'm
in juvenile hall headed
for the penitentiary.
    GEORGE TREVINO, sixteen, "Who Am I?"

Two Boys, Thirty Years, and Other Numbers

Gila County, Arizona
June 8, 1964

A MILDLY irritating, lewdly suggestive telephone call and a fifteen-year-old boy named Gerald Francis Gault: that's all it took to bring the nation's juvenile justice system to its knees.

At the time, Gila County was, to put it charitably, something of a backwater. Arid even in winter, it was a place of trailer parks and gritty two-lane roads peeling ruler straight through the scrubby fry pan of the Upper Sonoran Desert. There are no major cities here. The county's principal claims to fame include the fact that Zane Grey's cabin was located here, and that the county seat, Globe, had a neighborhood so contaminated with asbestos-laden mining debris that the U.S. government had to remove its families and entomb its soil beneath gigantic concrete caps. Conservative and insular, it is safe to say that Gila County has never been the sort of place in which obscene phone calls, even pubescent ones, went over very well. So when young Gerry Gault and a snickering friend decided to while away the afternoon by telephoning a certain Mrs. Cook to tell her just how much they admired her physique, the local sheriff did not hesitate to act on the irate woman's complaint.

The sheriff hauled the fifteen-year-old to jail that same day, charging him as a juvenile delinquent. No one explained to Gerald his constitutional rights before demanding that he confess. No one offered him a lawyer or a dime to make a phone call. No one even took the trouble to tell his parents what had happened. They simply came home from work and found him missing. After canvassing the neighborhood, Gerald's worried mother and father finally learned their son had been arrested. They went to the county detention hall, where a probation officer reluctantly told them that a court hearing had been scheduled to determine their son's fate.

A week later, without any formal charges filed and without ever hearing any testimony from the simmering Mrs. Cook, or anyone else, for that matter—in other words, without any actual evidence against the boy—the juvenile court judge for Gila County pronounced Gerald guilty and proclaimed him a delinquent.

During the hearing, the judge forced Gerald to testify—there would be no claiming the Fifth in his courtroom, thank you. Then, when the boy failed to incriminate himself sufficiently, the judge proclaimed him "habitually immoral." The judge based this finding upon his vague recollection of an allegation two years earlier—never proven or even heard in court—that Gerald took another boy's baseball bat and glove. Again, this ruling was made without evidence or testimony from anyone.

An adult found guilty of making such a lewd phone call—a misdemeanor roughly as serious as running a stop sign—could have been fined five to fifty dollars or, in rare instances, could have received a brief jail sentence under Arizona law in effect at the time. But the consequences for a juvenile judged guilty of such a charge and designated habitually immoral were profoundly different. As Gerald's horrified parents sat in the judge's chambers, stunned and intimidated into silence, the judge sentenced the boy to the state of Arizona's juvenile prison for up to six years.

Gerald had no attorney to represent him at this hearing, nor was he permitted to have one. He was presumed guilty, not innocent, from the moment he sat down on the hard wooden chair reserved for him in the judge's chamber. No transcript was made of this secret "trial." No transcript was needed, his parents learned later, because juvenile delinquents like Gerald had no right to appeal. He had no rights, period. Whatever the judge said, that was it. And Gerald and his family soon learned that this was not some high-handed, backroom Star Chamber peculiar to Gila County. This was how juvenile courts throughout the country operated, the judge curtly informed them.

Three years passed before the U.S. Supreme Court agreed to do something about Gerald Gault's case. When the High Court finally acted, its sweeping decision became a landmark: Juvenile courts throughout the nation were transformed by the simple notion that children should not be convicted of crimes without evidence of their guilt, without fair trials and lawyers and the chance to face their accusers. The turn-of-the-century intent behind the creation of a separate juvenile justice system—that it be informal, stripped of legal ritual, and dedicated to quickly helping troubled kids get back on track—was all well and good, the Supreme Court observed. But those noble intentions had spawned outrageous abuses—not only against poor Gerry Gault, but against thousands of other kids convicted more on whim than evidence, imprisoned on charges for which no adult could serve even a day behind bars.

"Under our Constitution," reads one particularly caustic passage of the Supreme Court decision, now know as In Re Gault, "the condition of being a boy does not justify a kangaroo court."

And so, on May 15, 1967, Gerry Gault's adolescent prank had the extraordinary effect of bringing every juvenile court in every state of the Union to a grinding halt so that lawyers and court reporters and all the other trappings of real courtrooms could be put into place. When they started up again, the way in which society dealt with its troubled youth had forever changed.

Thirty years later, the system has yet to recover from that one lewd phone call, or from the hidden price tag attached to the reforms it spawned.

Los Angeles County Juvenile Court
Los Padrinos Branch
April 27, 1994

Richard Perez, aka Shorty, a scrawny sixteen-year-old with an adolescent mustache atop an adolescent smirk, walked into the court Gerry Gault built exactly twenty-nine years and ten months after that fateful phone call in Gila County. It was Richard's thirty-first court appearance in Los Angeles's massive Juvenile Court, and his sixth criminal arrest. This time, though, he was in for murder, his world's surest right of passage to adulthood—or, at least, to adult court and adult prison.

Richard's criminal career began with a car theft in 1990, when he was thirteen. At least, that's when he officially entered the system. Truth is, he had been getting into trouble for years before that—cutting classes, throwing chairs and disturbing classrooms when he didn't skip school. Long before his voice had changed, he had begun to disobey his parents with impunity. He joined a street gang, stayed out all night, stole from his family. Under old juvenile laws, such classic delinquent behavior would have been enough to get him into the system at age eight or nine. Today, such conduct can't be used to incarcerate kids. If it's not a crime for adults to run away or skip school or to tell their parents to fuck off, it would be unconstitutional to make it a crime for children. "I'm sorry," a police desk sergeant had told Richard's mother once, when she called desperate for help with her wayward son. "There's nothing anyone can do unless he commits a crime."

So it took a car theft for the system to get hold of Richard, not at age eight, when programs to reform troubled kids work three out of four times, but at age thirteen, when the success rate is down to one out of four. Not that it mattered. Such measures of failure and success assume someone actually makes an effort with a kid. But the number of cases like Richard's has become too overwhelming in recent years—annually, more than 5,300 auto thefts are committed by juveniles in LA—and the Juvenile Court, busy with more serious crimes, cannot keep up. With priority given to the 237 homicides, 3,746 robberies, 5,621 burglaries, 675 sexual crimes, 3,374 felonious assaults, 6,044 drug crimes, and 2,412 weapons possession offenses—all committed by juveniles in LA in a single year[1]—a mere car theft, like the thousands of graffiti cases that fill the court dockets, goes to the end of the line.

And so, Richard was released the day he was arrested. Five months passed before he was summoned back to court to face his charges. During that time, he ignored a court order to attend school, to obey his parents, and to quit his gang. He figured no one from Juvenile Court would have the time to check, and he was right. He capped off his show of contempt by failing to appear for his thrice-delayed trial. "I knew they couldn't do shit to me," he would later observe. "I was havin' too much fun to bother."

A month later, the young fugitive was rearrested and brought into court, where he cut a deal and pleaded guilty to the reduced charge of joyriding. His single mother said she was sick of his foul mouth and gangster friends. "You keep him," she told the judge. He got probation, lived for a while in a group home, then went home with his father.

From the moment he settled his case, Richard busted curfew nightly, got high, and continued gangbanging, all in violation of his probation conditions. But his probation officer had nearly two hundred kids to supervise, which she accomplished primarily by talking to them on the telephone once a month (twice a month for the troublesome kids). She didn't even catch the phony address and disconnected phone number Richard had supplied as his father's—until Richard's dropping out of the ninth grade provoked her to actually try and visit him. No one in the system had checked on his home life before releasing him. The PO found an empty lot where his house was supposed to be.

Richard remained a fugitive for another month, when police caught him behind the wheel of another stolen car. Released again after a few hours in custody, he stayed on probation and landed back in the same group home, conveniently located near his gang turf.

Three months later, Richard and three other members of a new, violent street gang he had joined, called the Young Crowd, started a riot at a hospital. Intent on visiting a homeboy with a gunshot wound, they had tussled with security guards rather than wait fifteen minutes for official visiting hours to begin. "I'll be back, I'll do a drive-by, I'll kill your motherfuckin' asses," Richard shrieked to the guards and the nurses who turned him out. A new judge took over his case, kept him on probation, and returned him to the same group home with the same no-gangs, go-to-school conditions he had yet to obey.

Six months later, in August 1993, Richard, by then sixteen, was arrested for participating in a swarming attack on a motorist who stopped near a park on the gang's turf, only to be beaten badly, his car stolen. After his arrest, Richard sat in court in bold gang style—a kind of Charlie Chaplin positioning of his feet under the defense table—as derogatory a gesture in his universe as extending his middle finger at the judge. But no one noticed or cared. The result: case dismissed, more probation, same group home. Richard celebrated by having his gang moniker, "Shorty," tattooed onto his back, and by breaking a middle-aged woman's nose with one vicious punch so he could steal the six-pack of beer she had just bought from a liquor store that had refused him service.

"I wanted a beer," he later said, when asked if he felt bad about hurting the woman. The question seemed to perplex him. "If you're strong enough to take something, why not take it?"

This was Richard's fifth arrest, but no weapons were used in the robbery, so the case was sent to the back of the line with the other "nonserious" felonies, and Richard walked free again, told to come back in four months.

The Juvenile Court could have revoked his probation at this point (or long before, given his abysmal record), locking him up for months or even years in county boot camps or the state-run Youth Authority juvenile prison system. His contempt for a system that had never held him accountable was clear from the way he laughed in court when his latest victim's nose was mentioned. He flicked spitballs and threw gang signs in the courtroom when he thought no one was looking. His offenses had grown more bold and violent with each passing arrest. Yet, once more, the system turned him loose, as it had always done. And, finally, Richard graduated to the big time.

It happened two months after the beer robbery, before the overworked DA's juvenile operation had even waded through its backlog far enough to file formal assault charges. Two boys, David and Enrique, sat down in a small restaurant in the LA County city of Lynnwood to eat meat burritos and drink Cokes. A thin, short, Hispanic kid with a wispy mustache and a hand in his coat pocket materialized beside their table after a few minutes. The kid wore the uniform of the street: an oversized black hooded jacket, the baggy trousers hanging low, the underwear tops peeking out of the waistband. He had been milling around outside with members of the Young Crowd, muttering things like "traitor" and "nigger lover" because Enrique was Hispanic, while David was black—a pairing certain Latino street gang members find intolerable.

"Where are you *vatos* from?" the kid in the black jacket asked fifteen-year-old David. This is derogatory street code for "What gang are you in?" It is the standard question uttered before drive-by shootings and gang fire-fights on the street. It is a declaration of war.

"Nowhere," David said, the only potentially neutral reply.

The skinny kid in the black jacket jutted his lower lip and turned slightly toward seventeen-year-old Enrique. "Where are *you* from?"

Enrique put his burrito down. "Nowhere," he repeated.

Without another word, the kid pulled out a twenty-five-caliber hand-gun and fired three times, then ran out. One bullet slapped into the table a few inches from David. The other two slugs plowed into Enrique, who shouted, "I'm hit, I'm hit, go get my mom!" Blood spurted from his shoulder and chest. Forty minutes later, Enrique Diaz Nunez, an eleventh grader whose only crime had been eating a burrito with a friend, lay dead on a bloody emergency room gurney, his mother and sister weeping beside him.

A few days later, David drove with investigators past a crash pad kept by the Young Crowd. He pointed out a thin, short kid in an oversized black coat sauntering out the door. "That's him," David hissed. "That's him." They arrested Richard Perez on the spot and charged him with murder. He hadn't even bothered changing clothes.

At the police station after his arrest, detectives pulled out the inevitable Miranda card, explained to Richard his rights, and, hoping for a confession, asked if he had anything to say.

"Yeah, I have something to say," the savvy street urchin said, well trained by his many encounters with the system. "I want my lawyer."[2]

Administrative Headquarters
Los Angeles County Probation Department
Downey, California

Though he had no way of knowing it, Richard's criminal career had been closely monitored for years, part of a massive project within Los Angeles County Juvenile Court designed to figure out what happens to kids after they enter the system—to actually track what a child does after committing a first offense. How many girls and boys never come back after one arrest? How many cross the line another time? How many go the way of Richard, committing crime after crime until someone dies and the system finally takes notice? As simple and crucial as these questions are—for they would reveal how well or how badly Juvenile Court performs its job—no one could answer them. They had never been asked before.

So, in 1990, researchers began watching first-offenders arrested in LA County in the first six months of that year, Richard among them—11,493 kids in all. Five men and women sat in a special secure room at probation headquarters and read file after confidential file, tracking every one of those kids—for three years. They did not intercede in any case, but merely watched, omnipotent and removed, part of a grand experiment that let each case spin out as it always had, even horror stories like Richard's.

By the end of 1993, the results of their painstaking work had become so appalling to the Probation Department and the Juvenile Court—and so profoundly threatening to the future of both bureaucracies—that officials have made no public announcement of the findings. But they boil down to this:

A little over half—57 percent—of kids who are arrested for the first time are never heard from again. They go straight, shocked by the system, mostly ordinary kids who make one mistake, and know it.

Of the rest, just over a quarter—27 percent, to be precise—get arrested one or two more times, then they, too, end their criminal careers. But the last 16 percent—that's sixteen kids out of every one hundred arrested—

commit a total of four or more crimes, ranging from theft to murder. They become chronic offenders. They become Richard Perez.

But as depressing as these figures are, they are nothing compared with the study's real gut punch, the part no one in the system wants to talk about: The researchers glumly concluded that Juvenile Court seemed irrelevant to how these kids turned out.

Out of those 11,493 kids, about a third had their cases dropped immediately after arrest. For a variety of reasons—insufficient evidence, reluctant witnesses, extenuating circumstances, pretrial diversion, even actual innocence now and again—these kids walked away without ever seeing the inside of a courtroom. The other two-thirds were prosecuted in Juvenile Court, where the vast majority went on to receive the benefits of probation, placement in a group home, or full-blown incarceration. And yet—here was the awful surprise—there was no difference between how these two groups of kids fared. Either way, Juvenile Court or no Juvenile Court, just over half never came back after their first bust, about a quarter committed one or two more crimes, and the rest went on a rampage.

In other words, doing nothing, and throwing everything the system has at kids, produced the same overall result.[3]

As word of this stunning, humbling study slowly moved through Los Angeles Juvenile Court like a monsoon's leading edge, it became a rallying cry for two factions within the system: those who believe the days of a separate Juvenile Court should be numbered, and those who want large-scale reform without discarding the notion that children, simply by virtue of being children, deserve to be treated differently—even when they commit crimes. A third group—not to be underestimated, for it had long held the reins of power—wanted only to give into inertia, to ignore the study, to preserve a bureaucracy that could create without pang or blink both Gerry Gault and Richard Perez.

And so the year 1994 began with unaccustomed turmoil and uncertainty within the world's largest juvenile court, a place now no longer merely at war with its young charges, but also at war with itself.

CHAPTER 1

January 1994

Los Angeles County Superior Court
Juvenile Court Division
Thurgood Marshall Branch
Inglewood, California

THE first thing you learn about this place," Deputy District Attorney Peggy Beckstrand says as she conducts a brief tour of the battered juvenile courthouse she helps run, "is that nothing works."

It is 8:25 in the morning, a cold winter day, the sky as gray as an old skillet, an intermittent, muffled roar occasionally filtering into the building from somewhere outside—the steady stream of fat, full jetliners on final approach to LAX one freeway exit to the south. Inside, the locks on the courtroom doors are snicking back, fresh piles of manila-covered court files are being placed on the judge's benches, lawyers are wading through the hundreds of kids and parents and witnesses gathered in the courthouse today, looking for a client they've never met, a witness they've never spoken to, a parent who can't believe his or her child is a criminal, evidence be damned. Dirty mint-green buses with metal cages inside them are lumbering toward court from LA's three enormous juvenile halls, carrying boys and girls wearing color-coded county-issue shirts and jeans, the color indicating their proclivity for violence or escape. The baddest kids sport coveralls in neon orange; their parents—those lucky enough to have a mom or dad interested enough to attend their court appearances—grip crumpled brown paper sacks with street clothes inside, hoping for an early release. In five minutes, court will be called into session, and the atmo-

sphere is charged with a sweaty, anxious expectation, as if the entire building were a crowded elevator stuck between floors.

"We're drowning," Beckstrand flatly announces. She looks taller than
her five feet six inches, due in part to her textbook posture. Exceedingly
pale, with very long, very straight brown-blond hair, Beckstrand, a former
Montessori teacher with a ribald sense of humor, enjoys a reputation for
toughness that has left her decidedly unloved—and once sued—by her
counterpart in the Public Defender's Office.[1] "Look around," she says of
the chaos swirling in the hallways. "It just isn't working."

She is not talking about the physical state of the place—the cracked and
broken fixtures or the dysfunctional water coolers that dispense brackish
water at body temperature—but of the juvenile system's broader failings,
the constant aura of futility that leaves this career prosecutor regularly
muttering about walking away from it all. She is not the only one. Many
who work these halls have heard about the new study circulating through
the system that shows, among other things, that the Juvenile Court squan-
ders most of its time and energy, focusing on the kids who are beyond
redemption while ignoring the children who could best be helped. "As
if we needed a study to tell us the obvious," she says. Throughout the bureaucracy, everyone is buzzing about this study, expecting—or fearing—
that it will bring massive and fundamental reform to a place that has not
changed in many positive ways since the 1960s, and shows it.[2]

Beckstrand, for one, says she would welcome a shake-up, but she openly
doubts the system's ability to break its tired patterns. Her voice sounds just
as tired. "We're not rehabilitating these kids, and we're sure as hell not
punishing them. They can get away with murder here, and they know it.
The law-breakers are winning, and we—society, those of us who obey the
rules—are losing."

A young prosecutor she supervises grabs Beckstrand then, asking her to
resolve one of the crises that erupt here hourly, and they disappear into a
courtroom together. They pass without a glance a deputy public defender
huddled on a bench with the mother of a mentally ill girl who has been
charged with attempted murder after voices in her head instructed her to
attack her sister with a machete. The mother is crying and shaking her
head as the young lawyer explains why it will be difficult to keep the girl
from being transferred to the harsh confines of adult court, due to the
severity of the accusations against her and the fact that she is past sixteen
years of age. "She really needs help and belongs here in Juvenile, and I'll
do everything I can to make that happen," the lawyer says. "But the prob-

lem is, the law is very tough on cases like this. The best I can do today is try for a continuance. The district attorney holds all the cards."

It is a peculiarity of Juvenile Court that two such contradictory conversations can occur here simultaneously and with total sincerity. This is because each side in the process—the prosecutors, the defenders, the judges, the cops and probation officers, the crime victims, the kids on trial here and their families—sees itself as being on the one and only losing side. When a case ends in Juvenile Court, it is often hard to tell just who has won.

The setting fuels this sense of futility: This courthouse is a grim place. The gray concrete box that is the Thurgood Marshall Branch of Los Angeles's massive Juvenile Court squats next to a once graceful garden district in the city of Inglewood, a community now so profoundly distressed that parents, policemen, and civic leaders meet monthly to plot safe routes through gang turf for their schoolchildren. The courthouse occupies the sort of neighborhood where members of warring black and Hispanic gangs summon one another by beeper and cellular phone to drive-by shootings and schoolyard race riots. Three blocks from Marshall Branch, an eleven-year-old schoolgirl sporting eleven prominent gang tattoos was caught distributing flyers advertising a gang-sponsored drug, sex, and beer party. The computer-generated flyers promised "Hoochies that ram free" can enter for free—meaning young girls who provide sex on demand need not worry about the five-dollar cover charge, a deal the eleven-year-old happily promoted to her sixth-grade schoolmates. When a counselor who seized the flyers asked the girl if she was worried about AIDS, she said no, it didn't matter. She'll be dead before she's twenty, anyway.

Yet, this is also the kind of neighborhood where wealthy Angelenos regularly park their BMWs and Mercedeses, because the Thurgood Marshall Branch, one of ten juvenile courthouses spanning the huge bowl of the Los Angeles Basin, serves more than just its own troubled surroundings. Juvenile offenders from LA's most upscale communities are hauled into the same courtrooms as well, from Beverly Hills to Hollywood to Malibu to Rancho Palos Verdes—the gangbangers' parents sitting next to the bankers and moguls with their designer briefcases and tasseled loafers, all equally dazed by the odd mixture of chaos, informality, and impenetrable ritual so unique to Juvenile Court. Through a fluke of geography and bureaucracy, in one of the most racially and economically segregated regions of America, the three grimy courtrooms of Marshall Branch Juvenile Court have become the last great melting pot. Here, everyone finds a new common ground: fear. Fear of our own children.

It is a fear seemingly grounded in fact, as juvenile crime, particularly violent crimes by kids, had ripped through the cities and suburbs of America like a new and deadly strain of virus for which no one possesses immunity. The figures were staggering: a 175 percent increase in juvenile murder rates since the 1970s, with similar boosts in juvenile crime of all kinds. Just in the last five years, violent offenses by children—murder, rape, assault, robbery—had risen 68 percent.[3] Los Angeles, with an estimated street gang force of 200,000, a majority of them under eighteen, has been especially hard hit by this epidemic. Given such figures—and the expert (and very mistaken) predictions that juvenile crime would continue to escalate for a decade or more—it should surprise no one that the Juvenile Court each year focuses less on children in danger, and more on dangerous children, locking more away, sending more to be tried as adults, imposing stiffer sentences. And still, the fear grows. You can see it in the courthouse hallway, in the furtive glances exchanged in the never-ending line at the two dented and sticky courthouse pay phones, in the way people rush through the gauntlet of silent, staring youth who sit on the steps and railings at the courthouse entry each day. One glimpse says it all: This is not a place to come for healing. It is a place to flee, as fast as you can.

Confusion is the other principal state of mind here—and in the nine other juvenile courthouses serving Los Angeles County, with their forty-nine courtrooms and eighty thousand active cases,[4] a system that dwarfs adult courts in most jurisdictions, the largest juvenile justice system in the world. Sweaty hands wave crumpled subpoenas and court orders like pennants, dangled anxiously in front of anyone who remotely appears to be in authority, followed by this question: Where do I go? Because most of the people asked this question are not actually in authority, but merely happen to be walking the hallway in a business suit or policeman's uniform, the most common reply is a shrug, and so dozens of people roam about aimlessly, unsure where to go.

This is what they find as they wander the Los Angeles Juvenile Court, Thurgood Marshall Branch: a waiting room, a clerk's office, and one courtroom downstairs, with one wide stairway leading to the second floor, scarred by graffiti, as are the other gray walls of this place. There is an arthritic elevator at the other end of the building, but it stinks of old urine and seems to take several minutes to pass between the two floors of this disheveled courthouse. The bathrooms are graffiti museums, the mirrors so thoroughly etched with gang insignias that the lawyers brave enough to enter cannot see enough of their own reflections to straighten their ties.

The layout of the place mystifies all but the initiates: Superior Court Department 241 is on the first floor, and Departments 240 and 242 are on the second floor. There is no logic to this numbering scheme (other than judicial jockeying for the least shabby quarters), and there are no other room numbers for the courts—you have to figure out their locations on your own. There is no information counter, no posted court calendar, no map of the building, no guidance of any kind. Cryptic, hand-lettered signs, faded and yellowed with age, hang haphazardly from the walls, suspended by ancient, brittle pieces of Scotch tape, defaced by vandals and communicating nothing relevant to the day's proceedings.

The aged building, once a small municipal courthouse for adult offenders, outgrown, disused, and, finally, thrown like a gnawed bone to the space-hungry Juvenile Court, is brimming with children and their families today, their combined voices a riotous roar. The modest, casual clothes worn by most of the parents, and the bagged-out, gangster-chic clothes worn by many of the kids, make it easy to spot the lawyers in their suits and power ties, clustered together, cutting deals or interviewing witnesses three minutes before trial. These hurried mutterings in the hallway are what passes for trial preparation in this haphazard court of law, except for a rare few high-profile cases, "specials" in DA jargon. Snatches of conversations become intelligible as you push through the first-floor hallway, packed tight as a rush hour subway car, hot and claustrophobic: A father says, *You listen to the judge, boy*, followed by a shrill, *Fuck the judge. . . .* A woman's voice pleads, *Can my daughter come home today?* while someone's brother complains, *Why are they charging him with murder? He was just drivin' the car.* Next to him, a public defender wheedles with a DA, a salesman at the bazaar, pressing to close the deal: *Come on, you don't need a felony on this one, we'll cop to the misdemeanor, save some court time. . . .* The DA has her eyes closed, files tucked under each arm, trying to remember the facts of the case they're talking about, one of forty-seven she is supposed to handle that morning.

As each of the three courtrooms begins its morning calendar call, the blur of intertwining hallway conversations fades as lawyers and litigants hustle into court. There are enough stragglers, witnesses, and families waiting for their children's cases to be called to keep the hallways crowded and loud, and any respite in the noise quickly evaporates as the public address system kicks into gear. Throughout the rest of the day, conversations will be drowned out by an intermittent electronic bong, followed by the voice of one of the court bailiffs speaking over the PA summoning some child or his family or a witness or an attorney to court. During morning calendar call, the busiest time in the courthouse, the harsh screech of the loudspeakers reverberates constantly, so loud that not even the thick, heavily worn double wooden doors barring entry to each courtroom can stop the sound. These announcements frequently drown out the words of judges and lawyers in the midst of hearings, destroying any semblance of courtroom decorum, and proceedings constantly are delayed as attorneys leap up to telephone some other courtroom competing for their services via loudspeaker. The crush of cases is so great, and the public defender and the district attorney here are so understaffed, that it is not uncommon for them to have two, three, sometimes five or more cases scheduled simultaneously in different courtrooms, causing impatient judges to electronically bellow for them to come on down every few minutes.

Peggy Beckstrand strides through the chaos, up the stairs, and makes her way into the courtroom of Judge Roosevelt Dorn, the newly arrived supervising judge at Thurgood Marshall. Ostensibly, she is there to pay a courtesy call on the new judge, but her real purpose is to assess what she will be dealing with in the coming year. She sits down inconspicuously in the back of the courtroom, surveying the scene like a baseball coach scouting the competition, jotting down the occasional note but mostly just watching, taking it all in. On the bench, she sees a fifty-seven-year-old man, short and a bit stocky, with salt-and-pepper hair cut close to his head, unfashionably long sideburns, a scrubby, well-clipped mustache, and large gold rings on each of his thick, blunt pinkies. Aside from his booming voice, his most daunting characteristic is a pair of pouchlike cheeks that seem to puff up when he is incensed, a warning sign as unmistakable as the maraca chatter of a rattlesnake. Lawyers have pushed through the double doors to his courtroom, spotted those inflated cheeks and slitted eyes peering over his reading glasses, and they have spun around and left, preferring to wait until later to ask him to call their cases. Peggy has seen that look during past encounters with this judge, when they both worked in adult court. "With Dorn," she has already warned her staff, "it's not a question of *if* things will come to a head. It's a question of when."

"You may have been on probation before, young man," the judge says, his trademark baritone booming, a radio announcer's voice emanating from the little man peering over the tops of gold-rimmed reading glasses. "But you have never been on probation in *Judge Dorn's* court."

You can almost hear the royal italics in the way he pronounces his name and title, more preacher in the pulpit than judge on the bench, leaning forward, gripping a court file in his hand as if it were scripture. Department 240 is full this morning, its torn and lumpy rows of ancient auditorium chairs crammed with parents, lawyers, witnesses, cops, and kids accused of crimes. Judge Roosevelt Dorn—who wears the minister's hat on Sundays—is preaching as much to this audience as to the fourteen-year-old boy whose case is momentarily before him. Part of Dorn's strategy is to run an open court in the normally closed and confidential arena of juvenile justice. The kids waiting for their cases to be called must listen to Dorn lecture or lock up one defendant after another—the judge figures the message will sink in for at least some of them, much the way Madison Avenue figures repeating the same jingles will sell laundry detergent. It is not precisely legal, but any reasonable way he can frighten, cajole, or persuade these kids into abandoning criminal lives is fine with Judge Dorn, whether the law specifically allows it or not. The defense lawyers despise this practice as a means of intimidating their young clients—which, strictly speaking, it is—but though they have a legal right to request an empty courtroom, few of the lawyers have the grit to ask. Dorn has an odd way of getting his way—and of dealing with those who would impede his agenda.

The boy before him now is named Robert, a young car thief and robber on his way to worse crimes. He has violated his probation by cutting school to hang out with his street gang, one of the more common entries on the LA juvenile docket. The boy's frustrated probation officer knows just how to push Dorn's buttons.

"This is the second time I've had him in here for missing school, Your Honor," the PO says, glancing at the skinny kid sitting in his oversized, untucked Raiders T-shirt, stereo headphones reluctantly removed from his ears and hanging insolently around his neck. "He's been missing classes for weeks—starting with the day after he last appeared before you."

Dorn's eyes turn to slits at this, a hooded, reptilian stare he has honed with much practice. Several lawyers in the courtroom shake their heads, knowing what is coming, for this judge is particularly infamous for two things: He insists the juveniles under his control maintain stellar school attendance, and he cannot bear to have his orders ignored. "You cut school *after* you came before Judge Dorn?" he thunders. It is a personal affront— the kid has already lost. Sure enough, the judge waves Robert's lawyer and his litany of excuses into silence and says, "This minor has no intention of complying with the court's orders. Therefore, I have no choice but to remove him from the home and send him to camp."

The bailiff immediately rises to stand behind Robert, his days in the street abruptly ended, a stay of up to a year in a county-run boot camp ahead, because he had the misfortune of getting Roosevelt Dorn for a judge instead of almost any other. And Dorn is not through.

"You've seen those homeless people down on Fifth Street, haven't you? That's where you're headed, son, if you don't get an education. Don't you understand that if you don't get an education, if you don't go to college or learn you a good trade, all you can expect in this world is a lifetime of degradation and poverty?"

The kid is silent, sullen, staring at his hands as Dorn lectures. The judge doesn't seem to notice. His eyes are darting around the courtroom now, where several mothers and fathers are nodding and whispering to their children to listen to the man. One father whispers, "That's a good judge. That's what that boy needs." Someone else calls out, "Amen," as if she were in church, and a slight smile plays across Dorn's lips at this. His voice grows even louder and deeper.

"You're stealing from yourself, no one else," he tells Robert. "You're stealing your own future. If you keep on the way you're headed, you can only end up in one of two places: the cemetery, or the penitentiary."

He pauses then, lowering his voice, taking off his glasses. "I can send you to a place where you have to go to school every day, but I can't make you learn, son. You have to want to learn. I think the world of you, son. I love you. I'm sending you to camp to give you a chance to decide to help yourself. Because I love you."

This is vintage Dorn. The parents in the audience—Robert's mother among them—appear awed. They have never heard anything like this newly arrived judge before. None of his brethren crack down on truancy this way. The same woman who said Amen before says it again. But most of the kids in the courtroom look bored with all this talk of learning and the future. Some of them have heard the cemetery or penitentiary threat five or six times already, and their eyes are wandering. One girl yawns, then grins at a sharply dressed young man with a gold earring and a long rap sheet who has blown her a kiss from across the aisle. As for Robert, as tough a nut for his age as any kid who comes before the court, he seems unmoved, not quite concealing a smirk as he is ushered through the door to the holding tank. "It's not like they can take anything from me," he says later, back with his homeboys at Juvenile Hall. "Ain't got nothin' to give. Nothin' but time, that is. And I been doin' time my whole life, one way or the other."

Still, whether or not it had any real impact on Robert, this heartfelt lecture of Dorn's was a bravura performance. Certainly, the parents were impressed, maybe a few of the kids, even the often-jaded prosecutor Peggy Beckstrand. But the scene is marred in the end by one slight jolt of mundane reality, a little thing, really, that nevertheless seems emblematic of the despair and futility that inhabits this courthouse so much more often than hope, a stark reminder that the crush of juvenile crime can reduce this system to an anonymous assembly line. After the sentence has been pronounced, the clerk grabs Robert's file—one of sixty cases the judge will hear this day—but Dorn suddenly realizes he forgot some minor point, and he asks for it back. He stutters oddly as he does this, and it takes a second for those present to understand why. Then it becomes clear: though he may indeed love Robert, Judge Dorn does not know his name.

During the pause between cases, Peggy Beckstrand approaches a public defender manning the defense table. They need to confer on a murder case they are trying together—the *People v. Ronald Duncan*. The trial of the kid accused of murdering the owners of a nearby Baskin Robbins store has become the most infamous—and certainly the most brutal—case currently on display in the Inglewood courthouse. Although her duties as deputy in charge are primarily administrative, Peggy is handling the case personally, unwilling to entrust it to one of the young DAs barely out of law school assigned to her office. Something about the way that short, squat kid with the scraggly goatee walks grinning and waving into court for each hearing—as if he was in on a curfew violation, not a double homicide—just infuriates Peggy. She is determined to win his conviction, despite the absolute certainty that, no matter how great her labors, she will not find the outcome either satisfying or just.

"We're supposed to set a trial date today," Peggy reminds the PD, knowing the lawyer will complain about needing more time, standard procedure in Juvenile Court. Nothing happens when scheduled. Nothing.

"I'm going to need more time," the defense lawyer says, eyeing her opponent cautiously. Peggy and the head public defender in Inglewood have been battling recently; the PD's office just finished an unsuccessful attempt to have one of Peggy's young prosecutors censured for misconduct. The fallout has left the two offices quibbling over the most routine matters, further slowing down a process that only crawls on its best day. "Is that going to be a problem?"

Peggy knows there would be no point in fighting it. Defendants in Juvenile Court, particularly those accused of murder, are pretty much entitled to unlimited delays, unlike prosecutors, who must be ready at the appointed hour, or lose. Besides, Peggy cannot find her star witness in the case, a potential disaster on the horizon. She didn't want to telegraph this by asking for a postponement of her own, and she conceals her glee at being taken off the hook with a chagrined expression and a tired shrug. "I guess not," she says. "It's not like Ronald's going anywhere." The hypocrisy implicit in playing such games bothers her, but they are a big part of the process here, a shabby mirror image of adult court. In both venues, winning the case is everything. Figuring out what's best for a kid—and for the community— well, that isn't her job. Peggy's job is to get a conviction. Her opponent's is to do whatever it takes to get an acquittal. Only when that contest is resolved does the Juvenile Court take up the question of what to do about a screwed-up kid. Like so many other initiates of the juvenile justice system, Peggy despises this order of priorities, while feeling powerless to change it.

The two lawyers agree on a new trial date, knowing the judge will go along with whatever they want. "I think the family is hiring private counsel anyway," the PD says, "so I doubt that I'll be trying this case."

Peggy looks at her for a moment, then, with a bitter sincerity she didn't mean to show, says, "Lucky you."

With the question of the trial date for Ronald Duncan settled, Peggy lingers in Dorn's courtroom long enough to watch him give probation to a seventeen-year-old girl convicted of driving the getaway car in a bank robbery—a shockingly lenient sentence, Peggy fumes to herself. The girl is articulate and attractive, despite her cartoonishly long, red-lacquered nails extending daggerlike from each finger. But she also has prior arrests for threatening a teacher with her fists and a fellow student with a knife, and she is believed by police to have ties to the infamous Rolling Sixties street gang as well, one of the toughest, deadliest in LA, with branch "offices" nationwide for dealing crack, and a series of bank jobs and daring Las Vegas casino robberies to its credit. Both the prosecution and the Probation Department have asked that this girl be locked up in the California Youth Authority, widely considered the biggest, toughest juvenile prison system in the country. But Dorn is impressed by the girl's membership in a church choir and her plans to go to college, where, she says without a trace of irony, she plans to study to be a police officer or a CIA agent.

"I daresay very few bench officers would send you home on probation for this," Dorn says, and Peggy can't help nodding, then hoping Dorn didn't see her. "I'm giving you a rare chance. No one can love themselves robbing a bank. Sooner or later, you'll end up in the penitentiary or the cemetery unless you change."

The girl leaves all smiles, her own lawyer blinking in surprise at the outcome. But moments later, this same judge lambastes the prosecutor assigned to his courtroom for being too lenient with a thirteen-year-old first-time offender accused of breaking into a car. As often happens in such a case, the prosecutor horse-traded the case down from a felony to a misdemeanor, something few judges would care about, but which Dorn hates. Felonies carry longer sentences—they let Dorn take charge of a kid's life for years, rather than the few months that misdemeanors allow.

"You on the wrong side of the table, that's your problem," Dorn announces, employing the greatest insult possible for a prosecutor—accusing him of acting like a defense lawyer. Then he pointedly stares straight at Peggy as she sits in back. "Maybe no one has taken the time to explain to you how Juvenile Court works. . . . Next time, check with me before you tie my hands. *I'm* the judge, not you."

Most of the people in court crane their heads around to see whom Dorn is addressing. Peggy just smiles, waits until the next case is called, then walks out, if a little stiffly. It was all posturing, she chafes later. Dorn accepted the misdemeanor plea anyway, then imposed exactly the same sentence as he would have had the kid received a felony conviction: probation, a seven o'clock curfew, and the cemetery-penitentiary lecture. For better or worse, first-time auto burglaries are routinely pleaded down to misdemeanors—the system would seize up like an engine with no oil if such deals were not cut daily and every case went to trial. Dorn knows this—he was a prosecutor himself once, Peggy says. The criticism is just his way of announcing who is in charge.

As Peggy leaves, she stops in the hallway to chat with a juvenile probation officer who wants help with a girl gangbanger named Carla James. In the background, though, Peggy can't help but listen to the young thief Dorn just sentenced—a sharp-faced little kid in surf dude clothes and a blond mushroom haircut—leave court and say with dripping sarcasm, "Great judge." Then, safely through the door and into the raucous hallway, he blows a raspberry in Dorn's direction.

"You'd better cut it out," his father says weakly.

The kid, showing who in the courthouse is truly in charge, stalks off, but not before glancing over his shoulder and telling his dad with practiced scorn, "Just shut up."

CHAPTER 2

Home Girl

On the day Carla James became a casualty of juvenile crime, she earned an A on her English test, a B in math, and a mild rebuke for missing a history paper deadline, and then she stayed late after school. The staying late was not for the purpose of punishment, but so Carla could perform her regular volunteer work in the school office, taking care of files, answering phones, doing photocopying — generally making herself indispensable to the school staff. Carla was always offering to help out, the kind of kid adults naturally trusted, who did what she said she would do and did it well. Some of her teachers even joked that, some days, Carla seemed to run the place. Her face would split into a huge smile at that — everyone said her smile was dazzling — and she would nod and say something cocky like, "You're right. I do."

This day, though, Carla had been uncharacteristically quiet. She kept pausing in her work to root around inside her bulging backpack, as if she were afraid of losing something inside. Each time, she carefully snapped shut the pack when she was through, then stowed it out of sight. Five minutes later, she'd be rooting again.

"You look tired today, Carla," the school counselor commented, poking her head into the office area. Carla appeared startled for a second, almost guilty, then quickly closed and put aside her book bag. The counselor said, "Is everything all right?"

Carla looked up and smiled then, that broad, infectious grin of hers, a model's straight, white teeth gleaming. "Sure," the girl said. "I was just up a little too late. I'm fine."

The counselor nodded, studying the tall, thin, charming fifteen-year-old a moment. She had taken a special interest in Carla, ever since her normally excellent grades had begun to slip and her absences began to grow. They visited outside school and talked often on the phone. Carla had opened up to her for a time, revealing how troubled she was beneath her surface élan. She was especially upset about her mother's recent remarriage, five years after Carla's father died in a car wreck. Lately, though, the girl had been pulling back again, dodging the counselor. "We should talk," the counselor said. "Call me later?"

"Sure," Carla promised.

But Carla knew she would not call. She could not tell her counselor the real reason she was so tired, how she had not cracked open the front door of her house that morning until just after dawn, the sun still low and weak over the Los Angeles Basin, its light devoid of warmth, barely piercing air the color of watery brown pudding. She had stuck her head in, the living room silent and empty, no sounds coming from the kitchen, her mother and stepfather already gone for the day to work. Good, she had thought—she wouldn't have to hear the same old your life's headed down the toilet, nice girls don't stay out all hours speech from her mom. Carla knew her mother was beside herself over the suddenly late hours and disobedient behavior, assuming she was sleeping around. Carla did not correct this misimpression. That would mean having to explain what she really was doing.

Upstairs, Carla had locked herself in the bathroom, showered, then stared into the mirror for a long time. She had been wanting to do this all night, a burning curiosity that had gripped her as soon as the hot edge of fear at what she had done had dulled. Would she—would anyone?—see a difference in her face? Would it be obvious to everyone what had happened? Carla thought about the Shakespeare her English class had read a few months earlier, a lot of stuff she didn't understand, but that scene with Lady Macbeth, struggling in vain to wash the blood from her hands—that had stuck with her. She had even dreamt about it. Would it be the same now with her? Would it show in her eyes, her expression?

She had leaned close, bending over the sink, the medicine chest mirror close enough to steam up with each breath. The same old face had stared back at her, the same long blond hair, the same high cheekbones and ski-jump nose, the smooth skin untouched by makeup—the features boys kept telling her were so hot and that she couldn't stand, because they got in the way of her being one of the guys. She had searched for signs of guilt, of fear, of evil—for imaginary blood that could not be scrubbed clean—but, to her immense relief, she saw no change. She had not felt guilty, not much, anyway. What she really felt, she had decided, was bursting with life, her secret coursing through her like jet fuel. At school, she concluded, they would have no clue. They would see what they wanted to see, a good kid, popular and polite, a girl who loved school, who liked to help: Carla James, honors student. They would see it because it was true. It just wasn't the whole truth.

"I'll call you later," Carla lied, looking straight into the counselor's eyes, seeing genuine affection and concern there, and feeling a slight pang at her deceit. But at the same time, she felt relief, because Carla could see the counselor had no idea—she just thought Carla was tired. Her secret was safe. Before she walked through the door, excitement about the night ahead pushed conscience out of the way. She slung her pack over one shoulder, felt the comforting weight of the gun inside, and strode off the school grounds, returning to that new, separate life of hers, another night away from home, another adventure without end. Except it did end, and all too abruptly.

The next morning, Carla did not go to the school office before class as she normally did. Instead, two sheriff's deputies showed up. They had come about Carla. There had been a shooting, they said. A drive-by shooting.

"Oh, my God! How did it happen?" the counselor exclaimed, thinking, It's always the good ones who get hurt. The papers were full of stories like that: Honors student slain. She felt tears welling as office workers crowded around to hear the appalling news. She had sensed something was wrong, berating herself for not doing something more for a child she had come to think of as a daughter. The counselor whispered, "Is Carla all right?"

One of the cops looked at her strangely for a moment. Then he said, "You don't understand. We're looking for Carla James. She's not the victim of a drive-by. She's the shooter."

———◆———

"ARLA," Sharon Stegall is telling a visitor—right in front of the girl, as if she weren't in the room listening, "is what we're facing more and more these days. It's one thing to have kids who screw up because that's all they got to do, 'cause they have nothing at home, nothing at school, nothing but the streets and the homies and time to kill, no pun intended. But Carla"—Sharon pauses long enough to aim a measured glower directly at the girl sitting and fidgeting before her—"Carla has everything going for her. Good family. Nice home. Good grades. People who care about her, love her. And she still screws up. Now why is that, Carla?"

Carla meets her probation officer's eyes with a steady, even stare—no easy feat when the PO is Sharon Stegall, a large and intimidating woman well practiced at putting kids on the spot, who speaks with a gale-force delivery that paralyzes most delinquents. The judges in Juvenile Court may issue the orders, but it is up to the probation officers to enforce them, and Sharon is among the best. But, in that moment, Carla looks unafraid, wearing the unwavering expression of someone telling the truth—or of an extremely practiced liar.

"Aw, Ms. Stegall," the girl says quietly. "You know I'm straight now. Just ask at my school. I'm doing great."

"Oh, I'm sure you're running the place, as usual," Sharon says, shaking her head. "But what else are you running down, that's the question?" The probation officer earns a sly smile with that one, then turns away again, speaking about Carla in the third person once more, a deliberate tactic of intimidation. "If we can figure out how to deal with the Carlas of the world, we will have juvenile crime licked. It's that simple. But I'm not sure we can get through to this knucklehead. Not sure at all."

Carla rolls her eyes and laughs, running her fingers through her long hair, pushing it away from her eyes. The gesture reveals a place where her tanned skin is marred by a large scar in the center of her forehead. She got it when her head plunged through the windshield of a stolen car. The car had crashed while she and two homies, pursued by police, fled the scene of a drive-by shooting in which Carla had pulled the trigger (in court, Carla denied being the shooter, but later admitted to it in casual conversation). Had the bullet from her gun struck a human target, rather than glancing off a light standard and fragmenting into relatively harmless shrapnel, she would not be sitting and jiving with her PO about going straight. She would be facing a murder rap, her last chance used up.

But sitting here in Sharon's cubicle, beneath the Emancipation Proclamation poster and the enormous wall map with its pushpins showing the multitude of gangs that seem to carve the LA landscape into as many turfs as voting precincts, Carla looks and sounds for all the world like someone you would want for a baby-sitter. She instills that good gut feeling you need to have in someone before you entrust your most precious possession in the world, your child. And that trust would not be misplaced: Within a certain context, Carla is caring, loving, dependable, and courageous. That this same girl could point a .357 Magnum at somebody and pull the trigger without remorse is the maddening contradiction of Carla James. She is on the leading edge of two new and disturbing trends in Juvenile Court. She is part of a still-small but rapidly growing group of girls who commit violent crimes, once the exclusive domain of the boys. And she is part of a growing legion of kids whose criminal roots cannot be traced to any sort of abuse or deprivation, children who have potential, privilege, and solid families, yet take a turn toward darkness simply out of personal choice, who have the insight and ability to reflect about the immorality of what they are doing, then do it anyway. These are the kids who have Sharon Stegall and the rest of the juvenile justice system stumped—and scared.

And, like many of them, Carla is down to her last chance.

She would say she was going to the library to study. Or to her friend Laura's house to do homework. Or to soccer practice after school. And then Carla's mom would find out that the library was closed that day, or that there was no soccer—or no Laura. "I'll see you for dinner," Carla would say, then vanish until nine at night.

Somewhere between elementary school and middle school, somewhere around Carla's thirteenth birthday, the lying started. The coming home late from school. The hanging on the street corner. The holiday snapshots in the James family photo album show this transformation starkly: one Christmas, there's Carla with her two older sisters and two younger brothers, the kid in the middle with the glowing smile, the perfect clothes, the limitless future. A year later, there's this sullen, defiant stranger in bagged-out gangster clothes, forty-inch trousers hanging from her twenty-four-inch waist, all her old friends forsaken in favor of a new, dangerous, loutish crowd.

It was tough for Carla's mother to get a handle on her daughter. The girl had always been closer to her father. Unlike her older sisters, Carla had resisted her mother's attempts to interest her in Barbies and playing house and wearing dresses. Carla insisted on playing stickball and marbles and cards and whatever the boys on her street were playing. She took great pride in the fact that most of her friends were boys, not girls, and that she met them on their own terms: She threw a ball as good as any boy, she ran as fast as any boy, and she'd fight them ferociously if they ever questioned her ability or mettle because of her sex. Her mother fretted over this, but her father always told her she could be anything she wanted—and that she should not take any crap from little boys. Carla worshipped him for this. She was his little sidekick, working on the car, mowing the lawn, walking to the hardware store to mess with the bins of bolts and nuts and tools: If Dad was doing it, Carla wanted to do it.

His death in a car accident when she was nine devastated Carla, leaving her depressed and withdrawn for many months, then resentful of her brothers, sisters, and mother when they picked up the pieces of their lives and tried to move forward. In later years, once she became an initiate of the system and heard various counselors and POs theorize about her "antisocial tendencies," she began to blame her delinquency on her father's death. Parroting the pronouncements of various professionals she met along the way, Carla would say she never got over the grief of losing him, or the anger she felt at being deserted by the person she loved most in the world.

It seems a convenient explanation, but, in truth, this is just Carla giving the professionals what they want to hear, an excuse that does not match the facts. Carla's defiance at home and criminal behavior in the streets did not begin until nearly four years after her father's death. That was the year Carla turned thirteen and her body stopped looking like a boy's. That was the year her mother found a second husband who suddenly moved into Carla's world and expected to be treated like a father.

And that was the year Carla started coming home late from school, detouring past the corner where the hoods from the Tepa-13 street gang hung out. Carla got her first tattoo that year, a bright red heart on her rear end—a secret she managed to keep from her mother for two years. At age thirteen, Carla began leading two lives, with one—that of the young, dangerous, don't-care-if-I-die-tomorrow gangbanger—gradually edging the honors student toward extinction.

It took a while for the adults in Carla's life to realize her new behavior was more than mere teen angst. Both her stepfather and her mother worked long hours that kept them both out of the home a great deal of the day. By the time they concluded something was seriously wrong with Carla, she had graduated to frequent fights and suspensions at school, plummeting grades, and outright defiance when they tried to discipline her. Every time her mother tried to crack down, Carla ran away. During one three-day refusal to come home, Carla escalated her flirtation with the gang life. She jumped into the Tepa gang.

"Jumping in" is a literal term: to pass muster with the gang, she had to stand a minute fighting with several gang members, showing her worth, her courage, her ability to take pain. It is a standard initiation rite of street life, mirrored by an even more brutal "jumping out" ordeal. Normally, girls only have to fight girls, but Carla made it clear she intended to hang with the boys. That meant a double rite. First she had to take on three girl members of Tepa at once, which she did in such a wild and fearless way that she ended up landing more punches than the three of them combined. She sneered at her combatants when it was over and called them weak, sending two of them home in tears. Then Carla withstood a minute-long beating from two male members of Tepa, standing her ground, throwing solid punches of her own and shedding no tears even as blood streamed from her nose and her left eye swelled shut. She could hear some of the guys watching and muttering "Damn!" and she knew she had won their respect that day, the only coin of the realm that matters in a gang.

In short order, the same natural talent for making herself indispensable that had worked so well for her in school made her a popular leader within the gang. Smart, quick, a good planner, Carla found even older members of Tepa asking what she thought of some plan or plot. The power was intoxicating, something akin to being a general with an army to command. The fierce code of loyalty between gang members, and the sense of security and contempt for outsiders it breeds, became the center of Carla's life after that. And any guy in Tepa who forgot himself and spoke to her as if she were different or less worthy or, God help him, coddled or touched her in a way that suggested he might be aware of what lay beneath her gangster baggies, then that boy soon found himself flat on his back, Carla's knees on his chest and her fists drawing blood.

A new world opened up for her then. With Tepa, like any gang, the rules were clear. You knew what was right and what was wrong: You stood up for your homeboys, you showed them loyalty and respect and they gave the same to you. You never showed cowardice, and you never backed down on a point of honor. Disrespect demanded a quick and violent response. "No one tells you these things," Carla says now. "You just know them in your gut. You know what is right and wrong. And if you didn't know them, you didn't belong there in the first place."

No one had to tell Carla what to do when members of another gang drove by and peppered a group of Tepa homeboys with bullets, wounding one kid, Carla's friend (who recovered, killed a sixteen-year-old boy in revenge, and went to the Youth Authority). "He was my dog. He was my tight. I ran the streets with him. I had to do something." It was Carla who grabbed a gun—there were always guns, communal property passed from gang member to gang member—and who headed to a car with another girl and a homeboy. The guy tried to take the gun from her, but Carla refused. "If I'm going to do a drive-by, I'm going to do the shooting," she would later explain, as if discussing the advantages of playing left field over right field in baseball. "If we're going to get caught, you know, I want to get caught doing something worthwhile. Not some chickenshit murder charge just because I'm sitting in the car when the gun went off. Why go down for that? Might as well do the shooting."

Carla claims she shot someone that day, though friends wonder if this is mere boastfulness. She says the boy who was struck survived and recovered. She was never caught or charged with this crime, though she almost died that day. After emptying her revolver at a crowd of rival gang members, a barrage of bullets slapped into the car inches from her as they sped off. The other girl in the car crossed herself, thanking the Virgin Mary for protecting them, but it had never occurred to Carla that she would be struck down. She still doesn't really believe it's possible—Carla says she is too smart to be killed. After the drive-by, she stayed out all that night with a small garrison of gang members, hunkered down outside a homeboy's house, waiting for a retaliation that never came. Then she went home, showered, and went to school. Feeling calm, justified, moral, honorable. And thrilled.

She was at the time one month shy of her fifteenth birthday.

Carla still put on a good front at school, still was capable of excelling when she wanted to, still worked extra hours in the office to curry favor, though now it was as much to cover her new deficiencies in class as anything else, the result of more time on the corner, less with the books. At home, the pretense slipped away. She openly defied her mother, she treated her stepfather with studied rudeness, she refused to observe anything like a curfew, much less quit her gang associations. She stayed out for days at a time. The counselor at her middle school who had befriended her tried to help, seeing the girl's future withering daily, but she was as powerless as Carla's parents to stop the running away, the truancy, the refusal to obey.

In years past, Juvenile Court routinely reined in children like Carla early on, before they committed any serious crimes. Running away, incorrigibility, truancy—they are known as "status offenses," because they affect only a person whose status is as a minor, a child. Part of the logic used at the turn of the century to justify creating a separate juvenile court, and to stop imprisoning ten-year-olds side-by-side with forty-year-olds, lay in the acknowledgment that children are different from adults and therefore should be held to different standards. Not only would the sentences be different, but the offenses themselves would stand apart, too. Under that theory, running away or disobeying one's parents or skipping school could be crimes in a juvenile court, even though adults could not be prosecuted for identical conduct. Indeed, such offenses made up the bulk of juvenile court cases during the first half of the twentieth century. And as public policy, it makes perfect sense, because the experts knew in 1905, as they do now, that this sort of misbehavior is in virtually every case the precursor of more serious crimes, Carla being just one of countless examples. It is almost impossible to find a juvenile who committed a serious crime today who did not first commit a passel of status offenses. Going after status offenders and putting them under rigorous supervision or even imprisonment proved to be an effective crime prevention tool in juvenile courts nationwide, stopping many kids from committing worse crimes. Carla would have been a perfect candidate.

But the prosecution of most status offenses ground to a halt in the seventies in California and in many other jurisdictions as well, when laws were adopted that decriminalized them, under the theory that it was unfair to incarcerate kids for behavior that could not get them locked up as adults.[1] In part, this came as a logical extension of the Supreme Court's Gault decision giving kids the same rights as adults; in part, it seemed a way to save money by cutting back services, particularly by gutting the ranks of probation officers who previously supervised status offenders. The juvenile court can still theoretically prosecute status cases—the statutes are still on the books—but judges have no power to enforce their orders, because kids charged under them generally cannot be locked up like delinquents. The laws are toothless. So, many juvenile courts have dropped the pursuit of status cases, and the desperate parents who had once come to police or prosecutors for help and gotten it are turned away. When Carla turned fifteen, her mother had called the sheriff's station serving her neighborhood and begged for a deputy to come and arrest her daughter for refusing to go to school or to obey her.

"I'm sorry," the desk sergeant who took the call had responded. "But unless she commits a crime, there's nothing we can do. Now, if she does commit a crime, give us a call, we can take a report and get something rolling."

Carla's mother started to say, "But then it will be too late," but she was speaking to a dial tone. The sergeant had already hung up. Later, when she called the DA's office, all Peggy Beckstrand could provide was a list of agencies offering counseling services—and advice on how far parents can legally go in disciplining their children before it becomes child abuse. Peggy gets calls asking about that distinction several times a week from parents whose children are out of control. "I wish I could tell you the system can help," she tells them lamely. "But I can't. We don't have the answers."

Even when Carla got busted for robbery for taking another girl's backpack, the system could not help. Carla's mother had been almost happy when the police called. Finally, she had exclaimed, something would be done, and without her greatest fear being realized—that her girl, or someone else, would get hurt.

This relief was short-lived, however. The witness in the case—the girl who had reported the crime in the first place—would not cooperate when it came time to go to court, possibly fearing retaliation of some kind. As in adult court, Juvenile Court cases cannot stand on what witnesses tell police—the witnesses have to swear to it personally in court, so Carla could enjoy her constitutional right to face her accuser. It is another legacy of the Gault decision. Peggy's office had no choice but to drop the case. Carla walked.

Two months later, she was arrested after police watched her climb out of a stolen Jeep with a couple of other members of Tepa-13, then steal the T-top from another car. Charged with grand theft auto, theft of property, and two counts of receiving stolen property, Carla was released the same day of her arrest after the Probation Department ignored pleas from Carla's mother that she stay locked up for her own protection. Seven months passed without resolution of the case, a typical delay in Juvenile Court. Peggy's office had hundreds of backlogged files to wade through before it could even pursue formal charges against the girl.[2] Juvenile Court is supposed to be as quick and efficient as a hospital emergency room in stopping a kid's downward spiral, but Carla went on doing what she wanted, cutting school and hanging with her homeboys, confident she could sweet-talk the court commissioner assigned to hear her case into straight probation. She had already made a very good impression on him during a brief court appearance after her arrest, with the commissioner going on and on about what a fabulous student she was, what enormous potential she had. "He thinks he's going to lecture me a little and straighten me right up," she told the guys in Tepa after the hearing. "It's so funny. He's got no idea what's up."

It might have worked, too, but before her case could be set for trial, there was a second drive-by shooting, this one ending with her bullets missing their mark, Carla's head punching through a windshield, and two cops standing in the school office questioning the faculty about her whereabouts. They busted her later that day.

This time, Carla stayed in Juvenile Hall while her case wound its way through the system, safe from further trouble. Behind bars, her behavior ran true to form: She became a model inmate at Central Juvenile Hall, working for the detention officers, keeping the other kids in line. The staff could literally put their feet up and let Carla do the work.

Eventually, she was convicted of theft and assault with a deadly weapon by Commissioner Gary Polinksy, one of the three bench officers at Thurgood Marshall Branch. Peggy's office asked that she serve time in the California Youth Authority, the harshest sentence available for a fifteen-year-old.

"I've got four years and four months over your head, young lady," Polinsky told her, "and you could very well spend that time at the Youth Authority. Your behavior has been appalling."

Carla appeared properly abject while the veteran juvenile commissioner, renowned for his bouts of bad temper, continued railing about her path in life, but she did not believe for one moment that he would send her to YA. You just don't do that with kids who have "potential," she knew. Her more experienced homeboys had explained the law to her: they knew from their own courtroom misadventures that juvenile judges were required to impose the "least restrictive" sentence possible, which meant that Carla, who had not been sentenced to anything as yet, would never end up in juvenile prison her first time out of the box, not when there were other, less hard-core options available. And Carla got exactly what she expected: Polinsky sentenced her to up to one year at Camp Resnick, one of two dozen rural detention camps run by the Probation Department, where she would join many old friends from the street and gain even further respect from her gang for having done time.

Once there, Carla again impressed the staff in charge of watching over her with her charm, intelligence, and abilities, getting stellar grades in class and graduating the program with honors after only seven months in custody. Upon her release, she was pronounced a rousing success for the system. Clearly, she had learned her lesson. Carla smiled, promised she would never return, thanked all her counselors, and walked out, carrying a piece of paper that said her new probation officer was someone named Sharon Stegall.

"I'm doing great, Ms. Stegall," Carla promises her probation officer this day, on their first visit following her release from camp. "I'm back on track in school, I'm going to make up my credits, and then I'll be in college prep courses."

Sharon remains skeptical. Kids don't end up on her specialized gang caseload because they are so easily straightened out. Kids end up with Sharon Stegall looking over their shoulder because, if they don't shape up, their next stop could easily be the state penitentiary.

Most juvenile POs in Los Angeles have enormous caseloads, far too many kids to supervise closely.[3] Sharon, however, is on a special gang detail. Her load is limited to fifty kids, which in contemporary Los Angeles is considered intensive supervision. (Standards change as resources dwindle: In the sixties, many probation officers worked with fewer than twenty kids; thirty-five offenders, even minor ones, were considered the maximum number that could be supervised effectively by any one person.) Sharon and her colleagues on the Metro Gang Unit get the toughest, most hardened kids to supervise, the ones who have committed violent crimes or who have lengthy records and have resisted obeying regular probation officers in the past. Basically, she deals with the Sixteen Percenters—the 16 percent of juvenile delinquents in LA who are hard-core repeat offenders. All of Sharon's kids have been locked up in camp or CYA before coming to her. Few of them faced any meaningful consequences or supervision early on when it might have mattered. Now, though, these hard cases get the most intensive attention from the system available at this late stage in their criminal careers—when they are least likely to benefit from it. If five out of her fifty kids make it on probation in any given year, she considers it a rousing success.

"Making it" is defined as not disappearing, dying, or getting arrested for twelve months.[4]

"I don't know, Carla," Sharon says during that first meeting after Carla's release from camp. The probation officer has already had a long talk with Carla's school counselor, mother, and older sister. "I hear you are pretty slick."

"No, really, Ms. Stegall. I know now that I have to quit the life. I was just being a follower. Now I know my so-called friends don't really care

about me. I just want to do good in school so I can go to law school and be
a lawyer. I want to help people." Carla flashes that winning smile of hers.
"And I like to argue. I'm good at it."

"We'll see," Sharon says, her voice completely neutral. "Now I'm going
to go over your conditions of probation with you, and you'd better listen
up, because if you cross the line on any of them, I will hook you up." Sharon reaches into her purse and pulls out a set of stainless-steel handcuffs,
jingling them at Carla. "Now, you will obey all laws. You will submit to
being searched by any peace officer or probation officer with or without a
warrant. You will not consume alcoholic beverages or any controlled substance. You will not associate with any gang members, wear gang clothing,
or use any gang signs or gestures. . . ." The list goes on a good five minutes.
There are twenty-four separate conditions.

When the litany of dos and don'ts is completed and Carla walks from
the office, promising to be good, Sharon turns and says to a colleague, "I
give that girl a week before she blows it."

It turns out that Sharon underestimated Carla.

That same night finds Carla on a corner with her Tepa-13 friends, exchanging high fives and passing around a little homegrown, catching up
and kicking back. Then they show their long-absent home girl what they
have been up to while she was at Camp Resnick. One of her homeboys
lifts up his shirt and says, "Check this out."

His abdomen bears an enormous and still freshly scabbed tattoo, with
"Tepa" spelled in six-inch-high Old English letters emblazoned across his
belly like a billboard. Carla looks closely at the needlework, admiring the
artistry—and the nerve it took to get it. She knew that it had to have hurt
like hell, and every guy in the gang had one just like it. Several of them
were on probation with the Juvenile Court; the tattoos were blatant violations, an instant ticket to the hall for each of them if word got out.
Her probation conditions were specific: no gang tattoos. There is only one
thing Carla can say.

"So when do I get mine?"

Within a week, Carla is missing, her mother is frantic, and Sharon Stegall
is conferring in the hallway with Deputy in Charge Peggy Beckstrand.
They agree she needs to be locked up. It is one more case for the head
prosecutor to juggle as she prepares for her murder case against Ronald
Duncan.

"How is that thing going, anyway?" Sharon asks, after the two women decide to seek commitment to the California Youth Authority for Carla—if Sharon catches her before she ends up with a murder charge of her own to face. "That Baskin Robbins is right in my neighborhood. The owners were good people. You going to win?"

Peggy shrugs. It is the same question she asks herself daily. "I'm pretty sure I'll convict him, Sharon," the prosecutor says. "But I don't think anyone's going to win."

CHAPTER 3

Nine Days to Manhood

"It won't be long now," Ronald Duncan announces as he swaggers into the writing class on Unit K/L at Central Juvenile Hall. "Pretty soon, I'll be walkin' free."

"Yeah, you and O. J.," one of the other students says, smirking and cocking his head at the TV bolted to the wall outside in the dayroom, where tape of the ex-football player's infamous low-speed chase is on the tube once again.

Ronald ignores the remark. He is in unusually high spirits for a kid who just came back from court on the 8:00 P.M. bus, an exhausting day of thin bologna sandwiches and long waits in cold holding tanks punctuated by bewildering court appearances. He slumps into a chair, low enough to be eye level with the library table's surface, a compact sixteen-year-old with broad shoulders and a small head, a sparse collection of whiskers curling from his chin like mistletoe. He has a wide, yellow-toothed smile that he wears often, but his expression is unintentionally disconcerting, because his dark brown eyes never quite manage to point in the same direction at the same time.

"I'm tellin' you, I'm on my way out," he insists, but as is so often the case with Ronald, I cannot tell if he is serious or joking. The smile almost never goes away.

"Oh, yeah? Your trial go good today?" Chris asks. *"Or you just plannin' to bust out?"*

Everyone laughs, Ronald included, though there is an edge of nastiness to the amusement. He is not particularly popular in the class—quick to criticize, he never seems to write anything of his own—but there is little else to talk about in the lockup besides handicapping one another's cases and figuring out ways to smuggle dope into the hall. So when he falls silent, someone prods again. *"So how did it go?"*

Ronald shrugs. It is a chillingly nonchalant gesture for a kid with a double murder charge against him, for it is not pretense or bluster. *"It went pretty good. I told them I was innocent."*

The six other boys in the class nod. While in the courtroom, everyone here is innocent. Back on the unit, however, most of the kids say they pretty much did what they're in for, or something close to it.

"What'd you do, tell them you're no killer, just a punk tagger?" Geri Vance asks. In the Juvenile Hall hierarchy, graffiti artists—taggers—are lightweights, commanding little respect.

"Tag-banger," Ronald corrects quickly. *"We're a lot badder than just taggers."*

The other boys in the small classroom laugh again. Ronald often tries to impress the others with tales of his supposed criminal prowess, no matter how counterproductive that might be for a kid trying to get out from under a murder charge. He is wasting his time, though: Most kids who have been in the system as long as his classmates have possess finely honed bullshit meters. They can tell in a moment from Ronald's showy bravado and too-cool patter that before his arrival at the lockup, he never did much of anything wrong, always small and quiet and slightly left out, invisible in class, invisible to girls. He just had this slightly off-kilter appearance, and people always assumed the worst, giving him a wide berth, the way you would a quiescent yet mean-looking dog. In the lockup, they know better.

"Didn't you tell us you had blood all over your clothes or your backpack or something?" one of the other kids asks. *"How'd you explain that?"*

Ronald's grin widens a notch. *"I said I was walking home that night and I flagged down this van, so I could hitch a ride with this dude I know. And when I got in, there's blood all over and a sack of money on the floor. And he tells me, 'I did it. I killed them.' It's like, I didn't know until I got in the van, and by then, all the blood was all over me."*

The other kids are genuinely interested now, intrigued by the notion that you could climb innocently into a van and suddenly be thrust into the middle of a murder. It is not such an outlandish notion to the kids in this room: Three of the six students in the class this night are charged with murder simply for being willingly present when someone else did the shooting or stabbing. Now they wonder if they can learn something from Ronald they might be able to use in court. Enjoying the spotlight, Ronald continues to recap his testimony, slipping into the street slang he has carefully cultivated since entering the hall, hoping it will give him standing.

"So then they ask about the money I'm supposed to have stolen from my bosses, that I supposedly killed them for. And I say no, I got that from this dude's van. I told them that I just reached down and picked up some of the money sitting there on the floor of the van and said, 'Break me off.'"

The other kids stare at him, then shake their heads, immediately losing interest. Someone mutters the word "Fool," and Ronald looks confused. "What's wrong with that? Wouldn't you want to break off some of the money for yourself, too?"

"Man," Geri says with disgust, "no wonder they want to fry your ass, talkin' that kind of shit in court." Geri, facing his own murder rap, has written a series of eloquent letters to the court, polishing them in class, acutely conscious that he will walk into court presumed to be a monster, and that he will have a tough time combating that perception. "You go into court, you're not on the street, dummy. You think that judge is going to believe anything you say now? Break me off. He's gonna break you off, all right. Break you off right into prison."

Ronald just shakes his head at this piece of wisdom, still smiling his invulnerable, indecipherable smile. "Can't send me to prison," he says mildly, and this irks Geri even more. Because, unlike Ronald, Geri can go to prison.

The last student arrives a few moments later and I start the class with a five-minute writing exercise. Ronald declares his intention to write a quick page about a boy wrongly accused of murdering his bosses. "I'll call it, 'Innocent Blood,'" he says, inscribing the title onto a piece of blue-lined loose-leaf paper with a wobbly flourish.

For the next five minutes, he seems to be concentrating on his work, but when the time comes to read aloud to the class, Ronald is the only boy in the room whose page is still blank.

THE first time Peggy Beckstrand saw him, Ronald Duncan giggled and smiled over his shoulder at his parents sitting in back of the ancient courtroom, a skinny boy with those little kid arms you could wrap your thumb and pinkie around, no problem. It seemed hard to believe he could raise, much less successfully aim and fire, a double-barreled shotgun. The police had thought that right up until he happily showed them how he did it. That was a year ago, though, and since then, Ronald has bulked up in the hall, a product of forced calisthenics and starchy foods and the march of adolescence, new muscles and goatee and a slight paunch aging his five-foot-five frame.

"I didn't do anything, I swear," he tells his parents every time they visit, and they, of course, believe him. He is their baby, their youngest son, a kid who has never been in trouble a day in his life, but for the occasional detention at school, a cut class here and there. They dismiss his confession to the police. They have heard of terrible things that can happen to a young black male locked up in a police interrogation room; they know what happened to Rodney King. Ronald's father, a humble and soft-spoken gentleman with a deeply lined face and the hard calluses of a man who worked a lifetime with his hands, speaks with a quiet passion about his son's innocence, of how he *knows* with something that borders on religious faith that his boy, the child who came to him late in life and made him young again, could not possibly be a killer. He and his wife are no longer married, but they are living together again while the case is pending, their Ronald's future in the balance. The case is now the center of their lives, every hearing, every motion, every casual utterance in court. To them, Peggy Beckstrand is the monster—the humorless face of the state, trying to take their child away.

She feels their stares drilling into the back of her neck at every hearing. Peggy feels sorry for them, for the pain their family must bear, the look of incomprehension on their faces every time they hear the courtroom ring with the words, "Ronald Duncan: two counts, Section 187 of the California Penal Code—murder in the first degree." She wonders what the Duncan family sees when Ronald comes strutting into the room, grinning and waving like a kid getting off the bus from summer camp. At such moments, when disgust wells up within Peggy, she sometimes watches Ronald's mother and father rise and extend their hands toward him, reaching out across yards of empty space, the closest thing to an embrace they are allowed in court, where touching the accused is not permitted, the cold reality juvenile and adult systems share. To Peggy, it is as if she and the family are looking at two different children. Will they remain so blinded by love, she wonders, when the trial begins and she hauls out the pictures of what Ronald left behind on the night of the murder? Would *she* be so blinded if it were her daughter Courtney skipping into the courtroom? Even after all these years in the DA's office, it is the sort of question that can still haunt this former preschool teacher, this mother and grandmother, whose job is to be a prosecutor of children.

But then, there are the pictures. They haunt her, too, agony and loss captured in the harsh strobe light of a crime-scene photographer's camera. The last pictures of Chuck and Adelina Rusitanonta.

The image will always be indelible in Peggy's mind: husband and wife slumped in their old Mercury station wagon, engine still running, back door ajar. Shortly before 11:00 P.M., the car had drifted slowly into a lamp-post on a residential street. A man had run out onto his porch at the sound of two loud bangs followed by the sound of a car crashing, just in time to see a shadowy figure run away from the car and toward a van that seemed to have been waiting.

Inside the car, husband and wife were still wearing their matching Baskin Robbins shirts, impossibly huge matching holes blown in their heads by a pair of point-blank shotgun blasts, their blood and brains and bits of bone sprayed like graffiti onto the windshield, dashboard, and seats. Their facial features were wildly distorted, sagging like party balloons that had been overfilled, then deflated, by the volcanic heat and pressure of expanding gases leaving the gun barrel along with the buckshot. (Typical of her sometimes morbid obsession with the gritty details of crime, Peggy had gone to a medical library to study this ballooning phenomenon so she could explain it all in court in clinical detail—even though she knew the judge hearing the case would not be the least bit interested. This was a habit left over from a career of jury trials in adult court, where no detail could be ignored or issue taken for granted. "It's a matter of being pre-pared. Of being professional. If this were a *real* court," she says with biting contempt, "there would be no question. I'd have to do this.")

Natural suspicion, then hard evidence and witnesses (a talkative get-away driver, a bloody van), led detectives to young Ronald Duncan, the only other person working that night at the ice cream store. After telling a series of preposterous lies about walking home alone and getting mugged that night—and after police made an unfortunate and ultimately illegal reference to the killer receiving the death penalty that would come back to haunt Peggy—Ronald switched his story and confessed. He calmly explained how he rode home in the backseat of Chuck and Ada's car after they closed up shop for the night, determined to rob them, a sawed-off shotgun in his backpack along with his schoolbooks and unfinished homework.

As he would explain to his interrogators, a few minutes into the ride, having worked up sufficient nerve to carry out his plan, he pulled out his weapon and, without a word, fired at Chuck's head with the single-shot shotgun, the car still moving. The cops, who had found no murder weapon, had been taken aback by this, asking, *Are you sure it was single-shot?* Ronald had nodded: There was just one barrel. It wasn't a double or an over-and-under, he said. The awful implication of this would later stun Peggy as much as it had the police. It meant this fifteen-year-old boy had to shoot Chuck, who had been driving, break open the gun, take out the spent shell, put in another one, close the gun, and shoot Adelina—even as the now driverless car was drifting to the curb and crashing. Not to mention the fact that the vinyl interior of the Mercury station wagon had to have looked and felt like a slaughterhouse after that first shot. This provided clear evidence of premeditation, rather than a spur-of-the-moment act of irrationality. To calmly reload and kill a second time in the face of such carnage took a special sort of commitment.

"What was Ada doing during this time you had to reload?" one of the interrogators had asked. As Peggy later calculated it, the woman must have sat there for a good five to ten seconds wearing part of her husband's brain before Ronald got around to dispatching her, too.

"She screamed," a deadpan Ronald recalled. "After I shot her, it wasn't nothing else said."

Ronald admitted taking some of the store's receipts from a bank bag beside Chuck's body, but all the blood had finally unnerved him, and he only got a portion of the money, though it was a sufficient wad for him to show off like a game hunter's trophy the next day in school. Robbery might have been only part of the motive anyway. Ronald also said he was peeved at his bosses for criticizing him for being late. As a friend would later recall, "He didn't like being *dissed*."

One of the interrogators couldn't help but say, "Hey, you must've really hated Chuck and Ada to do something like this. And Ronald had smiled, then said, "No, I really loved them." Every time she reads that in the big blue Murder Book, it gives Peggy chills. Because she believes him.

Now, as the day of the trial approaches, Peggy has become increasingly obsessed with the case. The detectives have moved on to other investigations and seldom return her phone calls; it is now her responsibility alone to pursue Ronald. She takes the files home with her every night, sitting in bed with them, playing tapes and reading transcripts, falling into a fitful sleep with the trappings of murder spread all around her like a scrapbook. She even keeps the numbing crime scene photos in her top desk drawer, pulling them out whenever the place gets to her, a grim salve fortifying her resolve to put the shooter away. Here is a kid who was never abused, never deprived, raised in a solid middle-class family with all the clothes, stereos, color TVs, and opportunities he could want—a kid who, unlike so many of the truly pitiful children Peggy prosecutes daily, has no excuse for his conduct. Ronald's parents say there is a simple explanation for this: He is innocent. But Peggy sees Ronald as a conscienceless emblem of an era in which unspeakable acts of violence are carried out every day by juvenile delinquents—a legally mandated but quaintly outdated term for the sort of mayhem Ronald and his peers commit.

And it is that quaint designation of a shotgun murderer as a "delinquent" that is the source of Peggy's obsession with the case, for to her, Ronald Duncan clearly demonstrates everything wrong with the juvenile justice system. It has nothing to do with facts or evidence or law or coerced confessions. The issue is birthdays.

The murders occurred nine days before Ronald turned sixteen.

"Nine days," Peggy mutters to herself at least once a week. Each time, she examines the calendar again, hoping, somehow, she has miscalculated. She sent away for a true copy of Ronald's birth certificate, hoping for some discrepancy. It is sitting on her desk back at the office. But the nine days stand. And that inconsequential number of days means Ronald Duncan cannot be tried or imprisoned as an adult.

No matter what Peggy does in court, no matter how compelling the evidence, Ronald Duncan's punishment will never fit his crime. Through luck or design or simple accident of birth, he would remain swathed in the protections of Juvenile Court, which in California meant he would have to go free by age twenty-five. Period. There could be no appeal, no exception: That was the law in California. Are you sixteen or over at the instant the trigger is pulled? Then go to adult court, face life in prison without parole. Fifteen years, 364 days, 23 hours, and 59 minutes when the crime goes down? You're a kid, stay in Juvenile Court. Count the days till you're free.

The arbitrariness of it, the illogic, drove Peggy to distraction, as if there was any cognitive difference between a sixteen-year-old and a kid who was fifteen years, 356 days old. The fact that in forty-two states of the Union outside of California, Ronald would have been tried as an adult, and would be eligible for a life sentence (or, in a growing number of states, a death sentence), only enraged Peggy—and the juvenile system's growing legion of critics—all the more. Indeed, Ronald's case already had become a rallying cry, cited in Sacramento and in Washington as an example of needed change.[1]

"We have to live with this," Peggy complains at a staff meeting with her attorneys at the end of the day, "simply because someone, somewhere, decided decades ago, based on absolutely no scientific evidence, that only a sixteen-year-old can commit the crimes of an adult. And that someone who falls nine days short of the mark ought to remain in a system designed to reform wayward kids, not control and punish armed robbers and murderers. It makes no sense. It makes me sick."

Of course, fretting over Ronald getting a relative wrist slap for murder presupposed he would be convicted, something Peggy could no longer afford to count upon. She had at first considered the case a slam dunk: she had one witness who swore a blood-drenched, shotgun-toting Ronald flagged down his van on the night of the murder; there was a friend from school who swore Ronald admitted killing his employers the day after the murders; and then there was the centerpiece of her case, Ronald's taped confession to the police.

But here was the problem: The same Juvenile Court that could not impose adult penalties on Ronald gave him all the same legal tools an adult enjoys—and imposed on Peggy all the same legal burdens. The case would still have to be proven beyond a reasonable doubt. Ronald's lawyers were even now brutally attacking the credibility of the school chum and the van driver, who they claimed was no unwitting accomplice, but the actual killer. Worse still for Peggy's case, thanks to the bumbling police reference to capital punishment, which juveniles cannot receive in California, the defense had a very good shot at preventing her from using Ronald's confession in court. It could be "suppressed," to use the legal term—along with Peggy's entire case.

"We spend millions of dollars to prosecute juveniles with taped confessions," she rants at her staff meeting, trying to instill some fury in her small cadre of burned-out prosecutors left glassy-eyed at the end of each day by the sheer number of kids they prosecute. "We're wasting all this money on trials and proceedings and making sure everyone's rights are observed, even when we know, absolutely, that the kid did it. In fact, we spend *more* when we know they did it. It makes no sense. We've already decided to treat him as a juvenile, God help us. He's already won. Yet we still spend all this time and money proving the case, defending the case, litigating the case. And then there's nothing left over for the kids who really need help, who come in here on a car theft or a burglary and who get sent on their way with nothing more than a pat on the back, go on home to your gangs and screwed-up families. And then we're all so surprised when they come back on another charge. Or when they turn into Ronald Duncan. The system is stupid. Completely stupid."

Her prosecutors sitting around the file-strewn conference table stare back at their normally reserved boss with eyes wide, but no one says anything. They know she is nearing her breaking point, ready to quit. Most of them have already concluded that the Juvenile Court system is hopeless anyway, and they, too, are simply counting the days until their one-year tours of duty—their juvenile sentences—end, so they can move up the ladder at the DA's office.

After their year is up in this least desirable of all prosecutorial assignments, they know they will have served more time in the juvenile system than most kids do.

"God, I hate this job," Peggy mutters to herself after the meeting, an angry mantra spoken as she stands in her file-choked office, her aspirin bottle empty, her cup of tea long gone cold, head spinning with all that she must do. She rubs her pale face with hands so cold she brings gloves to work with her, though the temperatures have been in the seventies this week. She is tired of the green attorneys who work for her, tired of the defense lawyers who delay and confuse, tired of the cops who don't return her phone calls. Most of all, she hates the chaotic piles of files scattered throughout her office, because no matter how fast she deals with them, no matter how many young predators she puts away, more take their place. She thinks often of quitting. She even wrote the Peace Corps a few years earlier, figuring she could chuck the whole thing for a while in some distant outpost—only to find out she had no qualifications for such volunteer service. All she knows how to do is be a lawyer, the one thing the Peace Corps doesn't need.

Peggy used to have a simpler, cleaner mission in the DA's office, one she vastly preferred: She prosecuted sex crimes. Sexual assaults, molestations, rapes. Half the job was putting abusive, terrible people away, all of them adults, something she could do zealously, with a kind of angry joy she never quite mustered prosecuting juveniles. The other half of the job was looking out for the shattered victims of these crimes, shepherding them through the ordeal of testifying in court. In many of her cases, the victims—her star witnesses—were children. Peggy found she became as much a social worker as a prosecutor in this job.

One case in particular still haunts her—the face of the little boy she fought to protect carved into her memory. His name was Peter. He was seven when Peggy first met him. His father had regularly sodomized him for years. He had used a garden hose, among other implements of sexual torture. It was so bad, the kid could no longer control his bowels. When he had tried to tell his mother about it, she refused to believe her son, medical evidence be damned.

"You're ruining my life," Peter's mother told Peggy once the authorities found out and stepped in. Peggy wished she could prosecute her as well as the father.

The first time Peggy came by to interview Peter, he hid under his bed. He answered her questions, but he would not leave this refuge, the same place he would retreat to at night, hoping his daddy would not find him pressed against the wall in the darkness, though Daddy always did. After hours of this, of small talk and gentle coaxing, Peggy finally persuaded Peter to come out from the dust motes and shadows. She did this by sitting cross-legged on the floor beside the bed and offering him a chair, so he could sit high over her, safe and out of reach. He finally slid from under the bed, climbed onto the chair, and sat. It took three more sessions for him to look directly at her and make sustained eye contact, but Peggy slowly won the boy's trust. They forged a relationship, no small accomplishment when, of the two adults Peter knew best, one used him as a sexual plaything and the other called him a dirty little liar.

With that, Peter told Peggy everything. Nothing could be more chilling, Peggy would later say, than hearing a child recite his daily agonies, a bright, engaging boy whose life should have been full of promise, not hurt, and who, even after all that abuse, expressed no anger, only bewilderment. What had he done wrong? Peter kept asking. Why was he being punished? Nothing, Peggy kept telling him, you did nothing wrong. Her chest would ache when Peter asked that, for she knew he would never believe in his blamelessness. He would always figure he must have been very bad for his dad to do such things to him. All Peggy could do was to promise those things would never happen to him again, to promise to be his lawyer in the courtroom. His protector.

It was a tough case, hinging entirely on Peter's testimony, and when the day of trial arrived, Peggy worried he might not be able to tell his story, that he would see his father sitting at the defendant's table and freeze up. It had happened before in other cases. Molesters banked on it. So as they walked into court together, she kneeled down and whispered, "You know how old I am?"

Peter looked at her quizzically. He knew everything about Peggy. She had told him everything. How could she not? How could she ask him to reveal such unspeakable things without giving of herself? "Yes," he said slowly, "I know."

"Well," Peggy said, "you know how old people forget things sometimes?" He smiled then, nodded. "Oh, yeah."

"Well, I just forgot everything you've ever told me."

He smiled again, a stooped little boy who so often looked pained, but who would do anything to help his friend the prosecutor. "Don't worry, Peggy," the child said, his brows knitted in genuine concern over her memory loss. "I'll tell you again." And he patted her shoulder. The memory can still make her cry.

The defense lawyer kept Peter on the stand for two days. The father blew kisses at the boy. But Peter held up through it all, and the jury convicted the father on every count. It was the most satisfying victory of Peggy's legal career.

A few months later, Peggy was struck by a car as she left court, a glancing blow that left her dazed and sitting on the curb, dim faces looming over her like parade floats as people bent to see if she was okay. Through the haze and bewilderment, the only thought that kept going through her mind was the image of Peter's stunned and disbelieving father being led off to lockup. "Everything's okay in the world," she had muttered to herself as she sat bleeding on that curb. "At least that sonafabitch is still in jail."

But then there was delay after delay in his sentencing. Peggy got transferred before she could finish the case and another assistant DA took over. Peter's father hired a new lawyer, who claimed his first attorney had been incompetent. A judge granted him a new trial. And the new DA on the case, with no emotional investment, no knowledge of Peter, no experience of seeing that somber little boy hiding under his bed, fingered the file and figured it was too tough a case. He dismissed it. The molester walked free and Peter disappeared into the child welfare system. Peggy never heard what happened to him after that, though she could only pray he did not end up back with that father who tortured him or that mother who blamed him for ruining her life with lies. At the time, she considered it her low point as a DA.

"But, now," she says, "my job here in Juvenile Court makes me feel that way every day. Too many cases here end up like that. I can't protect anyone."

Peggy has moved from fighting for children who have been victimized by crime to fighting to imprison them. The irony is sometimes overwhelming to her. She knows many of the kids she now prosecutes come from backgrounds not all that different from Peter's. All too many were neglected, abused, discarded children before they became criminals. For all she knows, Peter has become a juvenile delinquent himself—he is what the experts call "at risk."[2] Yet she does not confuse her job with social work anymore. She sees herself at too much of a disadvantage to feel merciful toward the kids she now pursues. If she cannot save the Peters of the world, she would have to do her best to restrain the Ronald Duncans. This is what Peggy now believes: Lock the little monsters away. Protect the community at all costs. You only have to see photos like those in the Duncan case so many times before you decide murder is murder no matter the age of the killer, no matter how sad the story might be, no matter how much you yearn to help that kid hiding under the bed—because once you start excusing one of them, you can find reasons to give them all a break. That is the stark set of rules Peggy uneasily forces herself to live by every day. And if Judge Dorn or anyone else refuses to see that and to abide by the ever harsher laws and policies being put into place here, it is Peggy Beckstrand's job to take them down.

Peggy would have liked to concentrate on the crumbling case of *People* v. *Duncan* to the exclusion of all else, but no Juvenile Court prosecutor, least of all a DIC, a deputy in charge, could enjoy that luxury. She had her prosecutors to supervise, filing decisions to make, seemingly endless meetings to attend, and committees to chair. The distractions never stopped, and they were about to double.

After settling the matter of Ronald Duncan's trial date, Peggy Beckstrand's next stop is the hallway outside the two upstairs courtrooms. There is a niche next to the staircase here, with several wooden benches and relative quiet, and it is here that much of the court's business is decided. Here prosecutors talk to their witnesses for the first time, just minutes before trial, only then finding out if their cases are strong or weak—or if a key witness hasn't bothered to show up, a constant problem in Juvenile Court.

Defense attorneys huddle on the next bench with their small clients or their families, then try to cut plea bargains with the DA on the case. This slapdash process, in which two young, opposing attorneys—most of them a year or two out of law school—sit down on a bench with a pile of files and dispense with half a court docket, ends up deciding more about a troubled kid's future than any judge or formal court proceeding.[3] It is ugly and quick, a convenience for the system rather than a reliable means of healing our youth or pursuing justice. It happens with kids and families watching, standing off to the side, waiting for what amounts to a thumbs-up or a thumbs-down on the future of a child.

On this morning, an assistant district attorney looks to Peggy for guidance on an armed robbery case, an unusual stickup involving a sixteen-year-old honors student from a wealthy family from a coastal enclave in South Los Angeles County. The kid has no priors, the assistant says. Unlike most kids in Juvenile Court, John Sloan's family is intact, supportive, churchgoing, well connected, and desperate to do whatever it takes to keep their son out of a state prison system that would eat him alive. The case is the flip side of Ronald Duncan's—since he was over sixteen at the time of the crime, John can be sent to adult court, where he could end up doing more time for robbery than Ronald could for murder. The defense lawyer hired by the family wants the DA to drop its effort to have John sent out of Juvenile.

Peggy shakes her head no without hesitation. There won't be any deals on this one. Bad enough the law forces her to keep murderers when they happen to be under sixteen. She certainly won't voluntarily hold back on older violent criminals like John Sloan, not when California's extremely tough "fitness" law makes a transfer to adult court a virtual lock for prosecutors when a kid is over sixteen. Besides, she has talked to the victim of that robbery—his whole family was traumatized, his little girls are afraid to let him leave the house, afraid he'll never come home again. One nervous pull of the trigger that day, and this could have been a murder case, she reminds her deputy DA. "We're going forward with the fitness hearing," Peggy says flatly, looking the defense lawyer squarely in the eye. "Office policy. We don't withdraw fitnesses. If your client committed an adult crime, he deserves to go to adult court."

The answer is the expected one. The other lawyers nod like old bridge partners and head into court, while John's mother, who had been sitting nearby listening to the exchange, sits and weeps without uttering a sound, her eyes red and swollen, her hands gripping the purse in her lap as if it were a shield, waiting for a loudspeaker to hiss and spit her child's name so that she, too, can rise and enter this grimy and forlorn hall of justice.

It would not always have ended this way. At one time, before LA began to drown in a juvenile crime wave, Peggy and her colleagues did not feel the need to be so inflexible: Prosecutors used to pick and choose only the absolute worst kids to target for the adult system. A few years ago, John Sloan would never have faced transfer into the adult arena and its theoretically harsher punishments. Now, though, prosecutors here file fitness motions on nearly every kid over sixteen who commits a serious crime—over nine hundred of them last year, triple the number five years earlier. And the law is so tough, judges—albeit grudgingly—have become little more than rubber stamps for the prosecution's wishes. It is a trend mirrored nationwide, a deliberate shift in policy, letting the crime, not the criminal, dictate how a child is treated by the system.

Starting today, it is also a policy that will further distract Peggy Beckstrand from prosecuting Ronald Duncan, putting her—and the rest of the Juvenile Court—on a collision course with the new supervising judge at Thurgood Marshall, Roosevelt Dorn, judge of the Superior Court and minister of God, whose self-appointed mission is nothing less than rescuing the system, one kid at a time.

CHAPTER 4

Judge Dorn

"My mother and father made a lot of money off of ripping people off, and using scams such as cashing bad income tax checks. But the main cash that my parents made came from selling homegrown marijuana. We had a backyard that was full of marijuana plants that grew at least an average of four feet tall. My mom and dad sat around the house smoking marijuana and having sex all day long; even if I was right in front of them. My parents didn't care, they would just blow the smoke in my face until I got a buzz and left the room on my own." [1]

Geri Vance looks up uncertainly from the story he is reading, chapter two of his autobiography in progress. He is a handsome teenager with large brown eyes and a receding hairline, a brotherly peacekeeper on the unit, a favorite of both the staff and the other kids at the hall. He is bright and insightful, but there are enormous blind spots in his experience: he has never been to a museum or a baseball game or a public library or a doctor's office (unless you count the infirmary at Juvenile Hall). He reached sixteen without ever writing much of anything, but our class has opened a door. He is churning out ten and twenty pages a day now, handicapped only by the rigorous schedule of the hall, and the propensity of the staff to confiscate papers at night, promising to return them in the morning, then losing or destroying them. Geri has to hide his best work under his mattress as if it were contraband.

The room we sit in is dank and musty, like a seldom-used closet in someone's basement. There is a folding table and chairs. A few bedraggled paperbacks and a row of Gideon Bibles occupy a bookshelf bolted to one pale blue cinder block wall—props that enable the Juvenile Hall staff to label these uninviting quarters the "library."

Now Geri hesitates in his recitation, glancing at the other boys, unsure if he should be smiling and boasting about the passage he just read, or ashamed. The other kids are listening intently, their faces neutral, though there is some snickering when he reads the next passage. It describes the day he walked in on his father and a prostitute in bed, and how they reacted to the intrusion by ordering him to fondle the woman's breasts and genitals. He recalls that he was six or seven years old at the time. It was a scene that would be repeated many times.

"I knew it was dirty," Geri writes, "and I ran to my room and felt really bad and confused every time. But I liked it, too."

After one bathtub frolic with the prostitute, Geri tells the class, his mother came home and found him playing in his room with his father's gun, a gang-style bandanna on his small head and a marijuana joint in the corner of his mouth—imitating Dad, he said proudly. Geri's mother beat him with an extension cord until he bled. Then she took the gun, found her husband in bed with the hooker, aimed the pistol at the father's head, and pulled the trigger. The gun, it turned out, was not loaded. Geri watched his father knock it from his mother's hand, then savagely beat her while the prostitute sat naked and giggling, too blasted to get dressed and leave.

Geri and his mother left instead, fleeing the house that night and living for the next few months on peanut butter and bologna, staying in cheap motels, surviving on his mother's earnings as a prostitute (or that part of her earnings not squandered on crack cocaine). Geri did not attend school, but stayed in the motel room to watch his younger brother, Joachim, while Mom was out scoring tricks and dope. This lifestyle lasted until Geri was eight or nine, when his mom was sent to prison for cashing other people's checks, and Geri went to Juvenile Hall.

"I've been in the system ever since," Geri reads, putting down his paper. "That's the end of the chapter. I haven't gotten any farther yet."

I look around the table at the rest of the class, hoping to see astonishment or horror registering on some of the faces in the room, these boy with their unlined features and old, world-weary eyes. Instead, I see knowing looks of recognition, kids who had witnessed or experienced the same sort of life, or worse.

Someone tells Geri, "The Menendez brothers got nothin' on you," and everyone laughs. The Menendez case had been much in the news at the time, the two monied brothers from Beverly Hills who killed their parents, then justified their premeditated act by claiming their father physically and sexually abused them. Their uncorroborated story had so confounded jurors that no verdict could be reached—something Geri and my other writing students find perplexing. They, like many kids in Juvenile Court, can make claims of terrible abuse, all of it documented and indisputable, yet it does them no good. In Juvenile Court, being an abused child is no defense.

"It's all a double standard. You have to be rich and white for that defense to work," Elias says. He has previously advanced the theory that the single most important fact in a court case is the color of the defendant, something that virtually every kid in the hall seems to take as a given. Elias nods at Geri. "You think anyone is going to let him off because of what his parents did to him? A black kid? Shit!"

Geri smiles, embarrassed. "That's what my public defender told me," he murmurs. He then reveals to the class his experience in the distant Pomona Branch of Juvenile Court one recent morning. It was an important day for him—his fitness hearing—yet he had not met his lawyer until an hour before court was to convene. The attorney told him they had nothing to discuss: the outcome was a foregone conclusion.

"You're charged with murder, you're over sixteen, you're a black kid with a gun, and this is Pomona—white, suburban, middle-class Pomona," the lawyer said, as if explaining immutable laws of physics. "The judge is going to take one look at you and you're gone."

"But I didn't kill anybody," Geri insisted.

"I know. Doesn't matter."

At the hearing, Geri scanned the seats in the courtroom, looking for a familiar face, seeing none. His parents had long ceased being a part of his life; his grandmother was too old and sick to make it. His attorney presented little evidence in opposition to the DA's fitness motion. There were no expert witnesses, no psychological exams. No one asked Geri about his background, his willingness to reform, the trust and praise he had earned from the Juvenile Hall staff. The whole process of determining Geri's future—of choosing between mandatory release from the juvenile system at age twenty-five, or mandatory life in prison as an adult—lasted less than ten minutes. Without Geri ever saying a word, the judge pronounced him unfit, then told the bailiff to call the next case.

"Maybe if I had a different judge, it would have been different," Geri suggests to the class. *"I heard about this judge down in Inglewood, he's supposed to be good. Really tough, but good."*

"You mean Dorn?" Ronald Duncan asks. Several of the other kids nod knowingly. They have heard of Judge Roosevelt Dorn.

"Yeah. I wish I could have gotten him," Geri says. *"Who knows what might have happened?"*

◆

"C ALL the calendar," Judge Roosevelt Dorn intones at exactly 8:30, the first words he utters each morning after climbing the bench and settling into his huge leather chair, the day's files spread out before him like the tarot. Few Juvenile Court judges (or adult court judges, for that matter) in Los Angeles start so punctually, and Dorn's recent arrival in Inglewood has shaken the courthouse crowd from its previously torpid pace. The murmur of a dozen separate conversations in the courtroom gallery evaporates. The bailiff begins reading the names of the cases to be heard that day, one by one, checking off a box on his list every time a boy or girl answers Present.

The courtroom is jammed, as it is every morning, standing room only, a constant rustling of coats, of settling into lumpy chairs, of heads poking in the door wondering if this is where they should be. Every tenth name or so, no one responds, and Dorn immediately orders an arrest warrant issued. Dorn's predecessor was not so harsh, the defense attorneys grumble to themselves. But Dorn is a stickler for punctuality, and for many of the kids, this will be the first time anyone has expected them to be on time for anything. If the child shows up later in the day (as opposed to blowing off the hearing entirely, which happens in about one in ten Juvenile Court cases),[2] he or she will be taken into custody and locked up for a few hours, until the judge feels his message has been conveyed. "You'll not come late to Judge Dorn's courtroom again," he says to one of these latecomers, accused of emblazoning his spray-painted "tag" on several freeway overpasses.

"Yes," one attorney in the audience whispers to a colleague. "Next time he'll know not to show up at all." The lawyer starts to snicker, then falls silent and shifts uncomfortably when Dorn, who could not possibly have heard the remark, flicks a cold, prescient glance in the lawyer's direction, the teacher who can always detect the spitball's origin, even with back turned.

When the calendar call is through, the procession of cases begins in earnest. Lawyers line up in what once was a jury box (juveniles do not get trials before their peers, for obvious reasons), and compete with one another to have their cases called first, waiting to leap up and announce "Ready!" before anyone else, a kind of verbal elbowing to the head of the line. It is childish and raucous and the lawyers who get shoved aside pout and complain. Hearings for the kids in custody are supposed to have priority, but because the Probation Department is frequently tardy with both its buses and its intake reports—a child's entry into the system, the crucial passport to delinquency—this rule is often broken. Newly charged children are arraigned, their trial dates set. Older cases go to trial or, more often, get delayed, dismissed, or resolved through a plea bargain negotiated in the hallway, in which case the witnesses who wait through the morning are sent on their way, their days wasted for nothing. Perhaps they'll return for the next court date. Perhaps not.

"Call the first case," Dorn says, then closes his eyes for a moment. A very thin boy with thick spectacles is escorted from the lockup in back of the courtroom to the defense table. He sits with legs dangling from his chair, tapping the toes of his black, laceless Juvenile Hall–issue sneakers together in a slow fidget, gazing mournfully at the various players—the public defender shuffling papers for the forty-two cases she has to handle that morning, the assistant district attorney whispering to a witness in another case, the judge with his glasses now perched up on his forehead so he can scrub at his face with the palms of his hands. Dorn seems to be trying to massage away the weariness he feels from an early-morning start on the telephone, wrangling with county bureaucrats for a fresh paint job and an asbestos check for his ancient courthouse. The dingy courtroom with its cracked linoleum and sighing water cooler is still filled with parents, children, babies scrabbling and being shushed, surly teenagers with enormously baggy pants and tattoos snaking across their knuckles or up their arms, police officers sitting with arms crossed, knowing they will wait all day to testify in cases that will almost certainly be continued to another day, crime victims warily eyeing the juveniles accused of victimizing them. During a lull in the everyday din, when the cacophony of voices in the hallway and the courthouse's booming public address system briefly fall silent, you can hear the faint sandpaper sound of the dry skin of the judge's hands against his face. The boy begins to tap his sneakers together in syncopation with the rubbing. No one looks at him, speaks to him, or even seems to recognize that he is present, except for the khaki-uniformed bailiff hovering nearby, guarding against escape, or worse.

The boy is before Dorn for arraignment, his first appearance in court, a formulaic and purposely uneventful ritual. The hearing consists of a brief reading of the charges and an even briefer discussion of the contents of the court's juvenile intake form, a notoriously superficial, sometimes inaccurate two-page sheet that represents the system's sum total of knowledge about a child as he enters the court process for the first time. This is what the intake officers on duty at Juvenile Hall and in some police stations produce after each delinquency case is opened. With this, the judge must decide what to do with the child while the case slowly runs its course.

"It's a 245, Your Honor," the probation officer assigned to Dorn's courtroom informs the judge, referring to California Penal Code Section 245, assault with a deadly weapon or instrument. Tired of a bully at school, this skinny boy smashed a pipe over his tormentor's head. Then, still raging, he allegedly turned on a teacher before he was restrained. It is the boy's fourth such violent outburst in recent months, though the only one that caused major injury. The court and its investigative arm, the Probation Department, declined to act in the three previous incidents. Money and manpower is too scant to give much attention to "minor" offenses, so the system waits for someone to be seriously hurt before heaving into motion like an aged zoo lion. The boy is a twelve-year-old-bundle of anger.

Judge Dorn reads the brief summary available to him. It seems the boy once was an enthusiastic student, but a troubled home, the departure of his father, a mother who is more interested in dating than in raising an adolescent, have all taken their toll. Judge Dorn can see the boy needs help, stability, a caring guardian. He knows the biggest predictors of juvenile delinquency are a one-parent home and a failed educational experience. Studies of juvenile delinquents have confirmed this for years, as if he needed researchers and academics to tell him what he observes every day sitting on the bench: Virtually every delinquent he sees falls into one or both of these categories. But while the case is pending, the law—the boy's rights of due process—bar Dorn from doing much of anything, unless the public defender pleads him guilty on the spot. But the public defenders have a policy against doing this—first they must try to disprove or at least delay the charges. They say they are lawyers, not social workers, and their first duty is to attempt to win an acquittal—even when, strictly speaking, getting their clients off may not be in the kids' best interest. Their hard line in attempting to disprove every allegation and to exploit every legal technicality is what provokes the prosecution's lock-the-monsters-away hard line, and vice versa. And so, Dorn is left with but two options: He can release the "Pipe Kid," as a prosecutor referred to the boy in the hallway, and let him go home with his parents, or he can send him back to Juvenile Hall during the months it will take to resolve his case, on the theory that the boy is too dangerous to be free. The hall is just a temporary holding facility (though the new era of serious violent juvenile crime, combined with court backlogs, have made it far less temporary than originally intended, with stays now lasting months and even years instead of days or weeks). Services for the emotionally disturbed kids housed in the hall are minimal at best, consisting mainly of prescription drugs dispensed every night before bed, which have the additional benefit, to the staff, of making troublesome kids more manageable. The Pipe Kid cuts such a pathetic figure that Dorn is leaning toward sending him home instead, but then the mother brings him up short.

"I can't have him at home anymore," she informs the court, the large gold earring in her nose quivering as she speaks, her voice high and petulant. Her boyfriend sits next to her in his gray Budweiser T-shirt, staring at his hands folded across an ample fold of belly. Mother looks barely older than her son. "He won't listen," she fumes. "I just can't have him now."

The boy's head seems to turtle into his shoulders as she speaks, so eager is he to disappear. Someone in the audience clucks her tongue, and the mother glares in the direction it came from, though she can't quite locate the source of the disapproval. The judge nods without looking at her or the boy. "For the protection and rehabilitation of the minor, and for the protection of society, the minor is ordered detained," he announces, using that singsong voice people involuntarily adopt when they repeat the same phrase over and over, long past hearing the words. Then he returns to studying files at his bench and rubbing his face. The mother nods in satisfaction.

"We call kids like this NFC," a ponytailed narcotics investigator whispers to another onlooker in the courtroom gallery. "I see 'em all the time. You take a look at what they're doin', who their parents are, and you know: This poor kid's NFC. No fuckin' chance."

Three minutes after entering the courtroom, without ever uttering a word, without interrupting the DA's conversation with his witness or the defense attorney's shuffling of files, the boy leaves, escorted back to the holding tank. No one spoke with him or acknowledged his presence. There is a deliberately fostered anonymity to this, furthered by the practice of never calling the child by name, even as he or she sits mutely in court, life laid open for legal dissection. In Juvenile Court, a child is referred to simply as "the minor."[3]

Small, slumped, confused, the minor avoids the eyes of the mother who doesn't want him as he rises to leave. Before he can exit with the bailiff, Judge Dorn has called the name of the next case on the docket. A fifteen-year-old girl, visibly pregnant, rises in the audience and takes the chair at the defense table, the seat still warm. Dorn sighs and studies the file.

This is what most Juvenile Court hearings look like: Little substance, much legal ritual, all flow control—the judge sits at his bench like an air-traffic controller, keeping things moving. It was not always this way, but the Supreme Court's landmark Gault decision has transformed Juvenile Court from an informal forum on children into a formal court of law where the focus is more on procedures and legal technicalities than on the welfare of children and the protection of society.

A peek into the future: Six months will pass before the Pipe Kid will see his case resolved, an eternity for a twelve-year-old. He will celebrate his thirteenth birthday in lockup, his trial postponed and rescheduled three times. The public defender representing him will play Juvenile Court's delaying game, hoping one of the People's main witnesses—the victim or the investigating officer—will fail to show up one morning, in which case the charges must be dismissed, a common occurrence here. The tactic will fail this time, though; the witnesses will show up for the third time, only to be told they can go home for good: The boy will finally plead guilty. Then he will be shuffled off to the foster home Dorn would have sent him to right away had the law permitted it. But by now, Pipe Kid is so angry at the system that he runs away after a few weeks and commits another assault and a robbery, and the process must start over again. This is the futile pattern that absorbs so much energy and time in Juvenile Court.

Perhaps more than anything else, time is the enemy here. Every day, Dorn's docket, like most juvenile judges', is swollen by a workload many times greater than judges in adult court deign to tolerate—fifty or sixty cases a day is not unusual. No one judge can deal meaningfully with such a tidal flow of human tragedy—on a busy day, and given the ninety-minute lunches and frequent breaks most judges take, the average time left per kid falls between four and five minutes.

On this day, Judge Dorn will see a total of thirty-two kids—four of them charged with armed robbery, one with attempted murder, two assaults with a deadly weapon, seven children charged with graffiti vandalism, four auto thefts, four petty thefts, three probation revocations, one case of witness intimidation, one case of resisting arrest, one disorderly conduct, three batteries, one concealed weapon charge, and one girl fighting transfer to adult court for her crimes. The kids facing these charges range in age from twelve to seventeen. By the end of the day, Dorn will have dismissed three cases because the People were unable to proceed when witnesses failed to show up (one of the missing was a police officer), sent three kids home on probation, sent another to a foster home, placed four more in the county-run detention camps, refused two recommendations to send kids to the California Youth Authority prison system, accepted four plea bargains, held one full-blown trial, continued ten other cases to various dates the following month, and arraigned three girls and two boys on newly filed charges. In one morning—a rather light one by Juvenile Court standards—Dorn has resolved more cases than most adult courts in Los Angeles do in a week.

And he is just one judge in a vast system. Taken as a whole, the ten branches of Los Angeles Juvenile Court, in twenty-eight courtrooms, each a separate fiefdom with different standards, different philosophies, and wildly different outcomes for similar cases, will handle nearly eleven hundred delinquency hearings of one kind or another this day. The most common order issued in Juvenile Court during this tidal flow of hearings is a postponement, putting off action until another day, creating months of delays in a system that is supposed to arrest the downward spiral of young people with the speed and efficiency of a hospital emergency room. But there is one courtroom that, more often than not, avoids becoming an assembly line, one of the few in Juvenile Court in which postponements do not outnumber other orders from the bench: Judge Roosevelt Dorn's.

On his first day back in Juvenile Court, Judge Dorn banged on the courthouse door for a full minute before someone finally let him in. The hapless marshal who came to unlock the steel door shortly before 8:00 A.M. on this first business day of the new year had to stand there in silence as the diminutive, portly man in the gray business suit chewed him out for not having the building open on time. No one who worked in this particular branch of Juvenile Court had ever laid eyes on a judge this early in the morning before, but Dorn would brook no excuses.

"Things are going to change from this day forward," he bellowed, then stormed upstairs to inspect his new courtroom. The marshal could hear the judge's voice booming as he ascended the stairs, speaking aloud to no one in particular. "My God, the condition of this courthouse is shameful. Shameful!" A few minutes later, the court administrator was scurrying in Dorn's wake, peering into graffiti-scarred bathrooms and around grimy corners, taking notes as the judge pointed out what needed to be painted, moved, removed, waxed, and otherwise rendered tolerable by Dorn's un-yielding standards.

"There may be a budget problem with some of these things," the admin-istrator meekly suggested. The courthouse had been deteriorating for years without effort or care from the county. This place had not been a priority in an era of tax cuts and budget crises.

"I don't want to hear about budgets," Dorn shouted. "This is where young people come for justice. This is where we must show them we care. And this building looks like a place where nobody cares what happens inside! Well, that, my friend, is going to change."

A demanding dictator who does things his way only, Dorn arrived with a reputation for compassion married to unrelenting harshness, preach-ing love for his juvenile charges in his huge orator's voice one moment, then sentencing them to long stays in Juvenile Hall for minor infractions. "You belong to Judge Dorn, now," he was fond of saying with an ominous chuckle. Those who remembered his last tour of duty in Juvenile five years earlier recalled the surliest kids walking out of his courtroom saying, Yes, sir, and Thank you, sir, even as they were locked up for offenses the other judges routinely dismissed. Dorn once revoked a boy's probation and sent him to boot camp for six months for refusing his mother's order to take out the trash. "I'm putting you back in control, Mother," he said, eyes locked on the stunned teenager before him. "Next time, if you tell him to take out the garbage, he had better jump."

In years past, Dorn's high-handed ways and harsh sentences provoked the Public Defender's Office so thoroughly that its lawyers flatly refused to try cases in front of him, creating a huge backlog in Juvenile Court. At the same time, his reluctance to sentence delinquents to the Youth Au-thority—California's problem-plagued prison system for juveniles—and his even greater abhorrence of seeing children tried as adults made him almost as unpopular in the District Attorney's Office. When his court cal-endar dried up for lack of attorneys willing to practice before him, Dorn invoked a little-used provision of state law and declared "open court," inviting any parents having trouble with their children to bring them in themselves, so he could set things right.

And desperate parents came in droves, not just from the area his courthouse served, but from all over Los Angeles. Judge Dorn made their children wards of the court, his rulings of questionable legal merit but his paternal domination welcome to mothers and fathers with nowhere else to turn. Teachers in some of LA's toughest schools swore Judge Dorn's kids did better than any other problem students. In the end, though, Dorn was finally dragged screaming to a new assignment in adult court downtown, with critics charging improprieties, conflicts of interest, and a tendency to appoint a favored few defense attorneys who saw things his way. Dorn denied doing anything wrong besides forcing bureaucrats to roll up their sleeves, work a full day, and save some kids in the process, and he waged a four-year battle to return to the branch of Juvenile Court he once ruled in Inglewood. Adult court's purpose was to warehouse criminals, he complained, but in Juvenile Court, lives could still be changed for the better.

Now, at last, he is back, a pistol strapped to his waist to counter the nonexistent security measures in his courthouse, and a long list of new programs he intends to try, whether prosecutors and public defenders like them or not. High on his list: sending fewer, not more, kids to adult court and prison. "Appeal me if you want. Take your shot," he likes to dare.

Roosevelt Dorn sees himself as a teacher of sorts—in the courtroom on weekdays, in Bible class on Sundays at one of LA's largest and oldest black churches. He is active in the black community, president of the local chapter of a philanthropic organization of professionals called One Hundred Black Men, and one of a handful of African-American civic leaders who met with Los Angeles District Attorney Gil Garcetti to seek assurances that football-great-turned-murder-defendant O. J. Simpson would not be discriminated against, particularly on the question of imposing the death penalty, which Garcetti eventually decided against pursuing. (In casual conversation, long before Simpson's acquittal, Dorn stated aloud his fear that "O. J. might have been framed.")

One of nine children, Dorn was raised in rural Oklahoma, where his parents, a barber and a nurse, preached the gospel of education and the value of determination. Dorn holds himself out as an example of how both qualities can lead to success—even for a black man who grew up in a time and a place where signs announcing "Whites Only" were as common as summer thunder on the plains, and where chopping cotton was the only labor he was expected to seek. When he tells truant child after truant child in his courtroom that "Without an education, you are sentencing yourself to a lifetime of degradation and poverty," he is speaking from personal experience.

After joining the Air Force, then settling in California, he worked his way through law school while holding a job as a courtroom bailiff. His main experience as an attorney was as a LA city prosecutor, where he earned a reputation as a tough and uncompromising law-and-order zealot who never showed mercy. Appointed to the municipal bench in 1979, then the Superior Court a year later, his political patron was former California Governor Jerry Brown, a minor oddity given Brown's liberalism and Dorn's history of prosecuting antiwar protesters for disrupting college campuses during the Vietnam War. Once on the bench, Dorn requested service in the juvenile delinquency division of the Superior Court—something very few judges request—and made his own brand of child welfare his life's passion, transforming himself from a conservative prosecutor into a tireless and single-minded advocate for children.

He assigns blame for the problems of today's youth, in no particular order of preference, on poor teachers, ineffectual parents, a bloated yet ineffective Probation Department bureaucracy, politicians who champion popular "solutions" to juvenile crime—such as trying more kids as adults—even though ample evidence exists to show such tactics do not work as intended, and television ("the greatest evil in society today"). The answer, he believes, is to yank kids off the streets and force them back into school, where they can learn that they can succeed. Go to school or go to jail is the alternative he offers. The judge fosters his reputation for harshness purposely, he says, "so the minors—and the parents and the lawyers—know Judge Dorn means business." If people bristle or take offense at his words or his tactics, so be it.

It is safe to say that Judge Roosevelt Dorn believes in himself far beyond the point of brashness—he is a prophet. His words often seem as appropriate for a Sunday sermon as for a courtroom lecture. And though he packs a gun, he also says, "I fear no man. Man can just kill this body and set me free. I only fear my Father."

The lawyers, cops, probation officers, parents, and the delinquents themselves have looked forward to his return with a mixture of trepidation and hope. Anything that shakes things up has to help, many figure. Others, Peggy Beckstrand chief among them, are not so sure of Judge Dorn. "My instructions are to give him a chance," she told her prosecutors, enthusiasm notably absent from her voice.

"We'll give him a chance, too," Peggy's counterpart in the Public Defender's Office, Oksana Bihun, told her PDs during Dorn's first week. "We'll give him a chance to hang himself."

"All right," Judge Dorn says, after sentencing a petty thief to probation and arraigning three angelic little girls in white dresses—the oldest is twelve—on charges of armed robbery. "Are we ready on the fitness hearing?"

John Sloan's attorney and the prosecutor assigned to Dorn's courtroom both stand and announce ready, having heard from Peggy Beckstrand that the fitness hearing will go on. Judge Dorn orders his court bailiff to fetch John from the holding tank. While waiting, the judge puts aside a file and begins rubbing his eyes and massaging his forehead again, a habitual and disconcerting mannerism he has adopted while on the bench, as if he is exhausted or suffering from a severe headache. Peggy once asked him about it and he assured her he was not in pain, as it appeared, but that he was merely praying for the wisdom to decide a case correctly. The rubbing gets especially rigorous during fitness hearings. Most Juvenile Court judges dislike the fitness law, because it almost always requires them to do what prosecutors want—send kids to adult court—whether they personally agree with the outcome or not. This was what legislators intended: to rob judges of their discretion in such cases, shifting it instead to prosecutors, who could be counted on to take a harder law-and-order line. Most of the other judges grit their teeth and follow the law, even though personally they disagree with it and the blanket solution it imposes on so many cases. But Judge Dorn openly despises this process. With him, every fitness hearing is a battle.

The bailiff brings the boy in from the holding tank, hands clasped during the long march to the table. The courtroom crowd has thinned somewhat, but there are still people in every row, and their eyes follow John as he takes his seat, fixing his stare on the scarred gray defense table as soon as he sits down.

The judge opens his eyes and takes a long, measuring look at the silent, fidgeting teenager before him. He is a short, slim, exceedingly pale Korean-American youth with a shock of black hair tumbling over his forehead. He has a brown jacket on over his county-issue orange jumpsuit. During the brief silence, unaware that Dorn is studying him, John looks over his shoulder at his family, an entire row of parents, aunts, uncles, and a younger brother and sister, all in suits and ties or dresses. They exchange the tiniest of smiles with John. In this grungy courthouse with its unidentifiable smears and odors, the Sloan family appears to have been beamed in from a church pew. The judge looks them over approvingly, with the same expression of satisfaction he wears when he eyes his Bible class. John's mother is weeping softly again, her children comforting her.

"Minor is in court represented by counsel," Dorn says, setting the ancient ritual in motion. "The People are represented. Minor's parents are in court."

The dissection of John Sloan's life, motives, and actions is about to begin. These are the most scrutinized and tension-filled proceedings Juvenile Court has to offer. The fitness hearing lies at the heart of the most burning debate now swirling through the juvenile justice system—a debate about whether there should even *be* a juvenile court. The stated goal of a fitness hearing—bald heresy in a system founded so long ago on the notion that there is no such thing as a bad kid—is to save some children, and discard the rest. For good.

Although the official court record will show the focus of the hearing in the *People* v. *John Sloan* to have been on evidence and findings of fact and all the other required legal niceties of a fitness hearing, the underlying truth is that the boy's fate rests with a simple equation: measure the child against the crime he committed, then divide the total by Judge Dorn's willingness to break the law. For only a flat refusal to enforce a state law that virtually mandates his transfer to adult court can save John now.

The real question Dorn will be trying to answer—the one every participant in this process is aware of, though no one will speak it aloud for fear it would constitute instant grounds for appeal—is whether John Sloan is worth the trouble.

"Call your first witness," the judge commands, and it begins.

CHAPTER 5

Punks

"Santos needs to read his story first," Geri tells me one evening. "They told him he was going to County tonight."

County. Los Angeles County Jail, the adult lockup. Unless a judge intervenes, older kids like Luis Santos—"Cartoon" on the street—go to County once they are transferred to adult court, so that another juvenile can come claim the bunk, or the mat on the floor, that serves as his bed. After tonight, he will have to fend for himself among the adult criminals stacked into County by the thousand.

Cartoon looks at me shyly. He has a dark, wry face with a goatee and thick, bushy eyebrows that almost meet over his nose. Another face might look sinister because of that black V over his eyes, but Cartoon's face is full of mirth and intelligence. "If you don't mind," he says, "I'd like to read my story first. It's about the day I got torcido. Busted, I mean. I don't know how much longer I'll be here. They said the bus could come any time."

Cartoon looks around anxiously at the rest of the class. It will be the first and last time he will read to us. He has never written a story before, he tells us. "So don't laugh."

Well, it started like this. I was living with my home girl Smiley at the time. A couple of home boys and home girls were there getting ready for a party we

were gonna have there. The home boys were ironing their khakis and Pend-
letons, shining their Stacy Adamses, and the ones that had hair were putting
on Three Flowers. In the other room the home girls were doing their own
pedo, I don't know what, but when they came out they looked fine. Even
their hair smelled *bueno*. Then I spot my home girl Tiny.

*Cartoon's voice becomes almost a whisper as he reads, remembering the
party preparations and his first glance of Tiny behind the other girls. The
image of gang members ironing their clothes and dousing themselves with
hair tonic as their girls primp and preen lifts all the boys in the room from
their dour surroundings for a moment.*

Tiny. This *ruka* is fine. She has me sprung on everything of hers—her eyes,
face, body, laugh, attitude. Everything you can imagine was fine on her. No
I'm not overdoing it.

Well, I go up to her. "*Qué vole, mija, como estas?*"

"Fine, I guess," she tells me. I was determined to ask her to be my *hina* that
night, so I ask her to accompany me to the couch so we can talk some more.
She said all right. So we make our way through the now over-crowded room.
We finally reach the plastic-covered couch. It has a plastic cover on it because
when the home boys drink either they spill beer or they throw up on anything.

I was making up small talk so I can build up courage to ask her what I
needed to ask her. I felt a burst of courage come onto me, so I slowly inched
my hand toward hers, which was on her lap. I finally reached her hand. She
didn't seem to mind me holding hands with her, so I decide to tell her right
now. I say, "Tiny, would you . . ."

"CARTOON! CARTOON! Where are you *ese?*"

Damn. My home boy Payaso came storming into the room, and I couldn't
finish my proposal to my baby. He ran towards me and said hey, we gotta go
take care of something right away. "Quick, come on."

So I tell my home girl I'll be right back. "Okay, *mija?* But when I come
back, we gotta talk seriously, okay?" I felt bad about leaving just like that.
I'm sure she did too.

Well, as soon as I was out the house, my home boy tells me we have to
go collect something of ours that someone had, so I agreed. We got in the
car. It was weird, because Tiny came to the car window and said, "Cartoon,
don't go." She insisted, but my home boy drove away. I saw her slowly disappearing in the glare of the street lights. I hate to admit it, but I had a tear in
my eye. I don't know why, but I did.

My homie said, "So you like Tiny, *carnal?*" I said yeah, and he said, "Well, after today, you can settle down with her and your baby girl." (In case I didn't mention it, I have a baby girl.)

So we drove off to South Gate to pick up a couple of guns—actually, one gun, also one rifle. We got them and jumped on the freeway. Not only was my heart pounding from the anxiety of what we were about to do, but also because my home boy was going at 70–80 MPH on the freeway.

He gave me the rundown on what we were gonna do, which was to rob a house. I had the rifle, he had the gun. We got to this old apartment building. We parked the car in the back alley, and walked most of the way. As we walked, I didn't talk much, I was overwhelmed with fear of what we are about to do. We finally got to the front door of this one apartment. We found the front door open. I took my rifle from my waistband and my home boy took out his gun. And we walked in the apartment.

There we found ourselves giving three guys orders to get down on the floor, which they did. My home boy went and grabbed a guy by the shirt, pulled him up and took him to the other room. After five minutes, they came back, my home boy with four ounces of *yeska*, gold chains, and money. As I turned around to see what he had, one of the *vatos* grabbed my rifle and I was struggling with him as I yelled for my homie to help me. But he had left the premises.

Cartoon's reading is interrupted here by a burly detention officer, who opens the door and peers into the library. He eyes each kid, that sizing-up look cops and prison guards always seem to wear. The eyes settle on Cartoon. "Santos. Time to go."

A chorus of protests from the other kids draws a glare. I beg for five more minutes, and, after a moment, the man relents, shaking his head as if we were all wasting our time. But Cartoon gets to finish his story.

It was only I left there with three individuals which I was struggling with for my life. They beat me to the floor. I still had my rifle, they were hitting me with bottles and bats. Finally, they managed to take my rifle.

I was on the floor, dazed from the beating I had received. One individual placed the rifle in my mouth. At that moment, I saw my little girl, mom, my barrio, and the girl I loved. I knew I was gonna die, so all I did was throw up my barrio.

I heard one *vato* say, "Kill him, kill him." I saw the guy holding the rifle in front of me. I saw his finger squeeze the trigger. All I heard was click. . . . Click, click, click. Nothing. The gun got jammed on me.

Then they called the police on me. I laid there halfway dead from the beating I received, wondering why the gun didn't go off, why my home boy left me, but most of all thinking of my baby. Not to mention Tiny. She is always on my mind.

The police came, arrested me, placed me in the patrol car, took me to the nearest hospital. There I was for three or four hours, doing checkups on me. Nothing broken but my heart. Knowing I was coming to jail to do some hard time.

Cartoon looks up and says, "The End."

The room is silent. Every page of the little college blue book Sister Janet had scrounged up for each kid to write in had been used, even the unlined blue cover page, filled up by this world Cartoon lived in, where the juxtaposition between being too shy to hold a girl's hand and bursting into someone's home armed with a rifle is not considered extraordinary, and where making his gang's identifying hand signal—throwing up his barrio—is an honorable way to die. He has been a gang member since age eleven. He knows no other world. Seventeen at the time of his arrest, he is unfailingly polite, soft-spoken, and articulate, an eleventh-grade dropout with a long record of minor juvenile offenses, all of them impulsive and unplanned, set in motion by others—just like this latest one, this charge of armed robbery he now faces in adult court.

One by one, the boys in the class begin to applaud his story. Cartoon is beaming now. It is the first story he has ever written. It is the first time anything remotely linked to scholarship seemed enjoyable to him.

"I didn't know I could do this," he says, almost breathless. "Do you think I should write more?"

I tell him yes, absolutely. I praise his work lavishly. I tell him he has set an example for the class, that he has shown them, with effort and heart, that they all could tell stories with drama and humor and emotion. He looks like he is about to cry for a moment. He did not expect anyone to like what he wrote, he says. Now he promises he'll send more stories from County.

Two detention officers appear at the door then, arms crossed. "Let's go, Santos," the first one calls. "You're outta here." The almost giddy mood abruptly evaporates. Cartoon leaves, the excitement his story generated fleeing the room like air from a balloon. The other boys fall silent. There will be no more stories read or written this night.

A short time later, I leave Central Juvenile Hall. It is almost nine o'clock, and a cold snap has gripped the LA Basin, chill and damp enough to turn my exhalations into steam. On the loading dock, I see a line of eight boys waiting in the cold, stripped of their orange juvenile coveralls—along with their legal status as juveniles. They are wearing only white T-shirts and gray cotton trousers, and they are linked together by thick belly chains. They shiver in the dark, shifting from foot to foot, waiting to get into a sheriff's black-and-white van, bound for the Los Angeles County Jail. I hear one of them weeping, and what had been an abstract concept—this notion of trying juveniles as adults—suddenly hits home. This is how it is done, coldly, clinically, as if moving commodities from one warehouse to another. I spot Cartoon among these eight new "adults." He was not allowed to bring any personal items with him—not his story, not his letters, nothing—just a stick of deodorant and a toothbrush, whatever he could stuff into the top of his socks. You're not allowed to carry anything during these transfers, and your clothes have no pockets.

Something makes Cartoon look up then—he had been staring at his feet—and he sees me peering at him through the chain-link fence. He gives me a wave and a weak smile, and I wonder what will become of him.

I learn later that a judge sent him to prison for four years. I never heard from him again.

———◆———

THE evidence before Judge Dorn is clear.

Three weeks earlier, John Sloan departed the department store where he worked as a clerk, and met his buddy Richard. They had plans to cruise the night streets of the coastal city where John lived, as they had done many nights before. This time, though, they were not looking for girls or parties or places to hang. They were in search of a likely victim to rob and terrorize.

The two teenagers had planned it well, they thought. They were even dressed down like gangbangers in dark, baggy clothes, though the dangerous image they hoped to project seemed somewhat deflated by their mode of transportation for the evening. True gangbangers would have picked up a G-Ride—the hottest car they could steal, the "G" standing for "gangster"—but John had only his yellow Volkswagen Karmann Ghia, a cutely underpowered gift from Dad.

In John's waistband, though, he could feel the comforting, fearful weight of the .380 blue steel revolver he had scored for a hundred bucks on the street in LA. John had asked around at school and soon learned how to find a gun seller who catered to juveniles, a nameless man who tooled around certain neighborhoods with a trunkload of stolen weapons, dealing everything from Saturday night specials to AK-47s for gangbangers and anyone else with cash to burn and someone to kill. The dealer even threw in bullets, five of them, when John handed over the cash. A computer check of the serial number on the gun John picked up would later show no recorded owner, which meant it was stolen somewhere between the manufacturer and the distributor. Crates of weapons get walked off the docks of UPS and other shippers all the time, many of which then end up in the hands of kids—one of the gun industry's great, unreported scandals. Guns can be shipped with no more security than soap powder. Even for a kid like John, with no criminal record and no real street savvy—other than what he picked up from TV and music—finding firepower had been shockingly easy.

"How about over there?" Richard suggested, pointing to a parking structure that served a shopping center and a post office. It was a Sunday night, past 10:00 P.M., and the place was deserted. But there was a man driving into the structure, probably to mail some letters. He was alone. Perfect.

"Let's check it out," John agreed, stopping a block or so from the garage. Force of habit made him lock his car—thinking more about his stereo than of getaways—and the two boys dashed into the parking structure. They hid behind a green Pontiac near the post office.

Each boy wore surgical gloves copped from John's dad. Doctors always had rubber gloves around the house. The boys also had bandannas tied around their necks and pulled up over their noses Old West bandit–style, the old-fashioned kind that bikers and cowboys like to stuff in their back pockets. John's hands were shaking, even though he was certain he would never be caught. He was too smart. Always had been, all the way back to his days in the private elementary school, when his recitations of memorized Bible passages earned him red ribbon after red ribbon.

Even back then, the pressure had been there. The red ribbons were not a source of praise at home—they were expected. Like the A's on his report card. He was the oldest child, the standard-bearer, the perfect son.

"Let's get him right at the car," Richard suggested, as they watched a middle-aged Hispanic man pull in and park. John nodded. They would wait until the man was out of his car, vulnerable and exposed.

Things had gotten so complicated. His father was the original self-made man, having moved to America with his Korean parents at age seventeen. Just about John's age. The elder Sloan went right to work, earned enough money to put himself through medical school, then established a thriving practice and bought a home in one of Southern California's finest, safest, shiniest communities. Now it was supposed to be up to John to carry on the family's good name.

For a long time, he had earned the grades, joined in the church activities, watched over his younger siblings. He impressed teachers as a shy, sensitive, bright kid. He was a gifted artist, could draw anything. At night, he and his mother would read the Bible together before bed.

"Should we wait until he mails his letters, or get him right away?" Richard hissed.

"Let's wait," John said. He wanted just a little more time to think.

This was the problem: John saw himself as an American kid, born to French fries and skateboards and reruns of *Gilligan's Island*. But his parents were traditional Korean immigrants, with values that set them apart no matter how badly John wanted his family to assimilate. They couldn't understand that he did not want to follow in his father's footsteps, that he was sick of being the perfect son, that their expectations for him, once a source of pride, now seemed like an imposition.

A recent high school consolidation of three small campuses into one large one had made things worse for John—his new campus was racially polarized, making the immigrant heritage he wished to forsake all the more relevant. Anglos hung with Anglos at his school, Hispanics with Hispanics, Asians with Asians. Bigotry was fashionable. There had been fights, even something close to a race riot. John had been picked on by some Latino kids he took to be gangbangers. Only kids with gang alliances seemed secure and unafraid, he observed, their lives fraught with purpose and belonging. Somewhere along the line, he realized he wanted to be part of that.

That was when he met Richard. Firmly on the loser track, John's new best friend was a zero in school, chronically truant, with an arrest record for theft. Kicked out of John's high school, he attended a continuation school—a two-hour-a-day scholastic warehouse where the emphasis is on logging time in "independent study." But to John, Richard was freedom. Here was someone who didn't give a shit about his family, about school, about the future. Another child with an immigrant father, he was openly contemptuous of tradition. And from his brief stay in Juvenile Hall on his theft charge, Richard claimed to know all about gangs—how to dress down, how to throw your weight around, how you have to band together with others who have the same color skin to protect yourself. Learning to imitate the dress, manner, and attitudes of gangsters was not only fashionable, but an ego boost for John.

In the space of a few months, John became an uncommunicative C student, the honor roll a thing of the past. Teachers and counselors started putting him in the "at risk" category when they discussed his performance—at risk for failure, or worse. They urged him to live up to his potential, but he preferred to hang with Richard—at first learning from him, then leading him, and finally outdoing him. He didn't need money—he had plenty of cash available to him—yet there he was in that parking garage, stalking prey, ready to rob at gunpoint.

"All right, let's do it," John whispered, and they sprang up, raced around the Pontiac, and confronted a middle-aged man as he was opening his car door. John had his revolver out—he didn't even remember drawing it from his waistband—and saw that it was pointed at the man. He saw his victim's eyes grow wide with fear, and for the first time, John understood the truly seductive nature of gangbanging: the genuine power. This guy was about to piss his pants. Because of him.

"This is for real," John yelled. "We're not playing, Mexican motherfucker."

"What's going on?" the guy blurted, as if there were any doubt. Then he pleaded, "Look, I'll give you whatever you want. Just don't hurt me."

Richard, holding a switchblade in his gloved hand, took a halfhearted swipe at the man, not coming close to connecting, but still making him jump back. He said, "Give us your wallet, Mexican motherfucker."

The man handed his wallet over. This, John thought, was almost too easy. Then, realizing the man could simply hop in his car and follow them once they left, John demanded his keys. "Don't worry, we're not gonna take it," he said contemptuously. "We don't need no fuckin' low rider anyway." He hurled the key ring toward the other end of the parking garage to keep his victim at bay once they left. Everything had gone perfectly, exactly as he had planned.

It wasn't until John flipped open the guy's wallet that everything fell apart. It wasn't a wallet, after all. It was a leather case of some kind. And inside it, bright as a new penny, shone a large gold badge.

Now it was John who had to worry about bladder control. He had to stop himself from yelling, *Oh my God, we're robbing a cop.* He saw himself arrested, fingerprinted, and jailed, his mother and father peering at him through a visitor's window, eyes hollow with reproach. It no longer seemed a very amusing prospect.

There was only one thing to do: He and Richard both backed away, then turned and ran as fast as they could, the pounding of their footsteps echoing in the empty garage.

While Judge Dorn considers the case against John Sloan, Joseph Gutierrez paces and sighs in the crowded hallway outside, the fourth time he has come to Juvenile Court as a witness to armed robbery. He cannot sit inside and watch. Some hearings are closed to the public and, in any case, as a subpoenaed witness, he is not permitted to watch others testify, for fear he would be influenced or change his story. Each time, he has missed a day of work. Each time, he has been told to sit down and wait and to keep out of the courtroom. Each time, after hours of waiting, he has been told there has been a delay in the *People* v. *John Sloan*, that he has to go home and that he must come back again—not a word of explanation or apology offered.[1]

"This is how witnesses are treated in Juvenile Court," he gripes to a uniformed policeman waiting to testify. "Like we're the criminals." The cop nods absently, then returns to reading the paperback book he brought with him: *Presumed Innocent.*

"I've missed three days of work," a woman whose Mercedes was stolen six months ago pipes up from her seat on one of the second-floor benches. "Now they tell me the case has been transferred to another court, one that's closer to the kid who stole my car. They want to make things more convenient for him! And I'm supposed to go to another courthouse and start the whole thing over." She is rummaging in her purse as she speaks, talking more to herself than to anyone else in the hallway. Then she stands to leave. "This sucks. I'm thinking of just forgetting the whole thing. They can deal with that kid without me."

But of course they can't. If she fails to show up, there will be no case, and the boy who stole her car will be set free. That is why defense attorneys delay and transfer and insist on needless hearings—hoping witnesses will grow disgusted and stop coming. Defense lawyers in Juvenile Court use quirks in the law that force prosecutors to prove the obvious—that, for instance, a kid driving a stolen, hot-wired car did not have permission from the owner to shatter a window, hack the dashboard, maul the ignition, and drive away. That means calling the owner and forcing him to wait for hours or days for thirty seconds of testimony that consists of: No, he did not have permission to wreck and take my car. In graffiti cases, the owner of a wall emblazoned with gang insignias must be called to state the obvious: that he did not give permission to the vandals who defaced his property. If that property is a freeway overpass, then the state of California must appear to say it didn't authorize the six-foot neon message "FUCK HOOVERS," scrawled above the 405 freeway. Needless to say, the state of California often has better things to do than show up at Thurgood Marshall Branch. Private property owners in gang-dominated neighborhoods are understandably reluctant to testify in open court as well. No matter — the public defenders have a policy of insisting on such testimony, a legal loophole that wins dismissals of half such cases. Half.[2]

"We're not social workers," one of the defenders explains. "We can't worry about what happens after we win. If we get a kid off and he goes out and kills someone, that's not our fault. The prosecution should have done a better job."

Gutierrez has heard this logic before. He shakes his head. "This place is like some huge dysfunctional family," he says, still pacing. "I'm the victim. That kid shoved a gun in my face. And I can't even go in there and watch what's going on."

The cop sitting nearby looks up from his book again. "You don't really want to," he says quietly. "It'll just make you madder."

A short time later, Joseph Gutierrez is called into court to describe the night John Sloan robbed him.

"Were you scared, Mr. Gutierrez?" the prosecutor asks.

"Of course," the man on the witness stand says, recalling that moment in the parking garage when he thought he might die.

The government's primary witness against John Sloan has been on the stand about five minutes so far. He glances uneasily at Judge Dorn, who is rubbing his eyes again. The judge's eye-rubbing can communicate a host of different emotions and tempers; at this time, it seems a gesture of impatience, even annoyance. The witness says, "Of course I was scared."

"What happened after that?"

The gold shield Joseph Gutierrez carries is not a policeman's badge, but a city electrical inspector's, he tells the court. John and Richard apparently could not tell the difference. But though he was no cop, he says, his initial fear at being braced at gunpoint had turned to rage once the bandits left him standing there. He had gone on to do something extraordinary, something cops are paid to do, but ordinary citizens like himself usually avoid.

"I ran and got my keys . . . and I went to the trunk of my car and I got out my .45 Ruger automatic. . . . I cocked the gun and loaded it, and started the car and took off in the direction that they had run."

Joseph Gutierrez had simply gone out to mail some letters that Sunday night at a post office near his home. The area is one of LA's most beautiful and affluent, climbing a high, verdant peninsula overlooking the rocky froth of the South Bay, its neighborhoods stocked with estates that have housed such diverse luminaries as Ronald Reagan and Tom Petty, not to mention more millionaires per capita than any other Southern California community, Beverly Hills included. Gutierrez had moved his family to one of the more modest slices of this area as a hedge against crime.

"It doesn't get any safer than this," he had proudly boasted to his wife and daughters when they found a home they could afford there.

That sense of ease and security evaporated when John Sloan and his friend popped up from behind a dark green Pontiac, wearing gloves and bandannas, slinging a gun and racial epithets, seemingly full of hatred and violence.

They had caught him half in and half out of his car, reaching for the letters on his front seat, exposed and helpless. He had frantically looked around the parking garage for help or escape, seeing neither. There was no one to call to, nowhere to run, just an impossibly long moment of agonizing silence, a frozen tableau in which Gutierrez simultaneously thanked God that his wife and children were safe at home, prayed that he might see them again, and wondered what the hell two Asian gangbangers were doing in this neighborhood. When they called him Mexican motherfucker, he thought, I'm going to die right here, in some empty garage, just for a couple of letters. Just because their forebears came from across the Pacific, his from below the Rio Grande. But then, when they ran off, his own anger took over. He found the racist taunting particularly galling because his wife was Asian-American; he had always made it a point to teach their children not to judge people by color or ethnicity. He felt this was a hate crime, that he was targeted simply because he was Hispanic, that the real goal of the robbery was not to gain money, but to humiliate a Mexican-American. And without really thinking through the possible consequences, he had pursued them, gun in hand.

As he fetched his keys, he saw through the open-air parking garage where they were running, their bandannas now down around their necks, a yellow Volkswagen Karmann Ghia the only car in sight. Gutierrez rounded the corner and froze the two assailants in his bright headlights while John was still fumbling with the car door he had stupidly locked. Gutierrez leaned out of his car window and trained his weapon on them, then told them to lie facedown on the sidewalk. When they obeyed, he took John's gun away and made his captives put their hands behind their heads. A passing motorist called the police on his car phone a few minutes later.

"Did you get a good look at their faces?" the prosecutor asks.

Gutierrez looks at John, whose position in the courtroom is almost dead in front of the witness stand. John does not meet his eyes—he has barely looked up from the tabletop in front of him throughout the proceedings. "Yes," the thirty-seven-year-old city inspector says. "Many times. . . . That's the one with the gun."

"No more questions." The prosecutor sits back, satisfied. He is certain he has more than met the legal requirements for booting a kid out of Juvenile Court—requirements that amount to little more than proving the kid's age, and that the offense he is charged with committing is on a laundry list of twenty-four crimes for which the California legislature has authorized transfers to adult court.[3] In a fitness hearing, the prosecution need not prove guilt, and innocence is no defense (the theory being that no harm is done if a child is transferred to adult court and later found innocent—the switch in courts matters only if he is convicted and sentenced). Legally, John walked into court *presumed* to be unfit for Juvenile Court, one of the few legal presumptions in the criminal justice system that does not favor the defendant. The law virtually handcuffs Judge Dorn to the prosecution, which is why he hates fitness hearings so much.

John's attorney, Angela Oh, must attempt to undo this legal presumption if John is to avoid an adult-style punishment, and to do so, she launches a novel line of inquiry. She asks Joseph Gutierrez if he thought John and his accomplice were punks.

The witness looks confused. "What?"

"There was something about this interaction that suggested to you that these were a couple of punks, really, right?" the attorney asks.

Judge Dorn is looking amused and interested at this, and the prosecutor gets nervous, seeing where the defense is headed. For the defense to win a fitness hearing, the focus cannot be on disproving the charges—a trap some attorneys fall into—but on a legal test that examines five factors: a kid's past criminal record, the time left to rehabilitate him, the results of past attempts at rehabilitation, his criminal sophistication, and the gravity of the crime.[4]

No one doubts that an honors student with a supportive family and no prior criminal record is a good candidate for rehabilitation. That gets him past three parts of the test. But the prosecution, as it does in almost all fitness cases, is hanging its argument on the two remaining parts—armed robbery, with its potential for injury or death, is inherently grave, and a kid who buys a gun on the street from an arms dealer, then uses a mask and gloves to avoid detection, shows he is capable of planning and executing a sophisticated crime. Sophistication and a grave crime are all that is needed—failure of any *one* of the five parts of the test requires judges to transfer a kid to adult court, which is why prosecutors win fitness hearings nine out of ten times in Los Angeles. This is the draconian result law-makers intended when they redesigned the law in the 1980s under the assumption that too few kids had been landing in adult court before. And it is why Angela Oh desperately wants to paint John Sloan as a punk: Punks, she argues, are incapable of committing a sophisticated or grave crime.

"If I use the word 'punk,' do you understand what that means?" she persists.

The prosecutor, Deputy District Attorney Hyman Sisman, decides he has to put a stop to this. "Objection. It's irrelevant."

Judge Dorn agrees. "The fact that one may consider an individual a punk," he says, emphasizing the word "punk," almost drawing it out into two syllables, "does not mean that individual cannot necessarily be sophisticated in committing a crime."

Sisman sits down and relaxes again. But he seems to have missed the real message behind Dorn's comment. What the judge is really saying is that whatever Mr. Gutierrez thinks of John doesn't matter. Dorn's body language throughout the victim's testimony has grown increasingly hostile. At one point, he stood up, walked behind his chair, and watched Gutierrez from a distance, as if he did not want to be too close to the state's star witness. It unnerved the man in the witness chair; Sisman seemed to take no notice.

A few minutes later, Dorn reveals his feelings about Gutierrez even more clearly as Oh continues to argue that the man's willingness to pursue two armed robbers shows they were unsophisticated punks, and therefore still suitable material for the ministrations of Juvenile Court. Friends had lionized Gutierrez as a hero for capturing his assailants, but Dorn proclaims his act "something that no reasonable person would ever have done." It is a curious attack on a victim of a crime, especially from a judge who carries his own gun, even to court, and it should have served as a red alert to the prosecutor that he badly needed to bolster his case. Again, though, the prosecutor appears to take no notice, and he rests his case a short time later.

The defense calls Dr. Sloan to the stand. John's father is stiff and solemn, mortified at being in court. His entire family has been devastated by this thing John has done, he testifies. They are all bewildered by John's crime. He assures the judge that his son's behavior that night was totally aberrant, that they had no clue this was coming. There are no guns in the household, the doctor says, and John never expressed any interest in them before. I just could not understand this, Dr. Sloan says.

So he sought an explanation and, to an extent, he got one, the doctor says. John's father describes a recent visit with his son at Juvenile Hall. John talked about things he had never mentioned before, Dr. Sloan recalls—about pressures at school, about gangs and racial tensions and his fear of being assaulted by Hispanics and blacks. He talked of being held at gunpoint at a Taco Bell by some Hispanic teenagers a year earlier. More recently, he and three friends had been surrounded by Hispanic gang members. Several of them punched John and his friends, while others kept guns trained on them so they could not fight back, John told his father. John seemed to feel he had been targeted because he was Asian-American. He had never mentioned these incidents to his family before. Instead, he bought a gun for self-protection, the doctor tells Dorn. "John said he thought if he had a gun, then the gangs wouldn't bother him."

John does not testify about any of this himself, although he submits a letter to the court saying he had been attracted to gang behavior because it seemed "cool." It is difficult to tell if he is even following what is going on around him, so withdrawn and still has he been. But the defense theory is clear: John is being portrayed as the victim here, of gangs and of racism. This robbery was completely out of character, a mixed-up attempt to strike back at the people who had been tormenting him, a cry for help from a kid who couldn't fit in at home or in school. Or so argues John's lawyer.

It is a suggestion open to attack—one could question, among other things, John's convenient recollection of being assaulted by gang members a year ago, something he never mentioned to anyone before, and which is unsupported by any other source. Or how buying a gun, donning gloves and a mask, and robbing an innocent person fits in with the portrait of John as victim. But the prosecutor chooses not to pursue these points. He has no questions for John's father. Nor does he introduce counterbalancing testimony from the probation officer who wrote John's intake report, and who heard John confess that his only motive for the robbery was to get some money. Instead, Sisman, a thin, bearded redhead with a passionless courtroom demeanor, launches directly into his closing argument.

"This is not something casual," he argues in a clipped, mild voice. "This minor and his cohort were hiding in a parking structure at night with something covering their faces and wearing surgical gloves. They uttered racial epithets. . . . The fact that a resourceful citizen caught them is not mitigating. It just means these minors chose the wrong victim.

"The minor seems to think acting like a gangster is a cool thing to do. If that's what he thinks, then he ought to be ready to pay the price. The proper place for this minor is in adult court. . . . Under the law, there is no choice but for him to be declared unfit."

Judge Dorn barely glances at Sisman. He hates being told he has no choice.

"Defense argument?"

John's lawyer, well aware of Dorn's philosophical leanings, knows just what to say, deftly stepping into the opening the prosecution provided. Her first words emphasize not what Dorn must do, but the power he has to do what's best. "The court has the authority," she says, "to exercise its discretion in a way that will, in essence, save this kid. . . . He has never been in the system before, and he has certainly never been before *Judge Dorn* before. He will respond to your supervision."

There is no concealing the pleasure suffusing Dorn's face at this expression of deference. He is not rubbing his eyes now, or fingering files, as he has done during some presentations in the past. He is sitting up straight in his big chair, his attention focused on Angela Oh, jotting occasional notes on a yellow legal pad. Attorneys in the audience are nodding approvingly at Oh's masterful turn. Sisman's mouth is compressed into a thin line. Finally, he realizes he is in trouble.

"John used to get straight A's, now he's just average," Oh continues. "I don't know what has happened to John, but something has happened, and no one has paid attention. He comes from a moral family, a religious family, who had no idea. . . . What he did was stupid, it was naïve, and thank God no one was hurt. Even now, he doesn't seem to realize the lives he has impacted. But, basically, he's a decent kid. This is a kid on the edge. He can be saved. This court can save him."

Judge Dorn is nodding his approval at Oh, a perfectly coiffed private practitioner from downtown LA hired by the family. She is a rarity in Juvenile Court, where the vast majority of kids get overworked court-appointed lawyers paid by the state, since most children are legally indigent and their parents cannot be forced to pay for their legal bills, even the ones that can afford to. Oh has already impressed the judge by filing extensive written motions, affidavits, and a favorable psychological profile of John labeling him an ideal candidate for rehabilitation in the juvenile system (an expert opinion paid for by John's parents). All this had been neatly compiled in a bound volume with elaborate indexed tabs—again, a rarity. The assembly-line crush of cases is so great that most kids are lucky if they meet their lawyers before going to court, much less benefit from carefully researched pleadings. Dorn regularly criticizes defense lawyers for blowing off cases with little or no effort. Those who walk into Juvenile Court like Oh, ignoring the peeling paint and futility, treating it instead as if it were the most important forum in the land, find a certain edge in Judge Dorn's court.

The defense lawyer is now beseeching Dorn, passionate and heartfelt, asking the judge to compare John with most of the kids Dorn sees—the deprived and impoverished children, kids who have been abused, who have drug problems, whose only role models have been gangbangers and criminals.

"We understand why these kids end up here, or at least we think we do," the defense lawyer says. "But children like John have no framework to fit into our juvenile system. We're seeing more and more kids like this, who don't come from that background, and it's troubling. There is no easy explanation for their conduct, but it is a new phenomenon we're seeing more and more. We need to deal with it. . . .

"But prison won't do it. Prison won't help this kid. This kid is going to come back into society. The question is, do we want to help him, or to return him as a hardened criminal?"

Oh sits down, her presentation concluded. Everything she said is indisputable. State prison, with its hardened criminals, its predatory rape gangs, its rampant AIDS, is no place for a willowy seventeen-year-old. With an intact family eager to work with Dorn, with John's track record in school and his previous involvement with the church, he has far more going for him than most kids who, simply by virtue of their birthday, must be treated as juveniles. He is the sort of kid everyone agrees is most likely to be rehabilitated by the juvenile system, and most likely to be destroyed if punished as an adult.

There is only one problem: The law has changed since Dorn last sat in Juvenile Court. It is no longer interested in reforming John. The law says an armed robber over sixteen should be tried as an adult, unless hard evidence shows the crime was neither grave nor sophisticated. If the gun wasn't real, or if Richard had forced John to commit the robbery, or if they had forgotten their gloves and masks, or if they had suddenly stopped and apologized to Gutierrez and refused to go through with it—if the crime was clearly and demonstrably *childish*, and lacking in any potential for serious injury or death, then, perhaps, Dorn might have a legal way to keep hold of John. But there is no such evidence, and everyone in the courtroom knows it. It was a cold, calculated, and, except for a locked getaway car, well-planned crime, mature in its execution if not in its outcome, with fatal consequences but a finger twitch away, and no real extenuating circumstance—no real excuse—for Dorn to grab hold of.

Sisman gets in the last word of argument with one pithy comment: "The fact that the minor comes from an intact family and gets good grades is not justification for this sort of conduct. If anything, it only makes what he did more reprehensible."

Dorn quickly clears his throat. It is the sort of comment judges must reflexively agree with if they hope to stay in office. "Clearly, there is never, never any justification for this sort of conduct," Dorn says. John's mother resumes weeping at this, for it sounds as if the judge is about to rule for the prosecution—until Dorn finishes his thought. "But the issue is where should this minor be tried."

Sisman quickly interrupts, drawing a glare from Dorn. "The legislature says this sort of crime should be prosecuted as an adult offense, unless there are some powerful reasons not to. Those have not been proven here."

It is the last statement the prosecutor is allowed to make. "Well, there *are* some powerful reasons," Dorn roars. "Nothing sophisticated about what occurred here. It happens every day. You see individuals with a gun and mask go out . . . and do this all the time. Nothing sophisticated about it."

With the question of sophistication summarily dispensed with— apparently because armed robbery by juveniles is so alarmingly common— Dorn moves on to the question of the gravity of the offense, the other part of the fitness test John Sloan needed to overcome. Yes, armed robbery is a very grave crime, Dorn says, but that is offset by the fact that if he were transferred to adult court, he would probably get off with a very light sentence, a year or two at most, because of his youth and previously clean record. In Juvenile Court, Dorn said, I can keep him incarcerated until he's twenty-five, if necessary. That's eight years. Over in adult court, he's small potatoes. They might just drop the case. And if they do imprison him, it won't be in a rehabilitation program, as would be the case in a juvenile lockup.

"If the only thing you are interested in is a pound of meat, the only thing you are interested in is being vindictive, that is what you get. . . . The District Attorney's Office is always ready to file a fitness. . . . But I can't see any benefit whatsoever from him being tried as an adult. None whatsoever . . . I find the minor is fit to be tried in Juvenile Court."

Dorn's reasoning is eminently sensible, compassionate, seemingly indisputable. His analysis of sentencing patterns is true, too: California's tough juvenile fitness law has in many cases achieved shorter sentences, not longer ones, exactly the opposite of its intended effect. Except in murder cases, kids sentenced in Juvenile Court to the Youth Authority for major violent crimes tend to do more time than kids tried in adult court for the same offenses. (This is a function of "time off for good behavior" and other early-release gimmicks designed to relieve overcrowding in adult prisons and to cut sentences by as much as half—breaks juveniles do not get.) And, ironically, the vast majority of teens sentenced as adults to prison are "housed" at the Youth Authority anyway, so they can serve their shorter sentences safe from the violent confines of the state's adult prison facilities.

There is only one problem with Dorn's ruling: It is at odds with the law.[5] Ten years ago, his reasoning would have passed muster. But now the law specifically forbids judges from balancing one part of the fitness test—in this case, the length of time John can remain in the juvenile system—with another. If armed robbery is a grave and serious offense—something every other judge in Los Angeles Juvenile Court has concluded—then John should be on his way right now to adult court. Judges who haven't toed the line on this point in the past have been appealed and embarrassed—including Dorn's predecessor as supervising judge, who was slapped down on an appeal by Peggy Beckstrand for precisely the same sort of ruling as Dorn just made.

Sisman tries to say as much, but Dorn silences him while the prosecutor's knee joints are still cracking from standing up. "Counsel, I heard your argument. I have made my ruling," Dorn says. The judge turns away from him and asks his clerk for a trial date. Sisman is left sputtering.

Next to him, defense attorney Oh quickly whispers with her client, then, before the clerk can finish studying the layers of penciled entries on her battered desk calendar, the lawyer stands and announces that John is ready to plead guilty to all the charges immediately—as a juvenile.

Judge Dorn says he will be happy to oblige. He tells Sisman to take "the waiver," a lengthy series of legally mandated questions intended to safeguard against coerced or ill-informed guilty pleas by juveniles—but which amounts to fifteen stultifying minutes of monotone inquiries from the DA, proddings from the defense attorney, and uh-huhs from the kid. (*Do you know what a trial is? Yeah. Do you waive your right to trial? Uh-huh. Do you know you can call witnesses on your behalf? Do you waive your right to call witnesses? . . .*) Sisman goes through this numbing recitation at least twenty-five times a day, like all the other prosecutors here. Without objection or hesitation, he does it now on autopilot, voice flat and disinterested. John says yes to each question — the only words he speaks during the entire ninety-minute hearing — after which Dorn officially accepts the boy's admission and declares John a ward of the Juvenile Court.

John looks more confused than relieved as he is unceremoniously escorted back to the holding tank, but his family is overjoyed, smiling and hugging one another and pumping their attorney's arm. Dorn sets sentencing in three months, leaving time for an extensive diagnostic study to aid him in deciding what to do with John.

Deputy DA Sisman, meanwhile, slips out of the room at his first opportunity and crosses the street to his office, to complain to Peggy and to ask permission to appeal the ruling. Dorn watches him go, but he is unworried, confident in his vision of justice. He congratulates Angela Oh for a job well done, wearing a sly smile, as if the two of them are sharing a secret.

But the judge seems to avoid meeting the eyes of a large, forlorn man standing shell-shocked in the back of the courtroom — a man who has a very different opinion about the gravity of being robbed at gunpoint, a man who will never again feel secure in his neighborhood and whose daughters still cry when he leaves the house.

Instead, Judge Dorn grabs a file and says, "Call the next case," then, a moment later, as a new set of attorneys step forward to begin the ritual anew, the bailiff asks the victim of John Sloan's armed robbery to please leave the room while court is in session.

"God, that makes me furious," Peggy Beckstrand says when Sisman briefs her a short time later. "What's he saying, that just because armed robberies are a dime a dozen, it's okay? We're going to say it's acceptable behavior now for a kid to stick a gun in someone's face and threaten their life, because that's what everyone's doing? Can you believe a judge actually said that?"

She is up and pacing now, voice raised, hands waving, already framing in her mind the legal issues at stake. "There's no way we can lose an appeal on this. We've got to get a transcript." Then she looks hard at her prosecutor, and asks one question in a slower, more subdued voice. "You requested a stay, right?"

Suddenly, Sisman looks away, and Peggy senses this case is not going to be appealed successfully after all. She sounds like an exasperated schoolteacher lecturing a wayward student when she says, "Hyman, we just had a meeting about this, about making a proper record at a fitness hearing. We knew this was going to come up with Dorn. Tell me you asked for a stay."

After a silence, Sisman says, "No, I didn't. The minor pleaded to the 211."

"You let him plead?" Peggy is astonished. This is what Dorn must have been smiling about in court—he knew the prosecutor had made a fundamental error that left the ruling impregnable, no matter the legalities. "You didn't object?"

Sisman shakes his head. Unlike a defendant's broad right to appeal anything and everything, prosecutors have a small window of opportunity to try to overturn a trial court's unfavorable rulings. Sisman needed to stand up immediately and request a stay of all proceedings, which Dorn would have been compelled to grant. But by participating in John's guilty plea, Sisman gave up that opportunity. John's lawyer had cleverly locked in his conviction as a juvenile by immediately copping to the charge while Sisman was still reeling from Dorn's decision—and before any appeal could wrest jurisdiction away from the Juvenile Court. Trying him as an adult now for the same crime would constitute unlawful double jeopardy. Dorn and the defense attorney had outfoxed the prosecutor.

"Coming to me now," Peggy says, "is like saying in adult court, the jury acquitted him, let's appeal."

They discuss it further, and Peggy decides to pass the case on to the DA's appellate section to see if there is some way around this hurdle, but she knows it is hopeless. Sisman trudges out, dispirited—and under orders to reread his DA's manual, which clearly explains what he should have done in court that day. Even as other kids that same day were handed over to adult court on identically serious charges, John Sloan was guaranteed a far easier ride. Judge Dorn's perception of what was right had won out over what the statutes dictate.[6]

And with that, the war between the DA and the Juvenile Court judge had begun in earnest.

CHAPTER 6

Raised by the State

George Trevino clasps his hands behind his back as if they are bound by invisible handcuffs—the required posture for detainees in Juvenile Court—and trudges ahead of the bailiff, walking from the stuffy, crowded holding cell he knew too well to the courtroom he had seen far too many times. In that moment, he would give just about anything to trade places with someone like John Sloan, to have had the same opportunities, the home, the family. Most of all his family.

George spends much of his downtime—there is a lot of it in Juvenile Hall—trying to imagine what that would be like, having a mom and dad and his own bed that could never be taken away. Even as he walks that dismal hallway with its lumpy linoleum and odor of sweat and disinfectant—surroundings so familiar to him he had come to notice their absence more than their presence—he turns his thoughts once more to the sanctuary of What if?

What if he had never been a 300 kid? George used to ask God why he had to live with that unlucky designation, praying for deliverance, but that had been a long time ago. As the years passed, he tells me, huge blocks of his early childhood had melted from his memory. He now could no longer remember being small or playing with toys, or even if he ever had any toys to play with. His mother's face, his brother and sister—all had slipped into some black hole in his head. Thinking about that is too painful. The idea *that your family could disappear, not just in reality, but inside you, too, was paralyzing. If he let it consume him, he would just sit and weep for hours. So he fills the vacuum with daydreams instead, about having a home with a mother and father in it, people who made sure he was dressed and fed, who praised him when he did something well, yelled at him when he was bad. As he emerges from the holding tank door to stand blinking in the courtroom, George wonders what it would be like to have a mom or dad who cared enough about him to yell. Strange, George thinks, that he would crave such a thing, but he did. Most kids didn't know the riches they had. George knew.*

At age six, when a policeman found him abandoned in the filthy Dodge van that was his only home, his mother a fugitive later imprisoned for manslaughter, George Trevino became a "300 kid." That's what they called him, right there in court, one of those unintentionally dehumanizing verbal shorthands so common in the juvenile system. As he walked into court today, he heard the judge and the probation officer discussing his case in hushed voices. "Oh, he was in the 300 system before this happened," the judge said with a knowing, sad sort of finality, and everyone kind of nodded as if to say, Oh, that explains it.

The 300 kid is a synonym for a foster child, a dependent child, a beaten, battered, and abused child. The term is drawn from the California Welfare and Institutions Code Section 300, which empowers the Juvenile Court to protect abused and neglected children, to take them from their homes and put them in foster care as dependents of the court—with the court becoming, in essence, the child's new parent. Some families are eventually reunited. Some, like George's, are never made whole again. George was raised by the state.

And the state made George what he is today: While under the Juvenile Court's guidance and protection—as a victim, not a victimizer—a bright, law-abiding A student with a penchant for writing poetry was destroyed. For ten years, he was shunted from one temporary home to another. He was separated from his older brother and younger sister. He was entrusted to neglectful, drug-addicted guardians. He was allowed to roam the streets, to experiment with drugs, to drop out of school—all the while in the care and custody of the state. With each move, his pitifully meager possessions were packed into a disposable green Hefty trash bag, the foster child's luggage, which George was bright enough to see as a metaphor for his entire life. He considered himself a prisoner.

"I always wondered what it was that I had done wrong," George says, "but no one would ever tell me. I just figured they thought I would turn out like my mother, and they were just getting a head start."

*And when the inevitable finally came to pass, when this increasingly an-
gry, rootless kid took solace in the streets and got involved in crime, the
system geared up with all its power and programs to do what it always does
in such cases:*

It is preparing to abandon him.

———————◆———————

THAT George Trevino's juvenile fitness hearing is occurring in another
courtroom on the same day as John Sloan's is a good measure of how
common this once unheard-of procedure has become: In Los Angeles Juvenile Court, a total of five kids will be sent into the adult system today.
Nationally, the toll for this day alone will be forty-seven children branded
unsalvageable.[1]

"This case is more than sad," Juvenile Court Commissioner Jewell Jones
says—off the official court record, just discussing it with her staff while
awaiting George's arrival from the holding tank. "It's a classic indictment
of the system. He did not get what he needed, and that wasn't his fault.
And now we're going to send him out." She pauses, fingering the boy's
thick file absently, then sighs. "Oh, this one is giving me a terrible time."

"Would it help if I bring in the psychiatrist to testify?" George's court-
appointed lawyer, Anna Noriega, asks before the hearing commences.
"He's got a lot of good things to say about George. But I don't want to
waste his time or the court's if it's not going to make a difference. I'll just
submit his report." The respected child psychiatrist who evaluated George
said the boy would respond well in a stable, structured environment—
something the Juvenile Court, in all the years it controlled George's fate,
never managed to give him.

But the commissioner shakes her head. "Lord knows I think most of
these kids would be better served in the juvenile system than in adult
court," she says. "But, unfortunately, that is not the criterion I must use to
decide this case. The criteria are so rigid. I'm afraid I'll have a hard time
finding him fit."

Noriega nods. "Then I won't call the doctor. It's just that it's such a very
sad case."

"Yes," the commissioner says just as the black metal door to the holding tank opens and a tall, pale boy in green slacks and a sweatshirt enters the courtroom. "He was a 300 kid, you know."

When George Trevino's mother abandoned him and he became a Section 300 ward of the Juvenile Court,[2] the system had a goal: find him a stable, loving home as soon as possible. At age six, it was not too late for George.

But he never knew that stability. The social workers kept moving him from one temporary foster home to another. His mother, wanted for a variety of theft and drug charges, refused to come to see him or to tell the dependency court where she lived. An aunt who stayed in touch with George's mother while she was a fugitive kept promising to visit him, then failed to show up, bitterly disappointing George time after time. Predictably, his behavior grew worse. He began to lash out at his foster parents at various group homes, who would then ask that he be removed. Between the moves, he had long stays in MacLaren Hall, a lockup for abused and neglected kids—the closest thing to an orphanage in Los Angeles. He had caretakers, but no one to love or who loved him.

George's hopes rose again when an aunt and uncle in Colorado offered to take him, but the state agencies responsible for approving out-of-state placements dragged out the process so long, it eventually fell through. George fell into a deep depression after that, and he became very hard to handle, his temper explosive. "He sees himself as intrinsically bad and worthless, and feels tremendous guilt," his social worker wrote when he was seven. Another tantalizing chance at a new life—and a marked improvement in his behavior—came a year later, when the dependency court inexplicably abandoned its opinion that George's mother, Violanda, was unfit, and attempted to reunite the family—despite a social worker's report that found Mrs. Trevino led "a life filled with violence." Still, Violanda had surrendered herself to police, then struck a deal for probation, making her at least theoretically eligible as a parent. But on the eve of a sixty-day trial at living together, George's mother was again arrested and imprisoned, this time for fatally shooting someone outside a liquor store.

George's mother stayed in prison until he reached his teens and was released after finishing her manslaughter term, only to be incarcerated again for forgery and parole violations. She never regained custody of him, and was mostly barred from visiting her son, though when she was out of prison, she sometimes sneaked in to see him at school or in his placement by using a false identity. She eventually died in the penitentiary. He had no memory of a father. He died of a drug overdose before George turned two.

George's little sister fared better. Because she was a cute and precocious toddler when she entered the system, she was easier to place and was almost immediately adopted. George never saw her after that night when they were all pulled from that stinking van with its moldering blankets and wadded fast-food wrappers. Her new name and address were kept confidential, even from her own brother.

Growing up, George thought about her all the time, imagining the life she must be living, glad for her, jealous of her, grieving for her. After years of begging, he was allowed a fifteen-minute visit with her in a park in LA when he was fifteen, nine years after they had parted. They did not recognize or remember one another. It was awkward and silent, a meeting of strangers who shared blood and ancestry, but whose lives had nothing else in common. She belonged now to a solid, law-abiding family, stable and safe. She was a great student, a kid with a future George could only dream about.

"It was the first time I met her, and the last time," George would later say wistfully, eyes wet. Shortly after the meeting, the girl and her family moved to another county to escape George's mother, who was out on parole at the time and attempting to take her daughter back. Not long after the move, on Christmas Day, George's sister and two other members of her adopted family were killed by a drunken driver. George heard about it three weeks later, long after his only sister had been buried.

Thinking about his dismembered family makes George weep silently, his eyes crimson, the injustice of it leaving him quaking with an angry despair. He has lost his older brother as well. They were initially kept in the same foster homes, so at least they had one another, but they always ended up running away together. George idolized his brother, clung to him as his anchor. George would do anything he said. But the older boy was even more angry and difficult than George, sometimes violent, sometimes weeping uncontrollably for hours, calling for his mother to save him. By the time George was eight, the social workers separated the two boys for good. His older brother telephoned him and wrote letters for a long time, but the calls and cards gradually slowed, then stopped. George doesn't know where his brother is now. "He's somewhere in the system, in prison somewhere, that's all I know," George says. "He's a total loss. My sister, my brother, my whole family. Gone. Now it's just me."

George had done nothing wrong to become a 300 kid. He had not asked for a murderous mother or a shattered family. He was just one of a daily procession of abused and neglected children, one of twenty-five thousand who occupied LA's child welfare system with him in 1983—a system that, today, holds more than twice as many kids.

Despite the uncertainties of his future, the loss of his family, the constant moves from one foster home to another, one school after another, George thrived for some of the time he was raised by the state. Like many abused and neglected children, the trauma of his early life left him in need of medication and counseling for psychological problems, hyperactivity, tantrums. They called him "SED" in court hearings, which George learned meant "severely emotionally disturbed." For a while, he was heavily medicated. Then someone decided he wasn't so disturbed after all. He began to receive more moderate treatment and, finally, he began to heal. By the 1990–91 school year, when George was in seventh grade—and he was allowed to stay in the same foster home all year—his grades were all A's and B's, with good attendance and good behavior. He became the top student and role model at the Helping Hands group home, dressing each day in bow ties and sweaters, after school diligently tutoring and counseling younger kids. The owner of the group home would have been happy to keep George indefinitely.

But then the Juvenile Court made a fateful decision. In keeping with the system's primary goal of bringing families, even abusive ones, together, the court took George out of the group home in which he was thriving and sent him to live with his aunt and uncle.

For a while—even for a year or two—it seemed to work out. There was just one problem: George's uncle was a drug dealer who later succumbed to addiction and who died of an overdose during George's second year in the home. His aunt lost control after the suicide and began drinking and using drugs.[3] She would leave George to go score, the house in shambles. George responded the only way he knew how: He began staying away from the house, then skipping school, his once excellent grades plummeting. Then he joined a street gang. All this took place while he remained a ward of the court, his upbringing still the legal responsibility of the Juvenile Court. The social worker assigned to track George's case somehow never noticed any of this.[4]

Eventually, an older gang member took George under his wing. The older teen was tough, confident, brash—everything George felt he should be, but wasn't. This boy started a schoolyard brawl, and George leapt to his defense. George's new mentor cut another kid with a broken bottle, the police were called, and everyone got arrested, George included, though he was immediately released. A short time later, another gang member offered George and several other kids a ride in his new car. Two policemen confronted them at a gas station and arrested them all. The car had been stolen. Of the passengers, only George was truthful with the police and admitted he had known the car was hot when he saw the jimmied ignition switch, though he had no hand in taking it.

Despite George's minimal involvement—by the police department's own account, he was merely a passenger in the car and an unarmed latecomer to the schoolyard fight—he was charged with assault with a deadly weapon and, thanks to his forthrightness, car theft, both felonies. He was taken to Juvenile Hall, then Juvenile Court. Not the supposedly protective Juvenile Court dependency branch he knew as a foster kid, but a very different, harder place, the separate, larger side of the court reserved for delinquents, where people like Judge Dorn and Commissioner Jones maintained order.

He met his lawyer for the first time when he took his seat at the defendant's table. The judge was talking to someone else, and the harried-looking young blond woman from the Public Defender's Office whispered to George, "Sorry I couldn't talk to you before the hearing. It's been really busy. I'll be representing you today." She pulled a file from a large, messy stack of manila folders in front of her and studied it for a minute, reading it for the first time. Then she asked, "You are George, aren't you?"

The hearing passed quickly and without substance. There would be another pretrial hearing, but not for several months, thanks to the constant logjam of cases in Juvenile Court. The bailiff gave George a piece of paper with directions to the Probation Department, so he could talk to an officer about his case, and it was over.

"Look at the bright side," his lawyer had said. "Isn't that your aunt in the back of the courtroom? You'll be able to go home with her now."

Despite its brevity, there was a hidden subtext to George's first hearing as an accused delinquent. It had transformed him—in the eyes of the law, at least—from a child in danger to a dangerous child. No one blamed the nameless bureaucrats who took an A–B student and sent him to a home troubled by drugs; there is no such accountability in the system. No one asked how a ward of the court could become a gang member without anyone noticing. Only George was held accountable. His status as a 300 ward had ended, his file in dependency court stamped with one large red word: "Terminated." Officially, he was no longer a victim, he was a criminal, and that is how he would be treated forevermore.

The child welfare system failed miserably in George's case, but this caused no consternation. The public remained unaware of it, because, in the name of protecting children, the Juvenile Court zealously guards the confidentiality of 300 cases (not even delinquency court judges get to see these files). And within the system, none of the initiates much noticed, because what happened with George is so shockingly common. Every year, ten thousand cases are dropped from the dependency system in LA. A third of them get termination stamps because kids being raised by the state turn to crime.

That's more than three thousand kids in Los Angeles, every year.

It was downhill from there for George. Because of the confidentiality that swathes 300 kids, his first probation report does not even mention the fact that he was a ward of the dependency court for eight of his fourteen years. It reads as if he suddenly turned to crime at age fourteen for no good reason. The regular counseling and therapy he had received as a victim of child neglect ended. No one noticed: Now he was just a bad kid. He was released to his aunt, who, subsequent probation officers reported, had been jailed on drug charges. George ran away and never showed up for his court hearings, hoping the system would just forget about him.

And then, something incredible happened. The mother of one of his friends took him in. Her home was small and rather shabby, her income was meager, but Kathy Reveles offered George something he had never experienced: kindness, support, acceptance. She treated him like a son, got him reenrolled in school, gave him chores, a small allowance. When he misbehaved, she told him so, and George would apologize, begging her not to send him away. "That's not going to happen," she would always say. "This is your home now."

He never really dared to believe that, not completely anyway, until that day he shyly showed her a poem he had written, and she had hugged him and thanked him, as if it was actually worth something. Then George had said, "Thank you, Mom," and it felt right. Kathy had given him a big hug, and he didn't stiffen or push away or anything. George wasn't sure, but at age fourteen, he thought he finally loved someone. And maybe, just maybe, that person loved him back.

For a year, George stayed in school and out of trouble while in the Reveles home. He eventually returned to court and got probation for his old auto theft and assault charges, and Commissioner Jones allowed him to stay with his new "mother." But a few months later, a member of Reveles's household burglarized a home in the neighborhood. A stolen VCR turned up in George's room, and he was arrested and charged, too. A new probation officer assigned to the case decided Kathy Reveles's household was a bad influence, that her home was too crowded and unkempt, and that

George should be removed. "She's all I have; please, I'll be good and study harder," George begged, sobbing wildly during their interview. "Please let me go back home."

But the probation officer was adamant, and Commissioner Jones agreed. George was sent to a group foster home in an LA suburb, many miles from the Reveles home. At the time, notations in George's court file show someone finally noticed his need for counseling, that he was alternately consumed by anger and depression, hurling profanities at schoolteachers one moment, then weeping uncontrollably the next. The probation officer reported that George became "hysterical" during their interview. His school counselor begged the court to put George into some in-depth treatment program before something terrible happened. The Probation Department runs such a residential program, with secure space for a hundred kids and a waiting list of up to six months to get in. But George was never even considered for it. He received no counseling there, or anywhere else.

George hated his new group home. He was the only Hispanic kid; all the others were black and George felt like a misfit, unwanted and picked on. After a few months, George ran away. He returned to his old gang turf and soon fell in with a twenty-two-year-old gangbanger named Frank Villa. Villa and George recruited two other juveniles on probation to participate in a home invasion robbery. Their target was a used-car salesman named Shorty, reputed to keep large amounts of cash in his home.[5] Villa was to arm himself with a revolver, George with a .22 rifle, and one of the other juveniles, JoJo, with another gun. The remaining kid, Bambi, was told to knock on the door and to ask for one of Shorty's sons by name. As soon as the door opened, the others would storm the house, hold Shorty and his family at gunpoint, then make off with the money, Villa ordered.

Instead, Shorty shot Villa in the leg, the rest of the family pounced on him, kicking and punching, and the three kids working with Villa ran off.

Once behind bars, Villa quickly informed on the others, placing much of the blame on George and hoping to get leniency in return for cooperation. The police found George at Kathy Reveles's house; his other partners in crime were in the same neighborhood. The charges were extensive: There were six people in the house, including an infant, which meant six counts of attempted armed robbery. Because Villa fired his gun, attempted murder charges were under review as well.

George had reached his sixteenth birthday by then. The court system that had always given him such short shrift studied his record in minute detail now. In order to justify treating him as an adult, a new spin was put on his background by yet another probation officer assigned to his case—the sixth since he had entered the system. In the past, George's criminal involvement—in the assault, the car theft, and the burglary—had always been seen as minimal, which is why he stayed on probation and received virtually no supervision or services from the Juvenile Court. But now, the new probation officer wrote, "The minor appears to have a rather serious previous delinquent history. There is a previous assault with a deadly weapon. . . . It is clear that he is a threat to the safety of others."

As before, there was no discussion in this latest report of his childhood entrusted to the state. There was no mention of the unheeded pleas that George receive psychological counseling after he became a delinquent. There was only a harsh recommendation: Transfer him to adult court. Prosecute him to the fullest extent of the law.

Now it was up to Jewell Jones to decide.

In court, George shifts in his seat and glances mournfully at the empty chair next to him, the one marked "Parent." The bailiff speaks into the public address system: "Parents of George Trevino, please follow the yellow line to Department 251." Then, after a whispered command from Jones, he adds, "*Guardian* of George Trevino, please report to 251." After a moment, Kathy Reveles walks in, blond and plump with a wrinkled, kind face. She sits down heavily next to George, then begins to pat his shoulder as he wipes his tears on a sleeve. "I'm all he has," she tells the court.

George's lawyer, Anna Noriega, pleads with Jones to find a reason to keep George in the juvenile system. Unlike a John Sloan, who had so many advantages in life before he became the leader of a botched armed robbery, George has never been much more than a bystander to crime, his lawyer argues. He has never physically hurt anyone. He was an unsophisticated, minor player in a foolish robbery planned and directed by an adult, she says, and he is consumed by remorse.

"He has been a victim of the system. It's too soon to give up on this minor. He wants to accept the consequences of his actions. He doesn't want to go home. He wants to do better. That's the mind-set we need more of in Juvenile Court. Let's give him that chance."

The fact that he possessed a gun doesn't mean much anymore in Los Angeles, she adds. "If the crime statistics are to be believed, weapons are all too readily available to our children."

George tugs at her, whispering urgently. "Tell her it was unloaded. I told the police that. It was unloaded. I couldn't have shot anyone." But

Noriega sits down. She had made exactly the same pitch to Jones that John Sloan's lawyer made to Judge Dorn. But this was a different court, a different day.

The deputy DA on the case rises, looking uneasy. She is not an uncaring woman, but she represents a certain point of view in the system, one that supports the notion that punishment should fit the crime. She looks at George, ignores the knot in her stomach, and does her job. "Yes, everything that happened in his life may have been terrible," she says. "But there comes a time when it's on him. . . . The boy did need help. He's had a terrible life, I'm not contesting that. But on that day, he made a personal choice. On that day, he showed criminal sophistication. He is responsible, not the system. *He* committed the crime, not the system. . . . Those people in that house were terrorized. There was a baby in that house when the bullets started flying. If that's not a grave offense, I don't know what is."

It is a familiar argument, and a true one. Even George concedes that. "I made the choice, that's true," he says later. "I was there. I went in. Nobody forced me: I chose trouble. But you got to understand. They were my friends. They were all I had. I never hurt anyone. I never wanted to hurt anyone. But you just don't walk away from your friends."

It took a long time sitting in Juvenile Hall for George to articulate these thoughts. But in the courtroom, the words in his head are just a jumble. When the prosecutor sits down, he wants to yell out to Jewell Jones, to plead with her, to explain, to rail. He wants to tell her he is not hopeless, that he is not filled with hatred or violence, that he is not a number, a 300 or 600 or any hundred, but just a kid with no one and nothing, and who would do anything to make it otherwise. Just tell me how, he wants to scream. He wants to tell her what it's like to have the same dream night after night, that he's playing tag with his little sister, laughing, happy—then waking up and not knowing if the image in his head is a dim memory, or just something his mind cooked up to fill the black hole. Do you know what it's like to have no past? he wants to ask. And behind it all, like a ringing in his ears, is the question that really nags at him all the time, the one that has haunted him since he was six years old and his family evaporated. He wants to ask it, then and there and for good: What did I do wrong back then? What did I do to deserve this life?

But he says none of these things. How could he? And what would it matter if he did? As the prosecutor sits down, he just stares downward at the tear-spattered table, the words lodged in his throat like bile. He begins to sob again, silently, with Kathy's warm, large hand gently rubbing his back.

Commissioner Jones is silent a moment. She is a compact woman in her mid-fifties, with tousled auburn hair and a fondness for bright lipstick, brighter nail polish, and large, dangling earrings that sway hypnotically as she speaks. She greets everyone who enters her court with a cheery hello rather than insisting on judicial decorum. All the chairs in her courtroom are labeled with block-lettered strips of manila paper—one chair for the defense attorney, one for the prosecutor, one for the "minor/defendant." The parents get a pair of chairs, right next to the accused at the defense table—so they become part of the process, rather than being relegated to the audience, as in Dorn's court and most others in the juvenile system. A former probation officer, Jones is, unabashedly, what other judges refer to snidely as a "social worker on the bench." She spent most of her judicial career in dependency court dealing with 300 kids, so she is well aware of the forces at work in George's short, sad life, and she hates sending such kids to adult court. But prosecutors have tried to cow her liberal leanings of late by "papering" her—filing legal papers to have her removed from cases whenever transfers to adult court were at stake. Blanket papering of Judge Dorn by public defenders on every type of case had paralyzed the undermanned juvenile system years earlier, eventually forcing Dorn out of Juvenile Court until his recent return. In Jones's case, the DA relented after a few months, but prosecutors still treat her like a kid on probation. Decisions vary wildly from one courtroom to the next in Juvenile Court, depending on the judge, the prosecutor, the defense counsel, even the size of the docket or the space available in some program or home. There is no consistency—only luck of the draw. Today, it just so happens that the pressure on Jewell Jones to take a hard line is enormous.

"This case does indeed come down to responsibility," Jones says, picking up on the prosecutor's train of thought. "And the people with responsibility for George, myself included, did not make the right decisions for him. . . . God knows the facts of his life are horrendous. . . . God knows the system should have done better."

It seems, then, that the commissioner is about to find George fit for Juvenile Court after all. The prosecutor tenses—perhaps her office gave up on papering Jones too soon. She picks up her pen, ready to jot down anything Jones says—for use on appeal. The defense attorney, meanwhile, leans forward in her seat. Even George looks up for a moment, his sobs stopping. Jones is clearly grappling with what she has to do, right there in open court, the social worker in her battling with that five-prong test that makes it so hard to give a kid like George a break.

Then the moment passes. Jones looks directly at Kathy Reveles and says, "I'm sorry." The DA relaxes then, and Jones keeps her eyes averted from George, whose sobs have resumed. They are no longer quiet. His shoulders are heaving now in a mad shrug, his head resting on the scarred wood of the defense table. The DA hands him a tissue.

"Mistakes have been made," Jones continues, "but, unfortunately, that's not enough. The law is very, very tough. If there was some way we could give credit to kids for the crappy things adults have done to them, there would be a lot of credit in that column for George. Unfortunately, I cannot do that.

"George is sweet, he's compelling, he's dear, and he begged me to send him to you," Jones says, still looking directly at Reveles, wanting her to understand. "I did it, and I probably shouldn't have. Maybe I should have bitten the bullet and sent him to camp then. Maybe we wouldn't be here now if I had. Believe me, I lie awake at night wondering about things like that.

"I'm sorry," she says again, and now she is looking at the sixteen-year-old boy before her. "I have no choice." George must be tried as an adult, she rules.

"That is the order of the court," Jones says wearily. It is the expected outcome. It is what the law requires. No one will try to appeal it. If Jewell Jones can't be convinced, no appeals court is going to give George a break. Yet the lawyers, clerks, probation officer and judge, even the DA, all look as if they'd just been punched in the stomach. It is one of those Juvenile Court cases: no one wins.

Of the four people involved in the failed robbery of Shorty's house, George has fared the worst. Bambi and JoJo, whose criminal records were no better or worse than George's, were under sixteen; she got straight probation, he went to a Probation Department camp in the mountains outside of LA for six months. The adult, Villa, entered a plea bargain and got an eight-year prison sentence. That leaves George for the District Attorney's adult office to hammer, to pursue as a gang member, a violent felon, a sixteen-year-old danger to society. In adult court, he will face a potential sentence of twenty-nine years to life in state prison if convicted of every possible charge against him.

As the bailiff escorts him from Jones's courtroom, George, eyes puffy and wet, remembers something and turns to his lawyer. He says, quietly and without a trace of irony, "Thanks for your time."

Everyone else files from the courtroom without a word.

CHAPTER 7

War

     The surreally violent landscape of Los Angeles street gangs has been transformed this month as if by an earthquake. A deadly and notorious prison-based gang with tentacles throughout Southern California, the Mexican Mafia, has ordered something no cop or prosecutor or social worker has ever been able to muster:

    A truce.

    There will be no more brown-on-brown gangbanging, this gang of gangs has declared. No drive-bys, no hits, no contracts. Latino gangs constantly at war with one another, accounting for thousands of shootings and hundreds of deaths every year, would have to set aside their differences. It was time to work together, to build something greater, the prison gangsters had decided, and there would be no exceptions. Violations of the truce would be punished by death, quick and without appeal. And unlike the puny threats that emanate from the Juvenile Court, when the Mexican Mafia promises to come to your barrio and hunt you down, you take it seriously. Or you die.

    When law enforcement catches wind of all this, skepticism runs high. There is some hope at first that this truce, however unexpected and rife with ulterior motives it may be, will still bring about a decrease in shootings and murders in Los Angeles (statistics later prove this to be true, at least tempo-

rarily). But it soon becomes clear that the motivation behind the truce is not altruism: The purpose is to assemble an army.

With rival factions united and no longer letting one another's blood, a lucrative block of the drug trade currently controlled by black street gangs—the Crips and the Bloods—could be wrested away. Gangbanging against black gangs was to continue under the Mexican Mafia truce, and police intelligence uncovered a secondary directive to young gang members to stir up racial confrontations at schools, in Juvenile Hall, in the probation camps, and at CYA. The truce is a cover for a power struggle of epic proportions for the streets of LA.

A huge meeting has been called in Venice to hand down these directives. Delegates from every major Latino gang in the area are being dispatched to hear about the new order. In response, police patrols have been stepped up, with orders to use any pretense to stop and interrogate gang delegations. This is not precisely legal, but the gangbangers are in no position to assert their constitutional rights. It is part of the game.

On the day of this meeting, a pair of Los Angeles County sheriff's deputies stop a white Chevy Blazer headed toward Venice with four men and one woman inside, all of them dressed down in bandannas, oversized baggy pants, Pendleton shirts, and big, black engineer boots. The deputies make the passengers get out, and they saunter and slouch insolently, knowing they are untouchable (the delegates, expecting the police to be trawling the streets, have scrupulously avoided bringing guns or drugs to the meet, another Mexican Mafia instruction). The girl particularly impresses the police, so young, yet appearing as hardened as any veterana, coldly protesting being stopped and reluctantly giving her name as Sylvia Mercado. She barely looks sixteen, but something about the look on her face, the bandanna pulled tight down on her skull, the unfrightened look in her eyes, makes her stand out. The deputies have to let the car go—the driver and passengers had broken no laws—but in keeping with the unwritten policy to harass gang members whenever possible, the officers snap photos of the whole carload of them. All of the gang members pick up their shirts for the photographer, Sylvia included, displaying the large tattoos across their stomachs, announcing their membership in Tepa-13.

Back at the station, one of the patrol deputies mentions the incident to an officer who specializes in gang work. "We ran into this girl, she is without doubt the most hard-core gangster any of us has ever seen." The patrolman pulls out the packet of Polaroids they had taken and shows the gang expert. "Look at this kid. Name's Sylvia Mercado."

"That's not Sylvia Mercado," the other cop says. "That's Carla James. I investigated her on a drive-by last year."

The revelation that Carla is using an alias, dressing like a gangster, going to a major gang convention, and sporting a huge tattoo—in short, violating just about every condition of her probation—sets in motion a two-week hunt by Deputy Probation Officer Sharon Stegall, who finally nails the girl during one of Carla's infrequent visits home. When Carla showed up one morning, her mother quietly phoned Sharon while the girl showered and, a short time later, probation officer confronts probationer. Sharon forces Carla to display her tattoo, which provides instant legal grounds for arrest.

"You have the right to remain silent, do you understand that?" Sharon tells Carla as she snaps on the handcuffs. "You have the right to an attorney. And you have the right, apparently, to be stupid."

"It's my body," Carla says quietly. "I can wear my barrio if I want to."

A few weeks later, I catch up with Carla in the Sylmar branch of Juvenile Hall, where she is waiting to learn what the Juvenile Court has in store for her next. She has assumed her usual position of responsibility in her unit, a trustee who helps the staff maintain order, distribute meals, assign tasks, break up fights. Outwardly repentant, she insists she wishes to clean up her act, and has even filed the necessary paperwork to have her tattoo surgically removed, though somehow she never gets around to actually scheduling the operation. She says she wants a private doctor to do it, not some "county hospital butcher."

We sit in an empty hallway on a couple of plastic chairs, out of earshot of the staff, and Carla relaxes a bit, admitting that she is more ambivalent about quitting the gang life than she has let on.

"You have to tell them what they want to hear," she says. "I want the time to pass in comfort, so I do everything they want, I get all the privileges I can. You're crazy if you don't. That's how the system works. They want me to have learned my lesson. So I say, I learned my lesson. Wouldn't you?"

When I don't answer, she shakes her head. The people in the system, she says—the adults—don't understand her world. It's not like when you were kids, she says, and the baddest, toughest kid in school maybe carried a switchblade. Everyone has guns now. Everyone is more mature. And none of you understand about gangs. It's not all about shooting and committing crimes. It's about honor and loyalty and working for something bigger than yourself. In a gang, you feel welcomed, they open up to you, you are part of something, you are committed, you have power. Here, they don't understand that. They just think we're all monsters.

But what about the drive-bys, I ask, and the people who get shot, who die? Isn't that why people think gangs are monstrous? "You've been involved in drive-bys, on both ends of the gun. How can you justify that?"

"That's different. A drive-by isn't like a murder, where you get up in some-one's face and stab them or something. That's too cold-blooded. I could never do that. That's wrong."

I admit to being confused by this, and Carla looks at me as if I'm hope-lessly dense.

"In a drive-by," she explains, "you don't see what happens. You just pull up, blam, blam, blam, and you're gone. Maybe you hit someone, maybe not. It's not like you aim at someone in particular. You leave before you even see what happens."

"But if someone gets shot in the heart, they're just as dead as if you did it looking them in the eye, aren't they?"

"It's not murder," Carla insists. "I can't believe you don't understand this. If you don't see it happen, how can it be murder?"

I ask, What if her brother died in a drive-by? Would that be murder?

She considers this and, to her credit, admits she hadn't thought about it that way before. Perhaps, she says, there's more to it than she has realized. "Look, I'm not saying drive-bys are good, or that I like them or anything. I don't. I'm just saying they're not the same as cold-blooded murder, and that the courts shouldn't treat them the same."

Then she brightens. "But let me tell you this. If my brother did get shot, I'd have to go out looking for who did it. I'd have to get revenge. I'd have to do a drive-by myself to get back at the gang that did it. And I know that wouldn't be murder."

Part of me wants to just leave it like that, but I have to ask the question. "If it wasn't murder, Carla, what would it be?"

Carla smiles. "Justice."

———◆———

FOUR years, this minor has been before the court, and nothing has been done with him. Nothing!"

Judge Dorn is on a tear this morning, at war, it seems, with every faction in his courthouse. So far he has lambasted a defense attorney for being late, incompetent, and inattentive, threatening to cut him off from the gravy train of future court-appointed cases. Then he threatened to dismiss a gang murder case because a grizzled police sergeant had refused to give the public defender access to a key witness whose life was at risk. "I will not tolerate defiance of my orders," the judge bellowed, refusing to let the cop speak. "Turn over the information. Now!" Then, despite the fact this ruling favored the defense, he still managed to infuriate the entire Public Defender's Office later in the morning by eliminating previously common sentences of informal, unsupervised probation for minor offenders—then refusing to transfer cases to other judges who allowed what he calls "wrist-slap sentencing." And when one PD persisted, insisting on her legal right to request a different judge—to "paper" Dorn—he punished her by shipping the case out to the most distant branch of Juvenile Court available, Pomona, a minimum one-hour drive, even though the judge downstairs had space for the case on his docket.

Later this same morning, Dorn had probation officers grumbling because he decided they should make progress reports to him about his probationers every two months (and sometimes more often), instead of once or twice a year as other judges require—a way of forcing POs to monitor kids far more closely (and work far harder) than many care to. "Get used to it," Dorn rumbled when he saw one PO roll her eyes. "You will supervise Judge Dorn's minors properly, or I will have your department chief in here to explain why not." This is a favorite threat of Dorn's—he figures a bureaucrat will give him almost anything to avoid being summoned to court for a verbal drubbing, something he has already used to get new paint, new upholstery, and new furnishings for his long-neglected courthouse.

Next, word went out from Dorn's office that he was hosting an enormous meeting of police chiefs, probation officials, principals, school superintendents, and youth counselors in early February, where he would announce a plan to reform juvenile justice, pressing all those in attendance into service. The DA and the public defender, rather pointedly, were not invited, though both offices immediately began recruiting spies after obtaining bootleg copies of the guest list. They wanted to be ready for whatever Dorn had in mind.[1]

After that, the judge capped off his busy morning by upbraiding his favorite whipping boy, Assistant DA Hyman Sisman, for mistakenly sending a crucial witness home when he was needed to finish a case. Dorn refused to grant the prosecutor a brief postponement so he could summon the witness back to court, and instead acquitted two kids who had beaten and robbed a pizza deliveryman, danced a jig over his supine form, then ran off to count their victim's money and eat the pie with extra pepperoni they had ordered from their home telephone. "I have to acquit you only because the People did not do their job," Dorn announced for the entire courtroom to hear. Then he turned to Sisman. "Next time, when you state that you are ready to proceed, Counsel, make sure you are ready to proceed." The two boys, boldly attired in gangster baggies, hopped from court like school kids headed for recess, while the detective on the case—Mark Fuhrman, who would later become infamous for his racist tapes and his role in the O. J. Simpson case—wished them a sarcastic congratulations, then stalked off in disgust.

In short, Dorn is enjoying the sort of morning that makes it possible for public defenders to call him too harsh a judge, for prosecutors and cops to label him far too lenient, and for everyone else in the system to wonder just what the judge will do next.

His next target is the Probation Department once again—and its performance in the four-year-old case of one Eric Davis. "Nothing has been done with this minor," he bellows again.

Eric is a diminutive seventeen-year-old car thief turned carjacker whose criminal career has only flourished while under the supervision of the Juvenile Court and its investigative arm, the Probation Department.

Dorn is leaning forward, a look of revulsion on his face. He loads enough astonishment into his silky baritone to suit a first visit to the Grand Canyon. As he speaks, he shifts his stare between Eric and the thick Juvenile Court file on the boy, a mass of pink, yellow, and white forms indecipherable to the uninitiated, but a clear road map of failure to Judge Dorn.

"This is a classic example of what's wrong with how we deal with so-called 'minor offenders,'" Dorn says. "He'll be eighteen in a few months, and he's headed nowhere. Or worse."

No one in the courtroom says anything to this, though Dorn looks each principal in the case in the eye, daring them to respond. The system's performance in Eric's case is as indefensible as Eric's own behavior. That this is taken for granted by the prosecutors, defense attorneys, and probation officers present in the courtroom, that no one feels compelled to argue otherwise, speaks volumes.

"Look at this record," Dorn says, refusing to just brush it aside, as other judges in Juvenile Court often do. He has decided to make an example of Eric. "October 1989, the minor is thirteen, he attacks another boy with a baseball bat, arrested for assault with a deadly weapon. He is never brought to court. The Probation Department, in its infinite wisdom, puts this minor on unsupervised probation. For an assault that could have caused serious, serious injury. Outrageous! That is why I will not allow unsupervised probation to be abused any longer."

Gleefully overturning long-standing practice by his brethren on the bench, he had particularly irked the public defenders since his return to Juvenile Court by consistently refusing to grant informal, unsupervised probation to minor offenders, called "654 probation," from the California code section that authorizes it. In recent years, 654 had become a mainstay of the system. It did nothing for kids—essentially, the car thief or graffiti tagger or shoplifter granted 654 went home and, if he or she avoided arrest for six months, the case would be dismissed. It would be as if nothing had happened. In essence, 654 is a labor-saving device for the Probation Department and the rest of the court bureaucracy—with a high failure rate because, by definition, it provided no services or counseling to the kids who committed the crimes. Yet, most judges grant it with regularity—except Judge Dorn.[2]

"Waste of time," he says. "Lost time! Six-five-four never did any good for a minor. That's the time when we need to work with them, when they need all the attention we can give. Before it's too late!"

Dorn looks up over his glasses at the boy, who is doing a poor job of concealing a smirk. His public defender nudges him with an elbow, but he just pulls away. The judge returns to the file.

"Five months later, he's back, this time for grand theft auto. He goes home on probation again, supposedly under supervision this time. Still nothing done. The Probation Department does not even check his school record, which was atrocious. He should have been put in custody then and there." Another glare from Dorn. Eric shakes his head, pained and impatient.

"Age fifteen, he's arrested again, this time for carrying a gun—a misdemeanor," Dorn says, picking at another of his pet peeves, the California legislature's flaccid refusal to buck the gun lobby by making possession of a concealed weapon by a juvenile a felony. Switchblades, daggers, brass knuckles—those are felonies. But not guns, the weapon of choice in juvenile homicides and assaults.[3] By keeping gun possession a misdemeanor, the amount of time the court can keep a child under supervision shrinks drastically.

"Finally, the minor goes to camp for six months," Dorn recounts. "But then he comes home and is right back to his old tricks. Which brings us to today."

Eric is in court this day for car theft and resisting arrest. He and a friend led police on a wild, high-speed chase through Los Angeles in a stolen car. Two youths had taken the car at gunpoint from a terrified woman a few hours earlier while she waited for a red light to change. Eric would have been charged with the far more serious crime of carjacking, but the woman could only identify Eric's friend. She didn't get a good look at the other kid in the car. The likelihood that Eric was the second carjacker was great—his size and general appearance matched the woman's recollection—but that did not make for proof beyond a reasonable doubt. So Eric pleaded guilty only to theft. The reduced charge gave his probation officer the chance to recommend that he stay home on probation. In the months following his latest arrest, the PO reported to Dorn, Eric has been doing well in school and seemed to have turned his life around.

Dorn tosses this recommendation aside with disgust. "This probation report is not worth the paper it's printed on," he says. "Look at this: misspellings, poor grammar. Even the minor's name is incorrect. The probation officer did not even take the time to verify the minor's school record. Is this young man in school or not?"

Silence. Eric's attorney looks at him, but he says nothing. The judge turns toward the boy's mother, who sits in the back of the courtroom wearing blue sweatpants and a black leather jacket, a small gold hoop earring quivering in one of her nostrils. She had told the Probation Department that her son was a good boy whose only problem was that he had friends who stole cars and offered him rides, a statement Dorn openly mocked. Now his eyes drill into her, forcing the woman to look down at her lap. He repeats his question, louder. "Is this boy in school or not?"

"He's not enrolled," the mother finally mutters. "He hasn't been in school for five months."

"He's not enrolled," Dorn parrots in disgust. "He hasn't attended for five months—since the day of his arrest in this case. And yet the probation officer reports that the minor is in school and his attendance and grades are good. In other words, the minor just lied. And the probation officer simply took his word without checking. Incredible."

After a moment, he says the probation recommendation would be ignored. "Camp is the place for this young man," Dorn rules. "And that is where he is going to go."

Eric appears stunned—given the ease with which he had fooled the probation officer, he expected to get off, as always. Eric's mother begins to mutter angrily and incoherently in the back of the courtroom, but Dorn silences her with a stony stare. "The mother obviously has no idea what is going on with this minor. No idea. She is ordered to take at least ten parenting classes." Now it is Mom's turn to appear stunned. She whispers to no one in particular, "Can he do that?" A lawyer sitting nearby shushes her before she can make Dorn angrier.

The judge turns back to Eric. He does not look six months shy of his eighteenth birthday. He looks more bar mitzvah age than voting age, especially with the expression of disbelief now plastered on his face, in place of the studied gangbanger cool he normally tries to affect.

"Four years have gone by, and you are still on the same path, young man. But this time, you're going back to camp under Judge Dorn's supervision. There is going to be a change in your life. Crime is not the answer. Crime will only get you that quick trip to the state penitentiary or the cemetery. I don't want to see that happen to you. I love you as much as your mother. All right then, good luck, young man." The bailiff rises and leads the boy out.

"If I had handled that minor's case four years ago, when he was thirteen, he might be applying to college now," Dorn says later, sitting in his chambers during a break. "It is a tragedy that no one thinks it's worth the court's time to help a youngster who is assaulting other children or carrying firearms. That is a cry for help. But that boy got none, and now here we are, and here he is, almost eighteen, headed for the state prison next time if he doesn't straighten up. And it could have been prevented. It's just another example of the slipshod way some people are used to doing business around here. You see what's going on in this courtroom, what I've been handed to work with. It's shameful."

Dorn looks up from his desk, his round, jowly face almost cherubic. "But, then, that's why I'm here. To do something about it."

Roosevelt Dorn's message is simple: The Juvenile Court is the most important facet of the American justice system. The problem is, most people don't know it.

"But they will," Dorn promises. "The word is going out. I shall see to that."

Look at it this way, the judge says, leaning back in his chair, fingers steepled, delivering a lecture he has honed and practiced inside court and out. Virtually every adult with a criminal record, virtually every inmate in state prison, virtually every murderer on death row, started their criminal career in the Juvenile Court. Whatever was done with them at that time, way back before they became serious, violent offenders—way back when they were in the Juvenile Court—obviously didn't work. Why? "Because our priorities are backwards," he says, leaning back in his chair, warming to the subject. That is why crime is rampant, why violent juvenile offenses have climbed 50 percent between 1987 and 1991—double the increase among adults—and why the number of juveniles arrested for murder climbed 85 percent in those same years, four times the adult increase. This, Dorn believes, is directly attributable to the juvenile justice system's focus on the worst offenders, while the first-time delinquents get no attention at all.

"Instead of spending the time and the money and the manpower on the front end, when children first transgress—and when they can be helped and guided and set straight—we are waiting and waiting and doing nothing, until it is too late, and they commit crimes so serious that all society wants to do is punish instead of rehabilitate." Dorn assumes an expression of extreme disgust at this point. "And then you get the hue and cry from the politicians that we must try children as adults in order to fight crime, sixteen-year-olds, fourteen-year-olds, who knows where it will stop? When the fact of the matter is, the politicians have never committed the resources we need to stop crime in its tracks at the juvenile level, where it starts."

He points to the recent study of the court by the Probation Department—the infamous "Sixteen Percent Study" that found such high failure rates and futility, and showing that the most violent and intransigent 16 percent of juvenile offenders was taking up the lion's share of the system's time and energy. That's all wrong, Dorn says. And making the system even harsher will make things worse, not better.

"Instead of spending billions of dollars on more and more prison cells for adults, which is bankrupting our nation, we could spend a fraction of that amount here, with these minors, and cut crime in half. Every dollar spent here would save ten dollars down the line in prison costs, there is no doubt about that. Yet, Juvenile Court remains the unwanted stepchild of the system. They're talking about doing away with it entirely now, which would be a travesty. A disaster. Well, I intend to educate people about what this system is really about, and what it can do. I am the squeaky wheel. I will be heard!"

Which brings Dorn to his other main theme: openness. The doors to Juvenile Court must be thrown open to the public, sweeping aside the traditional confidentiality that protects the mediocrity and failure from public view. "The public has no idea how important this court is, or the shocking, deplorable conditions that exist in these courthouses. Or, with the right judge and the right program, how well this court can succeed. I want to educate them."[4]

Because he is certain that working with kids is the justice system's most crucial task, Dorn feels intense bitterness toward most of his judicial colleagues, who, as a group, consider Juvenile Court a low-prestige assignment, even a punishment. The assignments most prized by his brethren on the bench lie far away in the white-collar world of the civil courts, where the pace can be more sedate, the clients, especially the corporate ones, tend to be clean and well pressed, the fight is always about money, usually lots of it, and a judge can easily slide off the bench and into the partnership track at some major LA law firm that knows the value of having a former jurist on the payroll. That is where most of the judicial stars want to be, as far removed from the realities of Thurgood Marshall Branch as they can get. They shun Dorn's gritty domain, which is why there are only eight Superior Court judges filling Juvenile Court's twenty-eight delinquency courtrooms, with the slack taken up by appointed commissioners and referees, lawyers who assume the duties of judges to fill temporary shortages that are, in truth, permanent.

Some of the eight judges on the Juvenile Court bench are highly regarded and hardworking, but the verdict is less than flattering on a few of the others. Two have been criticized by lawyers for years for their less than energetic work habits, one of them infamous for his four-hour workdays, constant continuances of virtually every case before him, and his refusal to try more than one case a day. (By contrast, Dorn regularly holds ten or more trials in a single day, plus thirty or forty other matters—sentencings, guilty pleas, arraignments.) Because there is no effective way to discipline judges—like feudal lords, no one can tell them what to do within their own courtroom fiefdoms—such judges remained unchastised, except when lawyers refuse en masse to practice before them, the practice known as "papering the judge" because of the blanket of legal motions that must be filed to remove him or her from cases. The system is so jammed already that such a move is to the Juvenile Courts what blocking a lane on a freeway is to rush hour traffic: The effect is paralyzing. Sometimes this leads to a change in personnel, a transfer of judges from one outpost to another. Sometimes it just makes a mess.

The perception of Juvenile Court as an undesirable assignment doesn't stop at the bench. Some defense lawyers on the appointment list are little more than warm bodies occupying a chair while their clients admit to the charges. In most cases, the only written defense motions in the file are bills to the county for legal fees. These court-appointed lawyers are paid far less than their adult court counterparts, and the level of competency and experience among many can be shockingly low. O. J. Simpson's lawyers do not walk these halls, nor do any of Los Angeles's other legal luminaries. (Such lawyers would never work for the meager fees offered by the court — forty-five dollars an hour with a twenty-five-hundred-dollar cap, even on first-degree murder cases, compared to a sixty-thousand-dollar cap on murder cases in adult court.) Instead, Dorn and the other juvenile judges and commissioners find themselves scolding attorneys in open court for their incompetence and lack of preparation — then appointing them again, for lack of any alternative.

At the same time, the DA's Office, which has a cadre of investigators, forensic experts, witness coordinators, and victim counselors assigned to adult court, provides no such help to its embattled juvenile prosecutors or the crime victims who troop in and out of court each day — another bald statement of the system's priorities. High-tech tests of hair, blood, and DNA so crucial in adult court have never been employed in Los Angeles Juvenile Court — not because they aren't needed, but because the system cannot afford to pay for them. Except for the deputies in charge of each juvenile office, the least experienced prosecutors, sometimes only one year out of law school, often end up staffing Juvenile Court, trying murder cases and making decisions about kids' futures. Many are skilled and dedicated, but it takes years of trial work in adult court before a prosecutor is allowed to handle a murder case there. Juvenile Court, however, is as much a training ground as a court of law, where errors are more easily forgiven, and problem lawyers more easily hidden from sight.

The same weaknesses hold true for the Probation Department, the police, every agency that works in the juvenile system — it is an afterthought, Dorn gripes.

"But I have the answer to these problems. I can't change the whole system — not yet, at any rate — but I can change how things work in my courtroom. Call it a pilot project, call it whatever you want. But the change starts here. And if it works, then we can expand it systemwide. But there will be change in this courthouse. Be assured of that."

Judge Dorn's main engine of change, it soon becomes apparent, is hauling more kids into court more quickly for more minor offenses.

"We must get to these minors as early as possible," he tells probation officers, prosecutors, parents — whoever will listen. He has his staff send notices out to churches, counseling agencies, police departments—every agency that has contact with troubled and troubling children—telling them that Judge Dorn is back on the bench in Inglewood, and that open court is back in session. He distributes press releases, appears on radio talk shows, grants newspaper interviews, speaks to civic organizations, getting this message out: Parents who have lost control of their kids and have nowhere else to turn can come to the front of the line in Department 240, no questions asked. The status offense is back, and Judge Dorn has a new twist that puts some teeth back in the law, he promises.

The judge knows that it will take time to restore the line of parents and kids trooping to his door that made him famous during his first tour of duty in Juvenile Court in the 1980s, but he will not just sit back and wait for them to start trickling in. His next point of attack is to take on the constant problem of dismissed cases in Juvenile Court—the daily discovery that witnesses are absent and, therefore, cases cannot be proved. Many of these dismissals involve first-time, minor offenders, the very kids Dorn most wants to save, and though myriad reasons exist for this constant and shockingly immense problem, Dorn's fury falls squarely on the District Attorney's Office, which has the legal responsibility of bringing cases to trial.

Not long after the pizza-robbery dismissal, Dorn has to dismiss charges against a fifteen-year-old named Rafi who shoplifted a Levi's shirt from a department store, then, once arrested, was found to be carrying live ammunition in his backpack. The case had been pending for six months, but the DA's Office had never subpoenaed the policemen who arrested Rafi or the store security guards who saw the boy and a friend stuff the shirt into his backpack.

Deputy DA Sisman did not contact any witnesses until Rafi was sitting in the courtroom on the day of trial. The subpoenas generated by his office in this case, as in others, were never served. The prosecutor's attempt to remedy this situation consists of using a courtroom phone to call the department store security office, where no one answers. He then announces, "People are unable to proceed." The boy grins, and Dorn has to boot the case.

"But Judge," Rafi's mother pleads, not understanding how this could happen. "He's not going to school now. He's not doing anything but watching the cable. I feel he does need some kind of supervision. He's not doing anything, and he won't listen to me."

Dorn gives Sisman an icy look, then says, "Mother, at this moment, I can't do anything because the district attorney has not brought its witnesses into court. I assume they'll refile. I can't do anything until he's under the jurisdiction of this court. . . . Obviously, you need help with this young man, but I'm sorry to say I can't give it to you."

As the boy gives his mother a hateful look, then saunters from the room, Dorn instructs his probation officer to give Rafi's mother some do-it-your-self forms for charging her own son with a status offense, part of Dorn's new program of change. For now, though, forms are all the court has to offer the mother, a legal secretary who lives alone with her son and who doesn't understand what is happening to her boy.

Meanwhile, Sisman quietly fills out a disposition report on the case and checks a box at the bottom that says "No further action," effectively killing the case. There will be no refiling. Rafi's mother is on her own.

"If this were happening in adult court, Mr. Sussman"—Dorn occasionally mispronounces prosecutor Sisman's name, and it is not entirely clear this is accidental—"heads would be rolling. What is happening in your office?"

Sisman says there are reasons for the dismissal problems. Adult DAs have witness coordinators to keep track of subpoenas and witness lists; Juvenile Court DAs have to press overburdened secretaries into service to type subpoenas, in addition to all their other duties, and once typed, the sheriff's department may or may not get around to serving them in time. About a third of the notices to appear in court are delivered *after* the court date or are not delivered at all. Those that do get notice that they must appear in court are often treated shabbily, even when they are the victims of crime, subject to the delaying game some defense lawyers play. With enough delays and inconvenience, witnesses stop coming, and defense attorneys win a dismissal of charges. Hundreds of cases are dismissed this way every month in Los Angeles Juvenile Court—twenty-five in Inglewood alone in just two weeks. Kids who are dangerous, and kids who need help, walk free, unrestrained, unsupervised.

The worst of these dismissals is haunting Peggy Beckstrand's office this week, a kid named Norvin, fourteen and out of control, who was arrested months earlier for shooting an LAPD officer. Charged with attempted murder, the kid waited in Juvenile Hall while his lawyer requested repeated postponements until, finally, the two crucial witnesses in the case—two policemen—decided to go forward with their plans for a vacation cruise abroad. They were to be gone when the next trial date came up, but they figured it didn't matter, there would be another delay anyway. After all, it was only Juvenile Court.

Norvin's public defender, who had indeed been planning on another postponement, saw the two cops had not come to court and insisted on an immediate trial. The DA was forced to dismiss the case, and, though the charges were refiled immediately, Juvenile Court rules require kids be released from detention in every refiled case—even when a kid is charged with a violent offense. Even a kid like Norvin, whose stated ambition—after his arrest—was to kill a cop.

Within a week of his release, Norvin was rearrested for participating in a murder. A seventeen-year-old boy who passed him on the street made the mistake of looking at Norvin and his friend with something less than admiration, and they decided he had to die for it. A similar scenario in adult court would have led to public outcry, investigations, firings. In Juvenile Court, the case caused not a ripple. No one outside the system knew about it.

A few minutes after Rafi's departure, Dorn has to dismiss yet another case, this one against a gangbanger accused in three armed robberies. Again, none of the eyewitnesses were subpoenaed in what should have been an open-and-shut case. Sisman tried to put his case on anyway, but the one witness he managed to get into court was the wrong witness—he could not identify the boy on trial. Dorn's hands are tied, and he must watch the boy leave the courtroom, free and clear. The judge is beside himself.

"I don't know what's happening in your office, but something has got to change," the judge says, loud enough to make everyone in the courtroom drop what they are doing and stare. Sisman starts to protest that he is helpless when witnesses fail to show up as scheduled, but Dorn cuts him off. "What's happening in this courtroom is a travesty. A travesty for these minors, and a travesty for the People. It is unfair to minors, to parents, and to our citizens. Case after case has been dismissed because the People cannot proceed. I've had two today already, and the day isn't over yet. . . . Your office is programming these children for the cemetery or the penitentiary. You are telling them it's all right to break the law."

"We are having trouble serving subpoenas," Sisman says mildly.

"I'll put a call into Garcetti," Dorn rails, angered further by the prosecutor's casual response, referring to the elected District Attorney, Gil Garcetti. "I'll go to the press. Someone in the DA's Office isn't taking care of business. . . . This rarely happens downtown. It happens here all the time."

Another prosecutor waiting for his case to come up, Kevin Yorn, from the DA's special hard-core gang unit, can't resist standing up to try to defend his office's reputation. "I disagree with your assessment—" he starts to say, but Dorn cuts him off, waving his right hand as if delivering a karate chop.

"I did not make my statement for you to agree or disagree with me," Dorn says in a low, menacing voice. "The fact is that it is happening. I can't believe you can't subpoena witnesses in Inglewood, but you can downtown. This court needs to be taken just as seriously as adult court. More so."

A moment later, he tells his clerk to call Peggy Beckstrand. "I want her in my chambers tomorrow morning. We are going to do something about these dismissals, or I'll call a press conference. This travesty will end, one way or another."

CHAPTER 8

Juggling Act

PEGGY is in trouble.

It is time to go to court to begin the Ronald Duncan murder trial. She has prepared obsessively for this day. Last night, she dragged a rocking chair and a blanket into the bathroom, with all her papers and files, so as not to disturb her husband, Steven, a senior prosecutor in adult court downtown. He is intimately familiar with the long hours and obsessions that come with the job. But even he has not seen his wife so immersed in a case before. He found her still in the bathroom at six the next morning, stiff and shivering in her sleep. She had been pasting photos onto poster board for a courtroom exhibit—the deputy in charge of an entire DA's Office reduced to working with Elmer's Glue-All and Magic Markers on the hard tiles of her bathroom floor, because in Juvenile, prosecutors either make their own courtroom visual aids on their own time, or they do without. And Peggy is not one to do without.

Even so, even after all the sleepless hours and preparation and second-guessing, she believes her case to be in disarray. The sheriff's investigators who busted Ronald have dodged her phone calls, she says, too busy, they say, with "real"—that is, adult—cases. A crucial witness, Ronald's friend Marvin, is still missing. Ronald's new, privately retained lawyer has convinced her that the all-important taped confession to the police, concrete proof of Ronald's guilt, likely will be tossed out on a technicality. To fill the resulting gaping hole in her case, Peggy now must consider granting legal immunity to a young man named Jason Gueringer, who says he happened upon a blood-drenched Ronald on the night of the murder and gave him a ride home, making him an accomplice after the fact, a felony, though a relatively minor one for which he had never been arrested. Peggy had long resisted offering Jason immunity for a variety of reasons, not the least of which is the possibility that Jason might be a liar—that he might be an accomplice to the murder itself, not a mere witness, and had been holding back all this time. Officially, he remains a suspect in the killing, which is why he was never charged with the lesser crime. With the confession, she didn't need him. Now. . . .

And while she ponders all this, the endless series of crises and distractions of her job must be dealt with as well. Four other murder cases are reaching the make-or-break stage—plea bargain, or go to trial—including a boy who clubbed his mother to death, possibly because she molested him. Peggy is not trying those cases, but she must approve every major move her deputies make. Then there is an ongoing war between the fiery Commissioner Polinsky and the young prosecutor assigned to his courtroom. Each wants to discuss with Peggy a list of grievances about the other, some of them substantive, but most of them matters of style and personality—they despise one another. She will have to find some way to juggle prosecutorial assignments to separate them. There is the usual assortment of plea bargains to approve, lawyers to coddle and placate, memos to answer and write, county computers that freeze up and crash every few hours. The computer crashes mean the paperwork stops spewing from the printers, clogging the paper pipeline, making the subpoenas go out late (if at all), which means more witnesses won't show, and more cases will be dismissed, leading to more yelling judges, more meetings, more memos. More contemptuous kids committing more crime without consequences.

Which brings Peggy to her first order of business this morning, her meeting with Judge Dorn to talk dismissals. Her boss has already seen the erstwhile supervising judge of Thurgood Marshall on the eleven o'clock news complaining that the DA was programming children for the penitentiary while letting violent offenders off the hook. This is not the kind of publicity the DA is looking for, Peggy was told in no uncertain terms. "Deal with it," her boss instructed.

"Give me more people, and I will," she shot back.

When she arrives in Dorn's chambers, he goes on the attack as soon as she sits down. "The DA is not doing its job, witnesses are not showing up, minors are not showing up. The public defenders are waiting your people out and getting dismissals. It would be malpractice for them to do anything else. But the result is disastrous, not just for the People, but for the minors as well."

Peggy just nods, and Dorn becomes even more furious.

"You are understaffed here, and Garcetti doesn't care. I'll go to the press with this, I'll call a press conference. Don't think I won't. You're process-ing these minors for the state penitentiary." He has begun to shout.

Peggy bristles at this. "A lot of what you say is true, Judge, but I will never take responsibility for these minors' crimes. I come along *after* they've done their dirty work. If they're programmed, it's before I enter their lives."

"Oh, well, I know that," he concedes, backing down a bit, and no longer looking as angry. Judge Dorn tends to steamroll over people in his way, but he admires—to a point—those who stand up to him. "But what I'm telling you is that these witness problems are tying the court's hands with these minors. Something's got to be done."

"You're right about that," Peggy says simply, and her agreement defuses Dorn's anger further. She says she will talk to the bosses downtown, to see if they can spring for a witness coordinator to help keep pace with the huge number of trials Dorn is scheduling every day.

"Now you're talking," the judge says. "That's how business is done in adult court. Shouldn't be any different here." He is smiling broadly now. He promises to draft a memo to DA Garcetti to help things along. It is his way of announcing a truce. Peggy wonders how long it will last.[1]

She runs back across the street, plows through some paperwork, explains to one of her deputies that the office cannot afford to appeal a bad ruling in a shoplifting case, no matter how badly the commissioner erred, then prepares to return to court to start her murder trial. She pulls a pair of new shoes out of a shopping bag and puts them on—one of her pretrial rituals. She must have a new pair of shoes before starting a trial, though there are no jurors to impress in Juvenile Court. It is simply for luck, something she started early in her career, the way some baseball pitchers always wear a certain game shirt. In her wallet is a lucky one hundred dollar bill given to her by her mother during her last Christmas visit to El Paso. She would starve before she would spend that money. Peggy runs a brush through her long, straight hair, rubs her cold hands together for warmth, then gathers up her Duncan files, hugging them to her breast, ready to go.

Just then, her phone rings, bringing the first bit of good news she has heard all day. It is the one part-time DA investigator she shares with another group of juvenile prosecutors, whose main job is to serve subpoenas, but who puts in extra time chasing down loose ends in Peggy's cases when he can find the time.

"I found Marvin," he tells her. "He was standing in a phone booth right where some friends of his told me he'd be. He and his father will be there today."

"That's great," Peggy says. She had been worried about going to court without Marvin, afraid she'd have to watch her case dashed to bits, that she would have to shamefacedly tell the relatives of the victims, Sorry, I blew it.

"Just be prepared," the investigator warns, deflating the burst of elation she briefly felt. "Marvin's not exactly dressed for success these days."

Peggy hangs up, wondering just what she was in for. Marvin had always been a clean-cut, good-looking kid, kind of preppy, a perfect witness—but he had been living with his mother then. Now Dad is in control, a man who was less than eager for Marvin to testify, and who seemed to consider him a snitch for revealing Ronald's confession to murder. She picks up her files again and makes her way across the street, dreading the day ahead, her hands cold as ice.

Peggy Beckstrand almost quit over the weekend. She was a phone call away from packing it in. "If the Peace Corps hadn't rejected me, I'd be on my way to Africa right now," she told her husband.

She had interrupted her preparation for the Duncan trial over the weekend, driving to her office on Saturday to deal with the files, which were rapidly getting out of control. The previous year's collection of files had taken over the conference room, pulled from the cabinets lining the room to make room for the new year. They were stacked on the long tables in the conference room, hundreds of manila folders piled high in rough alphabetical order, waiting for Peggy's review before they could be boxed and stored for three years, after which they could be fed to the shredder. They had sat there for weeks, galling her, a constant reminder of the flood of juvenile crime she faced each day. The files had to be put into cardboard boxes the size and shape of large file drawers—there would be more than fifty of them before Peggy finished. One year's worth of juvenile crime, in one branch of Juvenile Court—a humbling sight.

So here was the supervising DA of one of the busier Juvenile Court branches in LA all set to go crawling around in her blue jeans on the weekend, boxing up files. It was menial, time-consuming work, but this was

Juvenile Court. There was no one else to do this: Either Peggy handled it, or the files just sat there, collecting dust and coffee stains as her deputies tried to find room on the table to have lunch. Besides, she had to read through each of the files before boxing them, particularly the dismissals, to see what the judges and commissioners had been doing to her prosecutors for the past year. Occasionally, her deputies attached notes to the manila folders: "This is outrageous" or "Once again, this bench officer shows he is ignorant of the law." She keeps copies of these in a separate place in her office—the outrage pile—so that she can make a list of them, to be turned into higher-ups downtown for purposes that are not entirely clear. She was simply ordered to start "keeping a list," apparently so that, when the time comes for reappointment of court commissioners or reelection of judges, the DA can have ammunition for ousting those considered most egregiously antiprosecution. The public defender, of course, is doing the same.

Peggy parked her white Corvette in the municipal parking garage, then walked around to the front door, so she could ring the security guard to let her into the otherwise deserted building, ready for eight hours of filing. But when she got there, she found a homeless man sprawled on the steps, blocking her entrance. She at first thought him asleep or drunk, not an unusual find in this neighborhood. His face was obscured by a tangle of matted hair, and he was dressed in clothes so filthy they had taken on the color of wet cement, except for the very odd purple shoes he was wearing, huge misshapen things. Then Peggy noticed the tattered pair of high-top sneakers on the steps next to the ragged man, and she realized with a jolt that those things at the ends of the man's legs weren't purple shoes, but hideously swollen and infected feet, stinking of gangrene. She tried to rouse the man then, yelling and shaking him, but he couldn't move or even talk clearly. He just mumbled something about having crawled out of the cardboard box he lives in that morning, looking for help. He had the strength to reach the steps, but then couldn't stand up to ring the buzzer for the guard. "My feet hurt," he moaned. "My feet."

Not sure what to do, Peggy tried to hand him some money, but he could not grip it. She buzzed the guard, then broke off a piece of the submarine sandwich she had brought with her for lunch. He managed to thrust some of that into his mouth, then croaked, "I haven't eaten in twenty days." Peggy could almost believe him.

After a while, the guard ambled up and unlocked the door. "I think he's dying," Peggy told him.

"Oh, him?" the guard said, looking down at the man expressionlessly. "He's been there all day."

Peggy looked at her watch. It was noon. She was furious that this guard could have let the man lie there for hours. "Call the paramedics. Now!" The guard, rather reluctantly, shuffled to the phone and called for an ambulance. A half hour later, the man was whisked away.

Peggy went up to her office then and hurled the rest of her sandwich into the trash can, appetite for food and for filing destroyed. She tried to imagine a hospital admitting the man, treating him with respect and kindness, letting him die in a warm bed with food and humanity around him at the end. But the fantasy lasted only a few seconds. Just as likely, she knew, some harried emergency room doctor or nurse could have taken one look at his reeking, stained clothes and wild hair, given him some antibiotics for the infection in his feet, maybe an IV to get some nourishment into his wasted body, then put him out the door to die alone in his cardboard box.

Suddenly, Peggy burst into tears, staring at all those files, each representing a kid, the paper trail of more lost souls she couldn't help. The man on the steps seemed to her the perfect metaphor for it all. Why had he come to the steps of the Juvenile Court for help? Had he been there before? As a parent? He hadn't looked that old, really—perhaps he had been there once as a delinquent himself. Peggy couldn't shake the thought that his life, too, had once been reduced to a manila folder stuffed into a box somewhere in this building. She went to her computer and started typing a letter of resignation. Who could do this for a living? What good was she doing?

Then she stopped, sat still for a moment, calmed herself. She forced herself to open her top desk drawer, to take out the crime-scene photos— the Ronald Duncan murder scene. She stared at them for a long time. Chuck and Ada Rusitanonta, their bodies broken and abandoned, stared back at her with sightless, dead eyes not yet closed by the undertaker. She had visited their store, talked with the sister and brother-in-law who had taken over the business, who treated Peggy like visiting royalty whenever she came to update them on the case, who called her "our lawyer." "We know you will punish whoever did this," they always would say. "Thank you."

After a while, Peggy put the photos back in the drawer and deleted from her computer the resignation letter she had been writing. Then she walked to the table covered with files, and picked one up and started reading. She was only up to the B's—there was a long way to go.

When she left the building five hours later, it was dark outside, the street cool and empty of traffic. In her conference room, fifty-three boxes sat neatly stacked, labeled in her flowing handwriting, ready for the closet and, later, the shredder. Then she drove home. She had a murder trial to prepare for.

"Bring in the minor," Judge Charles R. Scarlett says in his mild, distracted way, and the bailiff rises to fetch Ronald Duncan from the holding tank. Peggy nervously shuffles papers, idly listening to the continuous courtroom babble of lawyers, parents, kids, and cops coming together on uneasy common ground. As a deputy in charge, she hadn't tried a case in a long time, and she felt uncomfortable back in the prosecutor's chair. It didn't help that Scarlett, once one of Los Angeles's top civil rights attorneys and now one of the most senior judges on the juvenile bench, was stubbornly resistant to the get-tough policies transforming Juvenile Court, and could be counted on to rule against the prosecution on many close calls. He had retired a year earlier, ceding the supervising judge position to Roosevelt Dorn, but that had not removed him from the courthouse. He immediately became a "retired judge on assignment"—an unofficial retirement program judges in California have given themselves—allowing him simultaneously to collect his judicial pension while still working as a full-time bench officer. He even kept his old courtroom.

Nor did it help Peggy's cause that Duncan's private attorney, the former head public defender in Inglewood and very popular in the courthouse, was in a relaxed and jovial mood, joking with other defense lawyers, who were eagerly gathering in the back of the courtroom to see if the Duncan confession would get thrown out or if Peggy would give legal immunity to Ronald's getaway driver, Jason. Such legal maneuvering, though commonplace in adult court, is relatively rare in Juvenile—few attorneys have the time to litigate many motions at all, much less file briefs or perform legal research. This case was drawing a crowd, and the defense lawyer retained by Ronald's parents, James Cooper, clearly enjoyed the attention, discussing a new movie with the judge, a legal point with some young lawyers, and hurling the occasional gibe at Peggy: "You're not really going to give Jason Gueringer immunity, are you? Don't you know he's the one you should be prosecuting?"

Peggy winces at the comment—pure psychological warfare, as obvious as it is effective. She still has not decided whether or not to give the driver of the getaway van a free ride, though she knows, either way, Cooper will try to put the older boy on trial in place of Duncan. Before she can think of a retort, Cooper is already telling the judge another joke, earning chuckles. "Everything's a cocktail party with this guy," Peggy mutters. "He laughs and jokes and everyone has a great time, and pretty soon, the judge thinks he's at a cocktail party, too, and he forgets what's going on. Cooper wants us to forget that two people are dead. He's a genius at that."

Just then, the heavy door in the back of the courtroom opens. Echoes from the lockup, the sound of metal clanging and of shoes scuffing on linoleum filters into the room, then Ronald Duncan emerges, blinking. The boy wears handcuffs and a bemused expression as he is led by a khaki-uniformed bailiff to his seat next to his attorney, where the cuffs come off with a merry jingle. He giggles and smiles over his shoulder at his parents sitting in back of the ancient courtroom, with its faint smell of mildew and old paper, his expression, as usual, a chilling contrast to the grave charges against him. Cooper puts his arm around the boy and whispers something to him, after which Ronald assumes an erect posture and solemn facial expression.

His mother and father sit huddled in the back of the courtroom, trying to make themselves small and inconspicuous, radiating hopelessness and anger, glaring occasionally in Peggy's direction. Ronald's mother is fairly young and sharp-faced, with a tendency to shake her head and growl when she hears the DA say something unfavorable about her son. His father, divorced but living in the same home, is much older than Ronald's mother, quiet, careworn, in cowboy boots and sparse gray hair, a well-worn cap hung on his left knee as he sits in court. Mother and father occupy different rows and rarely seem to speak to one another. They have other children, at least one of whom has had trouble with the law. But not Ronald. He is their baby. The kid who never gave them a moment of trouble. Their hope for the future. They simply could not accept what their son had done. He told them he was innocent, and they believed him. They believed it was all a conspiracy, all racism, all coercion of their son, all favoritism toward Jason, who is a cop's godson, another reason why Peggy is hesitant to give him immunity. The appearance of favoritism would be overwhelming, confirming everything Ronald's parents believe. To his credit, defense lawyer Cooper keeps telling them as gently as possible that Ronald is unlikely to be acquitted, but the Duncans only blink with incomprehension when he says such things. They trusted this man—trusted him with the precious life and fate of their son—but when it came to discussing the likelihood of Ronald's conviction, they did not believe him, either.

"My son says he is innocent, and I know there is no way he could do this terrible thing," Ronald's father says just before the hearing begins. His voice is quiet, tremulous, his calloused hands turned palms up in a gesture of bewilderment, a man speaking from the heart, from bedrock belief in a boy he loves beyond the power of any law or evidence. He is not a small man, but at this moment, he looks brittled and hollowed by grief, as if a strong wind would send him skittering down the hallway like a dead leaf. "The judge will see it. God will see to that. He will see my son is innocent."

The buzz in the courtroom gradually stills as milling attorneys and other observers find seats. Peggy stands. She has the option of litigating the admissibility of Ronald's confession before beginning the trial, or during. Peggy chooses the latter. She wants Scarlett to know more about the case — and what is at stake — before asking him to make such an important legal ruling. Let him look at those evidence pictures first, she figures. Theoretically, they should not influence his decision on the separate issue of the confession's voluntariness, but Peggy knows better. Judges are human, too.

"The People are ready to proceed," Peggy announces. "Should I make an opening statement, Your Honor?" she asks.

"No, no need for openings. No jury here," Judge Scarlett says with a wave of his right hand. Opening statements are part of the theatrics of adult trials, like movie previews — highlights without substance, intended to influence jurors. They are rarely heard in Juvenile Court. There is no time for such frills. Scarlett settles back in his chair and steeples his fingers. "Let's get on with it."

So Peggy begins a textbook murder case presentation — revealing the evidence as if it were an onion, peeling back each layer, first with the discovery of the bodies, then an examination of the physical evidence, then the trail of testimony, events, and objects that leads inexorably to the defendant. It is how virtually every murder case is presented, a time-tested formula that applies in Juvenile Court just as it does in the adult world.

First to the stand is a man who lived in the neighborhood where the bodies were found. He testifies that he heard what sounded at the time like a car backfiring, but what he now believes were gunshots, followed by the sound of a car crashing into something. He walked out onto his porch, saw Chuck and Ada's station wagon smashed into a light post a short distance down the street, then saw a young black male emerge from the backseat and run away from the car. The man left his porch to approach the car, saw the murdered people inside, then took off after the fugitive, watching from a safe distance as the killer climbed into a blue van. The witness had the impression that the van had been waiting for the gunman, but he couldn't be positive.

As for the person he saw running: could have been Duncan, the witness says, but he only saw him from the back. Can't be sure. Peggy is satisfied, though. This testimony is just a scene-setter, establishing time and place for the judge, like the opening scene of a movie.

Next comes the first uniformed deputy on the scene, who describes the condition of Chuck and Ada's bodies and the bloody car, providing the legal basis for introducing those blood-drenched crime scene photographs into evidence. Peggy figures she can quash the cocktail-party mood with those. She had stayed up late painstakingly pasting the photos to poster board, then hand-lettering captions under each one in black Magic Marker. She had felt like a kid on an elementary school project. It paid off, though: Scarlett stands up and walks to the far side of his elevated bench, standing next to the witness stand so he can scrutinize the display as Peggy walks the deputy through each picture. The judge's expression remains impassive as he studies the pictures of Chuck and Ada in their Baskin Robbins shirts, heads imploded, gore everywhere. When he returns to his seat, though, Scarlett avoids looking at Ronald, which is not as easy as it sounds, because the boy's seat is directly in front of the judge.

But just when Peggy felt she had gained some momentum, the chaos so common in Juvenile Court asserts itself. Midway through the deputy's testimony, just as he is uttering the words "severe head trauma," the lights in the room, and throughout the courthouse, black out—an aftereffect of damage from a devastating earthquake that hit the Los Angeles area a month earlier. Even the red emergency exit lights wink out, leaving the room in total darkness, generating bewildered exclamations from the audience, a giggle from Duncan. The bailiff rises to guard the minor, but it is the deputy on the witness stand who lights up the courtroom, pulling a large flashlight from his belt and shining it around from the stand, focusing on the boy in the orange jumpsuit.

Eight minutes later, the power flutters back on. But it takes another half hour for the crowd, the witnesses, the lawyers, Duncan, and, finally, the judge to settle back in the courtroom. Several attorneys use the lull to rush to the front of the courtroom to ask Scarlett to conduct a few brief hearings for other kids, which he does. Peggy finishes with the deputy, but her momentum is lost, the pasteboard and photos pushed aside. Scarlett becomes so distracted after the blackout that he forgets who Duncan is and mistakes him for another kid accused of petty theft.

Peggy moves on quickly through a series of witnesses who talk of blood—blood found on Ronald's book bag, on a pair of Ronald's pants crumpled up on the floor of the getaway van, inside the getaway van, and on a Baskin Robbins shirt streaked with blood, found by a jogger on a street between Ronald's home and the murder scene. No sophisticated DNA tests were performed on this critical blood evidence, as is routinely done in adult murder cases. But the far less discriminating blood-type tests showed the stains could have been from Chuck and Ada. Peggy hopes it will be enough.

With those preliminaries out of the way, Peggy goes to the heart of her case: Ronald's friend Marvin, who had just been found by her office investigator after months missing in action.

Peggy had always liked Marvin. He was her hero, a reminder that not all children in her world were monsters. Marvin had done the right thing when it would have been far easier to just go along, to protect his friend, to remain silent and accept the forty bucks Ronald had offered him from the roll of cash he started flashing at school on the day after his bosses were killed. She didn't know what made Marvin different from Ronald, only that he was—and that as long as there were Marvins in the world, she had hope. Hope died easily when you prosecuted twenty-nine hundred juvenile delinquents a year.

But she had not seen him for nearly a year. Now her star witness saunters into court with a new swagger, mirrored by his disheveled father, who sits down in the back of the courtroom, a dusty baseball cap pulled low over his eyes—until the bailiff tells him to take it off. Father and son sport matching gold earrings in their left ears. The investigator had been right about Marvin's appearance. Peggy frowns at the boy's outfit—jeans and an oversized black T-shirt with a cartoon drawing of a man in a top hat holding a large mallet behind his back, as if waiting to brain some unsuspecting victim. She had asked that he wear his Sunday best. She hopes for his sake this isn't it.

But despite his less than ideal appearance, Marvin remains just as soft-spoken and convincing a witness as when she first interviewed him so long ago. He calmly recounts seeing Ronald with a wad of cash on him in school on the day after the murders, bragging about what he had done.

"He said, 'I killed Chuck. Chuck and his girlfriend.' And I was saying, Yeah, right. I didn't believe him. I started laughing and stuff. He said he hid in the backseat of the car, and he shot Chuck first, then his girlfriend started screaming, and he shot her. And he ran to a van, a waiting van. He said he was covered with blood and had to take off his clothes and run into his house in his boxers."

Marvin's testimony amounted to devastating evidence of guilt. His account—which he had told in similar detail the first time police questioned him nine days after the murders (on Ronald's sixteenth birthday, to be exact)—matched the physical evidence in the case perfectly. The blood in the van, the bloody shirt, Ronald's bloody clothes—all squared with what Marvin swears Ronald told him. Most important, Marvin's testimony mirrors Ronald's own confession to the police—right down to the detail about Ada screaming after the first shot, until Ronald silenced her by reloading and firing again. Peggy remembers again, with a chill, Ronald's comment to the police. *No, I didn't hate them. I really loved them.*

There was no way Marvin could have made up such an accurate story, Peggy planned to argue. Ronald had to have told him the details. She felt confident Marvin would withstand the expected assault on his credibility by the defense. The only thing that bothered her was the look of disinterest on the sixty-nine-year-old Scarlett's face. He looked bored and distracted throughout most of Marvin's testimony. At one point, the judge slumped so far down in his chair he was barely visible behind the bench, with just the top of his bald head sticking up so that everyone knew he was still there.

Still, sensing the solidity of Marvin's testimony, Ronald's lawyer surprised Peggy. Cooper didn't try to call Marvin a liar. Rather, he tried to show *Ronald* was the liar, shrewdly focusing on something Marvin had told the police early on—how he initially thought his friend Ronald had been telling tall tales. Under cross-examination, Marvin readily agrees that he had at first discounted what Ronald told him, writing off his story of murder as mere bragging about nonexistent exploits. It was only that night, when word of the murders appeared on the news, that he began to believe Ronald, telling his mother, then police, what he knew. Cooper suggests Marvin was right the first time—maybe Ronald really was just bragging. That was the real reason Marvin's account and Ronald's confession matched: not because Ronald told the truth, but because he told the same lie to both Marvin *and* the cops, Cooper plans to argue. And to tie this all together, the lawyer even offers a ready explanation for why Ronald would tell such a grotesque false story to his friend in the first place.

"You both belong to the same set, the same tagging crew, right?" Cooper asks.

Marvin nods.

"And sometimes you brag to one another, don't you?"

"Yeah, we're both in BSA—Beyond Street Artists," Marvin says. "You brag, you exaggerate to get respect."

"And if someone kills someone, or commits a drive-by, that gets more respect, right?" Cooper asks.

Marvin doesn't even have to think about it. He answers, "Yes."

Peggy winces. Not so much at what this testimony does to her case, but at what it says about Marvin. Here is a kid at a crossroads. A year ago, he had told his mother and the cops about the killings, because that was the right thing to do. But now here he is talking about equating murder with respect. He has a father who complained bitterly about him appearing in court, who called his own boy a snitch and derided him for failing to keep his mouth shut. Now that father has custody of him. Would Marvin be sitting at the defense table himself sometime soon, Peggy wonders, as Cooper presses on with his questioning, laboring to show Ronald was just a lying braggart, not a killer.

"And so Ronald is more respected now in your set?" Cooper asks. "Now that he has been charged in this case?"

"Yes."

Judge Scarlett, who has never lost his look of disinterest throughout Marvin's testimony, suddenly sits up and glances over at the witness. "You said you're in a tagging crew. Taggers don't do violence, do they?"

Marvin smiles, then proudly corrects the judge and the lawyer. "We're not just taggers anymore. We're tag-bangers. We have members of the set involved in shootings."

"So you're not just a vandalism crew?" Cooper asks.

Marvin is bursting with pride. He and Ronald exchange smiles. "Not anymore."

The first day of trial is drawing to a close, but not before settling the matter of Ronald's confession. When Peggy tries to peel back the next layer of her evidentiary onion—by introducing the boy's taped statement to the police—the defense, as expected, objects. Cooper jumps up and says the confession was coerced with threats that Ronald would receive the death penalty unless he cooperated. Having explained why Ronald would have lied to Marvin about the murders—to gain respect—Cooper now wants to show why he would tell the same lie to the police: self-preservation.

"Ronald denied guilt. Then the tape was stopped. When it came back on he confesses." Cooper arches his eyebrows and shrugs, as if to say, *We all know what goes on in interrogation rooms when the cops switch off the recorder—nothing good. Nothing legal.*

"That didn't happen," Peggy says, bristling.

"The proof is on the tape, Your Honor," Cooper retorts. "Just listen to it."

"If he was promised no death penalty, that's coerced. That's true," Scarlett exclaims excitedly, siding with Cooper, sitting up straight and tall now in his chair. He has not yet heard the tape of the confession or heard any testimony, but he has already staked out a position, a slight grin on his face. "He can't get the death penalty anyway. He's a juvenile."

"Well, listen to the tape, Your Honor," Peggy says, exasperation creeping into her voice. The judge waves his hand, a gesture for the attorneys to proceed.

When the tape is played, it reveals there is indeed a gap of five minutes that occurs just over midway through the two hours and twenty minutes of Ronald's taped statement. For the first half of the recording, Ronald denied being involved in the murders, instead telling a story—full of holes and easily disprovable—about being robbed and stabbed while walking a circuitous route home. This was his attempt to explain the blood on his things. When he refused to budge from that story, the detectives ended the interview and shut off the tape.

What happened next depends on who's telling the story. The two sheriff's investigators say they simply told Ronald he was under arrest and would have to go to Juvenile Hall. It was then, the investigators say, that Ronald volunteered to revise his statement. So the tape went back on. That, one of the two investigators swears on Scarlett's witness stand, is the only reason there is a gap on the tape.

Ronald has another story.

He walks up to the witness stand and takes the oath with a smile. The boy props his chin up on one hand and assumes a look of extreme concentration as he repeats his lawyer's argument and declares his confession to murder was a lie that the police forced him to tell.

"They cut off the tape and said, It's a double murder—I can get the death penalty for it," Duncan swears. "And if I confess, they won't push for the death penalty. Then they turned the tape back on."

When Ronald finishes his explanation, Cooper plays the very end of the taped confession, the very last exchange between the interrogators and their quarry.

"You haven't been threatened or promised anything?" Sheriff's Detective Robert Carr asked Ronald after he finished confessing to the killings.

It was the sort of routine query made at the end of almost every police interrogation.

"No," Ronald said on the tape. "Promise I wouldn't die, that's about it."

There it was. An inexplicable statement by Ronald, foolishly unheeded and unacknowledged by the interrogators sitting across from Ronald at the time. Neither Carr nor his partner responded to it. All they did was go on to recite the time and the date and to shut off the machine, this time for good. As soon as Peggy had seen it on the transcript months before, she knew it would be trouble; she knew exactly what was going to happen in court. Those seven words seemed to suggest that Ronald really had been promised something, or at least thought he had been.

"They said I wouldn't get the death penalty if I confessed to it. So I confessed to it," Ronald tells Judge Scarlett nearly a year after the tape was made. His expression and inflection are slightly sarcastic, as if he were explaining the facts of life to another kid his age, someone who should have already known the score. "Anything's better than dyin'."

When it is Peggy's turn to cross-examine Ronald, she goes to great lengths to point out every lie he uttered on the first half of the tape, hoping to erode his credibility. He lied about being robbed, he lied to Marvin, he lied about the facts of the murder. Ronald turns sullen and silent under her insistent questioning, forced to say, Yes, I lied, over and over, but I'm telling the truth now. "Anything's better than dyin'," he keeps repeating. After ten minutes of this, with Ronald exasperated and making faces, jutting his lower lip defiantly with each question, Peggy suddenly shifts gears with a mild query. "How many times," she wants to know, "was the death penalty mentioned in that interrogation room?"

"Once," Ronald answers, without hesitation. Once was enough.

It is the reply Peggy had hoped for. She then plays a section of the tape where the death penalty is mentioned, but in a more innocuous way than Ronald recalled—and long before the gap in the recording where Ronald claimed to have been threatened. On the tape, the detective simply stated that murder can carry a death sentence. For me? Ronald then asked, and the detective answered, For whoever did it. If the death penalty was only mentioned once during the interview, that was it—captured on tape, not whispered during a five-minute gap. What was on tape was no threat, at least not as Ronald had described it. And, in any case, after that mention of capital punishment, Ronald continued to deny doing anything wrong for another twenty minutes of taped interview. If his latest testimony is true—that the death penalty only came up once during the interrogation—then it could not have been mentioned again in a more threatening way during the gap in the tape. Peggy had caught Ronald in another lie.

But Scarlett is not so easily convinced. The death penalty should never have been mentioned at all, he says. It was wrong to bring it up with a juvenile. It doesn't matter that Ronald's confession is too detailed to be anything but the truth, the judge decides. Ronald could have been coerced by what he perceived to be a threat, Scarlett says.

Peggy tries to argue the point further, but the judge rapidly seems to lose interest, interrupting her repeatedly to take care of other court business. Trials in Juvenile Court, even murder trials, are not like the solemn events seen in adult court, where interruptions, even stray sounds, can send judges flying into rages. In adult court, interrupting testimony and argument to handle other matters while a trial is in progress would be unthinkable. There is a simple reason for this, beyond courtroom decorum. When life and liberty and public safety are at stake, causes in which both the individual on trial and society as a whole have profound interest, it is only right that the court give its undivided attention to the case at hand.

Juvenile Court enjoys no such luxury and maintains no such illusions. The courtrooms never stop bustling, with lawyers standing off to the side whispering into phones or huddled in conversations, and with judges juggling many cases simultaneously, even though their task is much more complex than an adult court judge's. Juvenile court judges must act as both judge and jury, deciding both legal and factual questions in a case. Yet their distractions are constant.

While Peggy tries to argue that Ronald was lying about receiving threats in the police interrogation room, Scarlett stops her no less than five times to hear other cases. He gives probation to a thirteen-year-old boy charged with graffiti vandalism. He congratulates a graduate from a county detention camp who has just been accepted to a community college. He placates an angry father who has waited a day and a half in court for his son's case to be heard, only to be told to wait some more. Then comes Max, a tiny kid, no more than ten, with a refugee's arms and hollow eyes, here to be arraigned for assaulting his mother. He has been in Juvenile Hall for several days, and his public defender wants him sent home. "But I like the hall," the boy whispers. The way he says it, so plaintive and stark, everyone in the courtroom stops for a second to look at him, the kid who wants to be in the lockup. The public defender shrugs and says fine. Max can continue living at the detention hall, the happiest home he has known in years.

"Okay, continue," Scarlett finally tells Peggy as Max leaves the room. She takes one look at the sour expression on the judge's face, and quickly wraps up her futile argument. The judge listens to Ronald's lawyer for a few minutes, nodding and agreeing the entire time, even repeating Cooper at times.

"There is no reason for bringing up the death penalty," Cooper says. "Why would he even mention it?"

"Why would you even mention it?" Scarlett echoes, staring at Peggy.

Scarlett is an affable, compassionate man, slow to anger and easy to get along with. But along with a perception that he is lenient in sentencing kids, he is known for holding police investigators to a very high standard — unfairly high, some prosecutors say, though defense attorneys disagree — and he unflinchingly punishes them whenever he judges the police guilty of misconduct. He rules that threats and coercion led to the Duncan confession. Despite Ronald's recollection that the death penalty only came up once, Scarlett concludes that a threat was made during the gap in the tape, and that the police are lying about it. Using the rules of evidence imported from adult court by the Gault case so many years earlier, Scarlett makes his ruling.

"There's only one way to interpret what he says at the end of the tape. I believe the minor. . . . Something was promised. Threats were made. The statement is excluded."

A short time later, the trial recesses for the weekend. The public defenders who had gathered in back of the courtroom walk out into the hall with Cooper, congratulating their old boss on his victory, notwithstanding the fact that the ruling could mean freedom for a killer. Peggy also congratulates her opponent. Then, as Ronald's parents gaze at her with undisguised hatred, his mother actually moaning aloud, Peggy announces that she would now have to give the getaway driver Jason legal immunity. He would be her next witness.

"You've got to be kidding," Cooper says. "He's the one you should be prosecuting. You're going to give immunity to someone who would be eligible for the death penalty if convicted, so you can get a kid who will be out in eight years? Come on, Peggy. That doesn't make any sense."

"You haven't given me any choice," she tells Cooper quietly. She glances at the Duncan family, and hears Ronald's mother saying something about cops taking care of cops, a reference to Jason and the fact that he is the godson of a police sergeant. "I want Ronald. He's the one who blew the heads off of two human beings, not Jason. It's not about who can do the most time. It's about who is most culpable."

Cooper nods at the Duncans. "They don't understand that. They don't think Jason should get a walk."

"Well," Peggy says, "tell them it's your fault. Tell them you're too good a lawyer."

She walks off then, an angry buzz in her wake, a long weekend of work ahead.

Now Jason Gueringer is the key to Peggy's case. Investigators first found him a day after the murders, when an Inglewood police sergeant named Harold Moret came forward with a bizarre story. Moret told investigators that his son, Peter, had once worked at the ice cream shop owned by the victims. A few weeks earlier, a neighborhood boy who had taken his place, Ronald Duncan, had told Peter he was angry at the shop owners for docking his pay for being late. He told Peter he planned to kill them. Moret said Ronald even asked about borrowing a van to use as a getaway vehicle. Sergeant Moret had seen the wanted posters put up in the wake of the murders. The van police were seeking in the case sounded just like one that belonged to a friend of his son's—a young man named Jason Gueringer, who happened to be Moret's godson. Ronald, Moret told the investigators, often tried to tag along with the older Peter and Jason.

The investigators then left Moret and drove down the block to Jason's house, where they were stunned to find the eighteen-year-old Air Force cadet in the act of busily scrubbing down the interior of his van. He looked up and appeared stricken by the sight of the two detectives walking toward him. Then they saw the sponge and bucket of murky water he was using were tinged pink with blood.

Faced with imminent arrest, Jason admitted he was engaged in a cover-up, but he swore he had nothing to do with the murders. He had been driving home from his girlfriend's house that night when Ronald ran out into the street and flagged him down. When he pulled over, Jason said, Ronald climbed into the van. Covered with blood and carrying a shotgun, Ronald had exclaimed, "Go, go, go. Take me home! Man, I just shot somebody." As a panicked Jason drove, Ronald peeled off his blood-soaked shirt and threw it out the window.

Jason said he had kept silent afterward, fearful—and correctly so—that he would appear more like an accomplice than an unwitting bystander. He had stuck to his story for the past year, but he would tell it again on the witness stand only if he received legal immunity, since the conduct he would be admitting to was a crime. By saying he knowingly drove a murderer home, then covered up the bloody evidence, he was admitting to being an accomplice after the fact. And there it had rested for the past year, with Jason graduating high school and joining the Air Force.

That he was never charged for this was, to the Duncan family, more signs of favoritism. The sheriff's investigators, however, said they always held off on the relatively minor accomplice charges because they suspected Jason of being far more involved. For one thing, the witness in the neighborhood, as well as Marvin, both said the van had been waiting for Ronald. And Jason's girlfriend said she never saw him that night. Early on, the sheriff's investigators made it clear that they would cut Ronald a deal if he rolled over on Jason, suggesting lack of evidence, not favoritism, was behind the failure to nail a cop's godson. Ronald, however, refused to give up his adult friend. Detectives never could find any hard evidence against Jason, and he was never charged with the murder. But neither was he cleared.

Now Peggy felt she needed him, and she was willing to take the chance that he had been telling the truth, despite some problems with his story. She had to go over her immediate supervisor's head to get an okay to offer Jason immunity, then get him on an airplane to Los Angeles from his new Air Force post in Colorado. Peggy went to the airport and picked up the lanky teenager herself, went over his statement with him and Investigator Carr, then dropped him off, satisfied that he had remained consistent in his story. "Just tell me the truth," she cautioned him as they finished for the evening, "and you'll be okay. The only thing that will get you in trouble now is if you lie."

Jason hadn't said anything to that. He just nodded.

At midnight on Sunday, just after Peggy took four aspirins and climbed into bed, dreading her next day in court, Jason calls. Peggy gives all her key witnesses her home phone number.

"Is my immunity agreement going to be in writing?" he asks, strain, perhaps even panic, constricting his voice like a sneaker tied too tight.

Peggy feels a knot settle in her stomach. "We'll make a record in open court. We're not going to screw you, Jason. The only thing it won't protect you from is lying."

Jason remains silent a long time. Peggy holds the phone and waits. Finally, Jason says, "We've got to talk."

"Can't it wait until morning?"

"No, I want to do it now."

"I can't," Peggy says. "I can't talk to you without the investigator present. Be in my office at seven-thirty."

Jason reluctantly agrees to wait. Peggy knows she won't sleep that night.

The first thing she asks Jason the next morning is "You didn't shoot them, did you?"

"No."

"You didn't know Ronald was going to shoot them, did you?"

"No."

"What, then?" Peggy asks, not allowing herself to feel relief at these two answers to questions that had tortured her through the night.

"I knew he was going to rob them. I was in on it. I was waiting for him. I was the getaway driver."

Peggy blanches. Jason has just admitted to being part of an armed robbery that ended in murder. Jason, an adult, who could face the death penalty in a capital case, has, in effect, admitted to murder.

And in her zeal to get Ronald Duncan, she knows she still is going to have to give this killer his freedom. Because as bad as he is, Ronald is worse.

She stalks from her office, then the building, to pace outside in the cool morning air, hating her job more than ever, the rational part of her insisting that she has no choice, but still feeling as if nothing in this juvenile system works, feeling as if she were drowning.

PART TWO

Softening Up

I was born on my favorite spot.
It's comfortable or mean, dark or bright, happy or sad.
I can go there when I want, how I want, and who I want.
This place scars my heart with good and bad.
This place is my mind.
   ELIAS ELIZONDO, Central Juvenile Hall

CHAPTER 9

The Big Fix

Bellflower, California
Pace School for the Disabled
Spring 1994

There she is. Andre can see her through the bus window, Walkman hanging from her neck by a cord, music blasting through the headphones at brain-jellying volume, body juking and jiving in the wheelchair. He watches as her eyes focus on his yellow bus, the vacant expression vanishing from her round face, replaced by an enormous smile. He sees her struggle to keep her head from lolling, to keep her hands from flapping uselessly at her sides, and she succeeds, after a fashion, Andre is happy to see. Then he watches her lips form the word "Andre," knowing she is calling to him, her tiny voice lost in the sound of diesel engine and spitting air brakes as the bus grinds to a stop.

He feels himself smile in a way that once would have been impossible for him, tickled by the idea that she is so eagerly awaiting him. Waiting for him to kiss her cheek in greeting. Waiting so she could shout, "Rock and roll!" over and over as he pushes her chair, knowing he would smile and clap at her mastery of this one sentence. Waiting for him to wheel her to class, to feed her lunch, to wipe her chin, to arrange her chair in just the right spot—"Our special spot," Andre whispers each day—so the sun warms her face. The pleasures are few in Miriam's small, limited world. What few there are, Andre helps provide.

The bus door creaks open. As Andre rises from his seat and jostles with the other delinquent boys headed for the door, he is gripped by a familiar sensa-tion, a feeling that this bus is his conduit between two warring worlds. The wheezing sound of the bus shutting down reminds him of a movie he once saw, about an outpost deep undersea where the inhabitants spent hours adjusting to the crushing pressure by sitting inside a claustrophobic yel-low tank not quite big enough for the six people inside it. Images of valves turning, air hissing from metal pipes: the bus, Andre imagines, is his decom-pression chamber. He walks onto it a member of Varrio Norwalk, master of the One-ways, the cramped, one-way streets that form the heart of his barrio and the turf of his gang, where a vato strong of heart and fast with his hands commands respect. Andre knows how to break into a car and start it without a key in forty-six seconds—he had timed it once when he was thirteen. He knows how to drive those cars down the One-ways so no cop could catch him, except for the last couple times, when the strange thoughts and distractions he had begun to feel with alarming regularity made him careless. And he knows how to drive slowly, with purpose, his homeboys peering out through tinted windows, looking for enemies from the rival gangs, so that they might shoot first.

Now here he is staring out a very different window with a different sort of eagerness, looking for a handicapped little girl who depends on him and loves him and thinks he is the best thing that ever happened to her. He had made fun of the stupid bus the first time he had to get on it, this rolling box the color of a highway stripe, tiny and cramped with too many kids—not a proper ride for a gangbanger of his distinction. At first, he had made fun of the school for geeks and retards the bus brought him to for two hours every morning. What did that DA and that Juvenile Court judge think they were doing, sending someone like him to such a place? Andre knew things about life and death and respect, he had seen young men die, blood running across hot summer cement. He had a record for multiple car thefts and high-speed chases, and he had done worse things, suspected but never charged. He had "made his barrio"—joined its preeminent gang—and he had the tattoos on his arms and his back to prove it. At sixteen, he had juice. What could be accomplished by sending him to this school for the handicapped? It wasn't right.

Then, gradually, unexpectedly, something happened. These kids in the special school weren't geeks after all, Andre began to see. They just needed someone. They needed him. And that was a whole new thrill for him, better than gangbanging or G-rides or ditching school, something he could feel proud of. At home, he found himself talking about Miriam and the other kids he helped walk and dress and take to the bathroom or the supermarket or clothes shopping. He started defending them against slurs from his home-boys, looking for little gifts to bring them, anything to make them smile. He began to like going to Miriam's school, looking forward to it each morning. Now it is going back to the One-ways, back to la vida loca that he dreads.

It has taken a long time for him to admit this even to himself. But, grad-ually, his clothes changed, from a banger's baggies to button-down shirts and crisply pressed black dress slacks. He has stopped smoking and drink-ing and carrying guns. He sneaks away from his friends to study college applications, dreaming of a future, any future. To his teachers' and pro-bation officer's surprise, he has changed—precisely at the time the system was preparing to give up on him. After all, none of the usual stuff had worked—arrests, detention, probation, and camp hadn't put a dent in his destructive course. Going to this school that forced delinquents to care for disabled children had been an afterthought. No experts or studies or com-mittees had produced the program—it had been cobbled together by two dedicated teachers sick of failure and bureaucracy, and who sensed power in this melding of one child's helplessness with another's lack of purpose. One more crime, and his next stop would have been prison, but something about this little wheelchair-bound girl has reached Andre instead. The system has won, not with jail cells or boot camps or harsh new laws, but with a young street tough spoon-feeding a little girl with cerebral palsy, a girl whose eyes at the end of the day are filled with love.

"Hey, Miriam! Qué pasa?" Andre cries as he jumps off the bus and jogs around several other boys to the little girl's side.

"Andre, Andre," she chants as he kisses her right cheek. "Rock and roll!"

"Rock and roll, Miriam," he agrees, then pushes her off to class with a quick glance back at the bus, wishing it would leave and not return, but knowing it will—and that he'll be back on board in two hours. In two hours, he knows, he'll be on his way back to the One-ways. Then the pressure will return, pressure for him to change back into something else, the homeboys coming by, calling him a pussy, telling him to get down and become, once again, what the judges and the cops and the probation officers say he should not be. The people in court make change sound so easy. They don't have to live in his world, where gang membership is for life, and quitting can have fatal consequences.

But today, now, he has two hours. And Miriam.

S UDDENLY, this year, everyone is a reformer.

Until now, Juvenile Court in Los Angeles, like the rest of California and most of the nation, has remained essentially unchanged for thirty years, except for laws that ship more children to adult court—which is not so much an advance as a return to an earlier practice.

Now, though, an extraordinary lineup of interest groups, politicians, and lobbyists wants to remake the system. After decades of treating juvenile justice like an unwanted stepchild, with its cast-off facilities, green attorneys, overloaded probation officers, and dyspeptic budgets, suddenly, the policy-makers are wondering aloud why juvenile violence is accelerating at three times the rate of adult crime, and how it is that the Juvenile Court isn't coping. Suddenly, the competition is on to find the Big Fix.

This abrupt realization of what seemed profoundly obvious to the juvenile system's insiders—who have complained for years without effect—seems to have swept the nation more or less simultaneously in the nineties. Major reforms of the juvenile system have begun springing up in most states.

The urge to fix the system seems to have hit with particular intensity in Los Angeles this year. The competing factions of reform are already grappling like rival gangs struggling for turf: Judge Dorn, for one, is assembling his own task force, working to build an odd little shadow court operating under its own rules and priorities within the larger Los Angeles system, focusing on the minor offenders the rest of the Juvenile Court tends to ignore. For him, Juvenile Court is the last, best engine of social change, one that can be made lustrous again with just a few commonsense improvements.

The governor of California, meanwhile, who has presided over a budget-busting program of prison construction (operating expenses: $3.8 billion a year and growing), is pursuing exactly the opposite course, backing a passel of new laws to fill the adult courts and adult penitentiaries with kids. To him, Juvenile Court is a dysfunctional relic that allows young predators to sneer at justice and kill with impunity—a law-and-order position that dovetailed nicely with his newly minted presidential aspirations.

The Los Angeles County Probation Department has its own separate initiative under way, an attempt to turn its harrowing study of repeat offenders (and its finding that the Juvenile Court is statistically irrelevant in stopping crime) into a useful new tool. By constructing a detailed profile of repeat offenders, the department hopes to learn how to spot and help the worst delinquents *before* they become the worst—a promising idea with some difficult ethical dilemmas attached, not the least of which is the notion of going after kids for crimes they *might* commit down the line. If it works, though, it could lead to a system that heads off delinquency before most kids ever reach Juvenile Court—a planned obsolescence everyone could welcome. Or, at the least, the fruits of this study would justify a reordering of priorities within the Juvenile Court, so that first-time offenders would be dealth with decisively, rather than being handed free pass after free pass until someone ends up hurt or dead.

And then there is the Los Angeles County District Attorney's initiative, the one effort that could make or break the juvenile justice system once and for all.

In the midst of the Ronald Duncan murder trial, and all that the Thirty-one Flavors case illustrates about the state of juvenile justice in America, Peggy Beckstrand has been summoned to a meeting with her boss. DA Gil Garcetti is assembling all his supervising juvenile prosecutors from each branch of the court to discuss a new attempt to sweep the juvenile slate clean. This, by far, is the most ambitious and far-reaching of California's juvenile reform efforts, with allies in the state capital ready to join with Garcetti to fashion new legislation that would shut down every Juvenile Court in the state and replace it with . . . something new. No one as yet is quite sure what that new something will be, other than it must go far beyond mere piecemeal tinkering with the existing system. It must be a wholesale, start-from-scratch remake that could build on what the governor and Judge Dorn and the Probation Department are doing, or discard these efforts entirely for a new system no one has yet fully envisioned. Garcetti is pushing for a statewide task force to study how to do this, drawing on experts from every side of the system, adversaries and allies alike, with the mission of rewriting the juvenile code start to finish.

"And that's what we're here to discuss," Garcetti tells Peggy and her seven counterparts from the other Juvenile Court branches he has gathered together for this meeting. "You know the system better than anyone."

Garcetti is a tall, thin, flush-faced man elected two years earlier to replace an unpopular predecessor he once served as a top deputy. The job makes him the most visible DA in America, thanks to Michael Jackson, the Menendez brothers, O. J. Simpson, and Court TV. But along with the glitz, he has inherited a massive operation with a ravaged budget, depleted morale, and a reputation of not being able to win the big one, having lost a series of widely publicized cases, from the McMartin preschool molestation case, to the Menendez brothers parricide mistrial, to the prosecution of the cops who beat Rodney King, to the never-prosecuted child molestation investigation of pop superstar Jackson. In the midst of what would eventually become the biggest loss of all, the Simpson case, he has decided the legacy he really wants to leave behind is in the long-neglected arena of juvenile justice.

To his credit, Garcetti has been doing considerable legwork for a man holding one of LA's top political offices, talking to judges, lawyers, child development experts, and, most unusual for a prosecutor, to some of the kids his office has put in Juvenile Hall. Prosecutors are not known for listening to what criminals have to say, but Garcetti realized that kids could tell him about the system from the inside. This led him to a particularly edifying—and unnerving—question-and-answer session with some of the kids in Unit K/L at Central Juvenile Hall, where most of the writing class lives.

The kids don't often get a chance to talk to someone with real power (there are their judges, of course, but they are viewed as robed symbols far beyond reach, "looking down on me like some great white god," one of the kids wrote in class) and the questions flowed. Why is everyone afraid of us? Why do they want to lock us up with adult criminals? Why does everyone think, just because you belong to a gang, that you're a criminal? But it was something one of the younger boys said that stuck with Garcetti long after he left the hall, a little kid who kept asking about murder. He was fourteen years old, though to the DA the kid looked eight or nine, smooth-faced and angelic—which made him all the more frightening to behold.

"If I kill someone," the kid asked, "can I go to the gas chamber?"

When Garcetti said no and turned to another boy, the same fresh-faced kid persisted. "Even if I kill more than one person? They still have to let me go when I'm twenty-five?"

"That's right. That's what the law requires. For now. That's probably going to change, though."

"But right now, even if I kill ten people, they can't send me to the gas chamber, they have to let me go?"

Garcetti changed the subject then, but the encounter stayed with him, and he tells his juvenile prosecutors about it, how it hit home to him that kids at every level of the system know the Juvenile Court often can't touch them. "You talk to youngsters," he says later, "and they tell you, repeatedly, that they got away with so much—that they commit crimes, but aren't arrested, or if they are arrested, when they are brought into court, nothing happens. That's common knowledge. If you expect that, that you can get away with a helluva lot, that affects your behavior. You start making the kinds of calculations this boy in Juvenile Hall was making. Or you don't even think about the consequences at all, because they don't matter. . . . That's why I want fully dedicated, full-time experts on this task force, nothing less. I don't want to do this half-ass. It's just too important."

That, he tells Peggy and her colleagues, is what today's meeting is about—he wants to pick the brains of the juvenile DA supervisors. "I want your input," he tells them. "We're wiping the slate clean. You are the emperor. What would you do?"

To Peggy and the other frustrated supervisors of juvenile prosecutions, who see their cases dismissed, mishandled, and mistried on a daily basis, this question is like asking a kid what kind of chocolate she likes. Not since Juvenile Court first was conceived at the turn of the century to stop the imprisonment and execution of children alongside adults has the stage been set for a top-to-bottom rethinking of how to treat delinquents. The suggestions start coming rapid-fire: Lower the fitness age. Alter the burden of proof to make it easier to convict. Create a two-tier system, one for wayward kids, and one for the thugs and the killers where punishment, not rehabilitation, is the goal. As the suggestions roll in, Garcetti sits back and says little else, content to take notes on a yellow legal pad as his experts in the field warm to the subject.

"I think we ought to have direct filing of murder charges in adult court, with no age restrictions," Peggy suggests, the Duncan case and his nine-day window of invulnerability still heavy on her mind. "Murder is different. Kids who commit murder should automatically lose their right to be kids."

"How about direct filing of *all* major felonies in adult court?" a colleague suggests, taking Peggy's idea a step further. "Why stop with murder?"

Again thinking of Duncan and his inevitable freedom at age twenty-five, Peggy reminds the group they should not focus solely on the front end of the process—the when and where and how charges are filed and tried—but on the back end, too, the conditions of release for juveniles.

"Murderers shouldn't just get to walk out the door at age twenty-five," she says. "There should be some sort of review, parole, perhaps—and the power to keep them indefinitely locked up if they're still dangerous. Killers shouldn't walk out the door with a clean record and no supervision just because of a birthday."

Similar suggestions follow, all with a common theme: The system needs

to be tougher on kids, imprisoning them longer, focusing more on protecting the public and less on protecting a youthful innocence that no longer seems to exist. For this group, the fix consists of pushing the juvenile
justice system back toward the nineteenth-century model, when adults
and children were treated exactly the same. Juvenile criminals are more
sophisticated and less remorseful than previous generations, the prosecutors seem to agree. Treating today's child criminals differently from adults,
Peggy says, "flat out isn't working."

The setting for this attack on the system is appropriately glum: the
musty and dark Eastlake Branch, largest in the system, a moldering, castle-
like facility attached to Central Juvenile Hall, the busiest, most crowded,
toughest branch of Juvenile Court. It consists of one long shotgun barrel
of a hallway, branching off into a warren of offices and courtrooms. The
shotgun barrel itself is crammed with people during court hours, close and
sweaty as a subway car at rush hour, filled with a constant babble of voices
as the attorneys interview their clients, negotiate deals with prosecutors,
and whisper with witnesses while waiting for their cases to be called. It is a
noisy, artless place, with smeary, colorless walls and an entrance equipped
with a metal detector and a luggage X-ray machine, neither of which is
working. (In a typical example of the juvenile system's odd priorities, none
of the delinquency court branches have functioning metal detectors or secure entrances, although there clearly is a need for them — kids taken into
custody after court hearings are routinely found carrying weapons. Yet, the
county's new state-of-the-art dependency court, which hears child welfare
matters only, no criminal cases — but which also just happens to house the
Juvenile Court presiding judge — has an elaborate, airport-style checkpoint
at the door, with guard, metal detector, and X-ray machine.)

The meeting is taking place in the courthouse's lineup room, where juvenile suspects stand in a row for witnesses to view through one-way glass.
It is no different from similar adult facilities in police stations throughout
the city, and it seems all the more appropriate for a discussion of dismantling the juvenile justice system.

But one of the prosecutors, silent throughout the discussion, waits for a
lull in the torrent of suggestions, then voices his discomfort and disagree-
ment.

"Unless we address some of the root causes, some of the social problems
that contribute to juvenile crime, none of these things is going to make a
bit of difference," Jim Hickey tells the gathering. The others look at him as
if he had just rolled a stink bomb into the room. Hickey looks at some of

their expressions and sighs. "Everyone says the children of the eighties and nineties are different, worse, more dangerous," he says. "I beg to disagree. The children are the same. They do horrible, unchildish things because they have had very horrible, unchildish lives for ten years. It's like a computer. Garbage in, garbage out."

Hickey is the supervising prosecutor at Los Padrinos Juvenile Court. He is a tall, gentle man, with a big mustache and sad eyes, the sort who brown-bags a meal every day so he can work at his desk through the lunch hour, who thinks murderers, whatever their age, ought to be punished as adults, but who resists his office's tough fitness policy when he thinks lesser offenders deserve a break, and who thinks working on truancy cases is just as important as working on major felonies. "Every kid who comes to Juvenile Court starts out with problems at school, and that's what we need to address," he reminds his colleagues. He is, in short, not in the mainstream of prosecutorial thought when it comes to juvenile justice—and glad of it.

"If some of these fourteen- and fifteen-year-old armed robbers were taken at age six and assigned to loving, good parents, things would be different," he says. "No single solution is going to solve this. We have to start addressing the root causes, or it's all moot—we'll never fix the system."

The room falls silent. A few look embarrassed by Hickey's comments. Several of the prosecutors exchange looks, one rolls his eyes. But Hickey pushes on. If we can just help families, if we can keep kids in school and off the streets, he argues, we'll do more to combat juvenile crime than a hundred new prisons could do. "And it should be up to us to say, Hey, we're for public safety, we're for stopping crime—and this is the best way to do it. By helping people have better lives."

That's not our job, the others snap. We're not social workers. We're prosecutors. Peggy Beckstrand, in particular, is vehement in opposing Hickey's sentiments. Sure, she says, a lot of us wish we could make better homes for people. "But that's not what we do. We're at the bottom of the barrel. The DA's Office cannot save all these people . . . Our job is to deal with the people who break the social contract. We're the barrier between all the people in society who haven't stepped over the line and who are abiding by the rules and the social contract, and the people who they're afraid of—the ones who do step over the line. And what we need are the right tools to do that."

In that barren lineup room full of prosecutors, the debate over Juvenile Court has crystallized as clearly as it ever will, striking at the ambiguities inherent in a system that wants to both punish and heal. Just as the defense lawyer's role is blurred in this place—is it really in an angry, violent, out-of-control kid's best interest to walk him out the door on a dismissal?—so is the prosecutor's role a difficult one to pin down. With young offenders, is it always in the interest of public safety to seek the prosecutor's traditional solution—the harshest penalty possible? Or is the public best served by finding ways to change a kid's lot in life for the better, even if that means opening the prison door?

"Love isn't going to fix these kids," Peggy says of the major juvenile offenders. "By the time we step in, it's too late for that. All we can do is protect the people who obey the rules. That's our obligation."

"I disagree," Hickey says. "Sure, we need to look for the sociopaths, and put them away. That's got to be our role. But the rest, we're still talking about *children*. The rest, they're salvageable. That should be our role, too."[1]

The Los Padrinos Branch of the Los Angeles Juvenile Court where Jim Hickey works is so physically and philosophically different from the Inglewood courthouse inhabited by Roosevelt Dorn and Peggy Beckstrand that it hardly seems part of the same judicial system. It lies not in a neighborhood crippled by violence and poverty, but in a serene corner of the city of Downey, a bedroom community on the southeastern edge of Los Angeles County. The juvenile crimes tried here are often serious—there are gang shootings and murders and other acts of unchildish children. Richard Perez had his fitness hearing here, and George Trevino. But, by and large, the cases here are not quite so relentlessly scary as the Inglewood docket. The prosecutors, judges, and defenders are not constantly at war here, either, finding more room for compromise, primarily because of the even, understanding tone set by Jim Hickey. Even this courthouse's name sets it apart, the only juvenile branch in the LA system where the officials in charge of such things chose a lyrical name instead of a functional one: Los Padrinos. The Godfathers.

Its location is as oddly out of place as its euphemistic name, surrounded not by gang turf, but sandwiched between a complex of squarish gray condominiums and a municipal golf course whose duffers occasionally pelt the blockish courthouse and its attached detention hall with wayward golf balls. None of the barely controlled chaos that reigns in Inglewood can be found here. Parents, children, and witnesses are relegated to a large waiting area with rows of uncomfortable brown molded-plastic chairs to hold them. Loudspeakers summon participants one case at a time, instructing parents and minors to pass by a guard desk and through black metal double doors, then to follow one of three colored lines imprinted in the scuffed black linoleum floor, yellow, red, and green. Each line leads to a heavy black metal fire door and a small courtroom beyond, so there is no confusion over room numbers, departments, or layout. Literacy is not required.

Off to the side, skirted by the procession of kids and parents following lines on the floor, is Jim Hickey's office, a large room with a bank of desks for two secretaries and two clerks, a chaotic file room, several side offices for prosecutors to share, and one private office in back, piled high with papers—Hickey's.

Usually, the door remains open to Hickey's private office, but today it is closed. The head prosecutor is talking with a man named Luis Silvestre, whose stepson has been murdered. Hickey is prosecuting two boys for the killing, intent on sending them to adult court.

Alfred Clark had been waiting in line at a McDonald's restaurant. Another boy had cut in front of him, then demanded he hand over his Sony Walkman CD player. Alfred had just tried to laugh it off. Alfred the high school senior honors student. Alfred the star athlete. Alfred the kid with the college scholarship and the girlfriend and the classmates and teachers who loved him, who was bound for great things. He never saw it coming.

The bullet sliced through his aorta and he bled to death there on the floor of a fast-food restaurant, French fries scattered around him, his eyes pleading and filled with disbelief while all the other kids in line scattered. The seventeen-year-old kid who shot him and took his Walkman—it was worth barely a hundred dollars—was caught the next day, no question about his guilt. He had no remorse. His eyes were dead.

Juan Macias, the sixteen-year-old who drove the getaway car, who protested his innocence, who said he had no idea his homeboy was going to shoot anyone—but whose gang name was Scrappy, with a long arrest record for car theft, burglary, and armed robbery that belied his credibility—had been a tougher call. At first, it seemed he might be telling the truth. But then Hickey heard a witness say Scrappy had stood in McDonald's and pointed Alfred out to the killer a few minutes before the shooting, and the prosecutor decided this boy should go to adult court as well.

Alfred's stepfather had come to all the hearings so far. He has stared into the bright eyes of the two accused killers, and felt a weary hate wash over him. He would see the case through to the end, a silent vigil for justice. Once, he had known nothing about gang wars or street crime or the ruthless coldness that drove young people to kill for no reason and to feel no regrets when they were through. He was a careworn man whose quiet, law-abiding life had not prepared him for any of this.

Today, Luis has stayed after the hearing to talk with Hickey about his overwhelming feelings of loss and bewilderment, to find some sense in it, somehow. But he can't. All he can talk about is what an incredible joy Alfred had been, tears streaming like they always do. Every day, he tells Hickey, he has to walk past the closed door of his son's room, willing himself not to shudder. No one in his family has been inside that room since the murder, months ago now. It is not that they are keeping a shrine. They just can't bear seeing Alfred's trophies, his schoolbooks, the acceptance letter from UCLA sitting on top of his desk. It was too much. Easier to leave it be, just as Alfred left it.

Only another parent can really understand this thing that has happened, this feeling that you just cannot go on, Luis says. "That's why I can talk to you. You have children." The portrait Luis has painted of his son is so clear, the family's anguish is so naked, that Jim Hickey is speechless. All he can do is nod, and clasp the man's hand. And then grieving father and professional prosecutor simply sit in that tiny room in silence, faces wet, weeping together, while Hickey's staff gamely tries not to look through the glass in the door.

Later, Jim Hickey sits in his office discussing the future of juvenile justice, a subject that consumes much of his thought these days, as well as filling his desk with reports and clippings and memos. His feelings for the family of Alfred Clark and his desire to see the killers punished severely do not diminish his belief that most juveniles are salvageable. He still believes the main role of any prosecutor is to represent the point of view of people like Alfred Clark's father. That holds just as true in Juvenile Court as in the adult system and, on this point, he and Peggy Beckstrand and all the other juvenile supervisors are in agreement. But there ought to be more to it than just that traditional focus, Hickey says. Juvenile Court demands more.

Look at the kids who committed the Clark murder, he says. Look at Scrappy. He has been in the system for years. He was made a ward, put on probation, twice sent to camp, returned to probation afterward each time, then got in trouble again. Every time he was placed in a structured setting, he did well, with good grades, good behavior. But then he would return to the same impoverished, crime-ridden neighborhood, the same lack of supervision at home, the same old homeboys urging him to return to his gang and his criminal ways. No one ever taught him all the little things you need to know to hold down a job: to be on time, to be dependable, not to call in sick all the time just because you don't feel like working that morning. Sounds like basic stuff, but Hickey knows, the way every other professional in the juvenile system knows, that the kids of Juvenile Court tend to be bereft of these basics—that's one reason why they have such lousy records in school.

Scrappy was bright, he had potential, Hickey says sadly. "But we didn't do the job we needed to do with him. He did his time, and that was it. And now one boy is dead, and two others are headed to life in prison. Everyone loses."

Then Hickey talks about another case, a kid who has a virtually identical criminal record as Scrappy, same age, grew up in the same sort of decayed neighborhood, experienced the same failure in school despite innate intelligence—a hardened gang member who never cared, one crime away from an adult prison term himself. Hickey is talking about Andre. The one difference between the two boys: Scrappy came home from camp and attended a run-of-the-mill court school where delinquent kids are warehoused all day because mainstream schools won't admit them. But Andre went to the Rosewood School, where delinquents work with handicapped children in addition to going to class—where he met a little girl in a wheelchair named Miriam. Scrappy is now going down for murder. Andre has moved up three grade levels in six months, is about to graduate high school, has gone straight for more than a year, and is in line for a job as a county clerk.

"It's a question of approach," Hickey says, scoffing at the newly popular military-style boot camps and the latest fad promoted by California lawmakers—taking gangbangers to the morgue to see murder victims. "These kids are already hard. They don't need to be made harder. The issue is softening them up. They need to learn how to care about life again. They've lost that. That's what we need to give back to them.

"We need to soften them up."

When expounding this theme, Hickey often sounds more like a defense attorney than a prosecutor. In part, this owes to his love of children, his belief in the bedrock principle of Juvenile Court—that most kids can be saved. He embraces this philosophy personally as well as professionally. The walls of his office are filled with pictures of his family—three children he and his wife have adopted abroad, kids who were orphaned to the merciless shanty neighborhoods of Brazil, where vigilantes sanctioned (and sometimes joined) by the police have been known to execute homeless urchins as if they were vermin. "They are my sweethearts," he says. "My joy." He is a strong believer in the power of voluntarism, in the healing ability simple caring and reaching out can accomplish, which is why he devotes so much of his time and effort as a DA to working with school boards and community agencies—trying to stop the cycle of delinquency in its earliest stages.

"When people stop caring, you get the kind of situation they have in Brazil, where children are killed and no one cares," he says. "I don't mean to suggest that could ever happen here, but we are becoming increasingly callous about children, and it troubles me. . . . Children in certain parts of our city are gunned down regularly. But where is the outrage? Where are our priorities?"

Hickey remembers trying a juvenile murder case years ago, before a Superior Court judge downtown. The case boiled down to one underpaid prosecutor versus one underpaid public defender, with no money for expert witnesses, or clerks, or researchers—a typical Juvenile Court scenario, then and now. In the same courtroom that day, the judge was hearing motions in a libel case filed by a well-known vacation resort, whose board of directors objected to an article in *Penthouse* magazine linking the resort's owners to organized crime figures. Six lawyers, well-dressed and making hundreds of dollars an hour, came to the hearing, backed up by an array of clerks, paralegals, and toadies of all sorts.

"It seemed really poignant to me," Hickey recalls. "Here we were, just the two of us, trying to decide this young man's fate, a capital crime, supposedly the most serious thing our system has to deal with, and here they were, a porno magazine and a spa for the wealthy, with all these resources at work. There was the system's priorities, for all to see. The judge couldn't wait to get us out of there, couldn't wait to get to the 'good stuff.' All the judges know the score. If they want to retire from the bench and be invited in as a partner in a good firm, or get into the lucrative world of private court for civil cases, you can't get there from Juvenile Court. The best and the brightest, except for a very few, don't want to be here. And, believe me, they're not. As much as we need them, they don't want to be here."

To Hickey's way of thinking, the Rosewood School's special program, in its own small way, reverses these priorities by conferring profound responsibilities onto children unaccustomed to being trusted to do anything. He tries to get every kid he can into Rosewood. "These are street thugs, serious offenders, some of the worst kids who come through here. Most of them have served time in camp or at the Youth Authority, and they're harder than ever. Then they end up feeding and bathing autistic and wheelchair-bound kids, working with them intensively, having these handicapped folks depending on them utterly. It works a kind of magic. It softens them. For the first time in their lives, someone is dependent on them. And it changes them. It's been going for four years, there's never been a problem, never anyone neglected or hurt. Rival gang members go there and work together side by side. Sometimes it seems like a miracle.

"There's just one problem. After a while, they graduate. Then they go back to where they were before. And the forces that made them criminals are stronger and more varied. The empathy they learn can vanish in a moment. But all you have to do is see the accomplishments of this program. That is the sort of initiative the system needs. That is what the system of the future ought to be looking at. Taking these kids and softening them up."

The Rosewood School occupies a large storefront in a tidy strip mall in the suburb of Bellflower, surrounded by a health club, insurance offices, a bookstore—a typical shopping center. There is one large room equipped with desks, computers, books, and a couple of blackboards, manned by two teachers working with twenty-seven students, all of them on probation, most of them boys. It is clean and bright, with hot lunches served free to the kids and a loosely structured lesson plan that allows each child to progress at his or her own pace. Most of the students are junior or senior high school age, yet many function at little more than a third- or fourth-grade level academically. A careful interview process screens out boys and girls unwilling to give the special program a sincere try; those willing to commit themselves can jump two or three grade levels in a few months. The goal here, like other court schools, is to have students earn enough credits to receive a diploma, or to build their academic skills—and their behavior—to the point where a regular high school will take them back, so they can have proms and SATs and all the things these kids once considered out of reach. Rosewood has a success rate about twice as good as other court schools—there are still plenty of failures, but more kids make it here than elsewhere.

The major difference between Rosewood and the other court schools becomes apparent at midmorning, when the students climb onto a small bus and head a short distance to the PACE school, where the disabled children await them. Supervised by counselors, the delinquents quickly attach themselves to groups of PACE students, taking some to eat, helping others in class, working as teacher's aides. For most of the Rosewood kids, their visits here represent the first time they have been relied upon to help another person, the first time they have been told that what they have to offer is worth something, the first time school has done something other than make them feel inferior. It is a small success, helping a paraplegic child eat a piece of toast, and yet one success seems to lead to another for some kids. If I can do this, some say, maybe I can do better in class, too. Not all of them make this leap, but many do.

Today, Andre and several other boys from Rosewood lead a procession of kids to the supermarket to buy groceries, helping them to choose packages, to use coupons, to pay at the register. En route this morning, Andre notices that one sixteen-year-old brain-damaged boy named Richard has adjusted his oversized trousers to ride low on his hips—imitating the "saggin' and baggin'" gang members he has seen in the neighborhood with their fondness for wearing pants and shirts ten sizes too big for their frames.

"Hey, no baggin' around here," Andre says, exchanging mock punches and feints with the boy, making Richard grin. "You think you're bad? You don't want to dress like that. Take it from me."

Richard looks sheepish when Andre yanks his pants up and cinches his belt, but then they shake hands and continue shopping, Andre's arm draped easily over the other boy's shoulder.

"I can't believe that's the same kid who walked in here, but that's the power of what we're doing," whispers Cedric Anderson, one of the teachers at Rosewood. When he first met Andre, the boy said his parents had given up on him, told him right to his face that he'd never amount to anything. Their communication with their son, like most of the kids Cedric teaches, had deteriorated to little more than yelling and punishing. "He was as hard as they come," Cedric says, putting his arm around Andre and dishing out the praise that is dished out as often at possible at Rosewood. "Now he has gone from a heart of stone to a heart of feelings, from hard core to soft core. He's going to make it—a kid whose own parents had written him off. I have no doubt he's going to make it."

Andre returns to his desk to complete some math problems, and the smile fades from Cedric's face. The future worries him. So far, no attempt has been made to replicate the Rosewood program that he and another teacher cobbled together, Cedric says, unable to conceal the bitterness in his voice. Its budget is in constant jeopardy, in line far behind programs geared more toward punishment than rehabilitation and prevention. Nor is it a model that the reformers are particularly interested in these days. The other court schools have not attempted to replicate the program. The Probation Department isn't interested. Juvenile judges outside of Los Padrinos haven't even heard of it.

Prosecutor Jim Hickey may believe in Rosewood and in the need to soften up tough kids, but the message is not being heard. His boss, DA Garcetti, has concluded his meetings and has become interested in creating a new system that would remove the worst kids from Juvenile Court, treating them like adults in a two-tiered system that punishes the worst offenders severely, and reserves the social services for the most minor offenders.[2] Kids like Andre would either straighten out after their first offenses—something Andre did not do—or get booted into the adult system under this plan.

As Los Angeles DA Gil Garcetti's juvenile point man, Dave Disco, explains it, the premise for creating a two-tiered system is based in part on a simple notion: Murder, whether by children or adults, as well as other violent crimes, should not be treated like an application for social services. Seventy-five percent of the cases in Los Angeles Juvenile Court are felonies. That's not what the founding fathers of juvenile justice had in mind when they created a system intent on rehabilitation rather than punishment. The founders didn't know that the behavior problems that most concerned school principals would shift in the last three decades from running in the halls and talking in class to carrying firearms and assaults on teachers.[3]

This two-tiered premise calls for reserving Juvenile Court only for the sorts of kids it was originally intended to serve, the hubcap thieves and shoplifters, and sending all the others—even the very young—to adult court, or something very much like it. It is in theory a sensible approach, cost-effective, fairly simple, and politically expedient. It might even work, at least for some of the kids, though it requires society to simply give up on an extraordinary number of its children. For in this system of the future—to be offered for study and possible adoption by the state legislature—kids who can be salvaged will be treated no differently from kids who are hopeless.[4]

In this system of the future, Andre and Miriam would never have met.

The Los Angeles County Probation Department's administration, with its study of Juvenile Court ineffectiveness and the 16 percent of delinquents who wreak havoc on the system in hand, wants to mold a very different sort of reform: not to give up on the worst of the worst, but to figure out who they are *before* they get in serious trouble, then throw everything the system has at them before it's too late. In such a system, most offenders—the 84 percent who do not become career criminals—would neither need nor get much in the way of services. Precious money and manpower would be saved to throw at the remaining kids who really need it. In this way, the child, not the crime, would determine what happens when a kid enters the system.[5]

The task of figuring out how to identify these worst kids before they do much of anything bad—a feat of behavioral prophecy that has eluded juvenile justice experts for ninety-five years—has in Los Angeles fallen to a soft-spoken former probation officer named Roy Sukoda. He firmly believes in creating a system that does not give up on any child, a core of optimism he retains even though the numbers he has been crunching from his department's three-year study get more dismal every day. Other than a handful of select juvenile justice professionals he addresses during occasional briefings, few in the system—and virtually none outside it—have ever heard of this man. But more than anyone in Los Angeles, Roy Sukoda has in hand the information needed to save—or to destroy—Juvenile Court.

"The Sixteen Percenters," as he calls the kids who account for most juvenile crime, "are shunted aside from the start. Typically, they start out demanding a lot of attention in school, behavior problems, academic problems, they disrupt. Gradually, they get shunted aside. That's the first time. Then when they reach age nine to eleven, maybe twelve, they commit a crime, usually a low-grade misdemeanor. At that point, there is a tendency to overlook the offense. The police counsel and release him without making an arrest, or the Probation Department looks at the case and decides to give the minor a break. That's the second time they are pushed aside. This is not such a break, though. In fact, that young person might have been better off being provided services then and there, intensive probation, supervision, special classes, counseling—something to keep them from becoming habitual offenders. But the opposite is done."

It is not until these repeat offenders have reached age fourteen, and have already committed three or more crimes, that the system takes action, meting out harsh punishments, Sukoda has found. Then it is too late for the delinquent, and too late for the people he has victimized. Sometimes through the best of intentions, sometimes through laziness or bureaucratic indifference, the system ends up with kids like Richard Perez, who commit crime after crime until a murder charge stops them.

The answer is to begin working with these kids at a very early age, before their first arrest, Sukoda says. As a theory, this is hardly revolutionary. It has been scientifically established for many years that a child's ability to avoid criminal behavior—his or her morality—is (or is not) locked in by age six, nine at the outside, and cannot easily be altered after that point. By age fourteen, the task is extremely difficult.[6] The Juvenile Court, on the other hand, typically meets the Sixteen Percenters for the first time just after they turn fourteen. Then more years pass before the system takes any meaningful action. The criminal mind-set has already been ingrained in many of them by then. And so an ordinary scientific principle becomes revolutionary in practice, because it would mean rethinking the whole notion of juvenile justice. Sukoda believes Juvenile Court must become a last resort rather than the first stop, with a network of probation officers and counselors stationed in schools and community centers to seek out future serious offenders before they break the law, pushing them to voluntarily join programs to help them avoid lives of crime.

Sukoda's study, preceded and replicated by others around the nation,[7] has led to a profile of the typical Sixteen Percenter: a kid with poor grades, a single-parent home (more than half of them had parents who were either divorced or never married, and only a quarter of them lived with both their natural parents), drug and alcohol problems, behavior problems at home and in school, and family incomes under twenty thousand dollars, which practically speaking qualifies for poverty in costly Southern California. A little over half of the kids joined criminal street gangs before their first arrest, twice the rate of kids who do not become repeat offenders.[8] None of this is particularly surprising—"A good probation officer has known all this on a gut level for years," Sukoda says—but the statistics can be used to create a kind of checklist. Third- or fourth- or fifth-graders with behavioral problems who match this profile could be put into special classes. Their families could be offered help, counseling, jobs programs. If gang membership is a problem, getting the kid into after-school activities to keep him off the street might be the answer. Judge Dorn's effort to rejuvenate status offenses fits in here, since it tends to pull in far younger kids, well before they commit serious crimes. In just ten months, strictly through word of mouth, more than four hundred parents have marched into court in Inglewood with their out-of-control kids, begging Dorn for help—a sure sign of a huge need. "The point is, to wait until these kids enter the system the old way is to wait until it is too late," Sukoda says. "We've lost them by then."

There are a couple of big roadblocks, though: There must be a sure way of identifying these "at-risk" kids without trampling on their civil rights. The probability that checklists, however carefully devised, will be seen as racially, ethnically, or economically biased is already causing turmoil within the Probation Department. Once identified, there must be a sure way of getting the kids and their families to participate voluntarily in special programs, a major obstacle. The glaring Catch-22 of the current system is its inability to order anything until after a crime is committed. And one of the hallmarks of these kids and their families is parental disinterest and refusal to acknowledge the existence of a problem—making voluntary programs a tough sell.

Perhaps the biggest hurdle, in Sukoda's view, is the simple reality that programs that punish are far more popular than those that prevent. Changing the system's course now would cost money, lots of it, without any immediate results. Ten years down the line, juvenile crime may recede under Sukoda's plan, but it would call for political and economic commitments no one wants to make. On the other hand, if you build a prison cell today, then fill it, the results appear immediate, even if crime continues unabated.[9]

In mid-1994, shortly after Sukoda presented a progress report on his study to Judge Dorn and other would-be reformers, Los Angeles County discovered it was going broke. The county government had exhausted its credit (it even mortgaged its courthouses) and could no longer continue a long-standing practice of quiet book-juggling and deficit-spending that had for years concealed a growing financial crisis. The order went out: Public safety (read: police and jails) must be preserved, but social programs must be cut. Prevention programs have to be shelved, including Sukoda's plans, it was decided. He could keep studying and recommending, but the likelihood of anything happening became nil. Probation caseloads would go up, therapeutic facilities would shut down—the focus of the system would have to remain on protecting society from the hardcore, dangerous few, with even less left over for the first-time offenders who could still be straightened out.

Just when the Sixteen Percent Solution study made it clear why the system isn't working, the very priorities that have made the Juvenile Court an endangered species got locked into place.

CHAPTER 10

Sister Janet

I notice Elias is missing when the writing class starts this night. The other kids tell me he is in The Box. A race riot swept through the Juvenile Hall school earlier today, black kids fighting brown kids, a pattern that has been occurring with alarming frequency in the other juvenile halls, in the Youth Authority, and on high school campuses throughout LA. Word among the staff and kids alike is that the Mexican Mafia is behind it, ordering a select few troublemakers to fan the warfare between the rival ethnic gangs. What started this particular melee remains in dispute—my students say someone suddenly yelled out, "Beaners suck," after which fists, then chairs, started flying. Others remember a slur against African-Americans as the original source of trouble. However it began, the ending was predictable and unambiguous: five or so staff members waded in and grabbed the combatants within reach. Elias had visibly participated in the fighting and already had a reputation as a troublemaker. He was an easy choice to serve as an example.

I ask the kids what it's like in The Box.

"It's like, if you were already worried that the rest of the world forgot where you are and who you are, The Box makes you sure of it," Geri says. "The only thing you can do in there, you know, is think—usually about how bad things are."

"Sometimes," Scrappy adds quietly, "the only way you keep from stressing out in this place is to not think. You can't do that in The Box. All there is to do is to think. I hate The Box."

The Box, I later learn, is a term only used by the kids, more descriptive than the official title, SHU—Special Handling Unit. It is a separate building near the back of the hall grounds, where boys and girls are kept locked individually in bare rooms without anything to read or do for much of the day. It is juvenile solitary confinement.

Normally, visiting privileges are canceled once a kid is in The Box. But the hall's Catholic chaplain, Sister Janet, has ways of getting around the rules and she manages to see Elias while the rest of us are in class. She knows he is facing a difficult decision.

"My lawyer tells me I should take a plea bargain," Elias tells her after they sit down. He puts his head down on folded arms on the tabletop and closes his eyes. "My lawyer says he got the best deal he can."

"I know," Janet answers. She has been in touch with the boy's court-appointed lawyer, Mike Shannon, since Elias first came here a year ago. Janet wanted to make sure he got the best defense possible, that the attorney assigned to his case understood that, as far as she was concerned, beneath Elias's anger and gang tattoos and criminal behavior, there was something more. Something worth taking time and trouble to salvage. "He's a very good lawyer," Janet assures Elias, "and a very good man. I'm sure he believes that the plea bargain is what's best for you."

She doesn't tell him that the lawyer, when talking to Janet earlier in the week, grew so frustrated he was almost in tears over Elias's case. "This sixteen-year-old kid is supposed to decide between going to trial—where he can't win and where he risks getting sentenced to life without parole—and taking the deal the DA's offered, a sentence of fifteen years to life. What kind of choice is that for a kid to have to make? When he gets out, he'll have spent half his life behind bars. But the pressure on the DA to crack down on this case is tremendous. The family of the victim has been relentless. I can't get him a better deal."

Janet usually avoids asking about the details of crimes—she says she is more interested in dealing with kids' futures than their pasts—but she knows the awful facts that brought Elias to her, that night in Hollywood, when he and a pickup truck full of homeboys and home girls went out on a "mission." That's what they called their armed escapades in search of robbery victims, heroic terminology borrowed from old war movies by kids at war with the world. There was nothing heroic about it, though, Elias says now—everyone had been messed up on pot and booze and things had gotten out of hand. They had been stupid and cruel. And some poor innocent on his way home from a convenience store with a carton of milk had died, stabbed on the street and left to bleed to death for a lousy seven bucks.

Elias had been in the truck with the others that night, had agreed they should do the robbery, had helped chase the man down. But then he had stood back. It was three other kids who tackled and robbed the man walking alone on the street. Elias hadn't done the stabbing, hadn't intended it or expected it, had been just as surprised as everyone else when crazy Tyelle pulled out the knife and plunged it into the guy's stomach. Even afterward, Elias never thought the man would die. As they drove away, he saw the victim get to his feet and stagger off, yelling for help. When the police arrested the gang members hours later and told Elias that no one ever came out to help the man, that he had walked around dazed and alone until he collapsed and bled to death, Elias broke down and started weeping uncontrollably in the interrogation room. He swore so vociferously about never meaning to harm anyone that even the detective who booked him for murder believed it. It was this remorse, more than anything, that convinced the prosecutor on the case to offer Elias a plea to second-degree murder and a fifteen-year sentence, which in this age of crime and punishment is considered a most generous offer. The others tried as adults in the case got twenty-five to life.[1]

"But part of the deal is, I can't get a YA number," Elias tells Sister Janet. "Only an M number." He is referring to a loophole in the law that allows adult court judges to sentence deserving kids back into the juvenile system. Kids who are "committed" to the California Youth Authority get a corrections file number that begins with "YA." Everyone else gets an "M" number, the abbreviation for male convict. The difference is immense. Kids with YA numbers get out at age twenty-five. M numbers do their time—no age limits. And though they can still be housed temporarily in CYA, there are no guarantees for M numbers. The state penitentiary is always right around the corner.

"I don't know what to do, Sister Janet," Elias says, looking up at her for the first time since she walked in. She sees he has dark circles under his eyes, as if his face were bruised. His arms are thin and his T-shirt hangs loosely— he has lost weight. "I was ready to take the deal the last time I was in court, but then I saw my mother sitting there, and my sisters, and aunts, the whole family. My girlfriend was there with my baby girl Ashley, and I just couldn't do it. I couldn't admit this thing in front of them. I couldn't let them hear me say I am a murderer. They don't think of me that way. I don't think of me that way. So I have another week to decide."

Sister Janet reaches out and takes his hand, a familiar ache in her chest. She loves these boys, has devoted her life to them, working with gang members in the streets of East LA for years, then becoming their advocate in Juvenile Court and Juvenile Hall. The prosecutors consider them monsters, their defense lawyers can be so jaded and overworked that they barely remember their names, most of them have families who gave up on them long ago, if they have families at all. And so Sister Janet fills the void, the chaplain of the lockup. Gray-haired and soft-spoken, she walks through the hall and even the most hardened gangbangers may drop what they are doing to take her hand or embrace her. She is a nun with a master's degree in filmmaking, who writes screenplays about her boys' lives, who has friends in the film industry, and whose nun's habit long ago was supplanted by smart knit skirts and fashionable business suits. Her quiet caring, her empathy for social outcasts, is unshakable. If racial tensions in the hall are rising, Janet seems to know it first. If there is an escape planned, someone may tell her about it. If a kid's lawyer needs a witness to plead on his or her behalf, Sister Janet is there. She has the Juvenile Hall wired. The kids tell her everything.

"Can you help me, Sister?" Elias asks.

"I'm praying for you, every day," she answers automatically. "And when it's time to go to court, I'll be there for you. It's not over yet."

When Elias finally accepts the deal a few weeks later—alone in court, head bowed—and returns for sentencing, Sister Janet and several volunteers from the hall go to the hearing to speak for him before the judge, pleading that he at least be housed at the Youth Authority for the first portion of his sentence. But Janet is up against the mother of the victim, Colleen Mansbridge, who has become a forceful and understandably bitter zealot demanding an all-out war on street gangs, and the harshest possible punishments for Elias and his friends.

"Gangs, like animals, travel in packs and are basically cowards," the grieving mother says in court, a compact woman in her sixties with light brown permed hair and a posture that seems to render her entire body into a balled fist. She shakes slightly as she speaks, not with an infirmity, but with rage. While she speaks, Elias sits in shackles in the empty jury box with one of the other convicted killers, head bowed, unable to look at the woman, his eyes tightly closed. Later, he says he didn't know if he should be angry, or if he should agree with this woman and her hatred.

"Our son's life was cut right out of him by these cowardly killers. . . . They are all culpable," Mrs. Mansbridge says. "They are all cold-blooded murderers. Elizondo won't get the sentence he deserves, but he will deserve the sentence he gets. . . . His juvenile status should no longer apply."

Later, out in the hallway, she confronts and denounces Janet for taking the side of a killer. "How can you do this, a Sister of God?" she asks, her face a mask of rage. She spits out one more sentence, then staggers off before Janet can speak. "I hope God can forgive you. I can't."

Mrs. Mansbridge is the living, breathing personification of the toll juvenile violence has wrought on society, and it is a chorus of similar emotion-laden voices, small in number but compelling in their fervor, that has come to dominate the debate on the juvenile justice system. Janet knows that no judge faced with such an awful scene is going to favor a convicted killer over a woman so blistered by anguish. Elias's lawyer seems to agree. He asks that the rest of the hearing be postponed, and the judge agrees.

Janet has time to write more letters, to make more phone calls. She asks the Youth Authority to reconsider its initial position on Elias—that he should be housed with adults, not children. She implores the judge to be generous. Most of this is futile, she knows, and yet, there is a benefit, something she looks for in all her "hopeless" cases. Even if her letters leave little imprint on the judges who receive them, they can hold huge significance for the kids, providing a more hopeful vision of themselves than they are used to hearing, a mental life preserver a few of them cling to for years. These letters, read in court, are often the only notes of compassion during sentencing hearings that otherwise paint kids as monsters. So it is with Elias. Janet has provided him a moral life raft. Still awaiting his sentence, he thanks her profusely for her efforts. If she believes in him, he says, maybe he can believe, too.

"I'm going to make it somehow," he promises. "Please pray for me."

------◆------

NONE of us want to see this place become a growth industry," the man campaigning for another term as California's governor intones, glancing around the acrid confines of Central Juvenile Hall with obvious distaste. With both hands, he grips the simulated wood podium plunked down on the uneven ground outside the lockup's modest chapel, then raises his voice. "These young punks need to be held accountable."

Pete Wilson, San Diego's mayor turned U.S. senator turned governor turned populist government "outsider," is locked in what started out as an uphill election battle this year with California State Treasurer Kathleen Brown, daughter and sister of two previous governors, the closest thing California has to a royal family. Recently, Wilson has soared in the polls, having goaded his once dominant opponent into shifting the campaign's emphasis from a discussion of jobs and education and the economy—her strong suit—to the need to crack down on crime, an issue the Republican incumbent figures he owns better than the NRA likes bullets. In keeping with this unrelenting anticrime agenda (and notwithstanding the fact that governors have relatively little to do with law enforcement), Wilson has arrived at Central Juvenile Hall today, taking over a slice of the lockup's barren grounds to hold a press conference to blast laws that treat juvenile criminals differently from adults.

With the media corps in attendance on a blistering hot, drizzly day, Wilson introduces two mothers of children killed by juvenile gang members, and a third woman whose son was seriously wounded in a drive-by attack— living, grieving testimony to the terrible human cost of the rising tide of youth violence. One by one, the mothers hesitantly approach the microphone and air their anguish, understandably eager to see maximum punishments for juvenile offenders put into place. The impression is left that, somehow, intolerably, the little monsters who shot their children got off with hand slaps because of their age. Enter Wilson, ready to fix this outrage.

"When we punish cold-blooded killers, their age shouldn't matter," he declares, as the probation officers and teachers who run Juvenile Hall— and whose livelihood depends upon the fact that the age of offenders *does* matter—shift from foot to foot in uncomfortable silence. "If you commit an adult crime, you'll do adult time."

It is a message that resonates, one that few citizens and even fewer politicians would care to challenge. This is why the Ronald Duncan case arouses such fury—there is no logic in treating fifteen-year-old coldblooded killers differently from sixteen-year-old ones. Wilson has picked an issue on which he cannot lose. But the governor conveniently neglects to mention a few facts that seriously undermine his pitch: namely, that the grieving mothers present today were victimized by juveniles who were *over* sixteen. All of them got shipped to adult court and life prison sentences under existing, supposedly lax laws.

Nor does Wilson mention that the new law he is pushing—which would lower the fitness age so fourteen year-olds could be considered adults—would not stop with murderers, but would wipe out whole swaths of Juvenile Court jurisdiction, allowing even some burglars to be transferred to adult court at age fourteen. Nor is it made clear that the two most outspoken of the three moms on hand—imported to this LA affair from conservative (and soon to be bankrupt) Orange County to the south—are angry not because killers are getting away with murder, but because some child murderers tried as adults get to spend the first part of their sentences in the California Youth Authority, away from older, predatory inmates in adult prison, until they are old enough or tough enough to avoid being assaulted and raped by older inmates.

Never mind that the importance assigned to juvenile murderers in the debate over the future of Juvenile Court is wildly out of proportion to their numbers. Murders make up less than 1 percent of all juvenile cases—and as many as 94 percent of those teen killers are *over* sixteen, which means the vast majority of juvenile murderers and other violent delinquents can be (and usually are) dispatched to adult court with no trouble under existing laws.[2] Sending fourteen- and fifteen-year-old murderers to adult court would address isolated outrages like Ronald Duncan, but it is not the big fix Wilson represents it to be. Statistically, it would have exactly no impact on crime, which is why the proposed legislation has quietly been expanded to include far less popular provisions, such as sending fourteen-year-old burglars to adult prison. It is also why Wilson brought with him mothers whose children were shot by sixteen-year-olds—that's all he could find. Wilson has stacked the guest list in his favor to avoid any dissent or disharmony, and such bothersome details never come up.

The moment provides some terrifically emotive film clips to add to the governor's television campaign spots—and to file away for the disastrous presidential bid Wilson has brazenly promised not to pursue (and which he would wholeheartedly pursue six months later, a lifelong politician selling himself unsuccessfully as an angry Republican outsider). On the muddy quadrangle of grass not far from the U-shaped, two-story brick buildings that house Geri, Elias, Scrappy, Carla, and all the other boys and girls who call this lockup home, Wilson's entourage of campaign aides scramble to check camera angles and bark into cellular phones, sweating profusely in their suits and ties and dark business dresses as Wilson exhorts the media to carry forth his message about the need to crack down on "young predators," a message he repeats time and again a year later during his presidential bid.

Across the field and safely out of the way, locked down in their rooms during the governor's visit, the kids he is speaking about peer through the scratchy portals of unbreakable acrylic in their rooms, windows etched by layer upon layer of initials and gang logos, noses and hands pressed against the panes as they try to make sense of the spectacle below. They know only too well that, though this is a party in their honor, they are not welcome to attend. Even the outspoken director of Juvenile Hall, who opposes Wilson's legislative proposals, is off the guest list at his own facility. There is only one thing the governor didn't count on.

Somehow, Sister Janet Harris got herself an invitation.

"What in the way of prevention programs are you proposing in all this legislation?" she asks during what was billed as a roundtable discussion, though none of the participants were actually expected to ask Wilson anything remotely controversial. Janet has the kind of voice that is both firm and soft, making you strain just a little to hear, which has the curious effect of giving her words more, not less, power. "And why are young people charged with burglary included in this law?"

Wilson looks uncomfortable, but only for a moment. Prevention is an important part of dealing with juvenile crime, of course, he says. And the best form of prevention is to get the message across that "adult crimes carry adult price tags." He has managed to get back on point, the consummate politician.

But one of the mothers—the only one from Los Angeles—will not let Wilson evade Janet's question so easily. To everyone's surprise, she says, "I think prevention and rehabilitation is crucial, not just cracking down on these kids. And I don't think burglary belongs in there, either. I think that's going too far."

"Well, I believe burglary belongs in the bill. But that's certainly something that will be debated," Wilson says lamely, knowing that the legislation is on the fast track in Sacramento, and that legislators are falling over one another to see who can out-tough the others in cracking down on juvenile crime. It is an unplanned and uncomfortable moment, and the entourage reacts quickly with much glancing at watches. There's another campaign speech in an hour, the aides announce that it is time to go, and the discussion abruptly ends.

But before Wilson and his people stride off to their waiting limousines, while he is still circulating among the guests and bidding them farewell, Sister Janet materializes by the governor's arm. His hand shoots out reflexively to grip hers, warm and firm, a smile fixed on his face as Janet leans close and whispers that she is praying for him and the other leaders of California to find ways to improve the juvenile justice system with compassion and wisdom. Many boys and girls who languish behind bars could be saved, she tells him, if only the people in power wanted it that way. He looks uncomfortable again, but he still nods and smiles, then thanks her. "I think we're going to accomplish that with these new, tougher laws," he says automatically, then turns briskly away. The newspaper and TV people immediately begin packing up for the next stop on the campaign trail as the governor and his staff race off, accidentally abandoning one of their grieving mothers in the process.

A television reporter sidles up to Janet then and says quietly out of the corner of her mouth, "What a dog and pony show."

"Put that down for the record," Janet replies. "Please."

There is a story about Sister Janet Harris. It dates back to the seventies, when Los Angeles County received a small federal grant to start a program to reform gang kids, and someone decided to put Sister Janet in charge. (Her guidance in this task: "Here's a desk, Sister, and a phone. Get to work.") She wanted to set up jobs and mentors and school programs for current and would-be gang members, but she needed support from the city of Los Angeles, which meant seeking out then-mayor Tom Bradley's help. She thought a former cop turned politician with humble roots, one of the first black mayors of a major U.S. city, would be happy to throw his support toward a program designed to keep poor and underprivileged kids from joining gangs and turning to crime. But Bradley—or at least his staff—rebuffed Sister Janet for months.

Then one night she spotted Bradley's unmistakable broad shoulders and blocky silhouette in a Beverly Hills restaurant. On impulse, she got down on her knees and crept toward him across the crowded restaurant, hands clasped in supplication, to convince him to participate in her gang program. "I'm begging you to help these boys," Sister Janet said, planting her elbows next to his wineglass, the mayor and his dinner companions gaping in astonishment.

She laughs ruefully at the memory now, a trifle embarrassed, but not the least apologetic. "It was important. And I wanted him to hear me." The mayor heard her, all right, and then, as Janet tells it, turned her down flat, leaving orders to keep Sister Janet away from him.

But someone else took an interest in Sister Janet's ideas and dedication—the former football great and actor Rosie Greer, who went on to become a minister. Greer, in turn, got Jackie Kennedy to show up a short time later to help raise funds for the gang program. The former First Lady ended up cruising the barrio with Janet in Greer's station wagon, littered with soda cans and fast-food wrappers. Before attending a press conference and a fund-raiser, Greer, Janet, and Jackie O. stopped in the barrio to play dominoes with gang members.

"The program really took off after that," Janet recalls. "I've been doing this ever since."

Sister Janet Harris is a youthful and slim sixty-three, with short silver hair, pale blue eyes behind metal-rimmed spectacles, and a manner that at times seems distracted, so immersed is she in the daily lives of the inhabitants of Juvenile Hall. Her workdays begin early and end late, filled with recruiting volunteers, organizing dances, planning church services and Bible study groups, staging plays and musicals, and lining up alternative lawyers and social workers for kids who have little contact with the professionals appointed to represent them. She spends hours a day roaming the different units in the lockup, and can only rarely be found in the cramped and chilly chaplain's office adjacent to the Juvenile Hall chapel. Still, her office is one of the few places on the grounds where the door stands open and unlocked throughout the day. Though theft is endemic in this place, her office has never been victimized.

She never planned on becoming an advocate for dispossessed children. As a teenager living in the Bronx, Janet had been an aspiring actress. Her father always told her she'd be on the stage someday. But on the eve of a critical audition for a Broadway play, just when those ambitions were close to being realized (or dashed, she says now), she decided against pursuing show business. Instead, she joined an order of nuns in California, the Sisters of the Presentation, where she took her vows, then attended the University of San Francisco. (Many people saw the two career choices as utterly contradictory, but not Janet, who as a nun went on to earn a master's degree in filmmaking and has collaborated on several movie projects, including helping with the film *Zoot Suit*.)

After college, Janet took a teaching assignment at a Catholic elementary school in an East Los Angeles barrio. Next to her convent stood a foster home for chronically delinquent boys, and it was here that Janet found her calling. A half hour of volunteer work at the foster home each day after school soon blossomed into three hours and weekends, time that left her energized and wanting more. She began spending time with gang kids, at first on her own, then through the LA County antigang program. She avoided the standard approach the church had always used with gang members and their families—Scriptures, preaching, prayer, penance— focusing instead on finding work for gang members, helping them get into junior colleges and trade schools, pairing them with volunteers and mentors who could offer them alternatives to violence and crime.

Gang members were at first dubious of this meddling white nun from New York. But when she refused to betray a confidence to police detectives seeking information on a gang killing—risking jail herself when the angry investigators accused her of obstructing justice—Janet gained enormous respect from the Latino gang members she was trying to reach. Several eventually came forward themselves with information for the police in order to spare her the handcuffs.

In the 1980s, Janet left the streets and began working in juvenile halls and, in 1989, she became chaplain at Central Juvenile Hall, becoming one of the few points of consistency the kids here recognize. Consistency is no small issue: Odds are a repeat offender will get a different judge, a new lawyer, another prosecutor, and a new series of probation officers (one to evaluate him before his arrest, another to investigate him before his sentencing, yet another to supervise him once he's back on the street). In theory, the court file is supposed to provide consistency that the human component lacks, a body of knowledge that helps the system avoid starting from scratch each time a child walks in the door. In practice, though, most judges and lawyers haven't the time or inclination to read anything in the file beyond the most recent piles of paper (the information superhighway has no on-ramps to Juvenile Court—in many respects it remains a manually typed, carbon-copy world, circa 1961). A ward's history before the court is often ignored or misplaced, especially when more than one branch of the court is involved (and worse still when there is a different jurisdiction). Continuity, cooperation, communication, even the mere sharing of files is an iffy thing between the disparate parts of the sprawling LA Juvenile Court—dozens of files, the complete and irreplaceable record of a child's life, are misplaced every month. Some of the ten branches of the court simply refuse to send them, and judges elsewhere have their clerks create "dummy" files, a name that aptly summarizes the sparse contents of such makeshift remedies. Kids who want to hide their pasts can do so easily, simply by slightly modifying a birth date or a name. At the same time, children who want and need help, and whose past should help them get it, are passed over—which is why a George Trevino, with his eight years as a ward of the Juvenile Court's dependency branch, could be hustled into the delinquency side of the court and be treated as if he had no history in the system at all.

These sorts of communication breakdowns work both ways. To most kids, the Juvenile Court is nothing more than a long stay in a dank holding cell, followed by a few minutes in a bright and noisy courtroom full of nameless faces speaking a legalistic language they can't follow. When the lockup bus brings them back to the hall, often after eight at night, many cannot say for certain the purpose of the hearing that brought them to court, or the name of the judge or the prosecutor they faced that day, or even the name of the lawyer representing them. But a good number of them know Sister Janet's name. They know if they ask her for help, she will do her best, no questions asked. They know she does not condone their crimes or violence, yet she still invests countless hours and endless effort on their behalf, trying to eke some measure of individual treatment out of a system that is best at crafting blanket solutions for the many. She makes a distinction between being a gang member and being a criminal, because, unlike virtually every other worker in the system, Janet has known many gang members who have never been arrested or accused of a crime. If the kids here take away nothing else from their stay in Juvenile Hall, those who come to know Sister Janet leave certain of one thing: that at least one person cares what happens to them.

For all too many, Janet has found, this is a new and startling revelation.

"This is just not acceptable," Sister Janet is saying to George Trevino this afternoon, her voice shaking with anger as they sit together in an empty classroom in the hall's school building. "I am not going to let this go."

George nods, glad to have Janet as an ally, but he also shrugs, the expression of a kid conditioned to accept as inevitable the hard realities of a system charged with both sustaining and restraining him. "It's okay," George says quietly, reversing roles and comforting Janet.

"No, it's not all right, George. Those poems are precious. They are important. They *mean* something."

As often happens with the personal possessions of the kids imprisoned here, the Juvenile Hall staff has lost George's poems. A bound and typeset version of twenty-five poems George painstakingly assembled is missing after a seemingly admiring supervisor on his unit asked to borrow it, then misplaced the boy's most prized possession. A few weeks earlier, his handwritten originals were seized as contraband and lost by the hall staff, making today's loss all the more devastating to the boy. Sister Janet has raised such a stink that the administration has begun searching every room and every boy and girl in the place, all nine hundred of them, assuming someone stole them, though Janet suspects the supervisor's carelessness is a more likely culprit. The same staff person had, months earlier, begged Janet to round up some donated books to give the kids. Janet spent the next several weeks pulling together a small library of several hundred paperbacks, which she then had delivered to the lockup's loading dock with the help of several volunteers. Three weeks later, Janet asked a boy if he had gotten access to the new books. "What new books?" the kid replied. Janet then learned that the supervisor had never bothered to fetch the donated books, though she had been told of their arrival immediately, and the residents of the hall had been clamoring for reading material for many days. When Janet went to see what had become of the books, she found them still sitting in open boxes outside on the unsheltered concrete dock, rotting and ruined by a month of rain and sun.

"The indifference so many of the staff here show these kids is incredible," Janet says, wanting George to understand that he has not been singled out. A day earlier, she tells George, one of the boys in the writing class, Chris, convicted of robbing a pizza man with several other juveniles—one of whom shot and wounded the pizza man at the conclusion of the robbery—was told to come over to his unit supervisor's desk. "Here," a detention officer told him, thrusting a dirty, used manila envelope at him without looking up from the paperwork on his desk. "This is yours."

Chris had been working all year to make up for his past truancy and school problems, earning high grades and completing all the credits needed for a high school diploma—an academic achievement not all that common in this place. His teachers have been encouraging him to think about college. He had been expecting some sort of graduation ceremony, some small recognition, but when he opened up the tattered envelope just handed him, he saw it contained his diploma. No congratulations, no handshake. This is a kid who grew up in the street, whose loved ones have been claimed by prison, murder, and suicide, who has no one but his keepers to look to for some measure of approval. "You could just see him shut down when he realized what the staff thought of his accomplishment," Janet says. "The thrill of his achievement—and it is quite an achievement here—just drained right out of him."

Janet made a fuss, of course—first congratulating him herself, with hugs and praise, and then by complaining loud enough to the hall administration, until someone agreed to organize a small ceremony for Chris and three other kids on the high-risk offenders unit who had earned their diplomas. It helped, a little. "Would it have killed them to show a little enthusiasm?" Janet wonders aloud with George Trevino. "Would it have killed them to put his degree in a clean envelope?"

George nods morosely. "You get used to it." He sighs.

George's court case has not gone well for him, either. A few weeks ago, he was convicted in adult court of participating in the home invasion robbery for which he had been arrested nearly a year earlier. The evidence against him, though suggesting he was more a helper than a leader, was nevertheless unequivocal on the issue of his involvement in a potentially deadly crime. He and three other people broke into someone's home. The adult leader had a gun. Seven innocent people, including children and an infant, were placed in jeopardy before one of the intended victims shot the ringleader, sending George and two other juveniles fleeing for their lives. Unable to do much to the two other kids because they were under sixteen, prosecutors piled charges on George as if to make up the difference: multiple counts of armed robbery, kidnapping, assault with a deadly weapon, burglary. Jurors never heard about George's woeful background as a foster child entrusted by the state to addicts, or the Juvenile Court's long-standing failure to provide George a decent home or much-needed counseling. This was deemed irrelevant. To no one's surprise, the adult court jury who heard George Trevino's case convicted him after less than an hour of deliberation. He has been told that he could face a sentence of twenty-nine years to life in prison.

He has one chance, though. The adult court judge has the power to return George to the juvenile justice system, committing him to the California Youth Authority—giving him the "YA" number that all the HROs covet. This is the sentence Elias Elizondo longs for but cannot get under his plea bargain. George still has a shot at it, though, and if he could get it, he would be out in seven years, at age twenty-five. He would be treated the same as Ronald Duncan, except it would be because the system chose to do so, not because it was *forced* to do so.

The two most important factors in determining whether the judge does that are the opinions of the Probation Department (which made the initial recommendation to send him to the adult court in the first place) and the California Youth Authority itself, which will hold George for ninety days, submitting him to a battery of tests, counseling sessions, and evaluations to see if he is still a salvageable human being.

Janet is working to see that he gets that last chance, but George is not hopeful—"I expect the worst," he says—and the process has gotten off to a poor start for him. When being interviewed by the probation officer charged with preparing a sentencing recommendation, George tried to show her his poems as an example of the positive work he has pursued in the hall. But the PO just tossed them aside, George tells Janet. The interview went downhill from there. George returned to the hall sobbing, then refused to follow orders from the staff, which landed him in The Box. That, in turn, led to a black mark on his record, which could easily be used to justify sentencing him to adult prison rather than CYA.

Lately, George has been gripped by a repetitive dream of playing with the sister he never knew, chasing her into a street, only to be hit by a car. He tearfully recounts it for Janet, describing for her the ache he feels each time this dream renews the grief he feels over his shattered family, torn apart and raised by the state. He wakes up at night, sobbing in the darkness, unsure if this dream is a memory or a trick played on him by his mind, turning his long-lost sister's recent death in a car accident into his fault.

"Oh, God, I don't have much hope, Sister," George says, tears squeezing out of his eyes as she embraces the boy, pulling him close.

They talk for a long time about his background. George is candid in admitting he made mistakes and poor choices. At the same time, he shrewdly assesses the juvenile system's priorities.

"The system didn't do much for me, but I'm still responsible for my predicament. I did the crime. It was just so easy. When I first got arrested, Juvenile Court was just a wrist slap. I knew they were sucking me in, that it was almost like a setup, so I would do something worse. Then they could get me. I knew it, but I still couldn't stop. I fell into the trap."

"Why do you think that is, George?" Janet asks. She is always trying to get kids to examine why they do things, to ask the questions they tend never to ask themselves.

"Trouble," George says after a moment, "was funner. I felt free." He shakes his head, bitterness welling up in him. "Now I can't remember what free feels like."

A short time later, the book of poetry George had put together turns up in the unit. He clutches his poems tightly, then asks Janet to make and keep some copies—just in case.

She flips through the booklet. Many of the poems are odes to adolescent love dedicated to one of two twin sisters who work as teachers in the hall, and who spent their off-hours typing up, printing and binding his work into a booklet. That someone would take the time and trouble to do this for him seemed so extraordinary to George, he has imagined an entire relationship out of this simple act of kindness. But some of the poems are poignant, angry self-portraits, and it is to one of these Janet turns. "This is the boy our system has created," she says, and begins to read aloud.

"Should I care about you,
do you care about me?
Should I care about a person,
that I've never seen?
Should I care about a mom,
who left me all alone?
Should I care about a dad,
that I've never known?
Should I care about a sister,
I never really knew — who died on Christmas Day?
Should I care about my uncle,
who died of AIDS cause he was gay?
I guess I should, but I don't,
if you were to die, you'd think I'd care,
no I won't."

"I fear for him," Janet says. "I fear he is about to be lost forever."

Janet is also working on Geri Vance's case. She retreats to her office to call his lawyer for the third time in a week, trying to get through to the man before Geri's case goes to trial. Geri has been complaining for months that his public defender in adult court, Al Johnson, seems disinterested in him. Geri thinks he might want to go to trial rather than accept the plea bargain and the lengthy prison sentence Johnson has recommended. But making and receiving phone calls at the hall is often hard, and Geri is having problems getting him on the phone to discuss his options.

Geri has adamantly clung to the same story since his arrest. He does not so much claim to be innocent as he insists there were extenuating circumstances. He says he was forced to participate in the armed robbery of a motel by two drug-dealing gangsters in his neighborhood. The older criminals had recruited him to deliver drugs for them, Geri says, but when he was ripped off and lost several thousand dollars' worth of cocaine, they told him he had two choices: pay them back by helping in the robbery, or die. He agreed, accepting a pistol for the job, and doing what he was told to do. But the robbery went awry, and one of the drug dealers was killed by an intended victim. The law allowed Geri to be charged with his murder.

There was no hard evidence to contradict Geri's story, except for the fact the victims saw only Geri and the dead man, though they could not say for sure that the third man had not stayed in the car as Geri claimed. And even they agreed that Geri was mostly passive during the robbery. But four things cut against him: Geri would not testify to the identity of the other man, because, he said, he feared reprisals against his younger brother or his grandmother if he named this criminal. (The police said the reason was the third man didn't exist.) Secondly, Geri had a long record of delinquency, dating back to age eleven, including numerous counts of petty theft and car theft. His repeated sentences to probation and placement in foster homes had not convinced Geri to go straight, and they made him a less than credible witness. Then there's the fact that Geri fired his gun, pointing it blindly over his shoulder as he fled into the motel parking lot with the mortally wounded ringleader behind him. The motel clerk had kept up a steady barrage of bullets as the robbers fled, and "I just wanted him to stop shooting," Geri says. "I didn't aim or anything." This seemed true—Geri's shot went far astray, hitting nothing—but just the fact that he fired at all looked bad and undermined his story of being coerced. Worst of all, his lawyer told him, completely apart from the evidence, was the fact that the conservative jury he was likely to face in Pomona, the suburb in which the crime took place, in all probability would not believe him no matter what he said. Just as his lawyer in Juvenile Court had told him, so did this attorney: "You are the jury's worst nightmare. Young black male with a gun." In all likelihood, a trial would end with him convicted and sentenced to twenty-five years to life, the lawyer warned during their one face-to-face meeting. After that, lawyer and client hardly talked, and Geri was a nervous wreck. "Please see what you can find out," he asked Janet.

She finally connects with the lawyer, and begins to explain how special she believes Geri to be, how he came into Juvenile Hall and made a genuine effort to take advantage of any program available to better himself, intent on proving he was anything but a lost cause. He was about to earn his high school equivalency degree, she told the lawyer, he had written a play that had been produced in Juvenile Hall, he was participating in writing classes, computer classes, music classes. "Teachers and detention officers at the hall love him," she says. "This boy deserves special consideration. He deserves some special effort."

The lawyer admits he had been unaware that Geri has amassed such an exemplary record, and he agrees to renew talks with the District Attorney's Office to see if he can coax a better deal for Geri.

A few days later, he calls back, ecstatic. Prodded by Janet and armed with the information she gave him, Johnson had gone over the head of the prosecutor assigned to the case, and convinced a DA supervisor to plead Geri's case down to attempted murder with a twelve-year maximum

sentence. (The attempted murder charge would be based on Geri's blind
shot over his shoulder as he fled, rather than the death of the robbery ringleader.) With time off for good behavior, Geri could be out by the time he
turns twenty-six or twenty-seven, maybe sooner, Johnson says—which isn't
much more time than he would have done in the juvenile system. Most
if not all of his time could be served in CYA. All he has to do is accept the
deal, go to CYA for the mandatory three-month evaluation, behave himself, then come to court to get his sentence, the lawyer says.

"It's a fantastic deal," he says. "Twelve years is unheard of in a case
like this where, quite frankly, the odds of acquittal are very slim, and the
probability that Geri could get a life sentence is very high if we go to trial."

Janet feels Johnson is probably right, that the courts could be—and often are—much tougher on kids like Geri. But she is fairly certain Geri will
be far less thrilled than his lawyer with the plea bargain, and she is right.

"I know I needed to chill for a while, that I needed to get my life together," the sixteen-year-old says after getting the news. "Being here has
been good for me—I know that. Three, four more years even, that would
be okay—I'd have a shot at getting an education, at making something of
myself. But twelve years, damn, that's a long time. I'm afraid I'll get like
some old con, you know, all buffed out on weights, crazy, institutionalized." He begins thinking out loud, puzzling out his options. He could
take the deal and hope that he gets the coveted YA number. Or he could
go for broke and plead his case to a jury. He shakes his head, overwhelmed
by the decisions a sixteen-year-old must make, on his own. He locks his
eyes on Janet's. "What do you think I should do?"

It's a question Janet hears often, and one she can rarely answer. How do
you tell a kid he has to give up twelve years of his life? Especially a kid like
Geri, who Janet feels strongly could walk out the door and into a group
home and a junior college and do just fine today—but who, after another
decade behind bars, could be broken and bitter, stripped of the optimism
and desire to succeed that he has found through a year in Juvenile Hall.

She wants to say the system is wrong to have given up on you and
shipped you off to adult court, where punishment and retribution are the
goals, that you deserve better. But that would relieve her own anguish, not
Geri's, and so Janet instead says, "I think if the judge can hear everything
you've accomplished here, hon, he'll give you every break he can."

Geri shakes his head. "Who's going to tell him? Not my lawyer."

"I'll tell him," Janet says without hesitation.

Geri stares at her a moment, then slowly nods.

CHAPTER 11

HOP

The beeper rouses Sharon Stegall just in time to see the alarm clock blink from 4:56 to 4:57. Her first thought—a familiar one, which is the real hell of it—is that one of her kids has been shot. Or had shot someone else. "Couldn't be anything else at this hour," she mutters to herself. "Couldn't be."

The number on the beeper confirms it: Hawthorne PD—the 'Thorn, home to some of LA's bloodiest gang wars, kids killing kids, seven dead in the space of a month. Two of Sharon's probationers have died, with another on the run. She had just sent one kid—a witness to one of the murders, street name "Blur"—into hiding in Florida, dodging a contract on his life at age fifteen. "He better turn up soon," one of the teenaged gangbangers stalking him had told Blur's terrified mother a day earlier—shortly after her house had been ventilated by a round of nine millimeters. "One way or another, somebody's gonna die."

Sharon expects that prophesy has just been fulfilled. She dials Hawthorne PD, waiting for someone to pick up, then croaks, "What?" In her circles, this early, niceties are a waste.

"Jefferson, Donny William, aka Li'l Dondi," a man announces, as if he were calling the lineup at a baseball game. The voice belongs to Hawthorne detective Jimmy Royer, a regular in Juvenile Court. "He's one of yours, isn't he, Stegall?"

"Yeah, he's mine," she says. Dondi is one of her probationers, a sixteen-year-old graffiti tagger, Blur's homeboy. He had nothing to do with any of the murders. If anything, he represents a success story in Juvenile Court— still hanging with a street gang, he nevertheless has stayed clean for months. "What about him?"

"Shot in the head at his apartment building by three Hoovers," Royer says, pausing a moment at Sharon's sudden, sharp intake of breath. She had thought she was prepared for it, but you never are. You never get used to children killing children.

"He's not dead, but he might as well be," Royer continues gamely. "Half his head's gone. He's on full life support, brain-dead. But they're still getting a pain response. You know, when they stick a pin in his leg. So they're not ready to pull the plug."

The Hoover Street Crips, a powerhouse among LA's street gangs, had put the contract out on Blur and one of his friends—who, just to confuse matters, was also known on the street as Blur. Sharon had taken to calling him Blur II. The Blurs had been together on Christmas Day when Blur II shot and killed a Hoover who had tried to jump them. Blur II vanished, Sharon's Blur went to hide in Florida, and the Hoovers went hunting. Last night, Royer says, they shot the wrong kid in their zeal for retaliation. Poor, unsuspecting Dondi, whose worst deed in life had been stealing cars and spray-painting freeway overpasses, had put down his Nintendo to answer the door, and walked into an ambush.

"Sweet Jesus," Sharon sighs, rubbing her face with her hands.

Sharon hangs up a short time later, makes some coffee, gets ready for work. This is how all too many of her mornings begin these days. When she started as a probation officer nine years ago, her principal piece of equipment was a notebook and pen, tucked into her handbag with her gold badge. Now she dons a bulletproof vest for the field, a can of Mace and a pair of stainless-steel handcuffs in her purse. Some of her fellow probation officers pack guns in violation of a loosely enforced department policy, but Sharon refuses to take that step. The day she has to use a gun to control her kids, that's the day she'll quit.

A few hours later, she sits in her cubicle at the grimy Centinela Probation Office. Today is client day, a procession of kids marching to her desk all day, with their endless excuses and screwups and, every now and then, tiny triumphs. Li'l Dondi had just been in a week before, a pleasant, husky kid slowly but definitely pulling back from the brink. He had been making it. Now his fate has left Sharon in a foul temper—she had tried to save one kid, *and another had paid the price with his life. It made her want to crawl back into bed and never leave. Instead, when a short, bashful kid named Randy comes in wearing an odd smile and a big chrome belt buckle emblazoned with a gang insignia, Sharon goes ballistic.*

"You gotta be kidding me, Randy," she shouts. "You come in here like this? Wearing that?" She suddenly pushes her face within inches of the boy's and stares at his eyes, pupils huge despite the bright fluorescents. "And you're high, too, aren't you? Aren't you?"

"No, Ms. Stegall, no, I'm not high. I swear." The kid is talking a mile a minute, explaining, absurdly serious, that he wore the gang insignia "because I wanted to be honest with you." In the past, he always took it off for his visits to the cubicle, but that was a form of lying, he says. "I just want you to know what I'm really doin'."

"What you're doing is standing up. Against that wall," Sharon yells. She stands Randy up, pats him down, and handcuffs him on the spot. "You have the right to remain silent, do you understand that? Or are you too high?"

"I'm not high, Ms. Stegall, I swear." But the kid knows it is too late. He wears a stoic, long-suffering expression on his small, smooth face. His ears turn red as Sharon continues her tirade, declaring him in violation of his probation for drug use and gang affiliations. He finally allows that he might have snorted some cocaine, just a little, before coming to his appointment.

"You may not understand this, but I'm trying to save your life. Do you know that?" Sharon says, softly now, intently. "I'm gonna get you off the street and save your life, whether you want me to or not. I'm not gonna have another one of my kids dead. Not today, anyway."

Then she marches him out to a county car, and takes him to Juvenile Hall.

———◆———

SHARON Stegall's branch of the Metro Gang Unit lies in a cheerless maze of a building surrounded by a huge parking lot set far back from a wretched stretch of Imperial Highway, listing like an abandoned scow in a sea of cracked and glass-strewn asphalt. The Centinela Probation Office, where both juvenile and adult probationers mingle together in a gritty waiting room, abuts a massive county welfare office where long lines snake out the door each day. Not even those crowds can fill the county-owned parking lot, however, which could serve a moderate-sized baseball stadium. This hulking place and its destitute environs are where the kids who are wards of the Juvenile Court in Inglewood must come. Each day, they fill up the waiting room, teenage mothers and fathers in their gangster baggies and tattoos, many of them hauling babies of their own, some of the infants and toddlers dressed down like gangsters, too.

The location of this probation office is a convenience for the county, not for the kids and their families — it is a long drive from the Inglewood court, a two-bus odyssey for the majority who rely on public transit. The distance provides a built-in, though unintended, incentive for probationers not to show up. Often, newcomers to the court will be told at 11:00 A.M. to leave Inglewood and to report to their probation officer on Imperial Highway before noon, where they must pick up some crucial piece of paper or provide some critical information in person. When, as is often the case, they cannot make it on time, the probation officer will have already left, and the kid is blamed for violating court orders. Or they come to meet their POs, but must miss school to do so, then get nailed for truancy. This happens daily (except in Judge Dorn's court, where the standing order to POs is to never schedule appointments during school hours, which makes its own set of problems, since probation hours roughly match most schools').

The problem has a simple solution: Move the probation officers. Kids ought to be able to leave a courtroom — or a classroom — and walk down the hall to see their new probation officer, Sharon believes. But such a sensible system has never been considered. It would require an investment of time and manpower the Probation Department increasingly cannot spare. There are probation officers assigned to every Juvenile Court judge, but none of them actually work with kids — they only push papers. They are "liaisons." Visionaries within this massive system talk about the decentralized probation department of the future, flexible, storefront operations scattered throughout the community, so that POs can once again know their charges, families, and neighborhoods, as was the case in the sixties, when most probation officers had twenty kids to supervise instead of two hundred. But the system has done nothing to address this end other than churn out a mountain of studies and proposals that have all the ingredients for success save one: the money to make them work.[1]

Centinela Probation is part of a tired network of offices spread throughout the Los Angeles area. Here, as elsewhere, the crush of cases is enormous, and kids' files — and the kids themselves — can get lost for weeks on someone's desk. The department is reeling from budget cuts and is in what seems to many insiders a permanent state of disarray, with the quality of probation supervision not always what it should be. Squabbles and racial divisiveness have at times reduced the department to warring camps, mirroring the ethnic violence that has polarized the juvenile halls and prisons. Even a softball game between different probation offices recently broke down into a black-on-brown fistfight. A full-time committee was created in recent years to circulate through the various probation offices, settling racial disputes among staff members on a regular basis.

Worse still, though the majority of POs seem to do the best they can in coping with a difficult job, the department at times seems incapable of policing rogues within its ranks. As Sharon tells it, one probation officer in her office fed her false information about a gang contract on her life, then left a threatening message on her answering machine. Several POs have been known to pad their caseloads with juveniles who are dead or imprisoned, lowering their workload while appearing to carry a full complement of probationers. Another is known to frequent strip clubs during business hours. Still others openly carry firearms in defiance of department policy.

On a more mundane level—but one that has a far greater negative impact on the juvenile justice system—probation reports are routinely late in Juvenile Court, with many rife with misspellings and factual errors, sometimes crucial ones. Several juvenile judges have openly questioned the literacy of some probation officers in Los Angeles. Probation officers are supposed to conduct independent investigations, but this is rarely done. Many simply rely on police arrest reports, even when writing presentence reports intended to guide judges in their sentencing decisions, at a time when far more recent—and more accurate—trial testimony is available. (A child may be arrested for armed robbery, for example, but convicted at trial of simple assault, a misdemeanor—yet, in many cases the probation report will be written as if the juvenile in question is an armed robber, because that's what the police reports assert.) Once an error is written into a probation report, it can be repeated many times over, since each writer uses the preceding report in a file for background information. Some errors become enshrined in this way, impossible to discover and ferret out of each and every report. There is little chance to correct some errors: Probation officers sometimes fail to check school records, fail to interview crime victims, fail to visit the homes and families of potential probationers. Thoroughness can often go out the window because juvenile POs in Los Angeles are faced with monumental caseloads that challenge their effectiveness and leave many burned out after a few years on the job.

At any one time in Los Angeles, about seventeen thousand kids are HOP—Home On Probation—the most common resolution to a case in Juvenile Court, not counting the do-nothing option. The results are often disappointing—about a third of kids who go HOP will be rearrested for something new. This accounts for the bulk of serious juvenile crime in LA and nationwide—every one of the chronic offenders found in the Sixteen Percent study was on probation at one point, while continuing to commit crimes. (Still, the results of locking kids up are even more disappointing: Nationally, about three out of every four juveniles incarcerated for their crimes will get arrested again after their release.)[2]

Given those odds, and the fact that Sharon Stegall's fifty probationers have all been locked up at least once before, it is no surprise that most of her kids end up failing. The Randys and the Carlas and the Blurs outnumber the kids who make it, until even the most modest successes begin to seem spectacular to her.

"I passed all my classes this semester," a young man tells her after she returns from locking up Randy the probation violator.

"Proof," the probation officer responds, holding out her hand for the boy's report card. The boy wears a wide, crooked-tooth smile that sheds years from his face. He had been a fugitive for a year, living on the streets, trying to beat a string of car theft charges. Now he's one of Sharon's stars. Still, in her line of work, you take no one's word for anything.

"I'll bring it tomorrow, Ms. Stegall," he promises, and Sharon decides he will do it. There is no faking the look on his face, the aura of accomplishment he is wearing like a halo. This is a kid who had been flunking every subject, including study period, before he was assigned to Sharon's watch. She has encouraged him, bullied him, intimidated him. She brought in his girlfriend so the two could gang up on him, play bad cop, worse cop, urging him to straighten up. On their first day, Sharon had told him she knew he could do better—the first time anyone had suggested this to him—and that she expected him to do so, or else—also a first. Then she had taken him for a ride in her Jaguar sedan. "You drive this?" he had asked. "You own this?" Sharon didn't tell him she had gotten it used at an obscenely low price because its previous owner considered it a lemon and that, in any case, the credit union owned the lion's share of it. What mattered was that it looked like a rich man's car, which was the message she wanted this boy to take home: that hardworking, honest people could live well. You didn't have to steal or deal to do it. The boy was not lazy—he was capable of boosting a dozen cars in a single day—and he got the message. He went to work. Now he is enjoying the payoff.

"You've come a long way," Sharon tells him as he gets up to leave. He has not stopped smiling since his arrival. But then she grabs the boy's hands, arching her right eyebrow at the black grime under his fingernails. "But let me tell you something. You have got to wash your hands and keep those nails clean. When you go to apply for a job somewhere, maybe McDonald's or whatever, the manager is going to look at this paw of yours and say, later, bro."

The boy looks startled at this, then blushes, mumbling something about not having the time to clean up. Sharon nods, trying not to embarrass him, but she knows the real reason for his unkempt appearance: The boy has no father, and his mother has never taken sufficient interest in him to teach him about personal hygiene. He has startling gaps in his knowledge—all Sharon's kids do. It's not their fault. They just don't have any adults in their lives willing to be bothered, much less serve as an example. Some don't know the name of the president. Others wouldn't know the Pledge of Allegiance from a limerick. Many remain ignorant of birth control and AIDS, despite aggressive education programs in LA schools. And this boy doesn't know how to keep himself clean.

"What you do," Sharon says in a completely neutral voice, carefully masking the profound sadness she feels at having to explain such things to a seventeen-year-old, "is go get you a scrub brush and some soap, and you go like this." Sharon makes scrubbing motions over her fingernails and knuckles. The boy watches, engrossed, taking mental notes, and Sharon swallows hard when she sees his earnest, intent expression. "Then you buy one of these little nail clippers," she continues, "they're about fifty cents at the drugstore. . . ."

A short time later, she watches him leave, thinking he has a shot at a decent life, though the pull of his old ways will always be strong, his old friends on the street beckoning. He is not at heart a criminal—though many of her other probationers are, kids with no moral compasses, who don't understand why it is wrong to steal from an innocent stranger or shoot at someone who disses them. That is the other consequence of growing up without any caring adults in your life—you may end up learning nothing about empathy. In the end, you may be unable to experience another person's joy or sadness or grief. There is only your own need, and fuck anyone who gets in the way—a perfect predator, but a lousy human being. Sociopaths are made, not born, it seems to Sharon, and in children, the results are frightening—kids who not only have no concept of right and wrong, but who don't care.

Sharon's probationer with the dirty nails knows the difference, though. He just needed someone to take an interest, to expect something more than failure from him, to hold his feet to the fire. To fill in the gaps. Once in a while, for Sharon, it is that simple.

But on this day, she feels none of the satisfaction a thriving probationer normally brings her, for she has learned anew today just how fleeting success can be in her business. Carla James is in lockup, on her way to who knows what. And poor Li'l Dondi is even worse off. He had been in a week earlier, doing fine, speaking about his new job, sporting a new leather coat, shyly talking about the girlfriend who pushed him to stay straight. It had been an ordinary, uneventful, mildly positive conversation, no hint of what was to come. He had sat there with his leg crossed casually, a kid Sharon was slowly but surely pulling back from the precipice. He had started thinking about the future, in small but clear ways, a pleasant, husky teenager who had been vaguely surprised when Sharon pointed out that he had stayed straight for an entire year for the first time since he was eleven years old. Then he had smiled with pride at the observation. "Gonna stay that way, too," he promised.

"But you're still hangin' with the same old crew, aren't you?" Sharon had asked. "Still got those same friends tryin' to drag you back down."

Dondi had nodded and shrugged. The judges always order kids to cut off ties with their old gangs and crime partners, but POs rarely try to enforce this condition for probationers who are otherwise doing well. Half those seventeen thousand juvenile probationers in LA would have to be locked up if they did. How do you go Home On Probation without going home?

"You know how it is, Ms. Stegall," Li'l Dondi had said less than a week before a bullet cut his brain in two. "You in, you in for life."

The rest of client day is a mix of good and bad. A girl comes in and reveals she is going to junior college, an unexpected and pleasant surprise. The next girl due in calls to say she is pregnant and won't be coming. Two boys fail to show up for their appointments. A teenager who swears he has quit his gang—"Those people scare me," he vows—says he is now afraid to go to school because he has no protection. He just stays home and watches television all day. Then another kid, nicknamed Poindexter because he is such a studious straight-arrow, shows up for his first appointment with Sharon after being convicted of carrying a gun to school.

"Why are you here?" Sharon asks, after looking over his record. He is an

A-student with no cuts, suspensions, or any other indicator of delinquency on his record. He has never been in trouble.

"Because I had a gun," he mumbles, staring at his shoe tops.

"Why?"

"Because I was afraid."

Sharon nods. He is no gangbanger. He is no sociopath. He got the gun from his mother's boyfriend, because he had been pushed around, beaten, and threatened so many times at school, he didn't know what else to do. He is deeply ashamed of having broken the law. But now the pressure on him to join a gang for protection—or to carry a weapon again—will be even more enormous, and there isn't a lot Sharon can do, except get him into another school and hope for the best. He is in the seventh grade.

Later, a stooped man with salt and pepper hair, leaning heavily on a cane, comes in alone to see Sharon. He supports four children on a cafeteria worker's $460 monthly wage. His oldest son is on juvenile probation. He sighs repeatedly as he apologizes in halting English to Sharon, then pulls from his pants pocket a crumpled plastic Baggie with three rocks of cocaine inside. "I wasn't sure what this was," he says. "I found it in Jesus's room, and my wife and I are worried. I think it's drugs."

Sharon grabs the bag and tells the man, "Yes, it's drugs. Very bad drugs. It's a good thing you didn't get stopped on the way over here." She is shaking her head. She likes this man, but his son, who entered the system at age sixteen and has since turned eighteen, is another story. He's a pleasant-enough kid, but he has sticky fingers. He smiled his way onto informal probation for a burglary two years earlier, then got arrested for stealing a car (case dismissed for lack of a witness willing to come to court), then got arrested again for grand theft after he and a friend brazenly walked out of a department store with five hundred dollars' worth of clothes piled in their arms. He got probation and, after working with another PO, was recently reassigned to Sharon's caseload.

By the time she got him, he had missed thirty school days in the past two months, failed to perform the eighty hours of community service attached as a condition of his probation ("I just didn't feel like it," he later tells Sharon—after she busts him), and he had refused to obey his parents, disappearing for four days. He had just returned, filthy and hung over. The Probation Department remained unaware of all this—his last probation officer had done no supervision and had told Sharon he was doing fine. Now here was Jesus's dad with a bag of crack and a desperate look on his face.

Sharon leaves the office a short time later, finds Jesus at home, handcuffs him, reads him his rights, and hauls him off to Juvenile Hall on a probation violation. He is angry and defiant, furious at his father, at Sharon, at the system he always assumed he would beat.

Later, though, when she sees him after a week in the hall, he seems transformed—calm, relaxed, almost playful. He isn't mad at his father anymore for turning him in. Instead, he says he feels almost relieved. "I needed to chill. Things were getting too crazy on The Outs."

"Isn't it sad these kids have to be locked up to become kids again?" Sharon muses later. "Out on the street, they walk the walk, they talk the talk, they harden over like rocks. But in the hall, there's no drive-bys, no peer pressure, they can relax. And they turn into little boys again. Until they get back out. Then it starts all over. It's so damn sad."

Twenty-five years ago, when Los Angeles's Watts ghetto neighborhoods erupted in riots, Sharon Stegall was a sixteen-year-old girl surveying the rubble that had been the grocery story where she had worked after school. As she stood there astride her bicycle, gaping at the desolation, a policeman suddenly appeared, gun drawn, shouting, "For the flip of a quarter, nigger bitch, I'd blow your head off."

She never knew if the cop took her to be a looter, or if he was simply motivated by a racist hatred. But she survived that day, though it colors her work as a probation officer—she knows her kids face the same sort of situations even now, children for whom violence appears from all sides, children for whom there are no good guys. The neighborhoods are war zones. Gangs lay claim to them. Policemen eye them not as kids, but as potential threats. They all know what "Assume the position" means, without having to see it in movies or on TV. Sharon visits her probationers and sees their little brothers and sisters playing not house or doctor or fireman, but drug dealer, crack house, and bank robber—their heroes and role models. Little kids actually standing there passing play money and bogus rocks of cocaine to one another over the counter, then pretending to smoke or shoot. She has seen this with her own eyes, this last gasp of childhood fantasy, modeled after the most successful adults on the block.

By the time these kids end up on Sharon's caseload, their ability to play and imagine can be completely destroyed. She sees it every day, the anger that wells up in some of her probationers when she asks them where they'll be in five years. They balk at the question, refuse to answer, but when she pushes them, all too many say, "Dead. Okay? Can I go now?"

There's the problem, Sharon figures. Most of her kids have no imagination left. They have no play in them, no power to see possibilities beyond the moment. And if you can see no future, if you expected to be dead by age twenty-one, what was the point of caring about anything? What was the point of having a conscience or feeling sorry for anyone you hurt if you were terminally ill? Sharon's probationers—like the kids Sister Janet meets in the hall—tell her that all the time, that it doesn't matter what they do, because they are, in essence, dead already. And this hopelessness, this living death, does not stop in the barrios and ghettos—she and her colleagues hear the same thing from the rich suburban kids, from children of privilege, even from the sons of two Juvenile Court bench officers. This is what makes so many of the kids of Juvenile Court so incredibly hard, so resistant to reform. This is what concerns Sharon the most.

And so she sees a good part of her job as rekindling in her kids a more wholesome ability to imagine, to grasp at a brighter future—giving them back something that should be innate. She tries to show them a different side of the system, a new realm of possibilities—that a black woman from Watts once threatened by a policeman's gun simply because of her race could go on to work as a federal park ranger and forester at Yosemite, as she had before becoming a probation officer. She tells them to drive down a certain street where they can see the name Stegall on a school building— her mother, an honored former teacher, had an entire school named after her, she informs them with pride. She talks to kids who have never strayed from their barrios about how she has traveled the world, started her own business. She shows them that Jaguar she drives. "I've done things these kids can only dream of," Sharon says, then corrects herself. "No, I've done things these kids *can't* dream of. That's what I'm up against. That's what I try to change."

It is what she almost finished doing with Li'l Dondi. It is what she is desperately trying to do with Carla James.

The courtroom is half full as Commissioner Gary Polinsky tries to sort through his clogged calendar. Sharon sits in the jury box waiting for her violation cases to be called—Jesus with his bag of crack and worried dad, and Carla James, with her tattooed stomach and infuriating resistance to change. The first case with Jesus should be an easy one, but Carla has charmed this Juvenile Court commissioner before. Sharon is worried she'll pull off another successful manipulation of the system.

First, though, there is an arraignment to be held. Sharon watches with interest as Polinsky tells his bailiff to bring out a fifteen-year-old boy named Kelvin Smith, known on the street as Doughnut, a classic repeat offender long ignored by the system, with ten arrests since age eleven for theft, burglary, battery, and trespass. The Sixteen Percenter pattern holds true in his case: Most of the early charges invariably were dismissed or dropped or led to minimal probation, allowing him to continue hanging with the Hoover Street Crips gang he idolized, committing more crimes, becoming a child with no imagination, one of LA's living dead. He could barely read at the second-grade level.

After his eighth arrest, Doughnut had finally landed in probation camp, where he failed miserably but was still released after five months to make room for older, more serious offenders. One day later, he stole a car and was arrested driving it. Yet, once again, despite his long record, he was released, still on probation, though he had never in four years obeyed a single probation condition or court order. His record was such a jumble, and his offenses sufficiently "minor," the system just couldn't find time to deal with Doughnut.

Now, six months later, his car theft charge still unresolved, he is back in court, this time accused of participating in the ambush of Sharon's probationer, Li'l Dondi. The Juvenile Court's abject failure had shot down one of its budding successes. Time for the system to pay attention to Doughnut.

At the moment, life support machines continue to keep Li'l Dondi's heart and lungs going, so the charge against Doughnut remains attempted homicide. But the first-degree murder papers have already been drawn up and are sitting in Peggy Beckstrand's office, waiting to be filed the moment Dondi dies, an epitaph for a sixteen-year-old written in advance of the inevitable. Seeing those papers gave Sharon chills, like seeing a tombstone carved for someone still living.

Slouching in a seat in the middle of the gallery is a tall, ponytailed man in a nylon baseball jacket. He is talking quietly with a woman whose face is contorted in anguish. The man is Hawthorne Police Detective James Royer, who beeped Sharon with the news about Li'l Dondi, and who later helped arrest and interrogate Doughnut. Sharon figures at first that the grieving woman must be Dondi's mother, but it turns out she is *Doughnut*'s mother. She ought to be furious with Royer for bringing her son in, but she has no one else to turn to in this place—no lawyer to represent her interests, no familiar faces, nothing but fear of the unknown. In Juvenile Court, the defense lawyers represent the kids, not the parents. The defenders even instruct kids to refuse to talk about their cases with their mothers and fathers, for fear they could be subpoenaed by the prosecution and forced to testify (unlike the marital privilege that protects spouses from incriminating one another, there is no matching parental privilege). Nor can parents participate in any discussions between lawyer and child, even when decisions are made about strategies that will profoundly affect a child's future—an ultimate irony in a court designed to bring families together. So Mrs. Smith has only Detective Royer to turn to.

In Hawthorne, he has a reputation as a fair man and a good cop, the sort who goes out of his way to help kids and families when he can, who tries to line up jobs for gang members who tire of the street life and who would gladly go straight if they could find any alternatives. Mrs. Smith views the system as so unfriendly that she is drawn to the man who arrested her son as her only ally. She is a single mother with two jobs and an abiding anger at a Juvenile Court she considers more an accomplice than a deterrent to her son's deliquency. Now, after so many years of inaction, she complains, the system wants to hammer her boy.

"How can they charge my son with doing the shooting?" she asks Royer, her voice a trembling monotone.

"It's called the felony murder rule," the detective explains. "Like when someone sticks up a liquor store and shoots someone, the getaway driver gets charged, too."

"But he didn't shoot anybody," Mrs. Smith complains. She already knew from Royer that only the two adult gang members with Doughnut actually pulled their triggers. Doughnut was armed with a handgun and present at the ambush of Li'l Dondi, but he never fired.

"I know he didn't shoot, but he was still involved," Royer tells the mother gently. "He's still responsible."

Mrs. Smith searches Royer's eyes then, pleading with him for some sliver of hope. "But how do you know?"

Royer shrugs apologetically. "Because he told me."

The woman grasps at one final straw, though her tone of voice makes it clear even she does not believe what she is suggesting. "Maybe he lied?"

Royer shakes his head sadly, as if to say he wished it were so. "Why would he lie? If he were going to lie, he would tell it the other way." He sees Mrs. Smith nodding slightly, accepting it, accepting that her son is part of a murder. She looks ashen. Royer clears his throat and whispers, "Look at it this way. He's fifteen. Good thing for him. It's a premeditated death penalty case for an adult, but the worst that can happen to him is ten years. Consider him lucky."

Mrs. Smith turns away, staring at the metal door her son will soon be walking through to enter the courtroom. She doesn't look as if she feels very lucky. She speaks again to the detective. "He's so scared, he has to have his night light on at night. What does that tell you?"

"I know what's in his heart," Royer agrees. "In his heart, he's not a killer. But he did it anyway. In the interrogation, I told him I knew he hadn't shot. He didn't even know how to use that gun. He didn't even know if it was loaded. So I said, 'I know you didn't want to kill that boy. Why'd you do it?' And he says, 'I didn't want to look punked out in front of my homeboys.'" It is a common explanation for juvenile murders, and a prime reason Los Angeles saw nearly eight hundred killings by street gangs in the past year.

Doughnut's mother shakes her head then, eyes closed. She doesn't know what is worse: that her son could be in such trouble, or that somehow her own flesh and blood had gone so wrong that he believed the lesser of two evils was to participate in a murder rather than risk being jeered at by his friends. She is a young woman with smile lines in the corners of her mouth, but pain has etched new furrows in her face. Without looking at Royer, she asks very quietly, "How old was the guy who got shot?" She winces when Royer answers, "Sixteen."

"The kid's brain-dead," Royer says. "Sooner or later, it's going to be a murder charge." He touches her shoulder until she looks him in the eye again. "Listen, if he tells the truth, he might get a deal, maybe he can get in some kind of facility and learn something. Otherwise, he'll go to CYA till he's twenty-five and come out a hardened gangster. They say it's supposed to rehabilitate, but bottom line is, it's prison. It's not going to help him. You don't want that to happen."

"I told him that," Mrs. Smith says. By her tone of voice, two things are clear: One, she trusts Royer on this, even though it is exactly the sort of thing cops always say to coax a confession; and, two, her son will not listen to her. He may not be a murderer at heart, but neither will he inform on his home boys. One of the reasons gangs recruit fifteen-year-olds like him to participate in capital crimes is their irrevocable status as juveniles. Doughnut cannot go to adult court. His homeboys will expect him to be a stand-up guy, protecting the two adults who could face death sentences.

When his case is called and he is brought in for arraignment, Doughnut doesn't do himself much good. He spots his mother sitting with the detective and refuses to look at her again. The hearing is brief, consisting of a reading of the charges, a determination by Commissioner Polinsky that Doughnut should remain detained, and the appointment of an attorney after the public defender declares a conflict of interest in the case, having represented Li'l Dondi in the past. Throughout, Doughnut scowls, mutters angrily to himself, shifting impatiently in his seat.

Polinsky spots Doughnut mouthing an obscenity at the detention order. "Your client seems unhappy," Polinsky angrily tells the newly appointed attorney. "He doesn't seem to realize he is in here only by the grace of his age. This is going to take time, and he is not going to be released." The commissioner then addresses the boy directly. "Do you understand?"

Chastened, Doughnut mumbles, "Yes, sir." For the first time, he looks worried, as if it has just struck him that this time, his journey through the system will be a very different one. He has just realized that, even though he cannot be sent to an adult court or prison, ten years' imprisonment in the California Youth Authority is a very long time.

A few moments later, he is escorted back to lockup. His mother waves, but he still will not acknowledge her, fear and defiance battling for control of his face. Sharon is glad to see Polinsky in a bad mood—she figures he will be less likely to fall for Carla's glib charm today. As far as she is concerned, cases like Doughnut's are a colossal waste of time, money, and effort because there is really no question where he will end up. There is an eyewitness and a confession. After six months or a year of delays, he will be convicted and go to CYA until he is twenty-five, or close to it. There is no other option for a fifteen-year-old accomplice to murder.

"It's just the system spinnin' its wheels," she mutters under her breath. The cops and lawyers sitting with her in the jury box say nothing, sitting there in stalwart silence, oblivious to the too-familiar spectacle unfolding before them.

She listens as Detective Royer tells Polinsky about another case he has coming up that day—a sixteen-year-old forced by his mother and stepfather to sell cocaine. The kid's dealing supports their drug habits, pays the rent, buys the groceries, he says. They encourage him to skip school. They even got him a gun to carry to protect his stash and their profits. Royer can make a case in Juvenile Court against the boy—the kid practically turned himself in, so desperate was he to escape his home—but the detective can't get the adult court DA to prosecute the parents for child endangerment. Insufficient evidence, he was told. And the kicker is, he says, for the last year, this kid was on probation, supposedly supervised by the court and a PO. Yet no one ever visited the home to see how he was doing.

"The kid's a classic victim," Royer complains. "And he's the only one that pays."

It's the kind of story that makes Sharon ashamed to admit what she does for a living.

Carla James is led in next. As Sharon rises to recite her violations for the court record, the probation officer is gripped by the overwhelming premonition that, in watching Doughnut's case, she has just witnessed an all-too-plausible preview of Carla's fate. Unless something is done here and now, she decides, Carla is going to end up charged with murder herself, bound for a long term of imprisonment like Doughnut. Either that, or the next time Sharon's beeper goes off at four in the morning, it's going to be tolling Carla's death, just as it had Li'l Dondi's.

"This young lady is out of control, Your Honor," Sharon tells Commissioner Polinsky, urgency in her voice. "She needs to be restrained."

Polinsky leafs through Sharon's report on Carla, then sees the Polaroid snapshot of the tattoo. He slams the file down and Carla, who had come in smiling, starts at the sound. He cuts off her explanations about it being her body, along with her sudden suggestion that she intends to have it surgically removed.

"You have come to the wrong court today, young lady," the commissioner rails, eyes still wide behind his horn-rim glasses. "I have had it up to here."

Carla watches as Polinsky returns to studying her file, each page turning with a sharp crackle of paper. The file is shaking in the judge's hands, he is so agitated—Carla has never seen this side of him before. She was used to being treated like a teacher's pet in Polinsky's courtroom, and had been expecting a mild admonishment and a sentence back to camp. Camp doesn't worry her: She'd have plenty of friends there, and she'd be running the place again soon enough, she figures, like always. But then Polinsky surprises her.

"You know, I could just commit you to CYA right now. I have more than four years over your head. You've had more than enough chances to succeed, and I'm not sure what else to do with you."

Carla stares at him openmouthed. She has heard stories about CYA. Carla's lawyer is sputtering. Even Sharon is astonished. Six months in camp was the most she had hoped for. This does not sound like Commissioner Polinsky, who very seldom sends any but the most egregious, unrepentant failures to youth prison, and who had counted on Carla to become a bright spot on an otherwise depressing caseload.

But like many others in the Los Angeles juvenile system, Polinsky is frustrated by the paucity of options for sentencing kids. For the privileged few who have parents willing and able to pay for out-of-county or even out-of-state treatment programs, where the cost can run into the thousands very quickly, there are special college prep programs with locked campuses, wilderness programs, secure drug and alcohol programs, therapeutic schools tailor-made to fit certain kids' needs—the possibilities are nearly endless. Judge Dorn is currently entertaining a proposal to sentence a young arsonist into a private program in another state—a kid who, had his father not been a wealthy physician, would have ended up in CYA. For kids with money behind them, justice—at least when it comes to sentencing—is for sale.

But for the vast majority of children sentenced in Los Angeles Juvenile Court—the Doughnuts and the Carlas and the Ronald Duncans—the county must foot the bill. And there are just four basic sentences for them.

There is HOP, by far the most common result in the thirty thousand delinquency cases brought to court each year. There is "suitable placement," a network of public and private foster homes supervised by the Probation Department and reserved for about twenty-three hundred mostly nonviolent kids who cannot live with—or do not have—parents. Kids who are runaway risks usually cannot go to suitable placement—there is no security. Then there are the twenty-six detention camps run by the Probation Department for forty-four hundred kids in a variety of rural settings from the desert to Malibu—locked, rigorous facilities that are good at keeping gangbangers in line while they are inside, but not designed for kids with emotional, learning, or psychological problems, or drug or alcohol dependencies. (This is something of an oddity, since most juvenile delinquents have precisely these problems.)[3] And the fourth and final option within the juvenile system is the California Youth Authority, the state's massive system of juvenile prisons, the largest in the nation, where rehabilitation is the nominal mission for its eighty-seven hundred "wards," but where gang wars, race riots, stabbings, and rapes are regular afflictions, mirroring, albeit to a smaller degree, the nightmarish world of America's adult prisons.[4]

With few exceptions, every peg has to be fit into one of these four basic holes. The nagging problem with the first three options offered by the LA system is that they are all short-term solutions at best. Sooner or later, they all dump the child back in the same environment where their criminal behavior began in the first place—the same gang-infested streets in the inner city, the same dysfunctional home in the suburbs, or the same abusive,

drug-addicted, or ineffectual parents. Follow-up supervision, once intensive, has been cut back or eliminated. Consequently, the failure rate is very
high. The fourth option, the California Youth Authority, can postpone this
inevitable return for years—but imprisonment is viewed as the juvenile
system's last resort, the last stop for kids beyond reach. Every kid that goes
to CYA is an admission by the Juvenile Court that it has failed.[5] And the
recidivism rate is even higher than for the first three options.

"You have been given every opportunity to succeed," Commissioner Po-
linsky tells Carla. "And it's not like you don't have the brains, or the ability.
We know you do, which just makes matters worse. You have no excuse.
You are making these choices, understanding full well what you are doing.
So you are going to CYA."

Then, seeing he has sufficiently terrified the girl—Carla's eyes are wide,
disbelieving—he adds these words: "For a ninety-day evaluation."

He had no intention of actually committing the girl to CYA—he just
wanted her attention. For the time being, he says, he will postpone sentencing while she submits to psychological and social examination at CYA
to help him choose the best possible sentence for her. In truth, he has
already made up his mind on what that should be; the real purpose of
Carla's CYA trip is to give her a look at where she could end up if she
continues to commit crimes. Polinsky wants to show Carla exactly where
her next felony will bring her.

"We'll see you in three months," the commissioner says. "Then perhaps
we can figure out what to do with you."

By coincidence of court orders and backlogged dockets, Geri Vance, Elias
Elizondo, and Carla James all end up at CYA for their evaluations at the
same time. The boys go to one of the state's two large reception centers
for processing new inmates, this one located in Norwalk, in southern LA
County.

Elias returns first. Even though his plea bargain bars him from being
committed as a juvenile, he can still be housed at CYA for the first half
of his fifteen-to-life sentence—if CYA will accept him. But he blows the
mandatory ninety-day evaluation, repeatedly disobeying orders from the
staff, lying about his background, and ending his stay by getting into a fight
with a gang member from Northern California (Hispanic gangs from the
two ends of California are traditional enemies). CYA wouldn't even keep
him the full three months—they sent him back to Central Juvenile Hall
in chains. Elias has erased the initial positive impression he had brought

with him—that he was a bright, sensitive kid with only one violent crime on his record and a huge potential for rehabilitation—and replaced it with the image of a gang-entrenched troublemaker unwilling to let go of his criminal values for even three months, when his entire future was at stake. His CYA caseworker—having received numerous letters and calls from the mother of the man killed by Elias's gang—writes a profoundly negative report about him to the court, making a direct sentence to adult prison almost certain. Why should CYA take a chance on Elias, the caseworker suggested, when all its facilities are overcrowded, and there are plenty of other kids willing to at least try to do better in order to stay out of the penitentiary?

Back at the hall to await his now inevitable sentence, Elias admits to Sister Janet he deliberately sabotaged himself at CYA, wanting to end up in prison so he could hunt down and exact revenge upon a killer. Just before leaving for CYA, he had learned that his beloved grandmother, who raised him and who tried, if unsuccessfully, to shield him from older uncles and cousins who led lives of crime, had been murdered by an in-law. All he could think about was finding and killing this man—especially after probation authorities refused to allow him to marry the teenaged mother of his daughter, Ashley, in a Juvenile Hall ceremony. These two back-to-back events had devastated Elias, capping a year and a half of tragedy in his life that began with a friend shot to death outside school, a boy who crumpled to the sidewalk and died in Elias's arms. A short time after that, Elias's best friend died in a drive-by shooting outside a convenience store. Just before his arrest, Elias's infant nephew succumbed to crib death (Elias memorialized him by having "Baby Stevie" tattooed on the back of his neck). Then came the night of robbery and murder that put him behind bars.

Too late, he has realized just how irrational it was to think he could go to prison and find his grandmother's killer. California has dozens of prisons and 120,000 inmates, more than any other state, more than most nations of the world. He would never see his grandmother's killer. All he had done was make things infinitely worse for himself, and for his family. Instead of a youth facility near Los Angeles—and near his daughter, his one remaining connection to the outside world unsullied by gangs and crime—Elias could well be sent hundreds of miles away.

Geri Vance has an entirely different experience during his ninety days. He goes to Norwalk determined to shine, knowing he is about to have what amounts to an audition—one that will determine the course of his life. It pays off: He earns excellent reviews from his caseworker and the team that analyzes him. They say they have no doubt that he would benefit from serving his sentence in a juvenile facility, and that he shows more promise and interest in reform than at any time in his life.

Geri returns jubilant, but with his own mixed reviews of the CYA system. He enjoyed the privileges there that outstrip those available in Juvenile Hall—the right to avoid school, to have radios and cassette players in your room, the ability to watch more television. But he also witnessed beatings and gang fights. There were several stabbings and assaults. He says he overheard two boys being raped in his unit during his three months there, crimes that were never reported to the staff—the prison code of silence and the mortal dangers squealers can face firmly in place. As in adult prison, kids are pressured to join gangs to avoid being preyed upon. The CYA corrections officers are armed with burning pepper spray to quell disturbances, and an incapacitating tear gas developed for the military called CS. (Indeed, some facilities have tear gas dispensers for mass spraying installed in their exercise yards to quell riots; more than twenty-seven hundred kids are sprayed a year at CYA facilities.) Whenever kids resist orders or threaten violence, an in-house team of burly corrections officers the kids call the "Ninja Turtles" because of their stocking masks come charging in and physically restrain the offenders. "Someone always ends up in the infirmary with something broken when they come," Geri tells the writing class upon his return.

"After a while, you start to see, everyone's just hanging out, they don't want to go to school, things pop over every little thing. The racial tension is tremendous. And if you don't hang with your own, the word gets around like that. You get a jacket, and it follows you all over the system. Then everyone's after you. So you're gonna have to take a side sooner or later. A coupla years, you can get by. But I'm afraid about staying there too long. How do you keep from becoming a part of it? From becoming institutionalized?" So many of the kids here seem to know this jargonesque word, and to fear it.

His best hope, Geri says, is getting committed to CYA, then transferred to its Ventura facility north of LA, where there is a four-year college program and a facility that tends to be less violent and war-torn by gang strife. Now it's up to his judge.

Ventura is also where CYA houses its small population of hard-core girl criminals, and this milder setting is where Carla goes for her three months' evaluation. (Out of 8,664 CYA inmates, only 282 are girls—a mere 3.2 percent of the total. This male domination of serious juvenile crime is documented in countless studies, including LA's analysis of the Sixteen Percenters, which found that girls make up only 6 percent of the worst repeat offenders.)[6]

Like Geri, Carla James also impressed the staff at CYA as a good student and worker. But whereas Geri was perceived as a young man genuinely interested in changing his life, Carla came across as less than sincere. "This is a very charming, pleasant, courteous and respectful youngster. She is responsive and cooperative, as nice as any youngster could possibly be, very sweet and personable," one psychiatrist assigned to her case wrote. But then he continued, "She is not candid, seems to be rather manipulative, and is rather marked in her denials. . . . Carla paints herself as being a follower who allows others to tell her what to do. There may be an element of truth to this. At least it is so when they tell her to do things she wants to do."

The analysis of Carla, in short, is right on the money as far as Sharon and a few others who know her well are concerned—though it adds nothing that wasn't already clear about Carla for years. And when it comes time to recommend what to do with her, the CYA evaluators are even less helpful. Their suggestions—after three months of supposedly intense diagnostic work, consist of such bromides as:

"She needs to take responsibility for her own choices."

"She needs to acquire a sense of empathy with those she victimizes."

"She needs to break off from gang affiliations and from gang-type thinking."

"She needs to acquire better companions."

"She needs to learn to become scrupulously honest with other people."

The conclusion at the end of this laundry list: "She has a long way to go."

These recommendations are little more than a wish list, and they could apply to just about any delinquent. Included in this prescription are no specific suggestions on how these goals might be accomplished—goals that, taken together, would constitute nothing less than a cure for juvenile delinquency, if not all crime. After all, if every criminal empathized with victims, chose better friends, took responsibility for their lives, and were honest, they would never break the law.

The only concrete recommendation in the report is that Carla should go to a closed and secure facility with a structured program, but one less severe than CYA. In other words, she should go back to camp—which has already failed to achieve any of the goals the CYA evaluators listed. But it is exactly what Carla wanted to hear.

Not that she would have minded staying at CYA. To her surprise, Carla found her stay in the Ventura institution far less intimidating than the stories she had heard about the place from her fellow gang members, whose experiences were limited to the system's more hard-core male facilities. "There's nothing there that scares me," she tells Sharon Stegall breezily upon her return, Polinsky's scare tactic having failed miserably. "I can do my time there standing on my head, no problem."

But Commissioner Polinsky surprises Carla one more time. Left with no usable, practical guidance after the three-month study, he goes on instinct alone, choosing to reject both CYA and camp for Carla. Instead, he sends her to a place called the Dorothy Kirby Center. A small, county-run program, it is one of the few options available in Los Angeles Juvenile Court that falls outside the four basic sentences.

Dorothy Kirby is a secure compound of ten cottages where kids live, work, go to school, and take part in an intensive, daily program of group therapy designed to change their behavior, their aspirations, their ability to imagine the future—to soften them up.

"If they can't do something with you," Polinsky tells her, "I don't know who can."

Carla must wait two more months in Juvenile Hall for a slot to open up in the small, much-in-demand Dorothy Kirby program (there are one hundred beds in the program, but a demand that could fill a thousand or more). She does not look forward to trading her comfortable position of top dog on her unit at the hall for an uncertain future at Kirby, though nothing can quite stem this girl's confidence and optimism. Though conciliatory during a follow-up visit with Sharon—one of the few people who seems to thoroughly intimidate Carla—the girl tells a different story once her probation officer is out of earshot.

"I think I'd prefer CYA as far as a place to live," she says after court, relaxing in the dayroom at Juvenile Hall. "Kirby is for psychos, and I'm no psycho. But the thing is, at Kirby, I'll be out in eight months, instead of three years or something at YA. What can happen in eight months?" She sits back and smiles broadly, already anticipating her return to the streets. She knows the juvenile system's secret: Programs like Kirby work only for kids who *want* to change. Otherwise, it's just a detour. "I just have to stay strong," Carla says.

After months of anticipation, Carla's big move finally comes. Kirby is not what she expected. The county van brings her to a ragged corner of a less than aptly named LA suburb, the City of Commerce, and deposits her at a walled campus of red brick buildings tucked next to a buzzing freeway. Carla gets a small room in one of the ten dormitories at Kirby, a building with a sign that says Amber Cottage, which she shares with nine other girls. Each cottage is named for a gem or semiprecious stone. At Amber, most of Carla's housemates are also gang members—one carjacker, two car thieves, one armed robber, three girls convicted of assault and battery, one probation violator who had her first child at age twelve, and one girl, like Carla, convicted of assault with a deadly weapon, though her offense was very different. (She is a hallucinatory schizophrenic honors student who tried to kill her sister with a machete, then threatened to slit her own throat with the heavy blade before police subdued her with a stun gun. The Dorothy Kirby staff initially declined to accept her, but Judge Dorn, as he often does, ordered them to take the girl anyway.)

Founded in 1961 as the Las Palmas School for Girls, the facility was renamed for its founder and made coed in the seventies, and now houses forty girls and sixty boys in its ten cottages. Every weekday, the Dorothy Kirby one hundred exercise, go to school, make and serve their own meals, and clean house. Then they go to work.

"Work" at Dorothy Kirby means working in group therapy sessions, once a day with a counselor and the other kids in the cottage, plus one night a week with parents, plus regular weekly sessions with visiting psychologists or psychiatrists for individual therapy. Calling this "going to work" is a deliberate choice of terminology with a familiar, though very different, meaning for gangbangers: Embarking on drive-bys, fighting with rival gangs, and pulling robberies and other gang "jobs" are often referred to as "putting in work."

"But the kind of work we do here," Rahman Shabazz, the counselor in charge of Amber Cottage, tells his girls, "is a lot harder than anything you've ever done on the streets. Going to work in group takes real courage."

As a Dorothy Kirby resident, Carla has been temporarily transferred from Sharon's caseload to Shabazz's care—that's how the kids address him, simply as Shabazz. He is a combination social worker–probation officer, as are each of the cottage directors at Kirby, a soft-spoken man with an easy smile that belies a long experience with the streets and its by-products. He comes across compassionate and supportive, and Carla instantly figures him for a potential ally who will want her to succeed—and who, therefore, would be vulnerable to being conned. Shabazz smiles and nods when Carla tells him how she plans to quit her gang, have her belly tattoo removed, go to college, and become a lawyer. "Sounds great," he tells her mildly. "Sounds like you got it all figured out."

"That's right," Carla says, looking her new PO in the eye. "I do."

But then Carla begins going to group—going to work—and she finds both Shabazz, as well as the other girls, not so easy after all. They seem ready to call her on her extravagant claims, pointing out that she has made such promises before and failed to carry them out. To her chagrin, the group tries to force her into corners she has never been backed into before. She grows angry and sullen after a few weeks of this, and Shabazz is well pleased at having struck a nerve. It is a pattern he is used to seeing. All the kids come in thinking they can put one over on the staff. Then they get angry when Shabazz pushes them and challenges them, forcing them to see themselves through other perspectives.

"These kids hate that"—he laughs—"because it means they have to be honest with themselves, and that hurts more than a bullet. . . . Here, they think it's going to be easy, that it's no boot camp here. But I make them submit themselves. I test their patience, their tolerance, I watch what they like and what they want to do, and challenge them to work for those things, to think about the future, to make it happen. It's a mental boot camp. Physical hardships don't faze a lot of these kids." He pauses to tap the side of his head with a long finger. "But challenge them here . . . and you can get results."

Once this process of criticism and self-examination begins, one of two things happens: A kid shuts down and refuses to work, and they leave Kirby no better off than when they arrived; or they start to see new possibilities—"running a good program," the kids call it. It's about a fifty-fifty split, maybe a little better, Shabazz figures. And there's always a turning point where—seemingly—he can tell which way it will go for a kid.

Carla's moment comes fairly early in her stay at Kirby, on a day when Shabazz shows a movie to the girls of Amber Cottage, an after-school special about a kid being terrorized at school by a bully. The protagonist decides to get a gun for protection, but ends up shooting himself while trying to fish it out of his school bag when the bully next approaches him. The boy is permanently paralyzed.

Reaction in the group is predictable. Several girls think the boy's decision to get a gun was reasonable, but that only fools shoot themselves.

Others, particularly Carla, think he didn't make enough of an effort to fight back with his fists in his earliest encounters with the bully. "I'd have bombed," she says, street slang for a pummeling attack with fists and any other weapons on hand.

"What about saying you're sorry?" Shabazz asks. "What about talking about it, reasoning, finding out what the source of the conflict is? There's usually some reason these things get started. Why not just apologize for it?"

Carla looks at him in astonishment. "Sorry doesn't work where I live," she says with contempt. "You got to earn respect. Sorry is backing down when you need to stand tall."

Shabazz nods his little nod, the one that signals not agreement, but amusement, as if he knows exactly what someone is thinking. Carla has seen that nod a lot lately. "So bombing is always a better way, then? That's the only way you can ever be strong? You don't think turning away from it takes another kind of strength?"

Carla sneers, but remains silent. Shabazz then tells the group about two former residents of Amber Cottage, Virginia and Claudia. Claudia had been a hard-core gangbanger from one of LA's oldest Latino gangs, White Fence, which can trace its origins back to the thirties, and whose members are third, even fourth generation. Claudia came to Kirby on car theft and weapons charges, her whole identity wrapped up in her barrio and her gang—a carbon copy of Carla, tough, smart, resistant to change. She just wanted to do her time, she announced on her arrival, then return to her gang. She didn't even bother to put up a pretense of cooperation, as Carla has.

But, Shabazz tells the group, over time, Claudia decided there were ways to be strong she had never thought of before—like refusing to be sucked into warfare over insults and turf and what neighborhood someone happens to be from. She realized that for her, gangbanging had been the easy way out, a way of avoiding real challenges, real tests of strengths, of compensating for a messed-up and violent family at home with an even more messed-up and violent pseudo-family on the streets.

Carla laughs at this, mocking Claudia and White Fence as a bunch of lightweight has-beens. But when she meets Claudia later, Carla falls silent, listening to the seventeen-year-old speak of how she at first hated Kirby and Shabazz, but how this place made her see herself, and her future, in new ways. She saw clearly, for the first time, that she was on a path going no-where she really wanted to be. What was she gonna do, gangbang at age thirty? The life was already getting boring at sixteen, the routine of lazing around with the homies peppered with sudden bouts of violence wearing at her, beginning to seem pointless and pathetic instead of exhilarating.

So now she is in college instead. Claudia says she has plans for law school. She wants to be an example for other kids in her barrio, "a strong brown woman making it—and making a difference."

"I want to make an example of myself," she tells the group, with all the fervor and idealism a teenager can muster. "I'd like to be Elijah Muhammad for brown people. Martin Luther King. I'd like to make that big of a difference." She laughs a little, suddenly self-conscious at the sentiment, which makes it seem less grandiose than it otherwise might have sounded. "I'm going to make a difference. I'm determined. That's why I'm aiming my sights so high. And if I can help some brown boy or brown girl start thinking the same way, that's what I want."

For once, Carla has nothing to say as she warily eyes this mature-seeming young woman, impeccably dressed, juggling school and a part-time job and dreaming of the future. After Claudia leaves, Shabazz tries to goad Carla by saying, "Claudia has come a long way to get where she is. I think some of you would like to get to that place"—he is looking at Carla as he is saying this—"but you don't know how to get there. Yet." Still, she has nothing to say.

Later, Shabazz tells the group about Virginia, the other graduate from Amber Cottage he had mentioned. Like Claudia, Virginia had, after a defiant start, run a good program at Kirby three years ago—she was smart, worked hard, participated in group, helped the other kids see things. But when she got out, she returned to her old gang.

"She just couldn't give it up," Shabazz says. "She was an honest-to-God, hope-to-die gangbanger for life. So she went back to the life, and just after she turned eighteen, she got shot in the head point-blank. Didn't kill her, but the bullet went through one eye, and messed up the other one pretty good. She's totally blind now. Can you imagine that? How awful it must be to be blind?"

He looks at each girl in the room. The thing about gangbangers, he explains later, is that while they may laugh off fears of dying, the idea of being disabled for life never really occurs to them. They may be criminals, but they're also children, and they are possessed of all the usual childish feelings of invulnerability. So Virginia's fate, the idea that they, too, could be left less than whole by their choices in life, leaves them queasy.

"Of course, Virginia's *still* gangbanging, blind and everything," Shabazz continues. "When her homeboys get ready to go, she just says, throw me in the car, give me the gun, and tell me where to shoot. You got to respect that, right?"

"Shee-it," a member of the group whispers, shaking her head. Even the girls of Amber Cottage are shocked at this story. Shabazz doesn't have to say anything more. His point is clear to Carla and the rest of the group. They can become Claudia. Or they can be Virginia.

A few weeks later, Carla pulls Shabazz aside and asks him if she could talk to Claudia again. "I just wanted to ask her a few things about college, you know," she says with a shrug. "No big deal." But she can't help grinning when she sees Shabazz doing that little nod of his.

CHAPTER 12

Judge Dorn's Solution

The makeshift library on Unit K/L is cold tonight, and oddly silent. None of the usual sounds of too many kids jammed too long in too little space are coming from outside. The TV room stands empty and desolate, the orange plastic and chrome chairs in neat stacks, the folding tables leaning against the cinder block walls, the scuffed linoleum mopped almost clean. Barely audible, an adolescent voice can be heard weeping down some distant corridor, loud gulping sobs that suddenly cut off with the thump of a steel door shutting.

The unit is in lockdown, with every boy confined to his room, stripped to his underwear. Contraband was discovered earlier that day—a homemade knife and a set of master keys, both hidden behind a loose brick in the kitchen, sure signs of an escape attempt in the making. The kids are master smugglers—they have marijuana and other contraband tossed over the walls to them, passed over during visits, tucked inside mattresses and holes in the walls. After the find in the kitchen, every room has been searched, all personal possessions confiscated, the hall "runners"—juvenile equivalents of trustees—stripped of their privileges. Sister Janet and I had to beg the burly and taciturn "senior"—the new night man in charge of the unit—into releasing the writing students from their rooms for an hour so we could hold tonight's class. Unlike his predecessor, who avidly supported the class and bent the rules each week to let us work past bedtime, this newly arrived senior seems to think it all a waste of time, perhaps even a threat to order on the unit. He sometimes appears suddenly in the library doorway, heavily muscled arms crossed, observing the proceedings with a dour expression on his face. The boys invariably fall silent in their jailer's shadow. Still, he agrees to let the class go on this night, and the boys slowly file into the room.

Most of the class is subdued. But just returned from his three-month visit to CYA, Geri is eager to read aloud from his autobiography in progress. As usual when Geri is reading, the class is enthralled—not only because his writing is among the best in the class, but because it sometimes seems he is telling all their stories. "I've gotten a lot farther along since my last time here," he says. "You have a lot more time to yourself at YA."

He has reached a point in his narrative where his mother, Mary, has been released from prison and is desperately trying to stay clean. Geri is a world-weary nine years old by this time, and he is constantly worried that his mom will lapse back into drug addiction and prostitution. She seems to be holding on, though. Then temptation suddenly appears during a visit to the home of one of Geri's friends. With that setup, his face assuming the look of uncertainty he always wears when reading aloud to the class, Geri resumes his story.

Just as we were ready to exit the room, my friend's mom Andrea jumped in front of us with a glass pipe in one hand and a plate containing crack cocaine in the other.

"What's the big rush, Mary?" My mom didn't say anything. She just stared at the glass pipe. Andrea began to wave the pipe in her face, then asked her if she wanted a hit.

My mom struck the lighter, then began to put the flame to the pipe until she remembered how much trouble it caused her. I could tell that she was very sorrowful because her hands began to shake, her eyes began to water, and the glass pipe fell to the ground and broke. I stood there watching my mom as she sobbed, until finally she snatched me by the arm and led me out of the house.

From that point on things seemed to be all right. My mom enrolled into a junior college . . . where she met a young fellow by the name of Sam. Sam was a nice man with a good paying job. He also used to box and every now and then he would show me a combination or two. I remember a time when Sam beat this huge white guy up for being rude to my mom. This was the shortest fight that I have ever seen! Sam hit the guy and the guy hit the floor and that was it. Sam was cool! Sometimes he would place me on his lap and let me steer the car. One time I wrecked into a parked car, but Sam didn't care. In fact, he said that the car shouldn't have been there in the first place.

About six months later, Sam and my mom got married . . . Everything seemed to be going great. . . .

November 4. My birthday. I had the biggest birthday party there could ever be. All of my friends from the neighborhood were there and all of my cousins. Sam dressed himself as a clown with a big red nose and big red Afro. He also performed magic tricks and comedy shows. The funniest part that I remember about the party is when Sam spiked the punch. All of the kids were staggering around the house like old drunk bums off of the streets. I couldn't remember too much of what I had done, but the next day all I knew was I had a migraine headache and my whole room smelled like puke. On top of that, Sam and my mom got into a big argument over him spiking the punch. The argument went on for a couple of hours until finally Sam just walked out of the door. It seemed as if my mom didn't appreciate anything that Sam thought was cool. . . .

After that, what seemed to be the perfect marriage turned into a case of misery. Everything that the two of them had to say to each other turned into a big argument. Finally Sam got fed up with everything and decided to break off the marriage. I began to cry very painfully because I had lost the best stepdad in the world . . . I didn't know if it was my fault or if they just didn't care about my feelings or what. Every time my mom meets a neat guy, he turns out to be the wrong one. . . .

I found myself talking back and smart-mouthing. I began to do whatever I wanted, whenever I wanted. I didn't come home after school until ten o'clock P.M. one day. Once I got home, I was expecting to get a whipping, a yelling, a slap, or something. But I didn't get anything at all. Not even a "Where have you been?" or an "Are you okay?" I remember a time when I pulled a cigarette out of the pack and began to smoke it just to see what my mom would say. She thought it was cute, then began to laugh about it right in front of my face. That really made me mad. I wanted to curse her out, to hit her or something. But instead, I walked away. As I was walking, I began to ask myself questions like, Why doesn't she do anything when I mess up? and Does she really care about me? I turned around and headed back in the living room to ask her these questions, but she was gone.

I began to search through the house and call out her name, but she was nowhere in sight. I went into her room and called her name but she wasn't there. Just as I began to turn towards the exit, out of the corner of my eye, I could see small trails of smoke coming from the cracks of the closet door. I slowly walked over to the door and touched it to see if it was hot. After that, I grasped the door knob and began to turn it until I heard a lot of movement coming from the closet. I took a deep breath and snatched the door open very quickly and stood there in disbelief. I couldn't believe my eyes. It was my mom sitting in the closet smoking crack. She was holding a glass pipe in her hand. Her eyes were big as two golf balls, her lips were chapped white, and she couldn't talk or do anything. I began to shed painful tears, asking God, Please let this be a dream. But this was no dream at all! It was like a worst nightmare come true. All along I had a feeling that something was wrong, but I never thought that this was the reason.

I ran out of her room, through the living room and out of the house crying for the fact that I thought that my mom had changed. But she hadn't changed at all.

I ran to the playground . . . and climbed to the top of a huge slide. I crawled over the safety bars, then balanced myself on the deck. I looked up and I could see my house with the screen door wide open just the way I left it. But I was crying and sweaty and I started to lose my grip. I gave a loud shout calling for my mom, but it was too late. I fell face first to the ground, landing on a broken bottle in the sand. The whole side of my face was busted up and blood gushed out. The next thing I remember is waking up in the hospital and the whole side of my face had painful staples in it.

Approximately two weeks later, this lady . . . interviewed me, then placed me in a foster home.

Geri puts down his papers and says, "That's as far as I got." He looks shyly at the other boys, who remain silent for a moment, then deluge him with compliments. Ronald Duncan is there that day, and he says, "They ought to make a movie out of your life, man," and everyone laughs and agrees.

One boy, though—Chris, the pizza robber who just received his high school diploma in a dirty and unceremonious manila envelope—is unusually quiet. He normally leads the critiquing sessions, but today, he seems preoccupied and upset after hearing Geri's story. He just stares vacantly at his own papers, so I prod him gently. "What do you think, Chris?"

He looks up after a moment. Chris is the class philosopher, as well as the closest thing to a jailhouse lawyer the unit has. Most of his essays are critiques of the justice system. "I was just thinking about foster homes," he says. "What it's like to get put in one. It's like you're no better than trash. You're so low, not even your own parents want you. At least when you're a delinquent and you get taken from your home, it's because of some crime you did. It doesn't mean your parents don't want you. But when you go into foster care, that's worse. That means nobody wants you. You're just out like the trash."

Several kids in the room are nodding as Chris speaks. They have felt this way, too, with all the anger and emptiness it implies, though no one has ever articulated it so well for them before.

"But when a kid goes into foster care, it's the parents' fault, not the kids'," I protest, my need to offer some comfort here, however inadequate, marching me into a tired cliché. *"Geri didn't do anything to deserve being taken away. It's not the foster kids' fault."*

But my students shake their heads — I clearly have missed the point, and not for the first or last time, these teenagers have left me feeling naïve. "That may be true, that it isn't the foster kid's fault," Chris says sadly, *"but that's how it feels."*

Geri nods. "You always think it's your fault. You always wonder if you could have been a better kid, then maybe it would never have happened — maybe they never would have taken you away. Hell," he says, averting his eyes from the other boys in the room, *"I still think that."*

———◆———

THE case files are stacked up like cordwood on top of Judge Dorn's bench, and the courtroom is overflowing with rustling, coughing, grumbling lawyers, cops, children, and parents waiting to hear the clerk read their names from the docket so they can get on with their lives.

Their impatience is of a particularly sour variety today because most of them realize their waiting will accomplish nothing. When their cases are finally called, there will simply be more continuances, more legal rituals, more dates to come back again to court to wait anew. It doesn't help that the courtroom is a furnace today, a crying infant stationed on either side of the room, the smell of hot dust in the air from the ancient heating system heaving asthmatically somewhere deep in the old building's basement. People keep crowding through the door of the courtroom, standing room only now, wondering why nothing is happening, why the judge's chair is vacant. Even the bailiff, whose job by definition is to wait, is drumming his fingers and staring anxiously at Judge Dorn's door.

And still, Dorn remains huddled in his chambers, where he has been for the past fifteen minutes in a private meeting with a mother and her recalcitrant daughter. It is the latest in his increasingly frequent attempts to keep status offenders from becoming crime statistics—at the cost of his regular docket. Every eye in the courtroom keeps drifting toward the closed door to Dorn's domain. Then, at the twenty-minute mark, faints sounds begin to emerge from chambers. Like an approaching thunderstorm, Judge Dorn's raised and angry voice can be heard pushing its way through the heavy wooden door, at first as an indecipherable rumble, then gradually rising in pitch. Finally, the words become loud enough to be clearly audible, even in the back of the courtroom, even over the howls of the babies.

"Anyone who is telling you to go against the orders of your mother," Dorn is railing, "must want you to be a prostitute."

The stirring throng in the gallery falls silent for a moment, straining to hear, a roomful of voyeurs picturing Dorn, cheeks inflated, glaring across his desktop at some child. The judge's voice dips below audible, then rises again. "Mother, you file the necessary papers, and I'll put you back in control. I promise you that. You think you know these streets, young lady? You know nothing. You don't know it, but you are headed on a quick trip to the cemetery, or the penitentiary, one or the other."

The door opens a few moments later. A sullen teenaged girl stalks out without a word or a look back, her long braids bobbing as she strides from the room. Her head is high and she is wearing the classic teen sneer, that perfect look of supreme contempt for the adult world, whose values she rejects even as she claims its privileges. The girl's mother follows like an attendant, face tight with embarrassment, eyes downward so that she need not meet anyone else's glance in that courtroom—as if the other parents there do not know exactly what she is feeling, the pain and helplessness and bewildered humiliation. She lingers only long enough to accept some papers from Dorn's probation officer and to mumble her thanks. She pushes out of the courtroom wearing the haunted look of someone who has just learned a loved one is terminally ill.

"It doesn't appear we've reached this young lady today," Dorn says absently. "Perhaps some time in the hall will convince her."

Then, without apology or explanation, Dorn climbs back on the bench and shuffles files, ready to resume his scheduled hearings after the protracted delay. He stares unmoved at the irritated looks of the attorneys who have been waiting at the defense and prosecution tables during his absence, and who now suspect—correctly—that Dorn, once again, is going to work straight through lunch, right up to the point his court reporter's hands cramp up into claws and she begs for a rest. The message is clear:

Dorn's informal in-chambers hearings are every bit as important to him as his official calendar. Perhaps more so.

"Call the next case," he says gruffly. His failure to cajole the girl into obedience has left him in a foul mood. He won't take it out on the kids who come before him, but the lawyers know they are in for a rough time. They hate his informal sessions, which have become increasingly frequent, up to several a day now. The Star Chamber, they call it. Or the Inquisition.

Dorn doesn't care. He calls these meetings the juvenile system's best chance to help families, and its surest hope for survival. They are the mainstay of his one-judge campaign to shift the priorities of Juvenile Court away from the formally charged repeat offenders and toward the kids teetering on the edge, the ones for whom violence and arrest, addiction or death, are clearly in the cards, but still—perhaps—avoidable.

The girl he lectured in chambers today has just turned seventeen and is refusing to go to school or to observe any sort of curfew. She refuses the simplest request from her parents. She has been stealing from them and, they believe, using the money for drugs. They blame her older boyfriend, a gang member, for pushing her down this path—the fellow Dorn accused of trying to turn the girl into a prostitute.

Her mother came to Dorn because she had heard through her church that he could step in when the police couldn't or wouldn't. When tackling such a case, the judge first tries a stern lecture, which, for many kids, is enough. Being hauled to that prisonlike courthouse, made to wait in the crowded courtroom, and then encountering a master of verbal intimidation like Dorn is enough to scare most kids. But if that fails, he tells the parents that he will help them bring a status offense case. All the parent has to do is fill out a complaint with the Probation Department and if a probation investigation confirms the problem, Dorn can use an old state law to declare the child incorrigible and put him or her on probation.

This is how Dorn believes the court can become a tool for prevention, intervening before a child commits a real crime—even providing a way of targeting the Sixteen Percenters before they embark on their chain of offenses and are claimed by the terminal illness of delinquency.

"Think of all the precious resources we can save by straightening these young people out now, before it's too late," he exhorts those who gripe about his plan. "Think about all the precious lives we can save. We can alter the lives of these minors, as well as their potential victims, for the better. This is the perfect prevention vehicle. But it is a lot of work, and so it has fallen out of favor. I hope to change that."

Later in the day, another status offender is brought before Dorn, this time a somewhat more malleable fourteen-year-old who has been staying out late and refusing his mother's orders, having fallen under the influence of an eighteen-year-old gangbanger in his neighborhood. The boy enters the courtroom a small bundle of fury with a shaved head, kicking his legs angrily as he waits in a seat in the gallery, wedged between his mother and his pastor. Dorn deliberately has him sit there for more than two hours, watching cases, listening to the judge repeat his lectures about choosing between education and poverty, of cemeteries and penitentiaries. The boy watches Dorn reward the kids who succeed, who go to school and earn passing grades they have never earned before. And he watches the ample failures, child after child sent to camp and detention as Dorn ruthlessly enforces his personal standards of school attendance, of unexcused absences, of keeping one's word and following the rules as laid down by Judge Dorn.

After a while, the pastor whispers to the boy, "Don't worry, your turn's coming," which, of course, instantly transforms the boy's anger into fear, just as the minister intended. Finally, after revoking a young car thief's probation for not going to school on time, Dorn greets the pastor and the boy's mother warmly, frowns at the boy, then rises from the bench and ushers all three into his chambers as several defense lawyers waiting for their cases to be called groan audibly.

Inside, Dorn lays it on thick with the boy, threatening him with detention if he does not straighten up—an idle threat at this point, since the boy has committed no crime and Dorn has no legal jurisdiction. ("But he doesn't know that," Dorn chuckles later.) Dorn also chides the boy for hurting his mother, for repaying her love with disrespect and contempt. "Why would you follow some reprobate in your neighborhood, who undoubtedly is going to end up in the penitentiary or worse, rather than your mother who loves you?"

The joint appeal to conscience and fear, combined with the sobering sight of Dorn meting out justice for two hours, has the desired effect. The boy leaves a changed child, outwardly at least. In front of Dorn, he hugs and kisses his mother, then apologizes, promising to change his ways. Dorn congratulates him for his maturity, then orders him to stay away from the eighteen-year-old who has been leading him astray, lest he find out what Juvenile Hall looks like from the inside out. ("It's not really an order at all," Dorn admits later. "But he doesn't know that.")

And so Judge Dorn, using the power of his robe and a heavy dose of intimidation, accomplishes what the law and the system normally cannot do: He puts a boy back on track. (A year later, the young man is doing well in school and has stayed out of trouble. His mother has no doubt about who deserves credit for that: Judge Dorn.)

Dorn's seemingly simple approach to preventing delinquency—the classic, paternalistic godfather role envisioned in the more innocent times that spawned Juvenile Court—was at the outset met with great skepticism throughout the system. First, there was the sense that kids today were just too sophisticated for lectures and tirades. And, beyond that, the bureaucracy that exists to screen cases and to select which kids enter the system, and which get to walk, is reluctant to cede its authority. Judge Dorn is setting up a wholly separate gateway to the system, one that bypasses the Probation Department and the DA and walks right in through the judge's chambers—and which uses the status offenses long ago discarded and ignored by a system intently focused on young, hardened criminals.

As he expected, soon after Judge Dorn began his new program, there were complaints that he was squandering precious court time and probation resources on kids who hadn't even committed a crime, while serious offenders were waiting their turn, their cases delayed. The criticisms escalated when Dorn, who has made it clear that placating him will always be easier than opposing him, persuaded the Probation Department to dedicate one officer to do nothing but handle his status offense cases. It was assumed that this PO would have little to do and could soon return to regular duties, but, to everyone's surprise but Dorn's, parents began showing up regularly at Dorn's door, their children in tow. Just through word of mouth at schools and churches, forty to fifty children a month were soon coming to Dorn, then trooping to his special PO for status offense investigations. The demand for such a service—and its potential for success—were far higher than anyone had realized. The interest in the community in Dorn's program has been so startling (and its success so great, though Dorn's claim of a 95 percent success rate has yet to be proven) that a task force on juvenile justice issues brought together by Dorn decided to recommend the judge's status offender program be duplicated in every juvenile courthouse in LA.

It might have happened, too. But the county government's sudden budget crisis derailed the proposal for now, perhaps permanently. For the foreseeable future, only Dorn and his two colleagues on the bench in the Inglewood courthouse will aggressively pursue status offenders.

Though Dorn has won over converts, others in the courthouse remain fearful, even outraged, by Dorn's private sessions in chambers. They see

Dorn as playing fast and loose with the rules, aiming for his own personal vision of what's right, rather than what's legal. While Dorn is dealing with another status offender case in chambers, a defense lawyer waiting in court gripes, "Here he is, in there with a kid, making threats, making orders he has no legal right to make, there's no court reporter in there, the kid has no lawyer—it's a kangaroo court. There are no checks and balances. Dorn's doing exactly what a judge did to Gault thirty years ago."

As much as Dorn would like to dismiss such criticisms as coming from recalcitrant bureaucrats and defense lawyers eager to protect a gravy train of court appointments, it is true that the status offense process Dorn is using lacks some of the checks and balances that other delinquency and criminal cases carry. Locking up status offenders is illegal, but Dorn finds ways to do it anyway, relying primarily on a judge's power to hold anyone who disobeys a judicial order in contempt of court. The problem with this, however, is the law still requires—for obvious reasons—that runaways, incorrigibles, and other status offenders be housed completely apart from delinquents who commit actual crimes. And there is no room for them all—there are only forty secure status offender beds in all of Los Angeles County, with Judge Dorn and the other two Inglewood judges quickly filling them all, leaving nothing left for the other twenty-five juvenile judges and commissioners who occasionally need to hold a child in that way.

"Judge Dorn does not live in the 1990s, he lives in the 1940s," the director of one of LA's juvenile halls griped. "He says, 'Lock 'em up,' and we have to obey his orders, but the thing is, the extra time and money we spend on his kids, we have to take away from other kids elsewhere. He's not operating in a vacuum."

Status offenders also fall under a different portion of the welfare code than other delinquents, one the District Attorney does not enforce. Instead, a probation officer—who does not have the same independence from judicial control that a DA enjoys—fills that role, acting as prosecutor of status offenders. And though a child is still entitled to a defense attorney, that lawyer does not enter the process until after Dorn has had his informal hearing without lawyers, and has, in essence, already made up his mind about a kid. It is Dorn, after all, who often suggests to parents that they file the necessary papers to initiate a status offense case.

The case of a sixteen-year-old problem child named Rolando exacerbated these fears, hardening opposition to Dorn's program, particularly among public defenders.

Rolando's grandmother brought the boy to Dorn. She had heard about the judge in Inglewood who ran an open court and who would help families with children out of control. Rolando's grandmother had raised the boy since age three, when the dependency branch of Juvenile Court took him from his mother because of chronic neglect. Like so many other foster children, Rolando started getting in trouble as an adolescent. At age fifteen, he joined a gang in the small city of Lennox on the edge of Los Angeles International Airport (a gang that is, coincidentally, the chief rival to Carla James's Tepa-13 gang).

Within a few months, he had racked up four arrests for vandalism and graffiti. He was released without formal prosecution each time. More recently, he had become a constant truant, and had stolen money and jewelry from his grandparents to finance a new drug habit—more than four thousand dollars' worth, his grandmother estimated. He sold the jewelry on the streets, using his earnings to buy rock cocaine and a particularly dangerous drug popular with juveniles, Sherm—marijuana laced with angel dust, an animal tranquilizer that causes hallucinations and, at times, wild, violent behavior.

Desperate for help and disgusted with the juvenile system's past performance, Rolando's grandmother and grandfather dragged the boy to Dorn and told him Rolando had stolen thousands of dollars from them in the past few months. Dorn questioned the boy, demanding he tell the truth, and Rolando confessed to stealing the jewelry and cash. Dorn then ordered him taken into custody by his bailiff so that the grandparents could go to the police department and file a theft complaint. Then the boy was turned over to the police so a formal theft case could be prosecuted by the DA.

Both prosecutors and the public defenders were incredulous at Dorn's actions in the case. No one actually had the nerve to confront the judge with this criticism, but privately they claimed Dorn had no legal right to detain Rolando *before* charges were filed. The judge had no jurisdiction. They also questioned the seemliness of a judge interrogating a boy accused of crimes, rather than backing off as soon as the grandmother made it clear she was talking about grand theft rather than a status offense. By urging (by some accounts, ordering) the grandparents to file a theft complaint with the police, they said, Dorn had become an advocate, sacrificing his judicial objectivity. And beyond that, because the boy confessed after talking to Dorn, the judge had become a potential witness in the case. He also had left himself open to charges that he used his judicial authority to coerce a confession from the boy, which, if true, would be a violation of Rolando's constitutional rights.

"It's a mess," Peggy Beckstrand sighed once the police brought the case in for prosecution. "And now we're stuck with it." Yet even she admitted that Judge Dorn had managed to do something for a child and a family that the system had previously been unable to help. Constitutional questions aside, no one really doubted Rolando's guilt. And for the first time, the kid faced real consequences for his actions. For the first time, he and his family had a chance.

"Dorn's goals are laudable," Peggy told her staff during one in a continuing series of discussions on how to deal with the supervising judge. "There's no doubt about that. What he wants to do is wonderful. The problem is *how* he does it. He doesn't want to play by the rules. He doesn't really want to be a judge. He wants to be king. And this is going to come up again and again. Wait and see."

Peggy's words were prophetic, and she didn't have to wait long in order to see them come true.

"They're inside me," Keesha Jordan began complaining at age twelve, at first infrequently, then more often as the years passed. "The voices."

And they were angry voices, difficult to ignore, chiding her, tormenting her, telling her—with increasing frequency—to do terrible things, unspeakable things. They made her curse her older sister Tina, vile words she didn't even remember learning, tumbling out of her in an unstoppable stream. She felt like a soda bottle shaken by invisible, malevolent hands at such times, frothing, overflowing, out of control. It got so Tina couldn't bring friends to the house—Keesha scared them too much.

Still, she got all A's and B's at school, she never cut class, she didn't hang out with bad kids, didn't do drugs. Keesha never even had a boyfriend, much less experimented with sex. In many ways, she had been a model child. Sure, she stayed locked up in her bedroom most of the time and occasionally had confused, sometimes violent yelling matches when no one else was present. But things could be a lot worse for a kid these days, her mother figured, what with gangs and guns and pregnant teenagers everywhere. Besides, there were more pressing concerns for the Jordan family. Forty years old and on her own, Mrs. Jordan was too busy with Keesha's little sisters, ages two and three, and with getting rid of an abusive ex-husband who had beaten her, Keesha, and the other kids for years. At the same time, Mrs. Jordan was fighting to stay off the drugs that had hooked her in the past. Who had time to take Keesha to some shrink for counseling? And who could afford it if there was time? Keesha's mother worked hard as a stock clerk to support the whole family, barely making ends meet with the $750 monthly salary she pulled in, most of which went to pay the rent. She was gone many days and evenings, and twenty-year-old Tina had to keep things together. It was easy for Mrs. Jordan to keep saying to herself, Keesha will outgrow this phase, she'll be fine, she has a bright future. Sometimes, she even believed it.

The kids who land in Juvenile Court share certain common characteristics: Most of their crimes are preceded by years of unheeded warning signs, and most of their parents possess high capacities for self-absorption or self-delusion. Keesha was no exception. It took the events of the evening of November 15, 1993, to shock her mother into realizing—too late—that Keesha was not going to simply outgrow her problems. But by then, the juvenile justice system had taken over.

That night, Tina Jordan had been watching television with her two baby sisters in a bedroom of the family's second-floor, two-bedroom apartment. Around six o'clock, shortly after Mrs. Jordan left for work, Tina heard a sound from the living room. Keesha, with whom she had bickered earlier, had taken a two-foot-long machete out of a closet, and was scraping it against the furniture. Tina could hear mumbling, too, as if Keesha were arguing with someone, though no one else was in the living room with her.

The scraping grew louder and more frantic, then suddenly stopped. Keesha appeared in the doorway, tall and strong, her black hair pulled back into a severe bun, the yellow light from the bedroom fixture glinting off her thick glasses. Her eyebrows were knitted in an angry V, and she brandished the machete like a broadsword.

"Get ready to die," she yelled. "I'm fixin' to kill you!"

She charged the bed as the babies screamed. Tina jumped up and away as Keesha swung the machete like a baseball bat at her sister's head as if to decapitate her. As Keesha moved toward her older sister and the machete whistled through the air again, Tina rolled across the bed, keeping it between her and her sister. She dodged two or three more swings this way, crying and pleading as she ducked and rolled, the long, flat blade getting closer every time.

"Please don't kill me, Keesha. Please, I don't want to die," Tina wailed, expecting at any moment to feel the machete carve her like the roast chicken they had for dinner a few hours earlier.

Instead, as abruptly as she had begun the attack, Keesha stopped pursuing Tina with the swinging blade. She took a position blocking the doorway of the bedroom. "If you want to live, then you'd better call the police," she muttered, and turned away, distracted by the voices only she could hear. Tina retreated to a corner of the bedroom, grabbed the phone, and dialed 911, the little girls still wailing on the bed beside her.

Eight minutes later, three Los Angeles police officers arrived at the apartment. They found Tina and the babies still barricaded in the bedroom. Keesha, wearing a nightgown with an old brown cardigan on top, sat in an armchair, her legs pulled up, the handle of the machete wedged between her thighs, the blade pointing straight up. She rested her chin on top of the point of the machete, so that one vigorous nod of her head would plunge the machete deeply into her neck.

"I have nothing to live for," she said, rocking in the chair, hunched and withdrawn. "I'm ready to die."

Fearing she was about to thrust the machete into her throat, one of the officers, armed with a stun gun, fired. The policemen were the ones stunned, however, as they watched in disbelief—and Keesha looked on with mild interest—as the stun gun's dart, which delivers a powerful electric shock, bounced off the machete blade and fell harmlessly to the floor. The officer tried again, with the same result, as if the machete were a magnet. Keesha began to grow agitated then. The officer held his breath, spread his legs, and fired again, twice in rapid succession, and though one of the darts again struck the blade and fell to the floor, the last shot finally lodged in Keesha's chin. She convulsed from the surge of voltage, dropped the machete, and sprawled onto the worn carpeting, where two policemen pounced on her and put handcuffs around her scarred wrists. Sobbing, Tina emerged with the babies and begged the policemen to take Keesha away.

After a checkup in a hospital emergency room, the police booked Keesha into Central Juvenile Hall on a charge of assault with a deadly weapon. Once there, an intake officer read the police reports, interviewed Keesha, and talked to Mrs. Jordan, who had rushed over from work. Then he wrote up a detention report for the court, Keesha's entrée to the system. The hurried report failed to mention Keesha's need for psychological testing and treatment, and she received none when admitted to Central Juvenile Hall.

The intake officers—as well as the police—have the option to interrupt the juvenile intake process and take an obviously disturbed child like Keesha to a psychiatric hospital for an emergency commitment, so long as there is evidence she is ill, and that she poses a danger to herself or others. Keesha clearly fit this profile, attempting both homicide and suicide in the space of an hour. Her blunt, expressionless face that night, and her talk of disembodied voices instructing her to do terrible things, made her mental problems obvious to all around her.

But seeking a mental commitment requires additional effort, time, and paperwork. The police or probation officer who brings the child to the hospital must wait around for hours, with no guarantee that the medical staff will take the kid. The hospital wards are crowded and there is enormous pressure to turn away indigent patients like Keesha if there is any question at all about the need for a mental commitment. If refused admission, Keesha would then have to be escorted back to juvenile intake to start the process all over. That's a great deal of time to spend on one new case. For all of Los Angeles County, with its thousands of square miles and its sixty-plus police departments and sheriff's stations making up to two hundred juvenile arrests a day, there are but twenty intake officers out in the field—for all three daily eight-hour shifts. Budget cuts have decimated their ranks, leaving most of the intake process to the juvenile halls, where the probation officers cutting the reports are in no position to get up and leave to take a child to the hospital. The cases and kids never stop stacking up at the halls.[1]

So Keesha went through the standard detention process. She had to strip, submit to a search, then run through the institutional showers. She was checked for parasites, dressed in gray underwear and an orange jumpsuit, and placed in the one of the hall's few female units. The only concession to her mental problems was a notation on her probation file and the hall's daily "pop sheet"—its computer printout of the system's two-thousand-plus juvenile population being held in pretrial detention—stating she might be prone to suicide. She would stay in the hall for the next two months while the system tried to figure out what to do with her.

Thirty-six hours after her arrest, a packet of information on Keesha—consisting of the police reports and the intake officer's detention report—arrived at Peggy Beckstrand's office, one case in a pile of about thirty others thumped on the front counter by the Probation Department's courier, sent over for possible prosecution. Such deliveries are made daily, not quite like clockwork, but close. There were no homicides in that particular pile, so Keesha's case was the most serious, violent crime presented that day. Based on the bare-bones information in the file, the DA's Office made the decision to file attempted murder charges against Keesha, and to seek her transfer to adult court, where she could receive up to life in prison. Given what Peggy knew at the time—the file focused entirely on the violence of the offense, with no information describing Keesha's mental state or her exemplary past—the decision seemed to make sense.

But not to Judge Dorn.

"Why is this case being prosecuted in this fashion?" he barks when Keesha's fitness hearing is called. The deputy DA starts to explain that his office routinely files attempted murder cases with an allegation that the minor is unfit, but Dorn, as usual, cuts him off. "I want to continue this and talk to your supervisor. This makes no sense. Look at this psychiatric report. This minor does not belong in the adult system. This child needs help.

"Transfer this case to adult court, and it will be lost."

Keesha looks confused, unable to comprehend what is happening, the only clue being the smile on her lawyer's face. She doesn't know how lucky she was to land before Judge Dorn, who sees the fitness law as the system's drastic solution for cutting its caseload and dumping its most troublesome kids—without bringing an equivalent amount of attention or help to the kids left behind. To Dorn, this solution is tantamount to heresy. He jabs a thick finger in Sisman's direction.

"Get me his supervisor on the phone," Dorn tells his clerk. "We need to make a stand here."

A short time later, Peggy has climbed the stairs from the Ronald Duncan murder trial and trudged before Judge Dorn. "Just read that psychological report," Dorn tells her. "There is no way this girl should go to adult court. She'll be eaten alive. Eaten alive! The people should withdraw the fitness motion. Surely you can see that."

Beckstrand reluctantly picks up the file and starts to read. Keesha's public defender, Leslie Stearns, has done what the Probation Department failed to do: She got a psychiatrist in to see Keesha, who prescribed antipsychotic medications that produced dramatic and rapid results. The hallucinations and murderous impulses have diminished, and her prognosis is good.

As she reads, Dorn tries to charm her with that honeyed baritone of his. It's for the best. I can do a lot more for her here, he told Peggy. Chances are, he suggested, changing tactics, she'll do more time with me than she would in adult. A judge there might see no one was injured, and just kick her loose. The busy DAs downtown won't want to be bothered with such a small-time case. Or she might get off on an insanity plea. Keep her here, I'll see she gets help, Dorn vows. It is the same logic he employed in keeping John Sloan in Juvenile, except now it is couched in the form of a request instead of an order.

"*Hmmmm*," Peggy murmurs. What the judge says may or may not be true, but Peggy still bristles at the pressure Dorn is exerting on her. Instead of finding Keesha fit for Juvenile Court, then taking his chances should

Peggy appeal, he is trying to goad her into an appealproof withdrawal of her fitness motion. She knows everyone in the courtroom is watching this interaction carefully, wondering if Dorn can bully a supervising DA, notwithstanding the constitutional separation of powers barring judges from interfering with a prosecutor's executive decisions, and the fact that Dorn's "request" could easily be viewed as a form of intimidation. Beckstrand's impulse is to refuse him on the spot.

First of all, she has never withdrawn a fitness motion before. Never. It is a matter of principle. She believes kids who committed such serious offenses as attempted murder proved, by their conduct, that they should be treated as adults. Most other states don't even blink when transferring kids much younger than sixteen, so California is far from the radical right on this issue. Even Attorney General Janet Reno, a longtime advocate for doing more to rehabilitate than to punish wayward children, tried fourteen-year-olds as adults when she was a DA in Miami. If anything, Peggy believes, more transfers of kids to adult court are needed in Los Angeles — desperately.

Secondly, if she rolled over now in front of everyone, there would be no end to it. Dorn would see a weakness, as would the defense lawyers, and they all would try to exploit it from this day on. This point alone dictated that she should stand firm. Fencing with a despot like Dorn would be a constant in her life from now on, and she was loath to surrender any advantage. Yet she stopped herself from saying no to his request, because she had a problem:

She had seen Keesha walk into the courtroom, awkward and sad, mouthing a tiny "Hello" to her mom in the audience, then sitting down, becoming motionless, inert. The girl then had to endure hearing people talk about her as if she wasn't even present, hearing her own lawyer say, "The medication seems to be helping. She's not hearing the voices anymore." Peggy genuinely felt sorry for the kid. And what if Dorn was right? What if the best place for Keesha — and the best thing for society — was to keep her in Juvenile Court? Would she have sought a transfer to adult court if the Probation Department had done a more thorough job in its investigation and reports? Perhaps not. She found herself thinking about Jim Hickey's kinder, gentler philosophy of juvenile justice. Could she allow policy statements and courtroom politics to get in the way of doing the right thing? One of the things that enrages her most about the juvenile justice system is its bouts of inflexible stupidity, its focus on process instead of results, its all-too frequent inability to do the right thing, even when the right thing is obvious to all. She did not want to become that which she hated most.

"The People will withdraw the fitness motion," Beckstrand finally announces.

Dorn is grinning now, cheeks dimpled. He opens his mouth, but before he can say anything in reply, Peggy adds, "It's not that we're going to do this every time."

"I can't get anyone to agree with me all of the time." he chuckles. "But if I can get it some of the time . . . well, then, I'm happy."

Once Peggy leaves the room, Keesha quickly agrees to plead guilty, sealing the deal, and Dorn sends her out to be screened for mental hospitalization, and for admission to the Dorothy Kirby Center.

The seemingly happy ending evaporates three weeks later when Keesha returns to court for her "disposition"—the Juvenile Court euphemism for sentencing.

She looks much better for this court appearance, her hair braided, her demeanor more animated—and more worried. Assistant Public Defender Leslie Stearns says Keesha has been sticking with her medication and doing very well in the hall. "She doesn't hear voices anymore," the lawyer announces. "She'll stick with her medication, because she knows she is better."

The problem facing Dorn, however, is what to do with Keesha. Despite his extravagant promises to Beckstrand of being able to hold her accountable longer than the adult court system would have, he finds that the Probation Department and the social welfare system he needs to help him accomplish this task are doing their best to avoid having to deal with Keesha.

The two departments are focusing on a technicality: Keesha turned eighteen within the past two weeks. Because her crime was committed before she reached this age of majority, she remains a "minor" in the eyes of the court, entitled to treatment as a juvenile. But no one else wants her. The county mental health screening committee that Judge Dorn ordered to examine Keesha waited a week to follow that order—just enough time for Keesha's birthday to arrive. Then, exactly on her birthday, a member of the committee called the Probation Department and said they were rejecting her case because she was an adult.

The Probation Department also waited until the day of Keesha's birthday to follow Dorn's order that she be considered for Dorothy Kirby. This delay allowed the Kirby Center to announce that it did not accept kids who had turned eighteen, either, so Keesha, who otherwise could benefit from the program, was rejected based on her birth date. Had they screened Keesha promptly, they could have taken her—it's okay to turn eighteen at Kirby once accepted in the program.

With the system trying mightily to reject Keesha, the probation officer assigned to recommend a disposition for the girl wrote Dorn a report suggesting he send her home on probation, with an order that she go to an outpatient psychiatric clinic. Keesha's mother would have to pay for this herself, a major problem, but lawyer Stearns asks Dorn to follow this recommendation anyway.

"The problem is," DDA Hyman Sisman interjects, "the older sister is still terrified of her. What if she stops taking the medication? If something like this happens again, it might not end with an attempt. Someone could be killed."

Dorn is troubled. Mentally ill young people frequently do resist taking the medication. They hate the dulling effect antipsychotic drugs can have, and Keesha is already chafing at the demands that she keep taking pills, insisting she is better and doesn't need them. Dorn is loath to agree with this prosecutor, but he says he has to protect Keesha's family as well as Keesha. Dorn announces that the only way he'll allow probation is if Keesha is sentenced to the California Youth Authority—a sentence normally reserved for kids with long records of major or violent crimes. It is the only other program left available to him that offers mental health services and security. He says he will "stay" this sentence. That means she can go home, but if she messes up, either through another violent episode, or merely by refusing her medication, then she goes to CYA. "CYA is the only place open to her now, unfortunately," he says.

Defender Stearns begins to argue, but Dorn cuts her off. "Those are the terms, Counselor . . . I have to be in a position to protect the family and the minor. If I don't get that, I'll have no choice but to do something I really do not want to do." The implication is clear: If Stearns refuses to agree to a CYA stay—a sentence of questionable legality—he'll just send Keesha directly to the youth prison, with no probation at all.

At this point, the court's assigned probation officer stands up at her desk next to the judge, approaches the bench, and whispers to him, though her words carry. "I can't say it on the record, Your Honor, because it's going against my department, but the minor would be better served at Dorothy Kirby." She goes on to explain that it is the department's *policy* to refuse anyone over seventeen, but that the *law* allows a judge to send eighteen-year-olds there, just like any other suitable placement. "You can order them to take her, and they can't say no," she tells Dorn. His eyes widen—he had not known this.

A whispered conference between the judge and the attorneys ensues. Then Stearns whispers with Keesha, who has been looking very worried at this talk of CYA. There is no mistaking the look of pleasure that suffuses Dorn's face at the notion of bullying the Probation Department into violating its own policies, while at the same time overcoming an artificial age division that is getting in the way of what this girl needs.

"It is the order of the court, for the protection and rehabilitation of this minor and the protection of society, that this minor be removed from the home," Dorn intones.

At this, Keesha turns to her mother, who is seated several rows behind her in the audience. Keesha begins to cry, as does her mother, large, silent tears running down both their faces. They had counted on probation; Mrs. Jordan had even brought a paper sack with fresh clothes for Keesha.

"The court orders the minor suitably placed with Dorothy Kirby," Dorn continues. "The court is ordering Dorothy Kirby to accept this minor and give her treatment." Then he adds a trademark Dornism. "If this cannot be done, I want the director to come in here and tell me why." Not just any flunky, but the director of the Probation Department, one of the three or four most powerful bureaucrats in the county. Dorn still delights in such threats, certain it will be much easier for the director to give him his way than to traipse into court. "They will help her, or give me a good excuse why not."

Keesha, who had sent a long, painstakingly written letter to Dorn on loose-leaf paper in purple ink explaining why she had to go home, is beside herself with grief. "But I'm better," she pleads.

Dorn shakes his head, but his voice is gentle now, sad but resolute. "Keesha, I would love to be able to send you home. But I have to do what I think is best to do."

The girl is clutching a sodden wad of Kleenex now, whispering again, "I'm better. I'm better. But I'm better."

"I know you're better," Dorn says. "I know. I want you to do even better still. This is not punishment. Please understand, this is for your own good. This is not like those other places. They have the best. You'll have your own room."

"Can I get free passes, to go home?" Keesha asks, desperate for some glimmer of hope.

Dorn fudges a bit here, saying yes, though he cannot know if this will be possible (it won't be, at least not for many months). "I'm doing this because it's best for you," he says. "I want you to get well, so you can go home. That is what I'd love to see."

He gives her a last smile, then sets her file aside. Dorn's kindly tone vanishes then, and it's back to business. He's calling the next case as Keesha walks from the courtroom, waving to her red-eyed mother and whispering, "I love you, Mom."

A few weeks later, Keesha is in Amethyst Cottage with Carla James and Mr. Shabazz, who nicknames her "Li'l Sweetie" because she is so unlike the other girls—a troubled, sick, but eminently healable young woman, not a criminal.

In Juvenile Court, this is success—the system working, not because of the court and its rule of law, but in spite of it, bureaucracy overcome by a cantankerous judge and a prosecutor willing to do the right thing instead of the legal thing.

At the same time Judge Dorn is breaking the rules for Keesha and others, the family of a seventeen-year-old former tagger is having a vastly different and far less satisfying run-in with the supervising judge at Thurgood Marshall Branch. In this boy's case, Dorn seems intent on a strict enforcement of the rules, no matter the consequences.

Christopher Jones had been convicted a year earlier for being a minor in possession of spray paint, a misdemeanor created in recent years by a legislature anxious to slow down graffiti. It led to Chris's first-ever appearance in Juvenile Court, though he had been chronically truant for years without penalty. The judge on the case—Dorn's predecessor in Department 240—didn't want him to do time in camp or the hall. But straight HOP was out, too, because Chris and his stepfather despised one another, and Chris's mother made no secret of whose side she preferred. She pronounced herself "sick of Chris's garbage," giving the judge no alternative but to send the boy to a group home to live.

A year later, Chris's mother telephoned her brother and sister-in-law, asking, How 'bout if Chris comes to live with you guys? He's finished his sentence in Juvenile Court, but he still can't live with us at home. He just doesn't get along with his stepdad. Andrea and Robert Jones liked their nephew Chris. They talked it over and said, Sure, we'll take him, but only if he agrees to our ground rules: He goes back to school, he gets a job, and he stays away from South Bay—the area south of LA where Chris's tagger friends hung out, and where his legal troubles began. With that settled, Aunt Andrea became the taskmaster Chris Jones never had.

"Education is the number-one priority in this house," she told Chris at the outset. "We're all in school here—junior college, adult extension classes, you name it. So join the club."

But she saw Chris was far, far behind where he should be. One year from graduation age, he had only 30 units of credit out of the 220 required for a diploma. So she put him in a special series of classes that would enable him to earn a GED high school diploma instead, replacing an impossible goal with an attainable one—the same way kids in Juvenile Hall can graduate from high school. Then she helped him get a job at a movie theater, and enrolled him in a vocational program that, once he had his GED, would teach him skills for the construction trade, so that he eventually could become self-supporting. It seemed curious to Andrea Jones that the juvenile system had spent a year with Chris, yet had not taken any of these steps. But Chris's mother had told her of many letters and phone calls to the Probation Department that had never been answered, and she just shrugged it off as another example of ineffective government.

Camp Andrea Jones, however, was anything but ineffective. Chris completely changed his attitude in three months. He dressed better, got up and went to school without complaint. He gave up tagging and his tagger friends. He even got promoted at the movie theater, where his boss raved about his work ethic. He had passed several of his GED tests and had only two more to go, scheduled in two weeks. Most importantly, Chris had begun to speak hopefully about the future. Living in a supportive and structured home for the first time in his life had done for Chris everything that the Juvenile Court could have hoped to accomplish, and in only a matter of months.

"You've really helped me, Aunt Andrea," he told her one day, giving her a hug, a rare show of emotion from the darkly handsome, quiet young man.

The next night, while the movie theater manager who employed him drove Chris home, a policeman pulled them over for a traffic violation. But when the officer radioed in a routine records check of the driver and passenger, he found there was a long-standing warrant out for Chris's arrest, issued by a Juvenile Court judge. Chris was taken into custody and brought to Juvenile Hall that night. Only then did Andrea Jones learn from her sister and Chris that he had run away from the group home the court had sent him to more than a year ago. Unwelcome at home, he had lived on the street for six months before coming to live with his aunt and uncle.

His mother had never been able to find Chris's probation officer to explain any of this, she said, and she had finally given up. It never occurred to her or Chris to take the simplest and most direct route to straightening out the mess: walking into court.

Because Dorn's predecessor in Department 240 had handled the case, Chris's fate now belonged to Judge Dorn.

Andrea Jones took off from work and school to be here for her nephew (Chris's mother would not leave her new home in Arizona to come). She has been sitting in court for two hours this morning, waiting for Chris's case to be called, and when she finally hears his name spoken by the bailiff, she blurts like a nervous schoolgirl, "I'm here!" and raises her hand.

Chris's lawyer, Leslie Stearns, makes a pitch for the boy's release, explaining his schooling, employment, and his change of life under his aunt's tutelage.

Dorn, face impassive, shakes his head at the public defender. "The minor ran from placement. No one bothered to return him, or bring him to court. If he was with the mother, the aunt or uncle, they aided and abetted him in violating the terms and conditions of probation. . . . Even if the mother had trouble contacting the probation officer, they knew where the courtroom was. And they did nothing. I cannot condone that."

Dorn then orders Chris kept in Juvenile Hall until a "Triple Seven" can be filed—a probation violation report, named for the statute number, 777—which the judge orders the Probation Department to prepare immediately. This is technically an improper order; Dorn is only supposed to request an investigation, and the Probation Department is supposed to independently determine whether a Triple Seven should be filed. But every PO knows that whether Dorn requests or orders a Triple Seven, the bottom line is that it better be filed, or there will be trouble.

Andrea Jones jumps up. Chris has already been in detention all weekend. "Your Honor," she calls out from the gallery, as all heads in the audience turn toward her, making her blush and stammer, "we thought everything was taken care of. We didn't know about the bench warrant. I've gotten him into school, into vocational training, I helped him get a job." She begins to sniffle at this point, her eyes watering. "His life is really on track now."

Dorn is unmoved. "We'll take that up with you at the next hearing." The judge asks for a hearing date from his clerk, then says Chris will be back in two days. Andrea Jones starts to protest anew, but Leslie Stearns, knowing Dorn can't see past Chris's original disobedience of a court order, grabs Andrea and whispers, "Don't say any more. We'll go over it more next time. You'll only make things worse."

After this, the case devolves into a classic and pointless bureaucratic morass. Two days after the first hearing, Andrea Jones comes back to court at 8:00 A.M. and waits all morning, then well into the afternoon for Chris's case to be called. She has spent the last two days arguing with Chris's mother for causing this mess, then trying to contact the probation officer preparing the Triple Seven. Every time she calls the Probation Department, she is told there is no Chris Jones case on record. She can't even find out the name of the PO who is supposed to be handling it.

The reason for this becomes clear as the court day winds to a close: No one is handling it. The file arrived at the Probation Department by courier from Dorn's court, but then just sat at the Centinela Probation Office, unopened and unassigned. Dorn is furious when he finds out. He has Chris brought into court from the holding tank, looking disheveled and unhappy, confused at what is going on. He waves weakly to his aunt.

Leslie Stearns begs Dorn to release him to his aunt at this point. She argues that the law requires a juvenile's release within forty-eight hours if no charges are filed, and that time is about to lapse, with no Triple Seven in sight. The DA agrees, happy to send Chris on his way.

But Dorn says he will do nothing without a Triple Seven report so he can know the truth about the boy's behavior for the past year. "Get me a Triple Seven in the morning, or the probation officer in here to tell me why," he tells his staff. In the meantime, he gets around the forty-eight-hour requirement by resurrecting the original "suitable placement" order that sent Chris to the group home. Dorn orders him sent back—a new suitable placement. Because the process of placing a juvenile takes weeks, the practical effect of Dorn's order is to keep Chris locked up in Juvenile Hall until a Triple Seven can be prepared. Then Dorn can cancel the placement order and do whatever he wants. Meanwhile, he orders everyone back the next day to resolve the case.

When Andrea Jones returns the next day, however, she still has not spoken with the probation officer on Chris's case, though she called and attempted to establish contact six times during the day. And after waiting in court all morning yet again, she learns Chris's case has to be delayed again. Dorn's clever ploy with the suitable placement order has backfired—it had the unintended effect of erasing the forty-eight-hour deadline for filing charges, removing any sense of urgency at the Probation Department. His case went to the bottom of the pile at the Probation Department, behind all those kids who still had forty-eight hour deadlines to meet. Another hearing is set in five days.

"This is a nightmare," Andrea Jones complains out in the hallway. "He's missing school. He's locked up. And for what? What's being accomplished?"

While waiting for the next hearing, Andrea Jones duns the Probation Department every day, without luck. Finally, on the afternoon before Chris's hearing, she is connected at random to a sympathetic PO, who agrees to search for Chris's file. He tracks it down on an unused desk at the Centinela office. Someone just stuck it there and left it, no one knows who or why. "No one's doing anything with it," the PO tells Chris's aunt.

She begs him to help and, hearing her desperation, he agrees, listening to her story, then staying at the office until 9:00 P.M. verifying everything she had to say—Chris's school performance, his excellent work at the movie theater, his work toward a GED. When the PO determines all this is true, he calls Andrea Jones back and asks, "Why would the judge order a Triple Seven on this?"

"I don't know," Andrea replies, "but Judge Dorn is pissed."

The PO then tells Andrea that, regardless of his own feelings on the matter, he must file a Triple Seven to placate Dorn. But he promises to recommend that Chris go home on probation and continue living with his aunt and uncle. "The judge will have to have a darn good reason to go against my recommendation, so you're probably in good shape." Andrea Jones is confident enough the next day to bring a change of clothes and shoes in a paper bag for Chris to wear home. She looks at some of the other kids in the courthouse and gets depressed, wondering what happens to boys and girls who don't have someone like her to push the system into doing something.

Finally, after another daylong wait in court, a fax of the PO's hastily handwritten report appears in Judge Dorn's courtroom.

Dorn speed-reads it, then tosses it aside without a second glance. "For the rehabilitation of this minor, the protection of this minor, and the protection of society, I am ordering him into short-term camp, closed, so he can't run away."

Chris puts his head down on the defense table. Dorn never even asked him a question.

Andrea Jones is stunned. She cries out, "That's not fair." Chris's lawyer shushes her, but Dorn ignores the outburst, and continues speaking to Chris about how he can do up to six months in camp, but that good behavior can earn him an early release. "You can't keep running. And I will not condone your violation of court orders. I will not simply send you home. If you had come in on your own, that would be another matter. But you did not."

Dorn hesitates, glancing briefly at Andrea Jones. Then he says curtly, "That's all. Good luck, young man."

"No wonder our juvenile courts are falling apart," Chris's aunt says a short time later as she leaves the building "This isn't justice. This is insanity. Now he's going to miss out on his diploma. He's going to have to start all over again. He's going to lose his job, his vocational training, everything. Living with us, Chris had accomplished everything the judge could have hoped to accomplish with his camps and placements. More. Why punish him now? It stinks. It just seems like revenge. What's the point?"

Assistant Public Defender Stearns is equally angry. Juggling files on her way back to her office, she gripes, "That's the thing with Dorn: It's got to be *his* idea, or it's no good. He'll give probation to a bank robber, because it's his idea. But here, he's got a kid who did it on his own, with his family instead of the court, and Dorn can't stand that. He's going to teach Chris a lesson even if it destroys everything good this kid has accomplished."

To Judge Dorn, of course, there is nothing unusual or inconsistent in his handling of the Christopher Jones case. Set aside the lousy performance of the Probation Department (it turns out they knew for months before his arrest how to find Chris at his aunt's home, yet never did anything) and all that is left in Dorn's view is a kid who ran away and who now wants to beat the system. "That is something this judge will never allow," Dorn says. If the court does not enforce its orders—in this case, an order requiring Chris to stay in a group home—then the judge's authority and power is destroyed, along with the ability of the Juvenile Court to heal children's lives. To Dorn, it's that simple.

But this case, along with Rolando's and Keesha's and others, fuels a perception in the courthouse, already nascent because of Dorn's past controversies and his heavy-handed treatment of lawyers who try to paper him, that he is a wild card, capricious and unpredictable. Right or wrong, prosecutors and defense lawyers in the courthouse begin to divide themselves into two camps: those who consider Dorn a savior, and the apparent majority, who see him as willing to bend or break the law when it suits him, yet just as likely to be harshly inflexible with some other kid, whether it seems warranted or not.

The private attorneys by and large remain neutral, because of a perception that to cross Dorn is to risk a cutoff of their livelihoods. Dorn controls which attorneys are eligible for court appointments and, these lawyers say, it is a time-honored tradition among judges to punish lawyers who paper them or appeal them too often by crossing their names off the appointment list.

"I have an obligation to my clients, when I believe they will not be best served by appearing before Judge Dorn, to do something about it," one lawyer whispers outside the courtroom after a terse and angry hearing with Dorn. "But I also have an obligation to my family to bring home a paycheck. I've been told not to paper Judge Dorn, that I'll be punished if I do. Then I'm no good to anyone here. So what am I supposed to do?"

In the end, this lawyer decides she will serve no one's interests by getting booted from the courthouse, so she settles on a covert strategy to elude Dorn instead. In each case she wants removed from Dorn's courtroom, she requests special hearings to determine if probable cause exists for the charges against her clients. Every juvenile has a right to these hearings, but they are not automatic, and few private lawyers request them because of the extra work they entail. Their advantage, however, lies in the legal requirement that someone other than the trial judge must conduct the probable cause hearing, to avoid tainting the trial later on. It is the equivalent of holding a hearing outside a jury's presence in adult court. Dorn has to send these kids next door or downstairs for these probable cause hearings, after which the cases are supposed to return to Dorn for trial. But once this lawyer has one of her kids before another judge, she quickly cancels her request for the special hearing and negotiates a plea bargain and sentence then and there, avoiding ever having to return to Judge Dorn, where sentences and conditions of probation are often far more rigorous. Peggy Beckstrand catches on to this trick fairly quickly, but does nothing to intervene—she has no desire to keep cases in front of Dorn, either.

The same defense lawyer also quietly begins feeding information about Dorn's behavior to the more job-secure, civil-servant public defenders, particularly an incident in which Judge Dorn locked up a petty thief in Juvenile Hall on questionable legal authority.[2] Other lawyers follow suit. It is around this time that both the Public Defender's office and the District Attorney's Office begin amassing long lists of anecdotal evidence against Dorn, at the instructions of their superiors downtown, in hopes of finding sufficient material for a formal complaint of misconduct—just as had been done five years earlier during Dorn's first tour of duty in Juvenile

Court. DAs assigned to his courtroom must return to their office and write a report every day critiquing Dorn's rulings and demeanor, then hand it in to Peggy Beckstrand; the public defenders must do the same for their boss. It becomes a race, then, to see which office moves first in publicly opposing Judge Dorn, an open secret in the halls of Thurgood Marshall Branch. If Dorn is aware of this—and he probably is—he gives no hint of it, nor does he give any ground.

The battle almost comes to a head after Judge Dorn flies into a rage when a new prosecutor on Peggy's staff resolves a scheduling conflict by asking a colleague to finish a trial for her. All that remained to be done was to call a final witness, then rest the case. But when Dorn convenes the trial and sees a different DA in his courtroom, he begins screaming about shoddy, unprofessional prosecutors, and threatens to have the absent deputy DA arrested for contempt. Then he dismisses the case, a strong-arm robbery in which the victim had been threatened with death if he testified (but where the evidence ended up falling short due to witness problems that had nothing to do with which DA happened to be in court that day). Finally, at Dorn's insistence, Peggy has to trudge over to the courtroom, where Dorn first gives her a silent treatment, then screams at her in open court and on the record, telling her she runs an unprofessional shop, and lecturing her like a probationer. No prosecutors will be excused unless they are in the hospital or carrying a note from their doctors, he declares. Peggy has to jam her hands in her pockets to keep her own temper in check. Dorn will not let her speak. Her place is to listen to him, he says.

Back at the office, her gut reaction is to go to war over this encounter, but upon reflection, she decides being humiliated publicly by a Dorn tirade, however unpleasant, is not sufficient cause. Instead, she sends a memo downtown, and her immediate boss in the DA's Office, Tom Higgins, ends up coming to Dorn for a quiet meeting in chambers. In the process, this senior prosecutor observes a young girl sitting in the courtroom in handcuffs, accompanied by a policeman. She is a runaway being brought to Dorn as a status offender in need of one of his in-chambers lectures. This, Higgins concludes, is blatantly illegal—status offenders may not be handcuffed, since they have committed no crimes—and if a sufficient stink was raised, it could doom Dorn's most beloved project, his effort to bring status offenses back into the Juvenile Court mainstream. The potential legal liability to the county is also enormous—if a child in illegal custody was to be injured, the lawsuits would fly. Peggy's boss now has some damaging ammunition to bring into chambers with him, and he feels sufficiently comfortable, once he has the judge on the defensive and sputtering about misunderstandings by the police, to tell Dorn that his outburst at Peggy was both childish and unprofessional. Dorn admits no wrongdoing, but assures Higgins that measures will be taken to prevent any more improper handling of status offenders, and the meeting closes on a conciliatory note. Dorn wants to work *with*, not against, the District Attorney to make the system work better, he promises.[3]

Afterward, relations between Peggy's staff and the supervising judge at Thurgood Marshall take a notably cordial, even jovial turn, and most of the courthouse regulars begin to speculate that it will take some hotly contested fitness case, probably a murder or other violent crime, to provide the impetus to push either the DA or the Public Defender over the edge into a direct conflict with Dorn. Something where the stakes are truly high.

In the end, though, the fuse is lit by nothing more than a fifteen-year-old wristwatch thief, and a simple question over visits. Judge Dorn had ordered a juvenile facility to bar the public defender's in-house social worker from visiting the young man. Such visits are normally a routine process no other judge had ever tried to impede, but Dorn does not see it that way. Attorneys from the Public Defender's Office point out that Dorn is interfering with their representation of a client and, by extension, violating the kid's rights. But Dorn will not relent. He says in open court, "No. You cannot take anyone to see the minor. Not without an order from the court."

It is a line in the sand. The Public Defender's Office could say Fine, may we please have your permission to talk to our own client? Or they could fight.

The head of the public defender's juvenile section downtown sees this as the opportunity he has been waiting for. He has long regretted his office's agreement not to pursue a formal complaint against Dorn five years earlier once it was made clear Dorn would depart Juvenile Court. He has watched with increasing distaste Dorn's harsh sentences and attempts to reform the system through reviving the status offense, and he thinks Dorn is neither representative of judges in the system, nor a model who should be emulated. Now he gives a two-word command to his lawyers in Inglewood: "Paper him."

That's all it takes to declare war on Judge Dorn and, in the process, cripple the entire Los Angeles Juvenile Court.

PART THREE

A Child's Disposition

In the last 70 years many dedicated men and women have devoted their professional lives to the enlightened task of bringing us out of the dark world of Charles Dickens in meeting our responsibilities to the child in our society. . . . The court now . . . invites a long step backwards into the Nineteenth Century. In that era there were no juvenile proceedings, and a child was tried in a conventional criminal court with all the restrictions of a conventional criminal trial. So it was that a 12-year-old boy named James Guild was tried in New Jersey for killing Catherine Beakes. A jury found him guilty of murder, and he was sentenced to death by hanging. The sentence was executed. It was all very constitutional.

> **JUSTICE POTTER STEWART,** in a lone dissent denouncing the Supreme Court's 1967 Gault ruling requiring Juvenile Courts to grant children the same rights as adults

It is, to begin with, absurd to think that one must be mature enough to drive carefully, to drink responsibly or to vote intelligently, in order to be mature enough to understand that murdering another human being is profoundly wrong. . . . We discern neither a historical nor a modern societal consensus forbidding [it].

> **THE SUPREME COURT,** 1989, sanctioning the death penalty for some juveniles

CHAPTER 13

Thirty-one Flavors

Like many cities in Southern California, Inglewood seems more municipal fiction than actual place, a roughly rectangular set of boundaries visible only on maps, surrounded on all sides by the tar and concrete fist of LA. Technically, it is a city unto itself, but to the casual observer passing down Hawthorne Boulevard or Manchester Avenue or Seventy-eighth Street, this home to the Fabulous Forum where the Los Angeles Lakers and the LA Kings play is indistinguishable from the rest of the continuous urban sprawl. There is no buffer or break or green space dividing it from the rest of the world, no clearly defined border, no separate identity beyond the City Hall letterhead and the slightly different shade of blue the police officers wear. And, certainly, its boundaries offer no relief from the big-city crime statistics that plague the Los Angeles Basin like a fever chart and which, more and more, are the work of small hands. The events of January 26 show that as clearly as blood pooled on a hot sidewalk.

It is just after 7:00 P.M., a balmy night, LA in winter, a waning moon peering through the day's rising smog. Four teenagers in a gray Oldsmobile Cutlass cruise down West Seventy-eighth Street, passing rows of two- and three-bedroom bungalows with drought-choked lawns and ground-floor windows caged by bands of black wrought iron. The Cutlass glides to a halt next to a man who is standing on the sidewalk talking to his twenty-three-year-old girlfriend. They are outside her house, holding hands, her daughter playing at their side. Their smiles fade as they turn toward the stopped car just in time to see the tinted windows on the driver's side, front and rear, lower in tandem. From inside, they hear a coldly indifferent voice, still creaking with adolescence: "What's up, cuz?"

The man on the sidewalk has the survival instincts of a lifelong gang member. He begins to scramble for cover even before the muzzles of two semi-automatic weapons materialize from the car's gloomy interior and jut out the windows, gleaming blue-black in the frosty streetlight glare. When those muzzles start to jerk and flash, spewing a dozen bullets in the space of a handful of seconds, the man eludes injury. His girlfriend, though, has not been honed by a life on the streets. She takes a bullet in the leg and falls to one knee. At the same moment, her two-year-old daughter, Kyiara Nicole, yelps and emits an odd, wet-sounding cough. Her tiny chest has been pierced by a single bullet. Mother scrambles to her feet, scoops up baby, and runs bleeding into the house, screaming for help, dimly aware that the crashing of gunshots has stopped, replaced by the retreating sound of a car engine racing. Kyiara's grandfather comes running through the house and into the living room, but it is too late. The toddler who loves puzzles and kittens and the Zoe character on Sesame Street and her granddad's whiskery face doesn't cry, doesn't speak. She just looks up at him for an aching moment, eyes wide, bewildered, a plume of red blossoming across the front of her shirt like those time-lapse photos of flowers blooming. Then, as he and her mother both reach out to her, Kyiara Nicole crumples and dies on her own living room floor.

A half hour passes. The ambulances and squad cars have arrived, the insect buzz of their radios filling the night air, neighbors gathered outside like a Greek chorus, kids straining to see inside the house, restrained by festoons of yellow tape. Less than a mile away, the same gray Oldsmobile reappears, this time pulling up to a crowd of ten schoolkids hanging on a corner. As far as anyone can tell, the schoolkids are not gangsters or hard-core criminals, just young people passing time, idle and harmless. The same two windows snick down with an electric hum. The same two muzzles rise and spit more bullets, and a boy and girl go down, wounded in the legs and back, while the other kids duck and scatter. The fusillade stops, and someone emerges from the car, a pale teenager with wild hair, who appears to the kids on the corner to be somewhere between fifteen and seventeen years old. He leaves the door to his car open; rap music with the bass turned way up thumps incoherently from inside the car. Wild Hair strides purposefully toward one particular girl, Tila French, a fourteen-year-old junior high school student who has fallen to the ground, a pile of books cascading from her backpack. Tila sees Wild Hair coming, the big gun carried loosely at his side, and she tries frantically to escape by crawling under a parked van. She is halfway underneath—that's how the police will find her body, wedged at the curb amid the oil stains and flattened cigarette butts and her own blood—when the kid with the gun stops, standing directly over her. With his feet planted, arms extended straight out in front of him, the gun in both hands, just like on the TV cop shows, Wild Hair yells, "You're not goin' anywhere, bitch." Then he calmly pumps three bullets into Tila's body. The last is an execution-style coup de grâce to the head, delivered as the other children, Tila's friends and schoolmates, watch and scream and wonder if they are to be next. But Wild Hair just jogs back to the car, which vanishes around a corner, its billowing exhaust fumes mixing with the stink of gunpowder, blood, and fear.

It is the worst night of violence the city of Inglewood has ever seen. Even in a region long jaded by daily carnage, these killings top the LA nightly news on at least a couple of stations, though only in a way reminiscent of a Guinness Book entry—so many killed, so many wounded, a new record for the city. The true horror of it is not conveyed in the brief television and newsprint accounts—the fact that children are killing children, violently, inhumanly, forcing one another to duck bullets, spraying whole crowds in order to take out a single intended victim, transforming urban American teenagers into the psychological equivalents of war orphans. Still, there is immense pressure to do something, anything. The chief of police announces publicly that Inglewood's 112,000 citizens should stay indoors after sundown until an arrest is made. It is an unprecedented declaration of unofficial martial law, which puts the detectives on the case on an untenable time clock. Their city is being held hostage—an arrest must be made. Fast.

And so, five days after the murders—and against the recommendation of a dubious Peggy Beckstrand, already struggling to convict Inglewood's other notorious murderer, Ronald Duncan—the detectives arrest a wild-haired kid named Hugh. One of the kids on the street corner has tentatively ID'd him as the shooter, and a jubilant chief of police pronounces the case solved. For the first time in recent memory, TV cameras appear in Inglewood Juvenile Court to record the great moment of Hugh's arraignment (which they miss because, as so often happens here, the bus fails to bring the boy from Juvenile Hall). Even so, the impression is left that it will be only a matter of time before the other three killers are caught. Rest easy, Inglewood.

There's only one problem: Hugh, the kid Peggy Beckstrand has been asked to help lock away for the rest of his life, just might be innocent.

———◆———

THE Thurgood Marshall Branch of Juvenile Court is as ordered and calm as a swap meet today as Peggy Beckstrand makes her way across the street to resume the Baskin Robbins murder trial. She has just returned from a sleepless weekend of worry—over the rocky case and her decision to give immunity to an accomplice, along with all the other distractions and duties of a job she no longer loves or wants.

Lugging a heavy wad of files, she has to wade past a throng of black-clad gang members sitting on the steps outside the courthouse, hooting and mugging for a group of reporters and news crews milling about the unfamiliar terrain of juvenile justice, awaiting the arraignment of Hugh, the boy accused of Inglewood's worst-ever murder spree. She silently gives thanks that they are not here for her Ronald Duncan trial, though she knows there is somewhere among them one persistent reporter from a small local paper who is assembling a story on the Thirty-one Flavors case. After talking at length with Ronald's lawyer, this reporter seems convinced Peggy is letting an adult killer, Jason, go free in order to pursue young Ronald in Juvenile Court, and that favoritism among the brethren of law enforcement may lay behind her decision to grant immunity to the godson of a policeman.

Inside, the building is jammed with anxious parents and milling children, a routine mob, no more and no less angry and furtive than usual. A blue-suited security guard keeps walking the crowded hallways and issuing futile commands for everyone to stay in the building's lone waiting room, which cannot possibly accommodate the hordes on hand today. Everything is running late: the buses from the hall are late, which means court starts late, which means the lawyers, who need to interview their clients before court begins, are running late.

Peggy pushes her way through the smeary glass door on the west end of the building and down the first-floor hallway, as packed and loud as an airport terminal at Christmas. Halfway to the sanctuary of the courtroom, a defense attorney approaches her to discuss two separate murder cases she wants dropped—one young gangster charged with a drive-by murder, the other, a former foster kid who may or may not have participated in a fatal assault. From a prosecutor's point of view, both cases stink, not because the kids necessarily deserve breaks, but because the evidence is iffy and the defense lawyer is one of Inglewood's best—two more balls for Peggy to juggle in the midst of her trial. "Let's talk later," the DA says, pushing on through the clogged hallway.

Sharon Stegall rushes by next, announcing over her shoulder, "You've got to do something about that sorry excuse for a prosecutor. . . . He's messing with my cases." Then she is gone, swallowed by the crowd before Peggy can reply. She knows the dismissal problem has been getting worse in here and that she needs to make a change, but she has no time—yet another ball to keep in the air. One too many. It is this wearing pull in every direction that grinds down the best-intentioned professionals of Juvenile Court, leaving them in constant danger of being swept away by an undertow of major crises and petty details. Peggy has finally settled on the most common solution to this dismal reality: She has put in for a transfer. Ronald Duncan, for better or worse, will be among her final legacies to Juvenile Court, and all her bottled anger and frustration at the system is finding its expression in this trial, making her seem far more brittle and exposed in the courtroom than people here are used to seeing.

Peggy finally makes it to Judge Scarlett's court, letting her back rest against the wooden doors that ease closed behind her, muffling the roar in the hallway. She stares vaguely at the crime scene photos on their poster board display, left over from last week's proceedings and still leaning face-down against one wall of the courtroom, those terrible pictures of Chuck and Ada, their heads exploded by shotgun blasts, their receipts from a day of selling ice cream pillaged from their car. She had kept the posters handy to use in her closing arguments, another day or two to go. But first she has to get past today, something she has been dreading: Today she has to put Jason Gueringer on the stand, her new star witness, tainted by past lies, new admissions, and an airtight grant of immunity—the cop's godson who is going to get away with murder.

Over the weekend, Jason admitted to Peggy that his original claims of being an unwitting driver for Ronald were all lies. He had helped plan the robbery from the start and had been a willing getaway driver. But he insisted he had no idea Ronald was going to kill anyone—on that point, he swore he had always told the truth. Still, his objections to murder didn't stop him from accepting three hundred dollars from Ronald for his trouble that night—at the time, he explained, he was trying to live on his own and was broke.

His new story, in short, made him as culpable under the law for two murders as Ronald Duncan, whether he knew they were going to die that night or not. Yet he would suffer no consequences. Peggy felt she needed him and, despite his lies, she reluctantly continued her offer of full immunity in exchange for his testimony against Ronald. He had made his new admissions under that immunity grant—they could not be used against him. And there was no other evidence against Jason. So the offer stood.

James Cooper, Ronald's lawyer, professed to be stunned by this decision. There are people doing life in prison—or on death row—who have done less than Jason, he complained when Peggy told him of Jason's new tale. Peggy cannot argue the point, for there are too many examples to count that prove Cooper right: Elias Elizondo, for one, got fifteen to life in prison for being with a fellow gang member who committed murder. George Trevino is looking at twenty-nine years behind bars for a failed robbery in which only the adult ringleader was hurt. Geri Vance, trying to avoid a life sentence, accepted a plea bargain that will take away twelve years of his life, simply because he was an accomplice to a robber killed by his intended victim. Yet Jason walks free, no criminal record behind him, a career in the military ahead. What could Peggy say to Cooper except "I know. I know. But you've given me no choice"?

Now word has spread throughout the courthouse about this turn of events. Every public defender in the building is in the courtroom watching. Ronald's original lawyer, Assistant Public Defender Nancy Liebold, is talking to a colleague loudly. She says she is outraged that Jason is getting a walk on a potential death penalty case. She points out how the immunity smacks of favoritism toward a cop's relative, even though she knows from her work early in the case that the detectives investigating the murders wanted her and Ronald to help them nail Jason—proof that a lack of evidence, not favoritism, shaped the course of the case. Had Ronald cooperated, Jason would be on trial now.

Peggy looks pale and grim when Judge Scarlett takes the bench and resumes the trial, mistakenly announcing it as "People versus Donald Duncan" for the third time. Ronald takes his seat next to his lawyer with his customary grin, waving to his mother and father. As usual, Ronald's parents sit in separate rows, but they react in tandem when they see Jason Gueringer arrive in the courtroom from the witness room upstairs. Ronald's mother stares at him with unmistakable hatred; Ronald's father wears more of a sad expression of betrayal, as if he cannot fathom how the son of a friend and neighbor could be tearing his family apart in this way.

Jason avoids looking at them as he enters. He is exceptionally tall and thin, ducking slightly as he strides through the double doors, a nervous blue stork in his Air Force uniform—blue tie and pale blue shirt topped by a darker blue sweater with cloth epaulets on each shoulder. He exchanges glances with Peggy, as if to say he knows he is in for an unpleasant grilling. She has already delivered a tape recording of Jason's new, revised statement to Ronald's lawyer, James Cooper, who told Peggy without hesitation, "I am licking my chops on this one."

The prosecutor ushers her witness to the stand so he can take his oath and spell his name for the record. As he does this, the courtroom doors keep opening and closing as various people stick their heads in to see if they belong, the roar in the hallway pushing into the room each time, then fading as the doors ease shut—the courthouse Doppler effect, one attorney calls it. Jason tries to ignore this odd wax and wane, perching on the stand uneasily, towering over the microphone, scanning the crowd of unfamiliar faces in the gallery. He spots his godfather, Inglewood Police Sergeant Harold Moret, the man who made the first queasy connection between Jason, Ronald, and the blue getaway van used in the murders and smeared with the victims' blood. Moret glares back at Jason from a center-row seat. He is aghast at what Jason has done, but he is unwilling to believe completely that this young man he has known all his life could be a criminal without hearing it himself, right from Jason's own mouth.

Jason licks his dry lips and looks away, focusing on Peggy. Then, under her gentle questioning and in a surprisingly calm voice, he tells the story of the murder of Chuck and Ada Rusitanonta. Unlike the previous witnesses, this is not police theorizing on the meaning of blood drops, or eyewitnesses saying maybe or perhaps, or friends reporting what someone said and might have meant. This is the real thing: Jason delivers the detailed story only an accomplice can provide, damning and grim.

He explains that, contrary to his original statements to the police, he knew about the robbery in advance, he planned it with Ronald, and he accepted money to be the getaway driver. Having also worked at the ice-cream store in years past, he knew the owners' habits well. He knew when there would be large amounts of money for the taking, and how Chuck liked to carry it from the store in a brown attaché he treasured and called his "James Bond briefcase." Jason even bought shotgun shells for Ronald a few days before the murders, at Ronald's request, he testifies.

He had originally told police that he was out driving that night because he had gone to his girlfriend's house. Now, though, he admits this was a lie, a cover story. In truth, Jason testifies, he drove alone in his blue van to Taco Bell for a quick dinner, wolfed down a burrito, then parked at a spot

Ronald had picked in advance. Just as the other witnesses had suggested, he parked there and waited for Ronald to come with the booty. But when he saw Ronald hop aboard in blood-soaked clothes, stripping down to his boxers and T-shirt and screaming of murder, Jason had been terrified, he tells the court. Still, he drove Ronald home and accepted a cut of the money. Later, he tried to scrub away the blood to save his own skin, only to be caught in the act by detectives, forcing him to cook up some quick lies to minimize his involvement. He had already instructed Ronald, "No matter what happens, keep my name out of it," and Ronald had readily agreed, eager, it seemed, to be a stand-up guy for the older, wiser Jason.

"I knew he was going to rob them," Jason swears. "I didn't know he was going to kill them."

It is devastating testimony of Ronald's guilt—with one caveat. And on cross-examination, defense attorney Cooper takes aim at the obvious flaw in Jason's story.

"Didn't you know," he asks, "that if Ronald robbed them, the store owners could identify him?"

"Yes," Jason answers.

"But that didn't give you cause for concern?"

"For my well-being?" Jason responds. "No."

Cooper arches his eyebrows and stares at Judge Scarlett, looking for a reaction to this implausibility. He gets none, but Cooper knows he has made clear the problem with Jason's story: How could he have hoped to get away with such a robbery unless the witnesses were eliminated? If Ronald robbed his bosses, they would call the police immediately, and Ronald would be arrested the minute he walked in the door. Had Jason really been willing to stake his freedom on the silence of a flaky fifteen-year-old tagger?

Unfortunately for Cooper, even if Judge Scarlett accepts this insinuation and concludes Jason must have known in advance that Ronald was going to commit murder, it doesn't do much for Ronald's case. Either way, Ronald Duncan is still a stone-cold killer. Indeed, if they agreed on murder in advance, it is worse for Ronald—it means there is no way Cooper can argue that the killing was an impulsive, panicked ad lib to what was supposed to be a bloodless robbery.

So Cooper tries to overcome this problem by next suggesting through his questions that it was Jason, not Ronald, who did the killing. But Jason is six feet eight inches tall, a full foot taller than the person seen running from Chuck and Ada's car on the night of the murders. It was Ronald with the bloody backpack and the money and the bragging the next day, not Jason. When Peggy's turn to question him comes again, she emphasizes these points, making it as clear as she can that there is no way Jason could have been the person running from the car that night.

Jason's testimony wraps up a few minutes later, but not without a nasty postscript. When Peggy asks why Jason wasn't honest from the beginning, he says, "I kept silent on my involvement . . . to cover myself."

"And now you have no reason to lie, do you, because you have immunity?" Peggy asks. "No matter what you say here, nothing can happen to you, isn't that true?"

It is a set piece, something prosecutors always ask of their immunized witnesses. But before Jason can answer yes, Cooper laughs, a short bark that sounds shockingly loud in the otherwise quiet courtroom. Peggy springs to her feet.

"I object to counsel's demeanor," she blurts, red spots flaring on her cheeks. She is in a foul mood now, and can't let it go, as she normally might have. "It's an attempt to intimidate the witness."

"I'm not trying to intimidate him," Cooper responds, chuckling again, just to tweak his opponent. They both know he can and will argue just as easily that Jason would say or do anything to stay out of the gas chamber, that the only reason he gets his immunity is because his story helps the prosecution. "It's not intimidation. I'm just laughing at the game."

Scarlett looks pained, but says nothing.

"It's not a game," Peggy says. "It's very serious and I object to his demeanor. I believe it's inappropriate."

Scarlett clears his throat and waves one hand vaguely at the space between the two lawyers. He looks intensely uncomfortable at the unpleasantness, and he seems vaguely surprised that a seasoned prosecutor like Peggy would become so emotional about a case. Scarlett, for one, has seen too many young killers to let one more bother him. "All right," he finally says. "Let's be serious."

A short time later, Jason hesitantly walks from the courtroom, his testimony over. He is not sure where to go next. Peggy follows him out and tells him to go to her office and wait there. She doesn't want to risk him getting into any confrontations with Ronald's relatives.

After Jason, there isn't much left for Peggy to present. Phai Wan Konsuer, the victims' nephew and a dayworker at the ice-cream shop, testifies briefly about his friendship with Ronald, how Ronald was chronically late to work, and how Ronald was the only one working with Chuck and Ada on the night of the murders. Phai recalls that when he left the store a few hours before closing, Ronald was wearing a Baskin Robbins shirt identical to the blood-soaked one found lying by the curb a mile or so from the murder scene. His testimony takes less than ten minutes, the only time any member of the victims' family will be heard in this case. Unlike adult court, where juries are given detailed portraits of the lives of the victims of crime, Juvenile Court does not acknowledge the existence of victims or their survivors. Input from crime victims is considered irrelevant here, a waste of the court's precious time and a violation of confidentiality rules. Minor offenders and accused killers alike are spared having to face the human consequences of their crimes.

When Phai leaves, Scarlett breaks for lunch. The courtroom had emptied out after Jason finished, and Peggy walks over to her office with the sheriff's investigator in charge of the case, Robert Carr. She is nervous and motor-mouthing, speculating about how Jason's testimony went over with the judge, still shaken by the judge's decision to kick out Ronald's confession to police. "I just don't know what Scarlett will do," she says. "I can't see how he could rule against us, but I just don't know about him."

Part of what bothers her is a conversation she had with the newspaper reporter who is writing a story about Jason's immunity deal. "I just hope Scarlett doesn't view the case like that reporter does," she says. "He kept saying, 'Wouldn't it be better to put one guy in prison for life rather than another in CYA for nine years?' And I said no, it's who did what. It's who is most responsible. You just don't sit down and weigh time, to see who can get the longest sentence. You look at who did what. But he didn't seem convinced. Is that how the public thinks, I wonder? You just weigh time?" Carr just shrugs.

Across the street, she and Carr sit down with Jason for a last conversation. The young Air Force cadet, a plane ticket back to his military base in his pants pocket courtesy of the District Attorney's Office, pulls up a chair at the conference table and asks, "What now?"

Peggy sighs and explains to her witness how Ronald, even if convicted of murder and sentenced to life imprisonment, has to be released by age twenty-five under California law—and that, in other states, he would be released even sooner, at age twenty-one, eighteen in some places. They will try to rehabilitate him, she says, for what it's worth, but even if he remains unrepentant, the calendar will set him free. Jason shakes his head in astonishment—an odd gesture, Peggy decides, for an admitted accomplice who won't do a day of time.

"But you were in a completely different position, Jason," she says, trying to sound good-natured, but not quite pulling it off. "You could be spending the rest of your life in prison for what you did. You were just over eighteen when this happened. They could have asked for the death penalty. All for three hundred dollars."

Jason shakes his head again. He looks rueful. "Not even that."

Peggy looks at him, searching his face for sorrow, for an apology, for something that looks like regret. She's not sure what she sees, and tries to drive home the point again. "Do you understand, if it had been Ronald testifying against you, you could have faced a death sentence, Jason?"

He nods. "That's what I figured."

Peggy is silent a moment. But she realizes there is no point in dragging this moment out. It's done. She made her decision. All she can do is cling to the belief that Jason has been truthful about the core of his story—that he didn't know Ronald was going to kill anyone that night. That's the only thing that makes the immunity arrangement palatable. Even so, she has done what prosecutors do every day: She has cut a deal with the devil in order to get someone she considers even worse off the streets. If you can't live with that, she tells herself, then you might as well get out of the business. Because sooner or later—and probably sooner—she will have to do it again. It is one of the consequences few could foresee thirty years ago, when all the rights and procedures of adult criminal court were superimposed on the Juvenile Court. No one back then ever thought much about brutal double killings by fifteen-year-olds, about confessions thrown out of court and accomplices offered immunity for murder. Now it's just another day in Juvenile Court.

"Okay, why don't you get out of here, Jason?" Peggy says abruptly, then softens it by adding, "Get on with your life. Stay out of trouble."

Jason turns toward Detective Carr, a questioning expression on his face. The detective smiles. "That's right, it's a done deal. You're through here."

After the man given immunity for murder works out the door, en route to a career in the Air Force, Peggy can't help but say, "I wish I could say I was through here, too."

She retreats to her tiny office to pick at a take-out lunch while hunching over files, a solitude quickly interrupted by the office filing deputy, Sandra Flannery, who is in charge of drawing up new cases for prosecution. Flannery is puzzled by the facts of a case, and asks Peggy for advice.

"This girl shoots at her nemesis with a BB gun," Flannery says, waving a police report at Peggy, "but just hits her car."

The absurdity of dealing with such a case in the same place and in the same fashion, with all the same rules as the Ronald Duncan murder case, almost makes Peggy laugh out loud. She thinks of what her own nemesis in court said a few minutes earlier: *I'm just laughing at the game*, and she regrets making such a big stink about it. He was more right than she cares to admit.

"How about a 245 with a deadly weapon," she answers. California Penal Code Section 245 — assault.

"Well, it's not really a dangerous weapon. And it only hit the rear of the car. It didn't do any real damage."

Peggy shrugs. They discuss a statute that outlaws throwing objects at moving vehicles, but because there was never any danger of causing a crash, that doesn't seem to fit, either. In the end, no charges are filed at all, the simplest solution in Juvenile Court, and the most common one: Let the kid go, and hope for the best. Hope she doesn't do it again. Hope she doesn't use a real gun next time. The filing deputy returns to her desk, and Peggy marches back to her trial.

Back at the courthouse, with time to spare before the trial resumes, Peggy runs into Sharon Stegall again. The probation officer wants to tell her about her Triple Seven against Jesus, the kid turned in by his father for having a Baggie of crack in his room. It should have been a slam dunk, Sharon says, but the DA assigned to Judge Dorn's court did not contact the police lab in advance of the trial to get test results, which meant they could not prove that the substance in the Baggie was an illegal drug. Everyone knew it was coke, but Jesus's defense lawyer would insist that proof be offered. Maybe it was sugar or salt or laundry detergent, the lawyer would say, and Dorn would have to dismiss.

"And if that's not bad enough, he hasn't even called the schools for a report. We know the kid hasn't been in school for a month, but we can't prove that, either. Now he has me calling all over, trying to assemble *his* case for him."

Peggy shakes her head. She has known for some time that she needed a new body in Dorn's courtroom. She just hasn't had any to spare.

"Kids are walking out the door who need to be here," Sharon says. "Dorn's eating that guy alive."

Peggy promises to do something as soon as she can, and she asks Sharon to try, in the meantime, to do what *she* can to bolster Jesus's probation revocation. In the end, Sharon gives up the impossible task of trying to get witnesses to rush to court at the last moment (just finding someone at LAPD's laboratory willing to locate Jesus's Baggie of crack could easily take all day). Instead, she starts talking up the case to the newly appointed lawyer, who is harried, running late, and less than familiar with the facts of Jesus's Triple Seven. One of the savvy public defenders might have walked the kid out on yet another dismissal—the deputy DA would likely have folded as soon as the defense insisted on a trial, and Dorn would have had yet another dismissal to rave about. Instead, Sharon tells the appointed private lawyer what a foul mood Dorn is in, and how he has been hammering drug cases all week. Having the father come in and testify against his own son will tear the family up needlessly, Sharon adds. Wouldn't it be better for this kid to stay on good terms with his dad, and get some drug treatment and structure in his life? The lawyer nods, spends about five minutes looking at the file, makes no inquiry about whether the necessary witnesses are present, then pleads a pliant Jesus guilty to four separate violations. The defense even agrees with Sharon's recommendation that Jesus go to camp for at least six months. Judge Dorn narrows his eyes a bit at the sudden absence of adversarial posturing, then sees it is in the best interest of the boy and accepts the plea without comment. Then he imposes the recommended sentence, adding his own provisions for drug counseling and special education classes during and after camp. In minutes, the case has gone from near dismissal to a full admission, thanks to Sharon's bluster.

"My wife and I are happy. We know he needs to be detained," Jesus's father says later, chatting in the hallway with Sharon. "At least now, he has to go to school. He needs this."

Sharon is less than pleased, however. "It's just the system at work, or not at work. What's the point in having probation if we're going to blow cases all the time? That boy could just as easily have walked out today. Going by the evidence, or the lack of it, he should have. The system just screwed up in reverse today. Neither side did its job, and the right thing happened. Sometimes I think that's the only time the right thing happens. Now go figure that out."

Outside Judge Dorn's courtroom, a large family is assembled—mother, father, aunts, uncles, an assortment of kids. They are here for Hugh, the boy accused of Inglewood's recent murder spree, who is due for arraignment. The bus bringing him from Juvenile Hall has finally arrived—five hours late, and long after disappointed news crews departed for other stories.

Hugh's mother is telling Assistant Public Defender Leslie Stearns that her sixteen-year-old could not possibly have done the shootings. "We know exactly where he was," she is saying, tears running down her face. "He was in Ventura, selling magazine subscriptions. He's not interested in gangs. He's interested in making money. Can't we take him home?"

Peggy overhears this conversation. The woman had called her earlier and said the same thing. Once again, Peggy is struck by the certitude in the woman's voice. Not simply that her son is innocent—most every parent that gives a damn about their kid thinks that, at least at first—but that she knows, for a fact, where he was and what he was doing. It is one of the reasons she has begun harboring grave doubts about this case. That, and the way Hugh was arrested. After he was tentatively ID'd by a witness to the street corner ambush of the schoolchildren, Inglewood detectives met with Peggy to discuss what to do next. Figuring Hugh had to be in hiding, they decided to get a search warrant for his house, hoping to find a cache of weapons—perhaps one of the guns used to kill fourteen-year-old Tila French and two-year-old Kyiara Nicole. But when they arrived the next morning, they found no murder weapons—just Hugh, sitting calmly at his kitchen table eating Rice Krispies and getting ready to go to school. He had not been hiding at all. Not sure what to do, the policemen decided to arrest Hugh then and there, a dearth of evidence notwithstanding. This, in turn, forced Peggy to file charges she thought were premature.

But defense lawyer Stearns is not nearly so impressed with talk of Hugh's magazine alibi. Everyone claims innocence at this stage, and it is hard not to be jaded. She merely nods and tries to comfort the family, but makes it clear that the hearing today is just an arraignment. Nothing substantive will happen today, she says, and no matter what happens, they could be sure Hugh will not be coming home today, not with multiple counts of murder and attempted murder over his head. This provokes louder weeping from Hugh's mother and his aunt. Stearns leaves them then, returning to the courtroom to frantically comb the file Peggy's office just turned over, looking for an excuse that would allow the public defender to dump this case and give it to a private, appointed attorney. "It's really a sick case," she whispers. "We're looking for a conflict, any conflict."

And it turns out there is one: a kid named Stuart—who survived the street corner shooting and who identified Hugh as the killer—is represented by the public defender, an obvious conflict of interest. The same law office can't represent a killer and the witness against him. By coincidence, Stuart is in court this very day for violating his probation for robbery by not going to school. Now he's in the holding tank, waiting to go to boot camp. The public defender begs off the case. But there is another problem.

"Wait a minute," Peggy tells Judge Dorn's bailiff, when she realizes that Hugh and the star witness against him are about to cross paths in the holding tank. "We've got to keep them apart."

She dashes outside, heels clicking on the tile floor as she heads to the holding area in the back of the building. Someone could easily get hurt or intimidated—or be persuaded to change his story, she fears. Breathless, Peggy manages to get down there just as Hugh is being brought off the bus and Stuart is about to be herded on. At Peggy's urgent, whispered command, the witness is pulled aside and out of Hugh's sight, and the two manage to pass one another without ever knowing it.

"Jesus, that was close," she tells the confused deputies. They have no idea that any sort of relationship exists between Hugh the alleged killer and Stuart the witness, and could just have easily put them in a room together without a thought. Peggy is about to explain this to the guards, but then she glances at her watch and realizes she is late for Judge Scarlett's court.

"Helluva way to try a murder case," she mutters, then disappears around a corner.

Little else is done that day in the Ronald Duncan trial. Judge Scarlett has some unrelated matters to clean up, and they leave him in a dark mood, unusual for this even-tempered veteran of the juvenile bench. First comes a twelve-year-old boy with four arrests under his belt (including an armed robbery), six months of truancy, six months of inaction by the Juvenile Court, a mother who sent him to court by himself, and a lawyer who thinks he ought to go home on unsupervised probation. (Scarlett gives him formal HOP but, given his age, there probably won't be much difference.)

Then comes a teenaged girl who tried to murder her mother with a butcher knife—an angry attempt to fulfill the mother's constantly shouted prophecy that the girl would turn out just like her father. The father, Scarlett is told, is a serial killer. Now Mom is wailing in court that she wants her daughter back home. (Scarlett puts her in a foster home, but he knows this is a temporary fix at best—juvenile law is purposely biased in favor of reuniting families, no matter how dysfunctional.)

"What a mess," Scarlett mutters after the family leaves his courtroom.

"As long as we keep returning these children to the environment that contributed to their violating the law in the first place, we should never expect to solve anything. Everyone in the courtroom knows it. But I do not have that power."

After fourteen years on the juvenile court bench, Scarlett believes the law needs to be changed so that judges can remove such children from their dysfunctional homes for years, perhaps permanently—not based on the severity of a kid's crime, as is the current practice, but on the basis of a kid's need. This is a radical notion, given the law's preference for keeping families together, and it is also a politically and racially volatile issue, because minorities are proportionally overrepresented in Juvenile Court, and therefore could be disproportionally affected by such a policy change.[1] Even for an African-American judge with a strong record as a defender of civil rights, such opinions are frowned upon. Scarlett recalls well what happened to former mayor Tom Bradley when he voiced similar beliefs many years ago, long before juvenile crime had arced out of control: Bradley was roundly denounced by even his most ardent supporters, and quickly backed off his statements.

When Scarlett finishes these other cases and finally resumes the Duncan trial, there is time only for some minor cleanup testimony, followed by Peggy's announcement that she rests her case. If Jason's testimony hasn't closed the deal, she figures, nothing will.

The next morning, the defense takes its turn. Ronald Duncan is the first and only witness.

The first time he testified, the focus had been on one legal issue—whether his confession to the police should be admitted or tossed out. Now, though, he could tell his whole story. His parents lean forward in their seats, eager, waiting, watching Ronald take the stand and his oath to God. Then he sits down and begins stroking his sparse goatee, assuming a look of intense concentration.

Cooper's first question gets right to the point. "Did you kill Chuck and Ada?"

Ronald shakes his head and gives a drawn-out and truculent "No," sounding like a small child denying a predinner raid on the cookie supply.

Cooper's next question, however, is an odd one—an open-ended request for Ronald to describe his knowledge of the murders. This violates a cardinal rule of courtroom examinations—questions must invite specific responses, not wide-ranging narratives that can take unexpected, sometimes legally impermissible turns. When Peggy objects, Cooper asks for a break, and the lawyers and Judge Scarlett retreat into chambers for a quiet discussion. Cooper informs the others that he asked such an open-ended question because of his own ethical concerns—he wants to avoid the possibility of eliciting perjury from a witness, something he is barred from knowingly doing. This is a tacit but nevertheless extraordinary acknowledgment by Cooper that his client might be about to lie. The only way off the ethical hook for Cooper is to let Ronald tell his story through an open-ended narrative. Peggy shrugs. Scarlett says, Okay, get on with it.[2]

When court is reconvened, Ronald tells his story. The courtroom is full again, mostly with lawyers and Ronald's family, his parents hanging on every word. "Now we'll hear the truth," his mother says to no one in particular.

Ronald starts his story of innocence by claiming that he did not wear his Baskin Robbins shirt that night. Therefore, the bloody polo shirt found by the side of the road could not be his. Or if it is, he has no idea how it was bloodied or how it could have gotten there. He says he walked home from work that night, rather than accept a ride from Chuck and Ada, and came nowhere near the murder scene. Halfway home, he saw a familiar blue van approaching, and flagged Jason down.

It was then, Ronald says, smoothing the front of his orange jumpsuit as he speaks, that he learned Jason had murdered his employers.

"When I got inside, he looked at me and said, 'I did it.' I said, 'Did what?' 'I did *it.*' And I looked down behind the seats and saw a plastic bag full of money."

Ronald knew, then, what had happened. Two people he claims to have loved had been killed, their money piled at his feet. When Ronald pauses, Cooper asks, "Then what?"

Ronald shrugs, as if the answer should be obvious. "My first thought was, Break me off." Ronald laughs then, as if the memory of it is amusing.

"What does that mean?" Cooper asks.

"It means, give me some. I got about two hundred dollars."

There is no mistaking the look of distaste on Judge Scarlett's face then, an expression mirrored by virtually all of the other people in the courtroom, except for those related to the witness. Ronald is oblivious to the effect he is having, which only makes it worse. Later, he would happily describe this scene in the Juvenile Hall writing class. It never occurs to him—on the stand, or in the class—that most people might expect a different reaction from him in that moment of discovery in the van, perhaps horror or sorrow or an impulse to call the police. It never occurs to him that there is anything wrong with *Break me off*. Even Ronald's father flinches when he hears this, the look of a man suddenly awaking from a dream etched across his face.

Cooper prods Ronald along with another "Then what?"—the question of a lawyer who does not want to suborn perjury. Ronald thinks a moment, then recalls how on the day after the murders, he again saw Jason, who instructed him, "If anything comes down, don't say anything. And I said, Don't worry, I'm covering myself." Once again, Ronald grins, the stand-up guy, taking the heat for his older friend.

Later, he says, his schoolmate and fellow tagger Marvin asked him if he killed Chuck and Ada. Contrary to Marvin's testimony about Ronald confessing to the crime, Ronald swears he told Marvin no, he didn't kill Chuck and Ada. He just robbed them—a lie, he says now, intended to earn him respect. "Gang kinda respect," Ronald explains. "To get a rep. To get more respect from our bigger homeboys . . . But I never said I murdered anyone."

There it is, then, Ronald's defense: Marvin got it wrong, Jason is the real killer, never mind my confession.

Cooper finishes up quickly then, and Peggy begins her cross examination. She has the look of someone performing a particularly unpleasant laboratory dissection.

First she confronts Ronald with all his many inconsistencies—how he was seen leaving for work in the Baskin Robbins shirt he claimed he didn't wear, how he failed to explain why his pants were inside Chuck and Ada's car on the night of the murder, crumpled and bloody, and how he neglected, during his direct testimony, to mention the blood on his backpack and how he once claimed to have been knifed on the way home from work in order to explain that blood.

"It slipped my mind," Ronald says tightly. "I'm under a lot of stress right now."

But when Peggy asks the next question, it is her voice that is quaking with stress, not Ronald's. "You didn't jump up from the backseat and shoot Chuck in the head behind the left ear and blow his brains out of his face?"

"No, I did not," Ronald says in a steady, clear voice.

Ronald has his chin propped on his hand again, a posture of insolence, the look of a kid seemingly certain he will elude justice. It makes Peggy furious, her hands clenched and white, her voice tremulous. "How did your friend Marvin know details of the murders if you didn't tell him?" she asks.

Ronald doesn't know.

"Does Marvin have any reason to lie?" she asks.

Ronald shrugs. "Not that I can see."

As Ronald testifies, smiling and sarcastic, both hands now propping up his chin, Judge Scarlett gradually inches farther and farther away from the witness stand, until, by the time Peggy finishes, he is as far from Ronald as possible without physically leaving the bench.

Peggy winds up her questioning by asking why he would say to Jason, 'Break me off.' Ronald's reply is smug and simple, a hateful child's response. "Why not?"

Peggy sits down and Cooper quickly puts his case to rest then. Scarlett glances at the clock, then at Deputy DA Wendy Derzaph, the prosecutor normally assigned to his courtroom, who has four other trials on his docket this day. The judge tells Peggy to make her closing argument, a process that is often an all-day affair in adult court murder cases, but which she accomplishes in about five minutes.

"The evidence is overwhelming," she says. There is the blood on Ronald's shirt, his pants, his book bag. There is Marvin's testimony that Ronald admitted to the crimes, in telling detail. There is Jason's testimony that they planned the crime together, and that he drove a blood-drenched and moneyed Ronald home from the scene. There is Ronald's stream of lies in the case.

"I was about to say he's clearly guilty beyond a reasonable doubt, but you can't say guilty in Juvenile Court," Peggy says. "We just say, petition sustained. Well, I ask you to make the equivalent finding of guilty beyond a reasonable doubt in light of the overwhelming evidence that Ronald Duncan is a murderer."

When his turn comes, James Cooper makes a game effort to earn his fee, talking of Jason's changing story, his motive to lie in order to get immunity and avoid the death penalty, the possibility that favoritism led police to Ronald when they should have pursued Jason. There's not much he can say about Marvin's damning testimony, so he avoids mentioning it, and instead complains about the lack of fingerprint evidence showing Ronald had even been in the victims' car that night (ignoring the fact that, had Peggy presented such evidence, it would have been meaningless, since Ronald had been in his bosses' car on many nights and could have left prints there any of those times).

"There is an absence of corroborating physical evidence," Cooper drones on. "You'll see that when the court reads the autopsy." Cooper knows, of course, that Scarlett will not read the autopsy report. He can see the judge rocking back and forth in his chair now, impatient, looking at the clock, after eleven now, with four trials and a full calendar still ahead of him. Cooper glances at the judge, stops talking, makes a vague gesture of surrender with his hands, then quickly winds up and sits down.

Scarlett turns to Peggy then with a big smile. "Do the People want to rebut?" He manages to load the inflection of this sentence sufficiently to make the unspoken subtext quite clear. No transcript will ever show it, but this is what the judge is really saying: *Don't waste my time with more talk. Let's just get it done.*

Peggy knows, then, for the first time, that she has won. She shakes her head and says, "The People submit it, Your Honor."

Scarlett doesn't waste a second. There is no retiring to chambers to deliberate or to study the evidence, no solemn ritual assembling of jurors to pronounce justice. Scarlett just does it. Without looking at Ronald, he says, "The court agrees with the People. The evidence in this case is overwhelming. The petition is found to be true, that the minor committed murder in the first degree, with enhancements, personal use of a firearm."

Peggy feels no elation at this. She just watches Ronald. He scowls as the judge's words sink in, a look, it seems to Peggy, of genuine surprise. Though Cooper told him over and over, along with his parents, that no other result was possible, he still appears stunned. He covers his eyes with his right hand, while his father, huge tears rolling down his lined face, begins to sob loudly, staggering to his feet and walking blindly from the courtroom. A minute later, still crying, but silently now, he walks back in, wanting to flee, but afraid he will miss something. Ronald's mother is weeping now, too, loudly sniffling. The bailiff hands her a tissue.

Cooper, meanwhile, is already talking about sentencing—"disposition," in Juvenile Court parlance. Adults are sentenced; children are "disposed of." Cooper wants a delay, insisting that Ronald must have a psychiatric report before disposition.

"But why bother?" Scarlett wants to know. "There's only one place he's going. There's no way in the world he's going anywhere but CYA."

But the judge gives in once Cooper asks for another conference in chambers, where the lawyer explains that, even though the sentence is automatic, failure to grant a psychiatric exam is reversible error. They'd just have to do it all over again. Peggy has to agree. Besides, Cooper says, making the prosecutor want to shudder, they'll need the psychiatric report for later. When Ronald comes up for parole. Scarlett grudgingly agrees.

As they prepare to return to open court, though, Judge Scarlett makes a remark that Peggy finds particularly satisfying. "This kid is so repugnant. I can't believe the lack of remorse. In my forty-year career, fourteen years on the bench, this is one of the worst killings I've ever seen."

Back outside, Ronald is motionless now, head down on folded hands, quiet, dry-eyed, disinterested. Scarlett has one more task today: He sets a day for disposition, choosing the first available date. But Ronald's mother begins to wail at this, a final blow. She screams, "No, no. That's his birthday. No!"

The judge quickly reschedules the sentencing, then eagerly says, "Next matter?" The resolution is anticlimactic, like a movie inadvertently shorn of its last few minutes of film. Ronald's father just sits in the gallery, face blank; his mother walks out of the courtroom, shaking her head, saying over and over, "They set him up, they set him up." Behind her, a cadre of lawyers is scrambling to its feet to see who among them can get his or her case called next, hoping to squeeze in a hearing before lunch, trying to keep the machinery of juvenile justice turning. Peggy walks past the Duncan family out in the hallway, feeling their stares on the back of her neck.

At the end of the day, Peggy leaves her office and drives to Chuck and Ada's Baskin Robbins store to explain to the family what happened in court. The prosecutor had previously suggested they stay away from the trial, not wanting them to see those awful photos or to hear the unpleasant testimony. They said fine, they trusted Peggy to see that justice was done, to keep them informed. Now she wants to explain to them that Ronald was finally found guilty and will be punished.

When she gets there, a small table is reserved for her, with special Thai coffee and Thai food set out, made in the family's own kitchen. Ada's brother Montri and sister Tina come out with a huge bouquet of flowers for Peggy, and she stays with them for an hour, explaining the verdict and the likely sentence, and the fact that Ronald will someday be freed, in nine years or less. She promises to do what she can to fight any early parole for the boy. Then, somewhat gingerly, she also explains Jason's involvement, his immunity agreement, the fact that he will not pay for his crime, but that, hopefully, he will never do anything like this again. Peggy is not sure these recent immigrants to America fully understand her deal with Jason, but they seem satisfied, even grateful that the killer has been convicted at least. They admit, though, that a year later, they still find the crime and Ronald's role in it inconceivable.

"I would just like to ask Ronald why," Tina says. "I would like to know why he would do this thing. Did he say he was sorry? Is he sorry?"

Peggy shakes her head, then has to watch the sadness creep across Tina's face. No, Peggy says, Ronald did not say he was sorry. Maybe he will someday. But not so far.

After that, Tina and Montri are interested primarily in talking about how wonderful Chuck and Ada were, remembering how everyone in the neighborhood mourned their loss, and how tough it has been for their two surviving children without a mother or father. And they cannot stop thanking Peggy. She is *their* lawyer.

But the next day, the local newspaper publishes a story highly critical of the immunity agreement with Jason, the article Peggy had been dreading. Neighbors have been coming in the ice-cream shop talking about it, how Jason planned the crime all along and is getting away with murder. Now Chuck and Ada's family isn't so happy with their lawyer Peggy after all.

"We want Jason in jail," Tina says angrily over the phone.

All Peggy can say is "I'm sorry." She offers the family the opportunity to come in and read the file, so they can understand what happened and why, but she knows they won't do it. Any sense of victory Peggy felt about the case vanishes after that, leaving only weariness. The feeling is compounded by a conversation she has a short time later with one of her deputies, who reluctantly tells her of a chat he had with Judge Scarlett. The young prosecutor, aware of Peggy's mixed feelings about giving Jason immunity, asked the judge if he would have convicted Ronald without Jason on the stand. He was hoping to find comfort for his boss, but it did not work out that way.

"Sure, I would have convicted him," the prosecutor reluctantly quotes Scarlett as saying. "The evidence was overwhelming. As far as I'm concerned, she didn't need to give the accomplice immunity at all."

CHAPTER 14

The Dorn Wars

Cecil Jacks walks into Commissioner Gary Polinsky's courtroom, a small, dark twelve-year-old with large doe eyes and a fidgety, can't-wait-to-get-out-of-here manner about him. He is anxious to leave court so he can return to the abandoned trailer home he calls his "clubhouse." A rusting hulk parked in a weedy vacant lot amid the broken glass, used condoms, and dog droppings, Cecil's clubhouse is the one place he feels at ease, in command, safe. "It's the place where I do my stuff," he says.

Eleven months ago, Cecil and his best friend, a fifteen-year-old budding transvestite named Danny, sporting lip gloss and fingernail polish, escorted a neighborhood boy to the clubhouse. The boy, Joshua, was fourteen years old and bigger than little Cecil, but he was developmentally disabled and mildly autistic. Mentally, he functioned as a six-year-old, if that. He is awkward and shy, and some of the kids in the neighborhood made a point of torturing him on days when there was nothing better to do, which appeared to be many. Cecil and Danny were among these, but one day, they pretended to befriend him instead. They even suggested he come do some "stuff" with them in the old trailer. He followed them like a puppy.

Once the door slammed closed on that leaning trailer, Cecil and Danny molested Joshua for more than an hour. They forced him to fellate them, sodomized him, even compelled him to kneel behind them and eat their

feces. That the ringleader—twelve-year-old Cecil—could even conceive of
such things had astounded police and prosecutors alike. Afterward, Cecil
and Danny had made Joshua swear to keep silent or, they said, they would
kill him. But when he went home, Joshua complained to his aunt about being sick to his stomach. He wouldn't stop brushing his teeth. After repeated,
anxious questioning, Joshua described what had happened in broken, tear-
ful sentences, first to his aunt, then to the police.

After a long investigation hampered by Joshua's disabilities and fears,
Cecil and his friend Danny were charged with various counts of sexual assault, then released to their families, who then called Peggy Beckstrand to
scream about their children's innocence and the racist propensities of LA
cops and prosecutors. They said they were good families—Cecil's father was
a tradesman, the mother a health care practitioner. And, in any case, Cecil
would never do such a thing. Why, Joshua still comes over and asks to play,
the mother railed.

These protestations slacked off when, while awaiting trial, Cecil was arrested again, this time for robbery and aggravated assault. Cecil had tried to
snatch someone's purse. When his intended victim resisted, he hit her with a
brick, then sped off on his mountain bike (also stolen). Even then, because of
his tender age, Cecil was not detained, but allowed to roam free for months,
continuing to terrorize his neighborhood, his classmates, his teachers.

Now, after months of delays, his trial date has finally arrived. But Cecil
knows all about Juvenile Court. "Ain't nothin' going to happen to us," he
whispers to his nervous-looking crime partner, Danny, while waiting for the
commissioner to take the bench. "You wait and see."

Soon enough, Cecil begins to smirk as he watches Joshua on the witness
stand, a pitiful sight. The boy is afraid, incoherent, rendering his testimony
interminable. He keeps putting the witness-stand microphone in his mouth
and sucking it. In the end, he stands up and faces the wall, testifying to the
faded walnut paneling about "sucking Cecil's dick" and "eating shit from
his behind."

When Joshua finally leaves the courtroom, Commissioner Polinsky, a
twelve-year veteran of the Juvenile Court bench, says he cannot convict anyone beyond a reasonable doubt based on the word of a witness like Joshua.
The prosecutor, Todd Rubenstein, argues in vain that it was simply the pressure of facing off with his attackers in court that was too much for Joshua.
He points out that the police detective who painstakingly interviewed Joshua
many times has gotten a consistent, coherent story from the boy in more
relaxed, less threatening settings. The DA also reminds the commissioner

that Cecil and his friend previously accused one another of assaulting Joshua—further evidence of their combined guilt. But Polinsky disregards these points. The whole case comes down to an unreliable witness, he says, and that requires him to find Cecil and Danny innocent. The commissioner says he feels terrible for Joshua, and that his ruling will make for the worst possible outcome for everyone involved. "But I have no choice," he says. "The law leaves me no choice."

It soon gets worse. The woman Cecil robbed was an illegal immigrant. She is too fearful to come to court, the prosecutor announces—she has disappeared. No witness, no case. The robbery charges, too, must be dismissed.

With that done, Commissioner Polinsky sternly lectures the kids, ringleader Cecil in particular. Shape up or you'll be back, facing worse, the commissioner tells him, but everyone in the room knows this for what it is— impotent rambling. Cecil has beaten the system, just as he knew he would. He is free. He openly laughs outside the courtroom after the lecture.

"All three of those kids need help," Polinsky later reflects. "And so do their families. But there's nothing I can do. I know those kids almost certainly are guilty, but I couldn't convict on the testimony I heard. We have to use the same standard as in adult court: guilty beyond a reasonable doubt. Without that, I can't order them to do anything. It's all so frustrating. They are time bombs."

The prosecutor is bewildered by the decision. "If everyone knows he's guilty, and everyone knows he needs help before he commits worse crimes, what kind of system still turns him loose? Polinsky could have gone the other way—it's not like anyone is going to go to the time and expense to appeal a conviction in a case like this. So how can a court commissioner arrive at a decision that everyone—including the commissioner himself—understands to be the worst possible outcome for everyone involved? It's nuts."

As he walks downstairs to see about another case, above him in the hallway, Cecil and Danny exchange high fives, then shuffle off with their families. Back home, their clubhouse awaits them. There's a lot of stuff to do.

———◆———

AS the Thurgood Marshall Branch's wheezing air conditioner slowly surrenders to the acrid swelter of Los Angeles summer, the courtrooms become close and stifling, traffic noise and exhaust fumes filtering through fire escape doors propped opened in futile quest for a cooling breeze. Shafts of pallid sunlight alive with eddies of dust enter through these doors, penetrating the customary gloom to leave the lawyers and judges blinking at the smoggy glare, and giving portions of the courtroom still in shadow a sepia quality, as if this courthouse were an ancient place, long disused.

This is the season when the pace of Los Angeles Juvenile Court slows to (some might say from) a crawl. This is when patience withers and the halls of this old courthouse turn clammy with a gummy film of moisture. This is the time the Public Defender's Office chose to begin its crusade against Judge Dorn, the time to blanket him with "paper."

This power to strike out at a judge stems from a simple right, a seemingly minor rule imported from adult court: Each side in a criminal case has the right to ask once for a different judge than the one originally assigned to a case, simply by filing a one-page form—"the paper." There are no questions asked, and no exceptions. Judges are assigned cases at random as they come into the system; the rule is intended to be used sparingly. But if lawyers use their paper en masse to target a specific judge, then it becomes a potent bludgeon. It is yet another unintended side effect of the Supreme Court's landmark Gault decision that gave children the same rights as adults, a seemingly minor procedural rule that has placed an increasingly impossible burden on the Juvenile Court.

At first, the papering of Judge Dorn begins on a selective basis, with the assistant public defenders who work in Inglewood requesting transfers of new, incoming cases only when they thought a different judge might grant informal probation, or when a poor school record was at issue—the two points on which Judge Dorn always crushes them.

But Roosevelt Dorn reacts as everyone should have known he would—escalating the conflict, rather than defusing it. This is, after all, a judge who finds it necessary to issue regular, imperial reminders to lawyers: "You are not running this courtroom, *Judge Dorn* is running this courtroom." His predictable response to being papered is to lash out by sending cases not to the other judges in the building, but to far-flung courthouses around the county, keeping the understaffed public defenders in their cars as much as in the courtroom.

That this combat began over a minor case and a minor question about a social worker's right to visit a client—a question an appeals court initially wavered on, then, after a long delay, summarily settled in Dorn's favor—is quickly forgotten. When the head of the public defender's juvenile section comes to meet with Dorn in his chambers, no white flags are in evidence. The lawyer, Mark Lessem, emerges and announces that a promise he made months earlier to the presiding judge of Juvenile Court—that he would give Dorn a chance despite grave misgivings—has been fulfilled. Now the gloves would come off. Judge Dorn is far out of the mainstream of judicial thought when it comes to kids, Lessem complains, a judge who represents neither what is typical in the system, nor what is best. He bullies and punishes and demeans, then calls it "working with kids," as Lessem sees it, and though Dorn could be viewed as pro-defense on some issues, particularly fitness hearings, the problems still outweighed the benefits. "He doesn't want to be a judge. He wants to be a king," Lessem says after their meeting. "When I went to talk to him, he nearly threw me out."

On even this point, the warring parties could not agree: Dorn recalls Lessem storming out of the meeting on his own. Afterward and in open court, the judge accuses Lessem of pursuing a personal vendetta against him for reasons unknown. Dorn says he had been approached by attorneys in the Public Defender's Office who told him they were being forced to paper him against their will, even though they knew he always gave a fair trial—comments the judge took to be true, though others suggested this was merely a case of savvy trial attorneys wisely using their downtown boss as a shield from Dorn's wrath. "Sooner or later, they'll have to try a case before Dorn again," one lawyer sitting in the gallery whispers as the judge reiterates his claim that he is the victim of a vendetta. "Why poison your own relationship with the man when you can blame someone else?"

In any case, after that brief meeting between Dorn and the head juvenile public defender, the papering becomes a blanket. Now, every new case that comes before Judge Dorn—one-third of all the cases filed in the Thurgood Marshall Branch, hundreds a month—have to be shipped out.

Once the blanket is in place, the scene in court becomes almost farcical, a constant state of confusion. No one knows anymore what court they are supposed to be in, when or where. On the defense table, the lawyers keep a thick pile of photocopied forms—the one-page legal motion used to request a different judge. Each time a new case is called, the public defender on duty picks up one of these blank forms, fills in the juvenile's name, and files the paper. There is no consulting with the client—this is about teaching Judge Dorn a lesson, not about what might or might not be best for any particular kid. Most of them, freshly arrested and dazed at their loss of freedom, appear not to really understand what is going on. No one explains it to them.

Each time he is papered, a small, tight smile creeps across Dorn's face, barely making his thin mustache move. If possible, he makes the defense attorney, the juvenile, the family, and witnesses wait all morning for him to reassign the case. If a lawyer tries to prod him into choosing a new courtroom, he merely says, "I haven't decided yet," and takes up some other matter. When he is finally ready to decide, he consults with his clerk to find the most distant courthouse possible with room on its docket. If he can send a case to Pomona, one of the two satellite courthouses he supervises—and the most distant and inconvenient one available—he does so.

And if the witnesses and victims and family have to travel across town to a new and unfamiliar courthouse along with the public defender on the case, so be it. Dorn has a lesson to impart, too. He makes it a point to apologize to the witnesses and families, then points a finger at the defense table and says, "The Public Defender's Office is forcing me to do this." It is not precisely true—he could be sending the cases to Commissioner Polinsky or Judge Scarlett, right there in Inglewood—but he achieves the desired effect. After a week of this, the public defenders are as popular as roaches here.

His Pomona ploy does not always work, however. The Pomona Juvenile Court has no judges, just referees and commissioners, and for some hearings, a juvenile has the right to insist that a full judge hear his case. When that happens, Dorn's clerk must get on the phone with one of the delinquency court administrators at the presiding judge's office, who must then contact the other judges, one by one, whining and calling in favors until someone finally says, Oh, all right, send me the file. Several judges make a point of reminding the administrators that they had warned against bringing Dorn back to Juvenile Court, that this kind of blowup would be inevitable once he returned. After several rounds of phone calls, the cajoling process starts to take hours—judges, the ultimate authority in their individual courtrooms, can always say no when asked to take over Dorn's workload—and this brings all other activities in the administrators' office to a halt as the search for court space expands. That, in turn, piles more delays into the system, as other crises go unattended—the missing files, the misplaced delinquents, the riots in Juvenile Hall, the endless stream of memos that keeps the sluggish system moving along—all must line up behind the Dorn War. In the end, Judge Dorn must grudgingly begin to send some of his cases to the other two courtrooms at Thurgood Marshall, exploding their dockets.

The spread of the cancer is then complete. Kids and families wait all day to have their cases resolved. Students miss school. Parents miss work. Witnesses are told to come back another day. Uniformed cops stand around, waiting to testify instead of attending to their patrols. The number of postponements skyrockets.

One young man must wait all morning for a piece of official paper saying he has paid his debt to society, performed all his community service, and completed probation successfully. Indeed, he is an unqualified success story for the system, a young car thief and truant who turned his life around, went back to school, graduated, stayed clean, and is now about to join the Marine Corps.

He just needs that one piece of paper to complete the induction process. He needs it today. He has been waiting seven months for it to arrive in the mail, as promised. Now, after repeated, unanswered phone calls to his probation officer, he has come to court for a final time.

He waits hours in Judge Scarlett's gallery, watching the court wade through its calendar, a tall blond with muscular arms and a smooth, ruddy face that straddles the line between adolescence and manhood. He is rebuffed repeatedly by the court staff when he asks for help. "Are you on the calendar?" the clerk ask. When he shakes his head, she says, "You'll have to wait." Later, during a lull in the action just before lunch, the young man once again ventures through the little swinging gate that divides the gallery from the lawyers' tables and approaches the clerk. She is nearly obscured behind a duck blind of papers and files, the telephone wedged between her shoulder and ear as if it has taken root there. The clerk looks up at his questioning look and shakes her head again. "Your paperwork is not here yet," she says, looking away before she even finishes the sentence. "Sorry." The tone of her voice says she is not.

"I'm the one getting reamed here," he replies, patience finally giving way to anger. "I've done my time. I just want to get on with my life."

Despite his angry words and raised voice, none of the lawyers glance up from the files and papers—they are too busy, too caught up in the chaotic mess sweeping the courthouse. At the end of his journey through the system, when he has done everything asked of him, there are no congratulations, no acknowledgments, no one to represent him but himself.

"It's on your probation officer," the clerk says defensively. "It was his job to submit the report long ago. It didn't happen until today."

"I haven't seen my probation officer in seven months," the eighteen-year-old says. He is red in the face. Even his scalp, visible beneath the

Marine-style haircut he has already gotten in anticipation of boot camp, is crimson with anger.

"Well," the clerk says, dismissive now, accusing, "perhaps you should have."

"He told me to stop coming," the kid says.

The clerk offers no apology for her groundless accusation. "Well, we'll get to it sometime today. But I just can't say when the order will actually be entered. Might be a few days before you get it."

The young man stalks off, shaking his head, pushing through the double doors. No one gives him a second look.

Judge Dorn has waged this war before, and he plays to win. With the papering in full swing, forcing him to transfer incoming cases, he steps up his status offender meetings in chambers and he takes on more private-attorney cases. He is prepared to wait out the public defenders, over whom he knows he has one key advantage: No matter what they do, he never has to leave his courtroom. The lawyers must follow the cases wherever he sends them, and Dorn has them driving all over Los Angeles's sprawling jurisdiction, trying to keep up.

The Inglewood public defenders soon find they cannot keep up with the tangle of transferred cases for which they are personally responsible. The court bureaucracy's paper mill cannot keep up with all the changes, either. Witnesses are left wandering. The detention hall buses drop off the wrong kids in the wrong courthouses. The defenders find they have more than one case scheduled simultaneously in courthouses many miles apart, forcing them to spend every spare minute on Dorn's courtroom telephone, trying to get continuances from judges all over LA.

"I knew I'd have to be in three places at once this afternoon," one public defender tells Dorn sheepishly after one such attempt at telephone juggling collapses.

"Talk to your boss about that," Dorn says with a grin.

"I know I have other matters in here," the lawyer pleads. "But I have a hearing in South Central at two."

"No, you don't," Dorn commands. "You have three trials in here. You do not leave my courtroom until these matters are finished."

When a judge is papered, his brethren often close ranks in his defense, refusing to grant the continuances lawyers need when forced to travel between courthouses. The lawyer has been ordered to be at another Juvenile Court branch at two, or else.

"That's not my problem, Counselor," Dorn says. "I'm not going to release you to go somewhere else."

"Then, Your Honor, may I ask which jail am I going to be spending the night in?"

Judge Dorn cackles.

The chaos soon spreads beyond Thurgood Marshall Branch and increases exponentially when the District Attorney's Office chooses this moment, a particularly ripe one, to begin papering one of their judicial nemeses. Their target is Juvenile Court Judge Sherill Luke of Pasadena, whose work habits have long been lambasted by prosecution and defense alike, without result.

For more than a year, memos have been sent to the presiding judge about Luke, in which prosecutors blisteringly described the judge as rude, tyrannical, and chronically lazy, with a workday rarely lasting more than three or four hours. He started late, took a long lunch, then followed up with an early departure. Every day. A log kept by one prosecutor for one recent month showed Luke going home every day but one by two-thirty, long before the courthouse workday was supposed to end. Cases were constantly postponed at the judge's whim, inconveniencing victims and witnesses, and costing the county unknown sums in wasted legal fees as attorneys sat around waiting—and billing—for hearings that never took place.

The presiding judge, Marcus O. Tucker, well known as a tireless advocate for children, but not as a particularly efficient or decisive administrator, had taken no visible action on these complaints, even though his own in-house data gathered from every courtroom in the system—a far more objective standard than complaint memos from angry prosecutors—revealed unequivocally that Judge Luke lagged far behind his colleagues in the amount of work he accomplished, trying far fewer cases and postponing far more than the other bench officers of Juvenile Court.[1]

So, in the midst of the Dorn War—in which prosecutors have cautiously remained neutral—the District Attorney's Office begins papering Judge Luke. Another game is set in motion, the object of which has nothing to do with the welfare of children or the protection of public safety. The goal is simple: Cripple the court. Drive the administration crazy. Use all the procedural tricks imported from adult court in order to drive a disliked jurist from his courtroom.

In the end, the DA's strategy proves to be the better thought out. The court is already reeling from the papering of Judge Dorn, and has been further hobbled by having two other juvenile bench officers on vacation, and yet another one hospitalized. The massive Juvenile Court of Los Angeles is, in effect, down by 20 percent of its regular capacity, which is on the best of days already strained to the breaking point. Now it can no longer keep up with its cases, and the system literally collapses on itself. The guiding philosophy of the court—to quickly and decisively stop children from destroying themselves and others—once again goes by the wayside, as the normal three- and four-month delays in processing cases expands to seven or eight. Cases that might otherwise have been pursued are dismissed or never filed, letting beginning criminals off the hook, encouraging them to try their hands again at burglary or car theft or robbery or worse.

Timing is everything when lawyers go to war with judges: Judge Luke has far less support than Dorn, and the presiding judge quickly acquiesces to the District Attorney. Judge Luke is replaced and departs for another branch of Juvenile Court, where he hears only uncontested arraignments—hearings so formulaic that the DA's Office doesn't even keep a prosecutor in the room.[2] A new bench officer with a more rigorous schedule moves into the Pasadena court, helping to spread the workload around. This lowers the strain on the system, making up, at least in part, for the papering of Judge Dorn, undercutting the public defender's strategy.

Dorn, meanwhile, stands his ground and slowly wins his war. He makes it clear that "Judge Dorn isn't going anywhere." He goes on with his in-chambers counseling sessions, his focus on status offenders, his insistence on dishing out large blocks of detention time to truant probationers, something the public defenders detest. He humiliates the public defenders further by winning the appeal on the visitation case that provoked the whole papering ordeal in the first place. Finally, after about a month of papering, with the public defenders suffering far more than the judge they are supposedly punishing, it is decided rather anticlimactically that "the point," whatever it is, has been made. The blanket papering of Judge Dorn ends, much to everyone's relief.

The general consensus is that nothing good was accomplished by this mass exercise of civil rights, this legal siege of Department 240, Thurgood Marshall Branch: The kids, the families, the victims, even the lawyers suffered, as did the image of Juvenile Court in all their eyes. The small reserve of goodwill still in the system drained away a little more. But the crush of cases continues through the summer-hot courtrooms. And Roosevelt Dorn changes not a whit.

CHAPTER 15

Lost Causes

        Tonight's writing class has a somber mood, the kids falling silent after some brief, excited chatter about an escape earlier in the week, a kid who made it over the wall of Central Juvenile Hall and down to the train tracks, out of sight, on The Outs. It's that tantalizing glimpse of freedom that quiets everyone in the room after a few minutes, the image of that small figure in gray sweats vanishing around a corner they will never see. Security will be tighter for a while now, they know, privileges fewer, the more lenient staff less likely now to allow a Domino's delivery in the night, like in the old days.

    A writing exercise yields little more than blank papers matched by blank stares from most of the kids. I'm about to call it a night, but then a new student says he has something he wants to read, a poem he shyly offers up to the table for criticism. It's a surprise, because in two previous classes, this boy hasn't said a word.

    Rodrigo Becerra is, at seventeen, bound for a long prison sentence in adult court for attempted murder. He is a classic Juvenile Court career criminal, six arrests over three years—car thefts, high-speed chases, carrying guns in almost all of them, a long-recognized abuse of PCP and other drugs involved in each crime. Despite all this, the Juvenile Court did little for Rodrigo: After his most recent arrest for getting blasted on PCP-soaked marijuana joints while on probation, the court sent him home on probation yet again. At the time, the probation officer who investigated Rodrigo's case noted how crucial it would be for this boy to get intensive supervision immediately. But the department did not get around to assigning a PO to his case for eighteen days after his release. This turned out to be two days longer than it took Rodrigo, street name "Stranger," to get high, pull out a gun, and seriously wound a rival gang member by shooting him in the neck, then emptying his gun as his victim tried to crawl down the sidewalk to safety.

In class, Stranger makes a simple announcement, an eerie prologue to his verse: He has no hope in life. Then he reads his poem, written in five minutes there in class, powerful and raw:

I'm a stranger in life
But I'm really well known
To all of my homeboys
Way the back home.

I'm the kind you don't trust.
I'm the kind that steals.
If I steal something from you
I don't care how you feel.

I'm a stranger to no one.
I commit a lot of felonies.
I go to jail brown and proud
And I'm treated respectfully.

I'm a stranger in life
'Cause I ain't got one.
I'm facing a life sentence
So it don't leave me none.

I'm a stranger to my family
'Cause they can't see me grow up.
If I think of how I'm hurting them,
It makes me throw up.

This is a stranger in jail
Sitting in a one-man cell,

Saying to myself, what is this feeling
That I never ever felt?

*As he reads, Stranger's voice is so soft, the rest of us must strain to hear
over the clatter and rustle that is always in the background at the hall, even
in this closed and airless cube of a library room, with its tired collection of
paperbacks and chipped Formica table with wobbly metal legs. His face is
flat and pale, dark eyes hollow and circled, lips compressed now that he has
finished. He holds his paper tightly, his eyes still focused on it even after
he is through reading, but he looks up in surprise when he hears the other
boys begin to praise his work, every one of them, all impressed that he could
compose something so quickly and so well during a few minutes in class.
He blushes deeply then and, for just a moment, this lost cause bound for
adult court and state prison named Stranger is suddenly Rodrigo again,
years melting from his face to reveal the seventeen-year-old boy underneath,
a kid who has survived by carefully hiding his hopes and dreams from view
so long that he has forgotten he had them, until now.*

*"I always wanted to write," he says with a bashful grin. Then the moment
passes, as does the smile, quick as a camera flash, and the Stranger is back,
sullen and withdrawn, beyond hope, beyond hoping. He is transferred out of
the hall before the next class meets.*

———◆———

JUST when it seems so painfully clear that the Juvenile Court is the
worst of both worlds, combining the gamesmanship and procedural
excesses of the adult system with the juvenile system's toothless lack of
consequences, just when the denizens of the system are ready to throw up
their hands at the fifteen-year-old killers who skate and the sixteen-year-
old robbers who get life in adult prison—just when the urge to scrap the
whole concept of Juvenile Court and run screaming from the building
becomes nearly irresistible, something happens to remind everyone there
is a reason to preserve this schizophrenic system. Just when the judges start
thinking about early retirement and the prosecutors start wondering about
going into entertainment law and the public defenders begin sending their
résumés to the top corporate law firms and Peggy Beckstrand starts dust-

ing off her Peace Corps application, something happens that shows them there is wisdom, after all, in maintaining a separate juvenile system, and in keeping all those onerous legal guarantees handed down on behalf of Gerry Gault.

These reminders always crop up sooner or later—the proud young man who strolls into the courthouse four years after his case concludes so he can show the judge his college degree. The young woman who writes from the Midwest to say she has kept a steady job and has been off drugs for three years. The former gang member who now acts as a mediator between warring gangs, helping to forge truces that keep young people from dying. The father who says in open session that the ordeal of Juvenile Court has brought him together with his son for the first time in years, making his family whole and happy again, a rare fresh start. All the kids who commit just one crime, then go straight for good—the majority in Juvenile Court.

This time, in the wake of the Dorn War and all its attendant confusion and futility, the reminder takes the form of three troubling murder cases and a tireless defense attorney named Sherry Gold.

Gold is a courthouse regular, having first served at Thurgood Marshall as a public defender, and now as a private lawyer on the appointment panel. She draws a sizable portion of the murder cases here whenever conflicts force the Public Defender's Office to bow out—a sign of the respect the Inglewood judges have for her abilities. For the most part, in juvenile as well as in adult court, murders are parceled out only to the most experienced and skilled lawyers on the panel.

Gold is a forceful presence in court, a small, slim woman with unruly blond hair and a persistence rare in the ranks of the low-paid appointed attorneys here. She is one of the few defense lawyers who regularly visit Peggy Beckstrand's office (to most of her colleagues, it is like crossing enemy lines, something to be avoided). But Gold is always there, clamoring for deals and breaks and a fresh look at the evidence—an irritant to prosecutors who, nevertheless, often gets what she wants through sheer determination. She has her own table at a cramped diner across the street from the courthouse, where she long ago ceased having to say her order out loud, and where she can be found between hearings huddled over her legal briefs, or with her head bowed close to a prosecutor, whispering negotiations to settle a case, alternately pleading or bullying, depending upon the strength of the evidence.

Sherry Gold writes a prescription for each of her cases, a kind of motherly checklist for kids who have never been mothered. When she takes on a new client, the first thing she does, even before the court gets around to it, is to check on the kid's school record. Then, if the boy or girl is out of custody, she gives the parents of her clients assignments: Enroll the kid in school, take him there personally each morning on time, talk to the teachers, pick up the kids after school if at all possible. "Make sure they come right home and do their homework," she says. "Make sure the teachers call you whenever there's a problem, so you can fix it before it gets worse."

At first, there is resistance to this parenting of the parents, these dicta from some pale, freckled Jewish woman with her blond hair and blue eyes and steamroller intensity. But Gold is patient, and she always explains the bottom line: When you have months to wait before a case comes to trial, putting in effort at home and in school before some angry judge gets around to *ordering* the same things can make an immense difference at the end of the case. He's been in school for months, Your Honor, Sherry Gold can say, hoping no one will notice that his enrollment occurred two weeks after his arrest. Appearances are everything: A kid who would otherwise have gotten probation gets off completely under the Sherry Gold prescription. Another who might have gone to camp but who suddenly has excellent report cards and a mother who knows all his teachers by name may get to go home on probation instead. A felon bound for CYA might have a shot at camp. All it takes is the appearance that the boy or girl in question is contrite and making an effort to change. No one has to know it's being done under orders from defense lawyer Gold.

"If you do what I tell you to do," Gold promises one mother, sealing the deal, "you'll have to come to court a lot less, and when you do come, the judge will be congratulating you instead of ragging on you for ignoring your child's education."

Most of the time, this simple ploy works. Some of the parents, previously worn down by their child's misbehavior, even become inspired enough to scrape up a coat and tie for their kid, which Sherry Gold calls the easiest—though most often ignored—method available for shedding months from a sentence in Juvenile Court. And for some of the kids and parents, what begins as a way to put one over on a judge ends up becoming an end in itself—the kids start liking school, the parents begin to enjoy being involved, the family starts to pull together.

When it comes to more serious cases, Sherry Gold does something else only a few of her fellow appointed attorneys seem to do: She performs her own investigation. For many of the lawyers here, case preparation consists of reading the police and probation reports, then trying to cut a deal. But Gold, a former city prosecutor who knows well how the police can sometimes cut corners on juvenile cases, always tries to eke a few dollars out of the tightfisted court for private investigators. Failing that—and even when she does get a PI—Gold does investigative legwork herself, interviewing witnesses, visiting crime scenes, challenging the police version of events in a way seldom done in Juvenile Court. The results can be startling—and troubling.

When the case of *People v. Leon Jones* came to her, the murder charge against the gangly seventeen-year-old truant and runaway seemed open and shut.

Late one January evening in the city of Hawthorne, the police received a report of a shooting. It happened on the same troubled turf that just one week earlier had claimed the life of one of Sharon Stegall's probationers— Li'l Dondi—and sent another of her kids into hiding. This time, two patrol officers pulled up to find a hard-drinking nineteen-year-old by the name of Larry Roberts lying belly-up on the sidewalk outside his apartment building, most of his face removed by a shotgun blast, charred blue wadding from the spent shell embedded around his lips like a second mustache. His left hand was still in his pocket, as if he was reaching for something, though no weapons were found on him.

Witnesses in the neighborhood said Roberts had been hanging outside his apartment building with ten or so friends, drinking forty-ounce bottles of Old English 800 beer wrapped in rumpled paper bags. Then he began arguing with three young men who were leaving an apartment complex across the street. Depending upon who was telling the story, Roberts either picked a fight because he didn't like the way the passersby looked at him, then got his buddies to rush the outnumbered threesome, or one of the three interlopers picked a fight with Roberts for "talking shit." Either way, there was no dispute about how it ended: Larry Roberts saw one of his foes produce a gun, yet refused to back down, thrusting his hands in his pockets and saying, "Fool, let's scrap." The man with the gun started yelling, either in fear or rage, then pulled the trigger. The shooter, witnesses agreed, was a tall, muscular, light-skinned African-American man in his early to mid-twenties wearing a beanie on short hair. After shooting Roberts, he ran off with his two friends while all the other homeboys scattered like bowling pins.

After stretching the inevitable yellow tape across the sidewalk where Roberts lay and canvassing the neighborhood, the police launched a search for this gunman and his two friends. They were able to trace two of them to a woman's apartment across the street, where they had been seen earlier in the evening. The woman was Carol Jones, Leon's older sister. She initially said she knew nothing, but when investigators found out she was using an alias and had been observed with two of the three suspects, she caved in and admitted two of the men had visited her before the shooting, and that one of them was her seventeen-year-old brother. He had just moved in with her after living with an uncle for several months. When she heard the gunshot, she had run outside to see if Leon was okay, then began to fear he had been involved.

The police tape-recorded their interview with Carol Jones, but the machine didn't work. They taped a second interview, then wrote a report based on their recollections, without listening to the tape. A particularly damning comment stood out in this report, concerning a phone call Carol received from Leon minutes after the shooting: "She asked him why he shot that guy. He told her, 'The guy said, "Shoot me!"' Then Leon told Carol he loved her."

The police took this as a virtual admission to murder, leading investigators to conclude that Leon, who had no prior criminal record, had been the shooter. They identified the other man who visited Carol with him as Frank McClure, a twenty-five-year-old man with five arrests and one conviction for unlawful firearms violations who, nevertheless, legally owned six handguns. They discounted him as the killer, but sought him as an accomplice. The third man remained unidentified. Thirteen days after the murder, the police found Leon hiding at the home of his fifteen-year-old girlfriend—mother to Leon's two-year-old son. He denied killing anyone, told numerous lies about his activities that night—he claimed to be playing basketball at the time of the shooting—and was booked for first-degree murder, a sure ticket to adult court and life in prison. One witness—the dead man's best friend—said he thought Leon looked like the shooter. An intake officer at Juvenile Hall pronounced him a threat to the community and ordered him detained in the high-risk offender unit.

When Sherry Gold first met Leon, he was surly and scared, insisting he was innocent, as most of her clients do, a tired refrain she at first did not take seriously. The case against him looked cold. His fitness hearing was scheduled in a couple of weeks, a normally automatic process in a murder case. At first, this appeared to be no exception.

But then Sherry began to have doubts. A quick check of his background showed a great deal of tragedy, yet no hint of criminal behavior.

His father—whose relationship with his mother had never been more than casual—hanged himself (or, as some in the family theorized, was hanged *by* someone else). Five-year-old Leon found the body. Five years later, officials from the state Children's Protective Service removed Leon from his mother's home because of her constant drug abuse and neglect of her children. Like George Trevino, Leon was then raised by the dependency branch of Juvenile Court. He was shunted between four different foster homes and various relatives, never in one place long enough to feel wanted, constantly switching schools and failing at each one, running away, consumed with anger at his mother for letting him be taken from her.

Juvenile Court is full of kids with backgrounds like Leon's. Crime can come easily to them. Yet Leon had never been arrested before, a mild surprise to Sherry Gold. After getting him to open up to her, to talk about his background—and then finding out through court records that he had been scrupulously truthful about his past—Gold decided he was a nice kid with problems, but that he was no killer. She decided she believed him when he swore he was innocent.

So she and a private detective went back to the neighborhood to reinvestigate the shooting. It was far easier than she expected: they quickly found five witnesses who said Leon definitely was not the gunman who killed Larry Roberts. He was just there, they said, a bystander. Even the best friend of the dead man, who had supposedly ID'd Leon, said he wasn't sure about who did the shooting.

All of the witnesses said the shooter was light-skinned with short hair. Leon is a very dark-skinned African-American, with a shaved head, shiny and bald. "No way it was him," one of the witnesses said.

And then there was the taped interview with his sister, Carol, in which, according to the police reports, she said Leon admitted to murder. When Sherry played the tape, she found Carol had said nothing of the kind. She hadn't asked why *Leon* had shot the man, as the police report said, but merely why it had happened. And Leon had answered, *He kept saying, shoot me*—something all the other bystanders heard as well. Truculent and unafraid, perhaps intoxicated, Larry Roberts had stood there and bellowed repeatedly, "Go ahead, shoot me," a challenge he apparently never expected to be met. But Leon had never told his sister that *he* did the shooting.

When Sherry presented her findings to Peggy Beckstrand, the prosecutor agreed to hold back on her motion to send Leon to adult court, embarrassed by the apparent shoddiness of the official investigation. The sheriff's homicide detectives on the case then had to reopen their inquiry. One month after busting Leon, they somewhat reluctantly admitted there had been a mistake.

They ended up arresting the other man with Leon that night, Frank Mc-Clure, and the third man, who they learned was named Kevin Davis. After protesting his innocence, then failing a lie detector test, Davis abruptly confessed to the murder himself, saying he acted alone, and that Leon just happened to be with him. He swore he shot in self-defense, certain that his victim was reaching into his pocket for a gun. Leon tried to stop the confrontation, Davis added, by urging the drunken Roberts to run away.

The confessed killer told police he originally had planned to give himself up and take his chances in court. But Leon and McClure urged him not to, promising to lie on his behalf.

When Peggy Beckstrand saw that updated police report cross her desk, she was unnerved. Had the investigation not been reopened, Leon could easily have been sent to adult court on a murder charge. A less pushy, less caring attorney might have failed to do the investigation Sherry Gold conducted. And in the old Juvenile Court, before it was transformed by Gerry Gault's dirty phone call and the adult court rights it brought, where there were no attorneys and the police reports were gospel, Leon most certainly would have been convicted of a murder he did not commit, while the real killer remained free.

This time, the system has worked. Peggy drops the murder charge against Leon, and files a new petition accusing him only of being an accomplice after the fact, for lying about the shooting to police and covering for the real killer. Instead of a potential life sentence in adult court, he faces at most three years in juvenile custody. The judge on the case even asks Sherry if she wants to move for his release from custody then and there, but she says no.

"He's got nowhere to go," she says. "I tried to get the foster care system to take him back again, but they dumped him. They don't want him anymore."

In the end, Commissioner Polinsky overrides a Probation Department recommendation that Leon go to CYA, sending him to camp instead. Leon ends up at Camp Kirkpatrick, where the specialty is sports and the teams routinely compete well in citywide and even state championships. Leon's love is basketball, for which he has considerable skills, though his constant moves from school to school and home to home never allowed him to excel. At Kirkpatrick, though, he has that chance. He makes the

camp team, hoping to parlay his talents on the court into a college education, maybe more, he writes in a letter to Sherry Gold.

It's the first time in a long time, she notes with satisfaction, that Leon
Jones has even thought about the future.

At exactly the same time Leon is being falsely accused of murder, another,
far more sensational murder case—the vicious drive-by killings of a toddler and a fourteen-year-old during a night of violence in Inglewood—is
also being turned on its head. This is the case of Hugh, accused of crimes
so ruthless that virtual martial law had been declared in Inglewood prior to
his arrest—a case that had already troubled a doubtful Peggy Beckstrand.
Now, another defense attorney willing to put in the extra time and energy
to conduct his own investigation, rather than simply making the court
appearances and taking whatever deal the DA has to offer, has found an
innocent kid gasping beneath the horrendous charges. As in Sherry Gold's
representation of Leon, this lawyer's fee will never match the hours he's
invested in the case.

"I can't really think about that—it's not very often that you get an innocent kid here," the lawyer, Gregory Humphries, explains, breathless after
a meeting with skeptical prosecutors who cannot bring themselves to believe yet another false charge of murder has made its way into their office
in the space of a few weeks. "This is not just a kid who says he's innocent.
He really *is* innocent. And with him looking at adult court and a life sentence in prison, you don't cut corners."

Humphries sighs, hefting his jammed briefcase, a short, curly-haired
man in a corduroy jacket and brown running shoes, dressed not to project lawyerly power and authority, but for crawling around crime scenes
and interviewing witnesses on the fly. "The pressure on this one," he says,
heading for the stairs, "is enormous."

Despite a premature arrest, the case against Hugh had at first seemed
more open-and-shut than Leon Jones's. The investigators from the Inglewood Police Department had determined that the same two guns used in
the drive-by that killed two-year-old Kyiara Nicole had also been used to
kill fourteen-year-old Tila French and to wound two of her friends as they
stood on a street corner.

More importantly for the state's case, two of the ten junior high students
who had been standing with Tila on that corner when the bullets started
flying eventually told police they were sure that one of the shooters was
Hugh. Yes, they had initially told police they couldn't ID the killer, but

they had changed their minds about that after a few days. Now they were sure he had been the one who marched up to Tila and said, "You're not going anywhere, bitch," then killed her with three shots. They knew Hugh from school, they added, and had always steered clear of him because he was so crazy.

When you say crazy, the cops had asked, you really are trying to say he was mean, right? The last thing they wanted was to set up an insanity plea. Under this prodding, the kids readily agreed that's what they meant to say: He was mean.

"Why would he want to kill a fourteen-year-old girl?" Peggy Beckstrand asked later on, during her first briefing with detectives on the case. One of the detectives was young and smooth-faced; the other was a big redhead who chomped on a soggy cigar throughout the meeting, though he never lit it.

"Well, she was in the arms of another guy, all kissing and hugging, and the other guy was from a rival gang," the cigar-chomper explained. "Hugh was jealous."

Hugh was part of a tagging crew called EWF, which was aligned with the Rolling Sixties Crips, one of the toughest street gangs in LA, the cops told Peggy confidently. The kid kissing Tila was from the Inglewood Bloods, the Crips' mortal enemies, the detectives explained.

"He shot her face off," the redhead said, the cigar wagging in his mouth as he gritted his teeth. "It was one of the most brutal murders I've ever seen."

Peggy grimaced. This was the kind of case she wanted done perfectly. They had to nail this monster . . . "Can the mother of the baby that was killed ID him?" she asked. "I'd like to charge him with both murders if we can."

The two detectives nodded in tandem. They hadn't actually done a lineup yet, but they knew she would do it, they promised.

"Good," Peggy said. She paused a moment, then asked, "By the way, what does EWF stand for?"

A grim smile crept over the detectives' faces. The young one said, "Every Woman's Fantasy."

"God," Peggy said, running over a checklist with the cops on what they had to do before busting Hugh. "Let's get this guy."

But then the police stumbled on Hugh when they went to search his home, and he was arrested before Peggy had given the okay and before the checklist had been completed. Immediately, the case began to seem less substantial than she had been led to believe. The prosecutor assigned to try it, Kevin Yorn, from the DA's hard-core unit, which handles major gang crimes, felt confident, but Peggy began harboring doubts. She found out that one reason the Inglewood detectives were in such a rush to make an arrest—in addition to the enormous pressure from the chief and the public chafing under a citywide curfew and crackdown—had to do with vacation plans. One of them had reservations to go abroad, and didn't want to lose his airfare.

When Greg Humphries looked at the police reports, he saw more reasons for doubts.

He saw the police had first heard the name "Hugh" several days after the killings from a kid named Marcus. Marcus was positive Hugh had done the shooting, he told the police. He didn't actually see anything, but his good friend Martell saw it all, and had told him crazy Hugh was the shooter.

The police then went to see fourteen-year-old Martell, who was absolutely positive that Hugh was the killer. Martell wasn't actually there, of course, but he had heard all about it. Hugh was a gang member and crazy and always high on drugs, Martell told the police. (This comment, uncorroborated and, it turns out, untrue, was what led the detectives to assure Peggy Beckstrand that Hugh was a hard-core Rolling Sixties member.) Martell knew all this, he told the police, because his friends Donte and Steve saw it all and told him Hugh did it. The word was all over school.

So the police followed the chain of schoolyard rumor to Donte and Steve. Donte assured the police he knew nothing. Steve, a convicted armed robber at age fifteen, had been on the street corner and was questioned right after the shooting by officers. (He was the boy Peggy would later rush to keep apart from Hugh in the courthouse holding tank.) At that time, Steve said he had ducked behind a car at the first gunshot, and had seen only the killer's feet. Days later, Steve said he believed the killer of Tila French had been his schoolmate Hugh because he recognized the shooter's distinctive haircut. Under intense prodding by detectives, Steve later amended this new story by saying he had seen Hugh's face, too.

Steve's girlfriend then came forward and said she had been present at the shooting as well, and that she, too, had recognized Hugh as one of the killers.

Though the police represented these witnesses as convincing, Humphries saw from the police reports just how the story had been passed from one kid to the next, a rumor about Hugh that spread throughout the school and the neighborhood until, finally, two witnesses suddenly came forward who had previously known nothing. As the lawyer investigated further, he learned that the two kids who first pointed the police toward Hugh, Martell and Marcus, had had several clashes with Hugh in the past. And the two new witnesses who identified Hugh as the shooter turned out to be their friends, and to have had their own run-in with Hugh, accusing him of stealing an electronic pager from them two days before the shooting. The lawyer saw in this a ready motive on the part of the two witnesses to assume the worst about Hugh, if not to lie outright.

Humphries also learned that, contrary to the detectives' assurances to Peggy Beckstrand, the mother of two-year-old Kyiara Nicole could not identify Hugh as the shooter. She never was able to identify anyone as the killer of her daughter, and so Hugh was charged only with the killing of Tila French and the wounding of two other kids on the corner that night.

And as for Hugh being "crazy"—which the police had interpreted as meaning violent and cruel—it turned out kids at school had teased him for being "crazy" because of his odd behavior a year earlier. A year before his arrest for murder, he had developed uncontrollable urges to smash windows—at home, at businesses, and at school. Hugh had been on probation at the time for graffiti, and when the window-breaking started, his mother kept calling his probation officer for help. But she could never get through. One day, Sharon Stegall picked up the phone instead of Hugh's regular PO, heard the desperation in the woman's voice, and agreed to go help. He had just broken twenty-five windows in the space of an hour, his mother said. When Sharon went to his house to talk to him, Hugh pleaded, "Miss Stegall, please help me."

She got him into a program that helped him control his behavior and changed his life. He returned to school and got a steady job in the evenings. Later, he called Sharon up and said, "I just wanted to thank you, Miss Stegall. You saved my life."

"I'll tell you this," Sharon said after she heard Hugh had been arrested in the Inglewood murder case, "that boy's no hardcase gangbanger, and he's no killer."

The final blow to the police case came when attorney Humphries traveled seventy miles north to the city of Oxnard, where Hugh had sworn he was selling magazine subscriptions door-to-door at the time of the murders. Hugh and his family had told the police this after his arrest, but they had not checked it out. Had they done so, they would have learned, as Humphries did, that not only did Hugh's boss verify his alibi, but there were also receipts from his door-to-door sales, and three new customers, who had met him for the first time that night, and who swore Hugh had been there at the time of the shootings. One of these witnesses who bought a subscription from Hugh was a respected employee of the California Youth Authority facility in nearby Ventura. These people were unbiased and unimpeachable, with no reason to lie.

At this point, Humphries tells prosecutors what he has learned, turning over the names and addresses of these witnesses so detectives could question them. By then, the trial prosecutor, Kevin Yorn, has joined Peggy Beckstrand in expressing doubts about the case, but the police resist unsolving the worst murder spree in Inglewood history, insisting that Hugh was their man and that his alibi witnesses had to be part of a conspiracy. When they grudgingly go to check the story out, they accuse the boy's employer of being a lying pedophile, then approach the alibi witnesses in Oxnard by asking whether Hugh had offered them a bribe to lie on his behalf.

"It's such a high-pressure case, they won't back down," Humphries complains to Deputy DA Yorn. "But he's a genuinely innocent kid who could be convicted of a terrible crime while the real murderers remain free. It's scary."

With a hearing imminent on shipping Hugh to adult court, Humphries demands the prosecution first demonstrate it had probable cause to keep him in custody. Yorn could easily prevail—only the state has the right to put on evidence at such hearings—but the prosecutor agrees to let Humphries put sworn affidavits on the record from his three alibi witnesses. When Judge Scarlett compares the prosecution case with what the defense lawyer has assembled, he says there is no contest—and no case. He finds no probable cause to believe Hugh a murderer, orders him released, and sends him home with his jubilant mother, aunt, brothers, and sisters. A detective on the case sits in the old jury box in Scarlett's courtroom, watching them celebrate, then bitterly denounces the juvenile justice system as insane, predicting Hugh will end up killing someone else within the week. "Wait and see. More people are going to die."

Instead, about a week later, the two witnesses who had accused Hugh begin to waffle. Steve is doing time in camp for a probation violation by this time, and has had more time to think about his testimony. Maybe they had been mistaken after all, he and his girlfriend admit. Then the police concede that Hugh has nothing to do with the Rolling Sixties Crips, either, and that EWF is just a band of geeky graffiti artists that Hugh rarely sees anymore, now that he is so busy trying to make money with his door-to-door sales. In the end, the police have to admit they were wrong about Hugh, that they had tried to send an innocent boy to adult court to face a life sentence in prison. He really had been selling magazine subscriptions when Tila French and Kyiara Nicole died, they say. Peggy Beckstrand orders the charges dismissed against Hugh.

The Inglewood Police Department, which had announced Hugh's arrest in the sensational case with such fanfare, makes no press releases about Hugh's release a month later, or the fact that the case remains unsolved to this day.

"Hugh's case is a classic example of how the cops put in less energy working cases for Juvenile Court. They did a rotten job," Peggy Beckstrand says after dropping the case. "But that wasn't immediately clear. If he had had a less able defense attorney, we might never have learned the truth. Hugh would have landed in adult court, and he probably would have been convicted. It's that simple. In a way, though, this case is an example of the system working. The checks and balances did what they were supposed to. Justice was done, right here in Juvenile Court."

She thinks about it a moment, then adds, "Thank God."

Incredibly, in the same month that murder charges were disproved against Hugh and Leon, the same thing happens in yet another murder case, another client of Sherry Gold's, another boy charged with a murder he did not commit.

This time at stake is the life of a fourteen-year-old neophyte gang member whose apt nickname is Shy Boy. He is a quiet, dark-haired kid with large eyes who does well in school, who has never been in trouble before, but who desperately wants to emulate the older gangsters he admires, the homeboy heroes who have respect in his eyes. Unlike Leon, with his agonizing history as a foster child, Shy Boy comes from a solid home and family; his mother, as soon as she learned her son had secretly joined a gang, put him on a strict curfew and began taking special parenting classes offered at the local police station to help steer her boy clear of trouble.

But Shy Boy had attached himself to a particularly violent Hispanic gang in a neighborhood miles from his own home, the Venice 13. And just when Shy Boy joined, Venice 13 had gone to war with an equally violent African-American gang, the Shoreline Crips. Both gangs claimed the same turf, the scarred and bedraggled Oakwood section of the beachside community of Venice—along with exclusive rights to the lucrative Venice street drug trade. This gang war soon escalated into a vicious racial struggle that spilled over into the community at large, claiming innocent victims. Drive-bys, firebombings, and other armed assaults between the two gangs had taken twelve lives in the space of three months. Six others were wounded, a home had been torched, countless lives endangered and threatened. Seven other Oakwood residents, with no gang membership and no reason to be attacked except for the color of their skin and the fact that they were ready targets on the sidewalk, had been shot at in Oakwood by one faction or another. In an even more ominous turn, so had four LAPD officers, though none had as yet been hit. But computer-generated flyers had been found posted around Oakwood, urging residents to provide safe havens in their homes to any gangsters heroic enough to kill a cop. Oakwood had become a shooting gallery, and Shy Boy was in the middle of it, prized by the Venice 13 because his age conferred upon him a certain invulnerability. Fourteen-year-olds in California still stayed in Juvenile Court, even for murder. Desperate to please, Shy Boy was a valuable tool to the older gangbangers.

The twelfth murder in the Venice gang war happened on a Sunday night, vicious and random like all the rest, a retaliation against the Shoreline Crips for the murder of a Venice 13 member a few weeks before. A stolen Jeep Cherokee with three Venice 13 gangsters inside drove slowly by someone they believed was a Shoreline Crip, a teenager standing on the sidewalk arguing with his girlfriend and the girlfriend's sister. The car turned around, came back, and stopped. Without uttering a word, the driver produced an assault rifle and pulled the trigger. Eleven shots later, the Crip was dead, the girlfriend was shot in the stomach and buttocks (she recovered), and the sister was weeping, screaming, and flagging down a patrol car.

A few minutes later, a woman who had seen the shooting and who had followed the Jeep in her own car, told another police patrol what she had seen. A short time after that, the police spotted the Jeep, now with only two people inside. After a high-speed chase, the car stopped. Shy Boy got out and was arrested, but the other person in the Jeep managed to get the car moving and escaped. Meanwhile, a few blocks away, the original driver of the car, an adult gang member who had tried to escape on foot earlier, was found and arrested. The sister of the wounded woman identified that man as the shooter with the assault rifle. She could not identify the others in the car, nor could the wounded woman.

Nevertheless, when it came time to file the case, police reports prepared by the LAPD detective leading the case identified Shy Boy as a shooter, claiming he had been in the car at the time of the murder, and that he had confessed on tape to murder. Based on these assertions, Peggy Beckstrand's office charged him in Juvenile Court with first-degree murder and multiple counts of attempted murder, assault with a deadly weapon, and discharging a firearm at a person from a moving vehicle—charges that would put him in CYA until age twenty-five.

The evidence seemed so convincing that Sherry Gold seriously considered taking an early manslaughter plea in exchange for his testimony against the other suspects in the shooting. But Shy Boy told her no, he would not rat on his homeboys, that he would stand up for them and take the blame for the killing. Sherry tried to explain to him that older gang members exploit young kids all the time, hoping they'll take the heat in Juvenile Court so the older criminals can avoid adult trials and possible life or death sentences. But neither she nor Shy Boy's mother could get through to him.

"You think that'll prove what a man you are?" Sherry said. "It proves how stupid you are. They're using you." But Shy Boy just turned away. He finally told her that even if he wanted to talk, he wouldn't. "They'd kill me," he whispered.

So, back against the wall, Sherry launched her own investigation and found, once again, that the evidence was not what it initially appeared to be in a juvenile murder case. Contrary to the police reports, there was nothing to show Shy Boy had been in the car at the time of the murder. He could have gotten in the car when the driver—the man with the assault rifle—got out after speeding away from the murder scene. Shy Boy was, in fact, behind the wheel when the police stopped the Jeep, but he definitely had not been driving when the murder occurred. And none of the witnesses to the murder recognized him as being in the car.

As for his supposedly taped confession, when Sherry got it transcribed— something neither the police nor the DA on the case had done—she found Shy Boy had not admitted to killing anyone after all, but merely said he had fired a pistol from inside the car. And there were no pistols used in the murder—just the adult gang member's assault rifle. However, Sherry found out that police dispatch records for that night showed someone else had reported being shot at with a pistol in a separate incident close by the murder scene. Perhaps that was the shooting Shy Boy had been referring to. This didn't exactly make him out to be a model citizen, Sherry Gold decided, but neither did it make him a murderer.

Had there been hard evidence that Shy Boy was in the car at the time of the fatal shooting, Peggy Beckstrand probably would have insisted he be tried for murder. Being in the car, armed with a pistol, with a fellow gang member firing fatal shots from an assault rifle, was more than enough to sustain a conviction against Shy Boy as an "aider and abettor"—a fully culpable accomplice. There were plenty of juveniles in CYA and state prison right now for doing little more than riding in a car with a killer—Scrappy, for instance, and Elias Elizondo.

But prosecutors can't put Shy Boy in the car at the right moment, and that saves him from eleven years in CYA. Given Shy Boy's youth and otherwise clean record, Peggy agrees with Sherry Gold that the evidence isn't there. Once again, she drops a murder charge. Shy Boy agrees to plead guilty to a single count of firing a gun from a car at another person, and Judge Dorn sentences him to camp for at least a year.

Instead of going to CYA or—had new laws lowering the fitness age been in place—to state prison, Shy Boy enters a camp with intensive school and counseling programs designed to lure kids away from street gangs. Whether this program will work for Shy Boy, no one can say. But afterward, when the court session ends, Shy Boy's parents cry and embrace in the hallway and promise Sherry they will hold their son's feet to the fire and keep him away from the gangsters. Then Sherry walks down to the lockup to say good-bye to her young client—he had made her promise to come down after the sentencing.

"I just wanted to thank you," he tells her. "You never gave up on me."

The lawyer tells him that the best thanks would be never to make work for her again. He smiles and nods and seems to agree. At least, that's what Sherry tells herself.

"It looked so bleak there for a while, but it's a classic example of the prosecution not being able to prove its case," Sherry Gold says later, parked in her usual seat at the luncheonette across the street, already at work on still another murder. "Yet justice was done in this case. If they had been able to prove their case, justice would not have been done. He would have spent eleven years in CYA, which is just prison by another name, and he would be gone, destroyed."

When Sherry Gold finishes her cup of brackish diner coffee and crosses back to court, she meets her latest client, one of two juveniles accused of the cold-blooded murder of an elderly woman who had been sitting at a bus stop after doing volunteer work at an institute for the blind. The killing has aroused considerable outrage in the community. Around the courthouse, they're already calling it "The Angel of Mercy Murder." At first blush, Sherry almost wishes she could prosecute this kid instead of defend him, but then she reminds herself how wrong first impressions can be in Juvenile Court.

"My name is Sherry Gold. I've been appointed to represent you," she whispers to the fifteen-year-old, as he stands handcuffed next to his crime partner, waiting for his arraignment before Commissioner Polinsky.

The kid turns to Sherry, sneering with contempt, unaware that he has been blessed through sheer luck of the draw with one of the best court-appointed attorneys working at Thurgood Marshall. "I wanna real lawyer," he hisses. "You work for the state. My mother's gonna hire a *real* lawyer."

Sherry Gold tries very hard not to say "Good."

Three weeks, three murder cases, all filed against innocent kids, all dropped by prosecutors when the errors were pointed out by defense lawyers. In a place where presumption of innocence often seems turned on its head, these cases are extraordinary. And yet there is no uproar, no demands for reform—as the inability to try fourteen-year-olds as adults has sparked—no rethinking of the slow dismantling of the juvenile justice system now under way here and nationwide. The public remains ignorant of these confidential proceedings, and within the system, no one seems to blink at these developments.

Yet, as everyone involved in these three cases agrees, any one of these kids could have gone to prison unjustly had they not received exceptional lawyers to represent them—representation that was never available in the original, informal Juvenile Court, and which still remains tough to come by in the current second-class system. Even allowing such kids to be trans-ferred to adult court—something many lawyers barely try to fight because it is a battle so rarely won—could have been disastrous for these kids. The-oretically, they would have had just as much chance of disproving the charges in adult court as in Juvenile, but the stakes are so much higher there, the climate so much harsher, the pressure to plead guilty to some lesser charge to avoid a life in prison so great, that the outcomes could have been very different. Prosecutors and defense lawyers know that, unlike the judges hearing cases in Juvenile Court, the juries who decide adult cases rarely have any sympathy for defendants accused of being gun-wielding gang members, no matter how shaky the prosecution case may be. Pros-ecutors depend on this factor; defense attorneys fear it. As Geri Vance's lawyer told him: *Black kid with gun? You're their worst nightmare, pal. I know you say you're innocent, but take my advice: Take the deal.*

At the same time the three erroneous murder cases are coming apart at Thurgood Marshall Branch, another case raises even more questions about the wisdom of pushing more and more kids into adult court, though for very different reasons. This time, there are no problems with the attempted murder case against Mark Lancaster—this seventeen-year-old is clearly guilty, the evidence overwhelming. And yet his case is no less troubling than the other three, providing yet another unheeded lesson about the juvenile justice system.

A few days before Leon and Hugh were arrested in their murder cases, Mark Lancaster spent all day drinking beer with friends and smoking *primo*—marijuana joints laced with cocaine. A chronic truant, he was failing all his classes and had been abusing alcohol and drugs, even sniffing glue, for years. His parents, now in their fifties, with two older daughters with college degrees and solid, independent lives, weren't sure what to make of Mark, who once had been such a good student, and who even now had them convinced he was a health nut far more interested in vitamins and exercise than drugs. With his odd, choppy haircut, ratty ponytail, and scruffy brown mustache perched unappealingly above pale lips, Mark had been drifting toward nowhere for years, though he had never been in trouble with the law.

But that day of drinking and *primo* was different. He left his friends and went for a walk, finding himself standing in front of a gas station. He approached an attendant and asked for change. Then, when the man's back was turned, he abruptly plunged a sharpened screwdriver into the attendant's back. Mark always kept this little homemade weapon in his pocket, though he never told anyone why.

The blade hit bone and bounced off, clattering to the ground and causing little more than a slight cut and bruise, though a difference of a few inches could have been fatal. Mark tried to run, but another attendant and a customer at the gas station caught him, then turned him over to police. Mark told detectives he had wanted to kill the attendant because he recognized him as the murderer of his best friend years before. Mark told them his friend had been shot in the back while trying to steal a six-pack from a liquor store, and that the gas station attendant looked just like the man who did it.

"I wish I had killed him now," Mark told the police. "If I had a gun, I would have killed him."

The police quickly ascertained that the gas station attendant had never worked in a liquor store. They could find no record of a shooting such as the one Mark described, nor had he ever mentioned it to his parents or other relatives. The police decided it was just a cover story. Mark later admitted that he had stabbed the wrong person—"Something in my head just snapped"—and that he was sorry, though he insisted that his friend really had been killed in a beer robbery. He must have still been high on the *primo*, he said, and mistook the attendant for the killer. No one believed him, though. The police said he did not seem high at all when they arrested him. Peggy Beckstrand authorized a fitness motion to ship him to adult court for attempted murder.

At the hearing, a psychiatrist testified that Mark should remain in Juvenile Court to receive treatment for his drug and alcohol problems. His crime was neither sophisticated nor particularly grave, the doctor suggested, having been rather feeble, poorly planned, and causing no serious injury. He was probably still high from drinking and doing drugs earlier in the day, the doctor suggested.

But Commissioner Gary Polinsky found the doctor's report infuriating. "You're accepting his word that he was under the influence, when there is no evidence of that," the commissioner spat, surprising the psychiatrist, whom he normally receives warmly. "What can you see here other than that he is a conniving, cruel individual who attempted to stab somebody in the back? That's the interpretation that I see here. . . . He's done nothing but lie, and has shown no remorse."

Mark's parents, both in their fifties, sit in the courtroom wearing red windbreakers, worry lines mapping pale faces. Mr. Lancaster, a former warehouse manager, has cancer, heart disease, and a bad back. He sits motionless, listening, and Mrs. Lancaster holds his hand and bites her lower lip. When the doctor is through, they get up and testify for their son, one by one, describing him as a good but troubled boy. It does no good. Mark avoids looking at them, stroking his mustache, biting a nail, disconnected from his surroundings, the same pose he maintains when a visibly disgusted Polinsky finds him unfit to be tried as a juvenile, and orders him shipped to adult court. "Is this not a hideously violent case?" he asks the boy's lawyer, then cuts her off, saying, "And what in the world mitigates that besides this story he concocted?"

As a juvenile sentenced to CYA for attempted murder, Mark Lancaster would have served about four years in juvenile incarceration under current CYA guidelines. In that time, even though there are long waiting lists for therapy programs at CYA, Mark could have received drug and alcohol abuse treatment (Los Angeles County has no secure facilities for juveniles with substance abuse problems—CYA is the only available option). At CYA, Mark also could have received remedial education classes—enough to get him a high school diploma, possibly more.

Instead, under state laws designed to punish rather than rehabilitate, Mark's case is transferred to adult court, where the penalties on the books are harsher. But once there, a prosecutor in Superior Court takes a quick look at the file, sees an irrational stabbing with no serious injury, and a kid with no prior record who has been in Juvenile Hall for a couple of months awaiting trial. Then he compares this case with the carjackings, shootings, and other hard-core adult crimes he has to handle. There is not much to weigh: He pulls Mark's new adult court attorney aside and offers a deal. Plead guilty to assault, and get sentenced to time served. Mark can go home that day, case closed. No harsher punishment. No more time behind bars. No drug abuse programs. Just go home to your parents.

Mark takes the deal. Like many kids transferred to adult court for crimes that fall short of murder, his sentence is far shorter than it would have been had he stayed in Juvenile Court.

Exactly the opposite result intended by the get-tough law has been achieved. Society is no safer, and neither is Mark.[1]

CHAPTER 16

The Ins

The writing class is full tonight, four new faces in the room to replace the recently departed, kids shipped out to begin their sentences, hustled onto buses with the abruptness of a gavel swing. We never know when a seat in the class will be emptied; there are no warnings to precede these departures, no chances to say good-bye. The system is so backlogged a kid can sit in the hall for weeks or even months after a judge officially pronounces sentence, their lives on hold, their names on The List. No matter how long the wait, when the transport van finally arrives, there is at most a few hours' warning, often just a few minutes, allowing some scant farewells followed by a frantic stuffing of their most treasured personal possessions into socks and waistbands—a photo from home, a stub of a pencil (prized contraband), a girl's love letter, read and reread so many times it looks like buttery parchment, the ink blurred, the folds ripped and fuzzy.

One by one, the original class members have vanished this way, here writing one week, gone the next. Chris and Louis got CYA; Elias and Robert, state prison; Ruben, finding in the class a new confidence in his ability to express himself, wrote a heartfelt letter to his prosecutor, who was so moved he agreed to knock seven years off the boy's adult sentence for murder. Others, though, disappear without word or explanation, some sentenced, some simply transferred to other branches of Juvenile Hall. We rarely hear what hap-

pens to them. On the brown metal library table, a small pile of poems and essays sits untouched, typed up with my now useless comments attached, the authors gone. I have learned to make each class self-contained, to treat each kid as if I will never see him again. Each class starts from scratch.

Once again, the class almost was canceled tonight, saved only through Sister Janet's pleas. There is tension throughout the hall this week—not the usual drill-sergeant-versus-reprobate antagonism, but something far more serious, electric in its intensity, an expression on some of the counselors' faces when they stare at their young charges that is new, yet unmistakable. The expression is hatred.

The reason: A probation counselor at another facility has been murdered during an escape attempt, bludgeoned to death with a metal table leg swung by a sixteen-year-old boy with convictions for auto theft, concealed weapons, and burglary. It is the first time anyone has died in the line of duty at the Los Angeles County Probation Department since it was founded in 1903, the first time the department's director has stood at graveside and handed a folded flag to a widow, the first time probation officers in LA have so keenly felt the dangers inherent in trying to contain and control dangerous, violent children with nothing but their wits and bare hands. The escape and murder happened at the Dorothy Kirby Center (in the cottage next to Carla James's), not at the higher-security Central Juvenile Hall. Still, distrust has flowed from the Kirby facility throughout the system, old assumptions about juveniles and security going out the window. Probation officers are now demanding personal alarms and aerosol cans of caustic pepper spray to control kids in the halls, the camps, and at Kirby. For now, though, all the staffers at the hall have is increased vigilance, and the kids feel this new pressure. The man who died, working the graveyard shift alone in a twenty-boy cottage, had always been known for his benign breaking of the rules, for bringing in candy and pizzas, for cutting the kids extra slack. There has always been someone on the staff of every juvenile facility who fills this role, the kindly counselor every kid likes—even the high-risk offender unit at Central Juvenile Hall had such people on staff. Until now. Now, for the moment at least, there is no slack, only hard stares and suspicion.

This new oppressive atmosphere has quieted everyone in the class—except for one newcomer, Little Criminal, fourteen years old with an eleven-year-old's smooth face, large-eyed and angelic. It is unusual to see such a young kid on this unit of hardened offenders, but he informs me with no small amount of pride that he is in for one count of murder, four counts of attempted murder, and enough other charges to fill several typewritten pages, all committed in one night of violence when he was still thirteen. He hadn't liked the way some eighteen-year-old kid in a pickup truck had looked at him. A gang member since age nine, Little Criminal took out a semiautomatic pistol and, once that was emptied, a shotgun, and killed the kid, wounding four of the dead teen's friends in the process. Little Criminal feels no more remorse for what he did than he feels for the dead bodies in the Stallone and Schwarzenegger action flicks he likes to talk about, which is to say he has no regrets at all, except for the fact of his getting caught. And even that is a source of pride, since taking the rap as a juvenile assured that his older homeboys would avoid going to adult court for his crimes.

I have never met him before, but something about Little Criminal is familiar to me, and I realize what it is when he starts to explain how he could have killed everyone that night, and he'd still get out of CYA at age twenty-five. "It's like, it doesn't matter how many people you waste, one's the same as five," he says, and I realize this is the same kid who so impressed—and disturbed—District Attorney Gil Garcetti when he visited Juvenile Hall earlier in the year.

"You talked to the DA a while ago about that, didn't you?" I ask him.

Little Criminal shrugs. He isn't sure who the tall guy in the suit was, but he was somebody important, yeah. "So that was the DA, huh? He didn't like my questions, but he said I was right, no matter how many people you kill, if you're my age, you get back on The Outs at twenty-five." The boy is smiling at this prospect, too young, perhaps, to fully appreciate just how long eleven years can be. He only knows he's doing better than most of the others in this wing of Juvenile Hall, with their adult trials and life sentences. Later, in a five-minute writing exercise, he hands in this poem:

Am I a criminal?
That's what people say.
I don't believe them, but
Its on my mind day by day.

The thought of being a criminal
Scares me at night
Thinking of humanity, wanting
Me locked up tight.

If they can define criminal
To themselves, one day

I can say to them
Little Criminal's no criminal.
It's just what people say.

"It's about when I get out," Little Criminal explains. "See, my record will be clean then. That's the law, too."

Geri, meanwhile, is unusually quiet. He has written some new chapters for his autobiography—I see the dog-eared pages poking out of a folder he is clutching. But he shakes his head no when I ask him to read. He just hands me the papers without comment.

When I look over the passages he gives me, I find them chilling, a no-holds-barred description of himself at age twelve, after the dependency court shuffled him around for a while, then gave him and his little brother Joachim to his grandmother. He describes his mind-set at that age, and I see that it is the same as Little Criminal's current outlook, conscienceless and cruel. It is not the Geri I have seen here in class. Somehow, it seems, he has changed since then. At least, everyone who has worked with him says so. Yet, having seen this other side of him, I can't help attaching a question mark. The curse of the juvenile system is never knowing for sure when it succeeds. Here, you can only know failure with certainty, the sound of handcuffs clicking shut on young wrists.

When no one else volunteers to offer up their work aloud, I read Geri's new chapters to the class for him:

I went to a toy store inside of the Central City Mall and bought a video machine called Nintendo . . . but the damn machine didn't work. This made me very upset and mad. . . . Without thinking, I went to my grandmother's room and searched for her gun. The last place I remembered seeing it was inside of a shoe box underneath the bed. I searched through every shoe box until finally, I found it. It was a shiny nickel-plated twenty-five automatic handgun with a pearl white grip engraved with a red rose. This was the most beautiful thing that I had ever seen in my whole life . . . as if it was a work of art created by the most famous artist in the whole world. . . .

Now I felt invincible about going down to the store and putting in work. I strolled down the street in a rage. . . . I thought about walking straight up to the clerk, then opening fire on him right there and then. But naw, that would have been stupid. The only results that I would have received from that would have been life imprisonment. As I continued to walk and think about this master plan, One-Time (the police) pulled up on the side of me and pulled out their weapons, ordering me to put my hands in the air and to go face down to the ground. . . . They took me to the station and booked me, but later on released me to my grandmother. . . . She had turned me in to the cops once she found out the gun was missing. I was glad I didn't go back to the hall, but I wasn't so happy about the whipping that I received when we got home.

In the silence that follows this reading, I find myself wondering if Geri realizes that, as long as he is in the system, and probably for years after-ward, one overarching question will color how others perceive him: Will the boy who would gladly kill a cashier over a video game, and who later would participate in an armed robbery of a motel (no matter the extenuating cir-cumstances) ever rise to the surface again, displacing the affable teenager sitting here now? When it comes time for a judge to sentence him later this month, I wonder, does he understand that question will be foremost on the jurist's mind? It will be there, just under the surface, an unspoken colloquy between prosecutor, defender, and judge: Why should I take a chance on this kid, and run the risk of a media storm and voter recalls and pickets if he should just happen to walk out and kill someone? Doesn't matter if most of the time taking a chance with a kid like Geri pays off, the judge could well reason, because it's the one in a thousand screwup that will make the papers. Why take a chance when sending him to prison would be so much safer, so much more politically apt, so much more in step with public opinion?

"Now we know how you ended up here," one of Geri's classmates offers at the end of the reading. "You were crazy."

"If you're sending your stuff to the judge to read," another kid suggests helpfully—I've been encouraging everyone to submit letters, essays, and sto-ries to their judges before sentencing—"you maybe should leave that one in your room, you know? Don't want to scare the man, make him think you're still a little asshole."

Geri nods, and mumbles okay, thanks.

After class, I learn from Sister Janet the reason for Geri's silence that night. A day earlier, a relative called to tell him his little brother had been murdered. He had not seen Joachim for more than a year.

———◆———

THE bus brings Geri to the Pomona courthouse early in the morning, where he is left to wait several hours in a holding tank, a hard bench to sit on, no one to talk to, alone with the fear that has lumped big and hard in his stomach like the Quarter Pounder he made the mistake of gobbling shortly before the motel robbery that brought him here a year and a half earlier. It feels like the damn thing is still there, indigestible and huge, gnawing at his insides, just like when the handcuffs wrapped around his wrists that awful night so long ago and the cops started talking PC-187. His stomach had flopped in just the same way. The memory comes back at him that quick and vivid, a physical sensation. The sweat of someone who realizes their entire future is about to be decided coats his body in a thin, sticky film.

Eventually, some deputies arrive to escort him from the lower levels of the courthouse to a large courtroom upstairs, where he sits in his orange HRO jumpsuit, not sure what is about to happen, sweaty and chilled in the air-conditioned room, scared to death. He knows his case is set for sentencing, but that's been true for the last several hearings, and it's always been delayed for one reason or another, a maddening source of both relief and anxiety. When he is told that his attorney from the Public Defender's Office, Al Johnson, is on vacation and won't be there today, he figures another continuance is in the offing, and that combination of disappointment and relief sweeps over him again.

But, instead, a colleague of Johnson's who knows very little about Geri's case—and knows Geri not at all—says everything's set, he'll sit in, we'll wind it all up today.

Geri later recalls not being sure what was going on, but he nods, okay, let's do it. After more than a year in Juvenile Hall, the notion of getting his life moving again—and avoiding another bout of fear in the holding tank—is a powerful one, and he shoves aside his unease at the unfamiliar person representing him in court. He barely knew Johnson's name, anyway, he tells himself—it wasn't like they had any deep relationship.

But whatever he expected to happen at the sentencing is not what he gets. There is no discussion of his performance in Juvenile Hall, the earning of his high school diploma, his work in theater and music, the fact that a lineup of counselors and staff members and volunteers would happily testify on his behalf. There is no submission of his poems or stories or plays. The favorable report he received from his three-month CYA evaluation is barely mentioned; Johnson later admits he never even took it out of the envelope.

Instead, there is just a cut-and-dried discussion between prosecutor, judge, and defense lawyer about his plea bargain reached months earlier. The murder charge was dropped, the lawyers remind the judge, replaced by a single count of attempted murder and a negotiated mid-range sentence of twelve years and four months. Judge Robert Gustaveson closes the deal, sets the sentence, and orders Geri housed at CYA, like other state prison inmates his age who are well behaved.

Don't worry about it, the substitute lawyer says, with time off for good behavior, and if you keep out of trouble, you'll serve your whole sentence in CYA—out in seven years, maybe less.

The hearing is over and Geri is back in the holding tank in the space of five minutes. "I didn't even have time to get my seat warm," he says later, back at the hall.

Once he has time to think about what happened in court, Geri becomes deeply disappointed about the hearing and his sentence. Several counselors at the hall had told him he had a good shot at getting the coveted YA number, rather than the state prison M number he ended up with. One could have meant freedom in four years or so; now he'll be lucky to get out in seven years. And, all that time, he will have to worry that one misstep, one fight, one detention officer who takes a dislike to him, could spell his transfer to state prison. You don't have to start trouble to get nailed, Geri knows. Sometimes just being there is enough. It's like basketball, where the ref misses the first foul, then spots the retaliation; the person defending himself in a prison fight just as often looks like the aggressor. And even if he keeps his nose clean, there have also been rumors that budget cuts could end up eliminating some spots at CYA for kids with M numbers—it is so much cheaper to put them in state prison at twenty thousand dollars a year per inmate versus thirty-two thousand a year at overcrowded CYA.

When Geri tells everyone in the class about his experience in court, I promise to find out why he was treated in such a peremptory way. And it turns out the reason Geri did not get his YA number is because no one ever asked for it. Geri's lawyer did not request Judge Gustaveson to consider returning Geri to the juvenile system and committing him to CYA, rather than prison—even though Geri appears to be as ideal a candidate for such a sentence as there is.

"We didn't ask because you can't do that," Deputy Public Defender Al Johnson tells me after returning from vacation, his desk piled high with cases, his time occupied largely by California's new Three Strikes and

You're Out adult sentencing law. "Once you're in the adult system, that's where you stay. He can only be *housed* at CYA."

The lawyer is aghast when shown Section 1731.5 of the California Welfare and Institutions Code, which says a judge *can* commit to CYA anyone under the age of twenty-one who has not been convicted of first-degree murder, and who has gotten a favorable three-month evaluation. Such a commitment essentially undoes a kid's transfer to adult court.

"I didn't know that law existed," the lawyer says, flustered. "What can I say? It was incompetent of me not to ask for that."

But after a few moments, Johnson thinks it over and assumes a different posture, defending his work on behalf of Geri and taking the position that it really doesn't matter in the final analysis. "No judge out here would do that anyway, even if I had put on a full-court press to get it. Pomona is too conservative."

Johnson says that the important thing was negotiating a plea bargain for Geri that eliminated the potential life sentence he had over his head. Going to trial could well have cost Geri his entire future.

"I was looking at a young man who I liked and who was talented, and I think we got a very good result. It's the best we could have hoped for. . . . Sure, I agree that there's better ways we could spend our money. In seven years, it's going to cost us $210,000 to keep him there. I think we could get more bang for the buck sending him off to college, or if we had invested in improving his life nine years ago. But we have to deal with reality. This is the best possible outcome for him."

Still, even if Johnson's assessment is correct, the public defender's failure to at least ask for commitment to CYA, along with his failure to present witnesses and evidence of Geri's good works and behavior, provides firm grounds for appeal and a new sentencing hearing. Other kids with far more serious charges have been committed to CYA from adult court, even in conservative branches of LA adult court—one tagger in the writing class, convicted at trial of a cold-blooded execution murder far more serious than Geri's crime, won such a commitment a month earlier. And he got it from a branch of the Los Angeles Superior Court in the city of Norwalk—a courthouse so conservative and generally harsh in sentencing that the kids in the hall call it "No-Walk."

When I explain all this to an attorney in the public defender's appeals section, she promises to investigate Geri's case and Johnson's handling of it, sounding confident in her ability to help Geri. Johnson, however, is outraged by this interference, and refuses to talk about the case further. Then the appeals lawyer calls back and says no appeal will be filed in Geri's case—not because it would lose, but because it probably would succeed, thereby so irritating the judge on the case that he might retaliate by giving Geri an even harsher sentence.

"I can definitely see a judge saying, Screw this kid," the appeals attorney says. "This kid ought to get down and kiss Al Johnson's toes for getting him this deal. He was looking at serious time. He ought to be happy with what he's got."

Geri shrugs this off, a sad smile on his face, though he admits to being amazed that some lawyer who doesn't know him thinks he should be happy about a twelve-year prison sentence. "Easy for her to sit in an office and say that," he says. "She gets to go home every day."

Sister Janet asks Geri if he would like her to try to find him a new lawyer to check out his case, but, after thinking about it a few days, he says thank you, but no, he's afraid that the appeals lawyer could be right, that it might just make things worse for him. The climate of public opinion is so angry and fearful now, he has been told, that it's not worth the risk. Adult court judges have been denounced and targeted for recall for committing kids to CYA, making such sentences even less likely than before. "I'll just do my time," Geri says. "And I'll do my best."

Every year in the United States, about 2.3 million kids under eighteen are arrested, shoplifters to murderers. This is a frighteningly large number—and one that, given a recent baby boomlet that is swelling the ranks of teenagers, is destined to grow.[1] But it is also a deceptive number, for once these boys and girls are in custody, they enter something the juvenile justice experts call "The Funnel."

At the mouth of The Funnel, big and fat, are those 2.3 million kids. But about a third never go beyond arrest—their cases are dropped, never forwarded to court, the kids "counseled and released." That leaves 1.5 million kids.

Each of them goes on to meet the Intake Officer, and the Funnel contracts further. Half of the 1.5 million kids referred by police for further action get dropped at the next stop—no Juvenile Court, no prosecution, their cases either dismissed outright or dispensed with through unsupervised probation, followed by dismissal. Seven hundred and fifty thousand arrested kids—whom the police wanted to prosecute—told to go home as if nothing happened. The Funnel is too small to accommodate them. They spill over and are lost.

That leaves the remaining three-quarters of a million kids to be formally charged in Juvenile Court. But the passage narrows even further here, and of those that are left, a tiny fraction (one in a hundred) go to adult court, and another four out of ten are dismissed or placed on informal probation by the court itself, with little or no supervision. A few of these kids are like Hugh, innocents falsely charged, but the vast majority are dropped simply because their offenses are deemed too minor or their cases too difficult to try, patients passed over as if this were triage in an emergency room: attend to the bleeders first, and let the rest sit and wait.

The Funnel continues to shrink for the remainder who go on to trial or plea bargains in Juvenile Court, with more dismissals and releases winnowing their numbers—the car thieves and graffiti vandals whose witnesses don't show, the molesters who walk because the victim is too disabled to testify.

At the very end of The Funnel, 330,000 kids out of the 2.3 million arrested are left to have their cases disposed of through probation, foster homes, or detention of some kind. Of the kids who enter The Funnel in handcuffs and are referred by police for prosecution, only 22 percent actually end up facing a meaningful consequence at the end (and that's assuming formal probation constitutes a "meaningful consequence"—a debatable assumption at best).

Strip away all the rhetoric about tough new laws and longer sentences and police crackdowns, and this is the bottom line on juvenile crime: When a kid is arrested, he or she can be assured that there is less than a one in four chance something is going to happen to them. Three out of four times, they will walk away. They'll stay on The Outs.[2]

Simple priorities are at work here. There are not enough courtrooms, detention facilities, or probation officers to adequately handle that one out of four cases, much less the three out of four it ought to be for the system to really have an effect. This is why, in Los Angeles, the 16 percent of kids who account for the majority of juvenile crimes can be arrested four or five times before any firm measures are taken. It is a futile set of priorities decried by everyone from the novice attorneys trying their cases here to U.S. Attorney General Janet Reno, who speaks passionately about society's refusal to put its children first and to build and pay for a system that works. And yet it is a set of priorities that has so far proven intractable and inescapable, and it is bringing the system down.

Even with The Funnel firmly in place, winnowing the cases down to a fraction, there are still too many delinquents flooding the dockets in most cities. In Los Angeles, the judges, prosecutors, and defense attorneys can't remember individual kids anymore, or faces or histories. They look at you as if you're insane if you name a juvenile and ask what happened with his or her case. "I can't keep their names straight for one day, much less kids from last month or last year," Peggy Beckstrand candidly admits. "They all run together." It is a comment that might not cause a second thought in adult court, but somehow it doesn't seem right in Juvenile; even Peggy admits that. "It's not supposed to be that way, but it is," she says.

Some of the more unusual and momentous cases might stand out, of course, but even then, only because the judge or the lawyers remember the facts of the crime, not the identity or character of the kid in question. A lawyer will sit down in the back of the courtroom and ask someone sitting in the next seat, "Is that the kid who killed his mother and left her face down on a heating grate for two days?" Or "There goes the kid who broke into thirty-two cars parked at the airport in a single day." Or "That's the girl who stuck her newborn baby in a suitcase and threw it in a Dumpster, but someone found the baby before it died. And, now, can you believe it, she wants custody?"

You can hear the lurid details of dozens of such cases in the back of every courtroom at Thurgood Marshall or in the hallways of Los Padrinos, discussed in hushed whispers by bored lawyers and cops and probation officers hoping to pass the time, trying to see if their companions retain any ability to be shocked, like medical students playing with cadavers. It is part of an attitude that increasingly permeates this place, the tendency to deal with the crime, not the kid. Do you really want to lock up petty thieves? the defense attorney asks. Aren't there better ways to spend the court's meager resources? Do you really want to let armed robbers free on probation? the prosecutor asks, just as sincerely. Isn't it better to lock them away to ensure public safety? The kids have been reduced to categories.

As a result the fundamental question Juvenile Court was designed to ask—What's the best way to deal with this individual kid?—is often lost in the process, replaced by a point system that opens the door, or locks it, depending on the qualities of the crime, not the child. Kids walk free when they are in desperate need of being reined in. Others get hammered by harsh punishments, whether they deserve it or not. Twelve-year-old Cecil goes back to his clubhouse, freed after his unspeakable molestation of a retarded boy. But Geri enters a courtroom, the judge and the prosecutor do some calculations from the penal code, and he goes to prison, out the door in five minutes, no questions asked.

The same forces are at work a few days later at Thurgood Marshall Branch, when the bailiff calls the case of the *People* v. *John Sloan*, set for disposition hearing.

"Which case is that?" a prosecutor asks a colleague.

"I don't recognize the name," the other deputy DA says, checking her notes. "Oh, here it is. That's the kid who did the armed robbery with gloves and a mask and Judge Dorn said it wasn't sophisticated because that sort of robbery happened all the time."

"Oh, yeah, that's right, that's the fitness case where we blew the appeal." The prosecutors look at one another, having remembered the facts of the crime, but unable to recall anything meaningful about John Sloan himself. "I don't know anything about this kid, do you?"

The other prosecutor shakes her head and hurriedly begins reading the file. Five minutes before sentencing begins and John Sloan's future is determined, the prosecutor is just finding the time to figure out who this boy is.

There are, however, a few differences between Geri's situation and John Sloan's. John has a supportive and affluent family; Geri is alone. John has a private lawyer who has devoted significant time and effort to his case; Geri had an overworked public defender with deficient knowledge of juvenile law and a vacation that conflicted with Geri's sentencing. And, most importantly, Geri can't even remember the name of the judge who sentenced him. John won't have that problem; he has Judge Roosevelt Dorn.

As his caseload has continued to grow, and with an increasing amount of his time taken up by his status offender program and private meetings in chambers, Judge Dorn has tried to streamline his courtroom. The results have been mixed at best. In a corner at the front of the courtroom, a green chalkboard has been set up, with the names of each case set for the day, with spaces for the attorneys to mark off whether they are ready to proceed or not, and for the bailiff to indicate whether a child has checked in on time or not. This way, the judge can call the next case with a mere glance to his left, rather than sorting through the piles of files on his bench, or relying upon the attorneys to shove and shout their way to the front of the line.

However many minutes this chalkboard saves, the courtroom is still crammed to capacity today. Two prosecutors, not one, have been assigned to handle the court's immense workload. Peggy has finally transferred Hyman Sisman, Dorn's favorite DA whipping boy, out of the courtroom, replacing him with two other prosecutors—the only courtroom in the juvenile system where the workload is so great, two DAs are required. This is the concession Dorn won when he threatened to go to the press over the stream of dismissed cases—an extra body in the courtroom. The jury box is still full of lawyers waiting to argue, uniformed cops waiting to testify, probation officers frantically scribbling, trying to complete the reports that were due this morning. Judge Dorn's probationers are still cutting school, and Dorn is still locking them up for it, day for day.

John Sloan enters the courtroom and sneaks a peek at the gallery. He focuses on his family, then quickly bows his head, pale face expressionless, shoulders hunched, as if he expects to be struck. He had last been seen in Dorn's courtroom three months earlier, when he pleaded guilty to confronting a Los Angeles building inspector in a parking garage, calling him a Mexican motherfucker, and robbing him at gunpoint. He was caught when his victim turned the tables on his assailants, pursuing and capturing John and an accomplice within minutes of the robbery.

At John's fitness hearing, Dorn had resisted following common interpretation of the law and found John fit to be tried as a juvenile, a ruling Peggy Beckstrand wanted to appeal but couldn't because her deputy DA in the courtroom at the time neglected to ask for a stay. The victim of the crime was outraged by this, but Dorn promised there would be no coddling, saying he could, if necessary, keep John imprisoned in the juvenile system far longer than the adult system ever could. Strictly speaking, this was true. But only theoretically.

Now John is back, having been to CYA for a three-month diagnostic study. The caseworker there reported being troubled by John's failure to appreciate the deadly seriousness of using a loaded gun and a threat of death to rob someone. John didn't seem to think what he had done was that big a deal, a disturbing caveat to an otherwise favorable report. Nevertheless, the caseworker concluded that John would be an excellent candidate for rehabilitation, and that, given the fact he was a first-time offender, he need not spend years confined in a youth prison in order to straighten out.

"The report is not correct," John's lawyer, Angela Oh, tells Dorn, trying to paint an even more positive picture. Unlike Geri's lawyer, Oh had no problem reading John's CYA report. "As you can see from his letter to the court, John *does* recognize the severity of his offense, and he's sorry for it."

Once again, John's family is assembled in court, his father the doctor, his mother, his younger brother and sister, all in suits and ties and Sunday dresses. Their lawyer, once again, is well prepared and briefed, with an array of plans to offer Dorn for releasing John on probation. She explains how he already has sufficient credits for his high school diploma and is ready to enter community college and to go to work on weekends. His entire family is willing to go into counseling with him, to resolve the conflicts between parents and child that seem to arise from their traditional immigrant values and his American-born sensibilities.

"His family is anxious for him to come home in some kind of out-of-custody program, so he can get back to his education," Oh says. "Academic testing shows he is in the ninety-second percentile, Your Honor. This is a young man who has not applied himself, not one who lacks the potential."

Just as she argued passionately three months earlier to keep John in Juvenile rather than adult court, Angela Oh now implores Judge Dorn to impose a mild sentence on the boy for his own good. "This is a child the father literally lost control of at age fifteen," she says. "That father says to me now he feels he has a new son. The incarceration John has had in Juvenile Hall has renewed their relationship and brought them closer. . . . I don't believe any more is required to accomplish the court's goals."

But though Dorn is inclined to keep as many kids as possible from transfer to adult court, he is not so easily convinced when it comes to relaxing his hold over a child's life. The rules of The Funnel don't apply in this courtroom, and Dorn only listens politely to the attorney, hears a brief opposition from the DA, then states his position. He has no intention of sending John home. But neither does he plan to impose the kind of lengthy sentence he suggested was possible at the fitness hearing.

"It is absolutely essential this young man be removed from the custody of his parents," the judge says, as John, pale and drawn in his orange jumpsuit, visibly sags at the defense table. "Long-term camp is the place for this minor, followed by probation and a ten P.M. curfew. And I'm ordering him to get C's or better in school, though that should be no problem.

"Now, John," he continues, then pauses for a few seconds, vainly waiting for the boy to look up at him. When John's head remains bowed, Dorn clears his throat and continues. "I'm going to give you an opportunity to earn your way out of camp early. Here's how: Work hard, try to become a leader, and it will be my pleasure to release you early, if you earn it. On the other hand, you can earn your way to CYA for five years if you go in with a negative attitude. All right, that's it. Good luck, young man."

Unlike Geri—unlike most kids charged with serious crimes—John has received a sentence that is tailored to *him*, rather than his offense. It is, in principle, what Juvenile Court was designed to do but seldom accomplishes. It happened in this case only because John had a determined judge, a wealthy family capable of hiring a private lawyer and expert witnesses, and a prosecutor who forgot how to preserve an appeal. Like some rare alignment of constellations, these factors don't often repeat themselves in Juvenile Court. Even so, the outcome leaves many people in the courtroom unhappy. John's mother is weeping, heartbroken that he won't be coming home. The prosecutor, meanwhile, is grimacing at another "wrist slap" for an armed robber.

And then there is Joseph Gutierrez—the victim of John's armed robbery—who walked into the courtroom at the very end of the disposition hearing. He had been caught in traffic, arriving barely in time to hear where John is headed. Gutierrez cannot believe it.

"That's just the icing on the cake," he says afterward, shaking his head. "Three months ago, the judge sat up there and made a big speech about how keeping that kid in Juvenile Court meant he would do more time than if he went to adult court. And now I come in here and instead of him going away for five or ten years, I hear he's going to summer camp. Unbelievable."

Gutierrez moves outside to a bench in the hallway and sits down heavily, hot and out of breath from rushing from his car to the courtroom. Now he wishes he had just stayed away. There was no discussion of his wishes at the hearing, no acknowledgment of the harm John inflicted on him or his family. No mention of guns and masks and gloves and racial epithets.

He says his three girls, ages seven, eleven, and sixteen now, are still fearful from that incident—afraid to go out at night, afraid at school, afraid of Asian-Americans, "because they could be like the two that stuck Daddy up."

"I give up," he says. "That kid's got money, he's got good lawyers, and that's how it works. This system is basically dysfunctional. The judge talks a good game, tells a good story about how he'll keep him longer than the adult system, but it was bull. That kid stuck a gun in someone's face—my face—and he's going to camp, he can even get out early if he's a good boy. That's not holding him responsible. That judge is guilty of exactly what he criticizes parents for—being too lax. This is why everyone is so disillusioned with Juvenile Court."

Gutierrez rises then, a tall, husky man with sad, dark eyes, ready to wash his hands of the whole process. He begins to leave, but then can't help but turn around, walk back, and make an admission. Despite all the delays and the anger and the outcome, he still thinks there may be some hope for the system.

"Nothing's totally black and white, I guess," he says. "The truth is, when I caught those kids, they were terrified. They looked like, well, kids, not hardened criminals. And over time, I've been starting to feel more sympathetic. It seems like this kid could have everything he wanted, except the thing he wanted most—love, and a family that understood him. He had the money, and all the things, but that love eluded him. And if it's true that his experience in this case has changed that, well, maybe this kid can still make something of himself. I hope that's what happens. If it does, then I guess this is okay. I can live with it."

While George Trevino spent his three months being evaluated at CYA, he jotted down some thoughts, a sort of free-flowing prose poem, then typed them up on a computer once he returned to Juvenile Hall. The end of it reads:

> Drain the blood from my veins but my heart will beat with pain, cold, shiver, arms hug chest, sleep, dream, nightmare, scream, eyes open, who holds you, who wipes your sweat and hushes your inner cries, no one, alone, deal with it alone, strong, weak, who said you couldn't be both?
>
> The light will come, but will cast more shadows, retreat, given in, give up, never, fight, absorb, suffocate, and move on.

Given George's stellar academic performance and mostly good behavior in the hall and at CYA, he should have every reason to hope for a lenient sentence. But he expects no mercy. He will not allow himself that hope. He has been in the system too long for hope, the abused and neglected kid, robbed of his childhood, entrusted to the state, which failed him, then dumped him, and has now decided he is beyond redemption, that his crime has made him an adult in need of punishment.

The jury had no trouble convicting George of taking part in an armed home invasion robbery. Jurors concluded he had joined with one armed adult and two juveniles to burst into a home and rob its occupants—a plan that backfired when the victims shot the adult, leaving George and the others to flee. The only part of the state's case that didn't succeed was the allegation that George had carried a firearm during the robbery. Some witnesses said yes, some said no, and the jury let him off the hook on that one, which reduced his potential sentence a great deal—though no one explained this to him. For months, he still thought he faced a life sentence.

Even with the gun charge dropped, he still faces more time than either of the other juveniles, who were under sixteen and stayed in Juvenile Court, or the adult gunman who cooperated with police and earned a reduced sentence of eight years. Yet another adult, who plotted the crime without physically taking part, also received a lighter sentence than George faces.

George's private, appointed attorney in adult court, William O'Donnell, is well aware of the law that would allow George to be returned to the juvenile system and committed to the California Youth Authority, rather than sentenced to state prison. He asks the judge to consider this, but offers little more than argument. Several counselors at the hall, George's teachers, various volunteers, and Sister Janet would have been happy to come to court to testify on George's behalf, to speak about his accomplishments in the last year in Juvenile Hall—his high school graduation, his poetry writing, his work as a mentor and tutor to some of the younger inmates—but the attorney never sought them out. There is no one to tell the court about his being nominated Student of the Year at Central Juvenile Hall, or of his becoming a finalist in an essay contest at the *Los Angeles Times*. Virtually all of the people who work with George at the hall believe he could benefit from treatment as a juvenile and should be spared a state prison sentence. But the lawyer never talked to them; indeed, they weren't even aware of George's sentencing until after it happened.

No information is presented to the sentencing judge about George's tragic past, either—how the dependency court was in charge of his childhood since age five, yet botched the job by removing him from a wholesome group home where he was doing well, and entrusting his upbringing to a home troubled by drug abuse. That his problems with school and delinquency intensified at this point in his life is indisputable—but this was never made clear to George's judge.

"George was the star among the kids who came through here," recalls Logan Westbrook, the director of the Helping Hands group home, where George lived and flourished for two years before being sent to live with his aunt. "He excelled in school, he was a mentor to the younger children here. He was our success story. We opposed him leaving, but the dependency court had other ideas."

Westbrook would have been happy to testify on George's behalf. "But no one ever contacted me."

Indeed, the probation report filed in the case makes no mention of George's childhood experiences, other than to outline the minor juvenile offenses he committed before the home invasion robbery. The report—

intended to guide the judge in passing sentence—paints George as a sociopath beyond redemption, erroneously claiming, among other things,
that George had been raised by a street gang since age five, when in reality
he had been raised by Los Angeles County as a dependent ward of the
court. No mention of this can be found in the probation report, nor of his
more recent and more positive year spent in Juvenile Hall while awaiting
trial and sentencing. Instead, the probation officer states baldly, "There
are no mitigating factors," then recommends a state prison sentence to the
maximum amount allowed by law.

The CYA report that follows George's three-month evaluation is somewhat more positive, though its only reference to his childhood history is to
say he comes from a dysfunctional family and has been in placement since
age five. Still, two of the three evaluators reported that George would do
well if sentenced to CYA, that he could be rehabilitated there and benefit
from its programs. They also wrote that he would have no hope if sent
to state prison with its array of more sophisticated criminals. (The one
dissenter on the CYA evaluation team, a psychiatrist known for his conservative views on delinquency, felt George was a very hardened and sophisticated criminal, full of rage and violence because of his tragic childhood,
and therefore was a poor candidate for rehabilitation.)

In any case, the portrait of George presented to Judge P. H. Hickok at
his sentencing in the Norwalk Branch of Superior Court was both inaccurate and incomplete. George's lawyer would later say it didn't matter, that
the prosecutor was out for blood, and that no sob story about George's past
and his good works in Juvenile Hall was going to make a judge go easy on
a kid who participated in an armed home invasion robbery.

"Nobody wants to hear it anymore," O'Donnell says. "It's a shame, but
that's the way it is."

Given his jury verdict, the maximum sentence George could get was
ten years, down from a potential twenty-five to life. The law allowed a
sentence as low as five years, but Judge Hickok gave him all ten, just as
was recommended by the erroneous probation report. The judge would
not commit him to the California Youth Authority but, as was done with
Geri, he ordered George housed at CYA while serving his prison sentence.
If he behaved himself, he should be able to complete his sentence there,
though there are no guarantees.

Afterward, George sits in the exercise yard at Juvenile Hall, reflecting
on his case and his childhood. Much of his early life is still a blank to
him, but, ever since his trial, he has been seeing recurrent images from his

childhood, sudden recollections that come to him at odd moments. One day he woke up, lying in his bunk at Juvenile Hall, eyes still closed, and he could see himself at age twelve, wearing a cardigan sweater and a bow tie, a little boy looking in the mirror, making sure his little clip-on tie was straight for school. The memory of it clung to him all day as he walked through the motions of life in the hall, wondering if this image was a real memory, or just something he dreamt up, some wish for a childhood he never had. When he mentions this to me, I tell him his memory is true, that the owner of a group home where he once lived told me about the sweaters and ties he used to wear.

George looks pleased at this, and relieved. "I thought it was real," he says. "But it's so hard to be sure. There's so much pain back there, I don't like to think about it too much. Memory hurts."

Though seemingly resigned to his sentence, George remains bitter about his experience in Juvenile Court. He feels "set up" by the court's decision to repeatedly release him on probation after he committed minor crimes, leading him to believe there were no consequences awaiting him.

"That's how the system programs you. They let you go and they know that just encourages you, and then they can get you on something worse later on. It's like, they set you up. Of course, I'm to blame, too, for going along with it. I didn't have to do those things, I know that." He assumes a look of concentration, trying to focus his thoughts. Sixteen when arrested, he will soon turn eighteen. He cannot conceive of spending the next six years (his earliest possible release) awaiting freedom.

"I didn't have to do those things," he repeats. "But the system didn't have to make it so goddamn easy."

A short time after his sentencing, George learns he has won the *Los Angeles Times* essay contest he entered, placing first in the high school category, and first place overall. Not just for incarcerated kids, but for high school students throughout Los Angeles. In his entry, he wrote:

The world's blind, neglecting its land. The human race has turned on itself, destruction's loud, but the world's deaf! Change can be found if it's truly being searched for, we as one need to communicate, guide our youth, because what we do today is setting the path for our children.

A few weeks later, George Trevino is shipped out of Central Juvenile Hall, another convict with a prison sentence to serve, a kid with no family, no visitors to see him, no roots left for him to cling to, no one to guide him or set his path. His unofficial, adoptive mother—the woman who took him in when he was living on the streets—tried to come to see him, but he asked her to stay away. He says he doesn't want anyone he cares about to write him or visit him, at least not for a while. Not until time has eaten away at his sentence, and he can envision being on The Outs.

"If I see people I love, it will only make it harder for me to pass the time," he says. "It will only remind me how much I wish I could be free, with them."

He turns away then, looking out across the hall's grounds, at the other kids playing softball and catching rays, the posturing and shoving and posing for the girls across the way. His narrow face tightens, the wistful sadness that had been there earlier vanishing, and it is easy to see how someone who didn't know him could discern a hardness there, seeing callousness where there really is only emotional callus, layers built up over the years, a shield against more hurt.

"It's easier to be alone," he says quietly. "I'm used to it."

CHAPTER 17

The Outs

In the same week George Trevino learns he has won a city-wide essay contest while awaiting the start of his prison sentence, U.S. Attorney General Janet Reno comes to Los Angeles, a person of power and position and a world so far removed from George's that he has no conception of it or her. Yet, alone among national figures, she has made it her business to try to alter the way the country views and treats kids like George—and Geri and Carla and the other children of Juvenile Court.

"If we don't wise up," she says in her usual manner—half hammer-over-the-head bluntness, half passion, a dash of sarcasm—"we'll never have enough money to build all the prison cells we'll need."

She is a tall, imposing block of a person, awkward and awe-inspiring at the same time. Having met with the mayor of Los Angeles, and preparing to don a cap and gown to address the graduating class at UCLA, Reno is sipping coffee at her hotel, her security detail guarding the door as she discusses one of her main interests as Attorney General—the juvenile justice system.

In the year and a half it took George's case to wind its way to its sad conclusion, Reno has pointed out, in speech after speech, that half a person's learned human responses are picked up in the first year of life, and that the whole concept of reward and punishment is learned—or not learned—by age three. What good is punishing kids later in life if they don't connect it to *their conduct, she asks, if the lack of nurturing, guiding adults in their early lives has left them totally deficient in matters of morality and conscience and empathy? We've got to reshape the system to begin the process of helping children steer clear of criminal behavior far earlier than is happening now, she says. And it has to happen everywhere—in day care centers, in hospital neonatal units, in classrooms and principals' offices, with cops on the beat, with juvenile judges like Roosevelt Dorn, willing to counsel kids in chambers before they become criminals, with an army of volunteers willing to go into detention halls and camps and youth prisons to work one-on-one with troubled young people, to become that one, positive adult in their lives who gives them hope and approval, a sense that someone, somewhere, finds worth in them. It's hard to take a chance on kids who have committed crimes, she says, but we have to suck up our guts and gamble on our children.*

Not that the hard-liners are all wrong. Yes, Reno says, the true sociopathic children—she figures one in ten violent, serious juvenile offenders might qualify as bad seeds who cannot be rehabilitated—need to be locked up and dealt with harshly (though she says the current fitness system that simply fixates on chronological age and a laundry list of crimes does not accomplish this—there will always be the child-monster who beats the birthday cutoff by a year or a week). And all juvenile criminals, even minor ones, need to face definite, real, and rapid consequences, something the system is not doing well at present, she says. But in the nine out of ten cases that do not involve sociopaths, Reno envisions a whole spectrum of ways to help and heal children and families before they land in Juvenile Court, requiring a new way of thinking about the juvenile justice system, a cradle-to-grave approach. Waiting until some child commits his fifth offense is just not cutting it. It's wrong, it's stupid, and it shows our nation's lack of commitment to its children, Reno says.

"Too often in the last thirty years America has forgotten and neglected its children. Twenty-one percent of the children in America live in poverty, a far greater percentage than any other age group. That's our future, that's our workforce in twenty years, those are our people who will be in prison in twenty years unless we do something about it."

Before Janet Reno, juvenile justice—and children in general—have never really been a national priority. The real money has always been committed elsewhere, wars hot and cold, drug wars, space races, Social Security and medical coverage for the aged. There is the occasional blue-ribbon commission or congressional committee that produces some hand-wringing pronouncements about the dire problem of youth violence and crime, but the *essential futility of the system's predominant pattern—reacting to the worst juvenile offenders, instead of the first—goes on uninterrupted. Rare are the national figures who care to make children their signature issue. Janet Reno, for her efforts in this regard, has been attacked by conservatives in Congress, who deride her as more social worker than prosecutor. And though she sees some sparks of hope around the country—a handful of promising programs and a dawning realization that preventing juvenile crime beats imprisoning juvenile criminals any day—there is still a predominant tidal force in favor of reducing or killing the nation's separate juvenile justice system, so that more kids can be treated as adults and locked away. Her calls for reform of a different kind have yet to yield any major changes.*

"Locking everyone up is not the solution," she sighs, staring into a cup of coffee gone cold as The Box at Juvenile Hall. "It's just the symptom of the problem. It's the proof that we're doing something wrong."

A few days later, Juan Macias—Scrappy—bids the writing class farewell. He was convicted in adult court of assisting in the murder of honors student Alfred Clark, shot dead at McDonald's over a CD player. Scrappy still insists he was unaware of his friend's plans to kill Alfred, but few beyond Sister Janet believed him. "You got a gun, Scrappy?" his homeboy had asked. They had done petty crimes together before, been through probation and camp. He was a little crazy, but Scrappy still said Sure, and his friend said, "Can I have it?" Again, Sure. Then they went to eat, his friend had some words with the kid with the CD player, then told Scrappy, "Wait in the truck, homes, I'll be right back." The sound of gunfire had constricted Scrappy's chest—he guessed immediately what his friend had done. Moments later, his red-faced friend had rounded the corner, bulleting toward the truck, elbows and knees pumping, wild expression on his face confirming Scrappy's worst fears. "I did it," his friend had exclaimed. "I wasted him." Scrappy drove away fast, then hid the gun for his friend. Even as he jammed it into an old tool box and shoved it out of sight, he kept chanting to himself, Stupid, stupid, stupid. But what was he going to do? Turn his friend in? A week later, he was in the hall. Two years later, he was convicted by a jury and sentenced to twenty-six years to life in prison.

In writing class, Scrappy always crafted tender, amusing stories about a bashful boy named George who likes chubby girls because they are less likely to dump him. He wrote longingly of just lying in bed with such a girl, watching old movies on TV in a motel room, a nice, safe, clean room where no one would shoot at him. He spent two years in the hall, waiting for his case to come to trial, earning his high school diploma and becoming a model resident, volunteering as a mentor and tutor for young kids. Yet he also heard the DA talking about him in court, using words like "heinous" and "malicious" and "vicious." He saw the hate in the eyes of Alfred Clark's family. *Could that be me they are talking about?* he wondered.

Maybe, he later tells me, this is payback for all the bad things I've done before without getting caught. Haltingly, he describes how, years ago, he once watched a fellow gang member leave a party, drunk and furious, swearing he was going to go outside and kill a girl who had pissed him off. Scrappy did nothing to stop it, though he could have intervened with a word. The next day, the girl was found beaten to death on the sidewalk. Fourteen years old, killed for nothing. Scrappy sits hunched over at the hall, remembering, saying the guilt over this has eaten at him for years (though it never would occur to him to turn his friend in to the police—in Scrappy's universe, that would be dishonorable).

"Maybe God is punishing me for not doing nothing, you know?" he murmurs. "Maybe I'm paying for that by being here now for something I didn't do. I figure whatever happens now, maybe I'll deserve it, you know?"

Sitting in the hall's Special Handling Unit, the last stop for kids sentenced to adult time, he is smiling and calm and surprisingly at ease, given the long incarceration stretching out before him like an empty highway through the desert. He says he will try to use every program and service he can squeeze out of the system—particularly during the first leg of his sentence, which will be at CYA—to try and better himself, and to earn the earliest release possible. "If I give up on myself, I might as well just be dead," he says. "I don't want to be dead."

Then he gives me a copy of an essay he just wrote, one that tries to explain how he feels about how he came to be where he is. It is entitled "Regret."

I stand looking out the window at the walls that separate me from the world. I see an old homeless man shuffling across the bridge. He walks with his head down as if he was going through some type of pain. A pain that won't let go. Much the same as the pain that clings onto a mother when she's not able to face she has lost a child.

The night merely lets me see that his hands are in his pockets. I wonder what he could be thinking. The word "regret" comes to mind. Is he now paying for a wrongdoing in his life? Does he regret? Or does the pain cause him to regret? Is he tired of experiencing the problems and the pain it causes? Does he hope to drift away—away to a place that would leave him at peace? I sense in him the loneliness I feel, even though he finds himself in the world that has its freedom.

As I see the old man walk away, I stand there trying to hold the tears that water my eyes. But the feeling is so strong teardrops come gushing down, like a father trying to fight the tears at his son's funeral, but he eagers to weep.

I close my eyes, only to see a flashback of the time that caused me to go through this unwanted pain. I fall into a dream that burns my heart so slowly, as someone being tortured by a memory and aching at the visual memory of wrongdoing. I see the young man that departed from his mother and the wonderful dreams he wished to reach. The hopes and dreams the mother had for her child would never be reached. A mother never wishing to go through the pain of losing a child. The pain the mother goes through flashes off my body, like a light being turned on and off.

Experiencing the mother going through the awful pain causes me to force the words, "I regret" out. But is it easy just to say the words "I regret" and not feel any kind of physical, emotional, or mental pain? Has a person really regretted after saying the words? Do the words touch the deepest of a person's heart to really mean them? Or has the person only said the words because the pain doesn't seem to have an end to it? Does it only take one person to hurt another for the pain and loneliness to keep going in circles? Could the mother and lonely old man have done something in life to deserve to feel the pain and loneliness they feel?

As I open my eyes I sense life has its own way of teaching each person. If life is a learning experience, why lose a child, your freedom, and why feel hopeless to learn? Now I wonder: If people didn't feel pain after a wrongdoing, would they regret?

———————◆———————

I N Inglewood, another normal day is unfolding at the Thurgood Marshall Branch of Los Angeles Juvenile Court. Peggy Beckstrand is filing five weapons charges against five kids, all of whom were caught carrying pistols onto the campus of the same junior high school during the same week.

She also finds herself helpless against a kid known on the street as "Sniper," a member of an extremely violent street gang called Asian Mob Assassins. Though he is suspected of running stolen automatic weapons and of committing at least one murder and one attempted murder, Peggy can't prove anything but his illegal possession of two concealed semi-automatic pistols. In California, that remains a misdemeanor, even for juveniles, and the best she can do with Sniper is send him to camp for six months, assuming she can even convict him on the minor charge. Sniper thinks this is quite hilarious. "Why are they even bothering with this small-time crap?" he demands to know after his arraignment, casting an amused glance around the tired trappings of Thurgood Marshall. "Like I really care what goes on here."

The public defenders, meanwhile, are up in arms again at Judge Dorn, this time for his practice of imposing one-day sentences to Juvenile Hall for every school day a probationer misses. For some insistently truant kids, this can add up to a month or more of detention by the time they are hauled into court—even though the public defenders believe the law limits such stretches of detention to a five-day maximum. They have begun papering Dorn again, but only on a very selective basis—minor cases where informal probation would be the sentence in most other courts, and Dorn's beloved status offender cases, a tactic that genuinely grates on him.

At the same time, next door, Commissioner Polinsky has been asked to put a scare into a fifteen-year-old boy whose once high grades and active participation in varsity sports have dropped precipitously, replaced by cut classes and long hours spent in front of the television. He is a handsome, curly-haired kid in baggy chinos and big black Nikes, his expression bored as Polinsky forces him to watch a morning of court action. Just before lunch, the commissioner orders the boy into chambers for a dressing-down. Next stop, Polinsky warns, could be Judge Dorn's status offender program if you don't wise up. Then we'll see how bored you look.

As the boy disappears into chambers, his father sits in the audience looking miserable, hoping this show of force (essentially toothless at this point) will help. "He tells me he knows the system can't do anything to him for cutting school," the father says. "I only hope this convinces him otherwise." An hour later, he leaves with his son, who looks less than impressed. But Dad is due back at work—as a judge in another branch of the Juvenile Court.

Meanwhile, downstairs in Judge Scarlett's courtroom, it is time for the final chapter in the Thirty-one Flavors murder case. Ronald Duncan is due in for his disposition, a hearing that should be as cut and dried as George Trevino's—in its own way. But where the system was programmed to hammer George for a burglary no matter how deserving of leniency he might be, the system is just as arbitrarily programmed to be relatively lenient with Ronald Duncan for fatally shotgunning his two ice-cream store employers.

Scarlett looks blank when Duncan's name is called by his clerk. Too much time and too many other cases have passed his bench in the three months since Ronald's trial, and he doesn't remember the case or the boy. He looks at Deputy DA Hyman Sisman, transferred to this more sedate courtroom from Dorn's domain, and asks what the sentencing range is in the case. Peggy Beckstrand, sitting nearby, answers instead. "Twenty-five years to life times two, plus ten years for personal use of a firearm."

Scarlett is startled for a moment, not expecting to hear from the deputy in charge, then says, "Oh, that's right, you tried this case." He clears his throat and says, "The court will call the Ronald Duncan matter."

In the gallery, Ronald's mother whispers, "Jesus," and shuts her eyes. The bailiff brings out Ronald in his orange jumpsuit, grinning as always, waving to his relatives, who still cling stubbornly to their belief in the boy's innocence—or at least something close to innocence.

In preparation for this hearing, Ronald talked to a probation officer about the offense and his background, there being no remaining legal reason to assert his right to remain silent. At his lawyer's insistence, he also spoke to a court-appointed psychiatrist. Both PO and analyst generated similar, grimly negative reports about Ronald.

In both interviews, Ronald admitted that he lied in his court testimony, as well as in all his previous statements about the murders. He still insisted that he did not pull the trigger on the shotgun that obliterated the heads of Chuck and Adelina Rusitanonta, but now he has finally conceded that he was part of a plan to rob them at gunpoint. In his latest story, Ronald claims he and Jason Gueringer—the policeman's godson who received immunity and became Peggy's star witness—planned to stage the robbery at the ice-cream store. But Jason showed up late, Ronald told his interviewers. Frustrated, he and Jason followed the store owners' car, then tried to rob them when the car halted at a stop sign. When they resisted, Jason shot them, according to Ronald's new story. He said he and Jason were supposed to split the money later, but everything fell apart when the police were tipped off about Jason and his bloody van.

In telling this story, Ronald not only admitted being a perjurer—since he had denied planning the robbery during his trial testimony—but he also was admitting to murder, whether he knew it or not. Even disregarding all the evidence that puts the gun in Ronald's hands and taking his newest story as literal truth, he is still guilty of murder for taking part in an armed robbery that resulted in two deaths. The felony murder rule makes him just as guilty; who pulled the trigger is irrelevant.

Ronald made no mention of being bullied, threatened, or coerced by the police into confessing. It was as if that had never happened.

When the probation officer asked Ronald if he thought there was anything wrong with planning an armed robbery against two people who had given him a job and had treated him with love and kindness, he said, "No. They were in business and they could always make more money."

The probation officer reported that, even now, Ronald does not think he did anything wrong, and that he doesn't feel he deserves to be locked up at CYA, or anywhere else, for that matter.

The interview with the psychiatrist yielded similar results. The doctor described a home life torn by divorce, where Ronald lived with his father most of the time, and desperately missed his mother. He said he wet his bed until age twelve or thirteen, and he recalled getting in trouble for setting a fire—two indicators of a potentially disturbed and violent adolescent. He talked of receiving daily beatings for messing up in school, and recalled being kicked out of one junior high school for possessing crack cocaine, though the incident was never reported to the police. One of the baffling aspects of Ronald's case—his lack of any criminal record before he committed murder, a pattern seldom seen—was thereby explained. It wasn't that he had never done anything wrong before. He just never got caught.

More recently, while living in Juvenile Hall, Ronald's small-time membership in a tagging crew turned into full street gang membership in a Bloods gang, he proudly claimed during his psychiatric interview. He said he participated in at least one race riot in the hall.[1]

The psychiatrist urged the court to recommend an intensive therapy program for Ronald at CYA, so that he could be shown the need to take responsibility for his crimes. The probation officer—one of the top juvenile investigators at the department, known for taking on high-profile cases and researching them thoroughly—was far harsher.

"The minor cannot be trusted and is a habitual liar," she told the court. "The minor has changed his story on numerous occasions and continues to do so even after being found guilty. The minor has even manipulated his parents into thinking that he can do no wrong. . . . The minor needs to be punished to the full extent of the law . . . in a secure and structured environment, supervised twenty-four hours a day."

There isn't really any question that this is exactly what will happen to Ronald. Because he was nine days short of his sixteenth birthday when he shot Chuck and Adelina, the law doesn't allow him to go to adult court. As a murderer, he has to be sentenced to life in prison, since the juvenile code mirrors the state's penal code. But as a juvenile, he has to be released at age twenty-five, at which age he walks out the door, free and clear, life sentence notwithstanding. No parole, no probation, no record. There is no room for any other sentence.

Still, Peggy Beckstrand and James Cooper get into a heated argument over whether Ronald should be sentenced concurrently to a total of twenty-five years to life for both murders, or whether the terms should be consecutive—"stacked," to use courtroom slang—so the sentence becomes fifty years to life.

It is an essentially meaningless argument, and Scarlett looks bewildered at it. "What does it matter?" he asks. "He's out at age twenty-five anyway."

"I just don't think they should be concurrent," Peggy argues, ignoring the low mutters from Ronald's mother. "It is absurd. To give the message to this minor that one of the lives he took doesn't matter—it's wrong."

Scarlett tries to reason with her, explaining again that, as a practical matter, there is no difference. A juvenile life sentence, or two of them, still means he will go home at age twenty-five. But Peggy continues to protest. Scarlett finally waves her off, saying the sentences will be concurrent, twenty-five years to life, plus five years enhancement for the use of a gun, a total of thirty years to life.

Peggy still won't let it go. "The People object," she says, standing up, her face red. Ronald is sitting and smirking, shaking his head. Defense Attorney Cooper says nothing, content, knowing it won't matter what Peggy says or what Scarlett does. Peggy plows on. "To the victims' family, this matters a great deal. The law has given us nothing to handle this case properly, but I just don't want to send the message that one of these people's lives doesn't matter."

"I agree with you. I agree with you," Scarlett says wearily. "This is one of the few states in the country that allows someone to commit murder and go to prison only until age twenty-five. But I'm not going to change that here, and neither are you. That's it."

And with that, the hearing is over. Ronald has been disposed of. He has

nothing to say to the court, no statement or plea—even though at the conclusion of his trial, Cooper had promised all sorts of revelations. Ronald
supposedly wanted to tell the whole story. Now, though, he is content to
just sit in amused silence.

As Scarlett rises to leave the courtroom, Ronald's father jabs a gnarled
finger in Peggy's direction and says bitterly, "They went after the small fry,
and let the adult instigator get away. It's not right."

Ronald's parents still believe in their son's innocence, even after he admitted being part of the plan to rob his employers. "When he spoke of
planning the attack," they told the probation officer on the case, "he was
just playing because he was upset. He loved his bosses."

Cooper overhears Ronald's father make a similar statement as they leave
the courtroom. The defense lawyer shakes his head and steps out in the
hallway with Peggy. "I explained to them that what Ronald has admitted to
is the same as if he pulled the trigger under the law, but they won't accept
that. They can't accept it."

"Neither does Ronald," Peggy says bitterly. "After all this, after a year of
fighting, after the trial and all this expense, to achieve a result we knew was
coming, and what do we learn at the end? That you can kill one person,
two, it doesn't matter. The result is the same. Out at age twenty-five."

Actually, Cooper corrects her mildly, it's possible he'll get out at age
twenty-three. That's when he's entitled to his first parole hearing. Just
about six years from now.

Peggy just stares at him, trying not to shiver.

The South Bay Community Day Center is housed in the former Jonas
Salk Elementary School, a long-abandoned LA County school building
designed for no known reason to resemble a brick-and-concrete Stone-
henge—a bizarre semicircular grouping of sagging classrooms whose
metal doors open up onto a barren concrete patio outdoors, cracked and
uninviting. In recent years, this dilapidated complex, unwanted and unloved, was converted into the South Bay CDC—a court school for delinquents on probation who have just left detention, camp, or the Youth
Authority, and who have been cast out by regular schools.

Unlike the bright and cheery Rosewood School, with its computers, its
dedicated teachers, and its program that puts delinquents to work helping
disabled children, South Bay is nothing more than an excuse to keep kids
off the street for a few hours each day. It consists of two classrooms, two
teachers, a secretary, a couple of administrators, and twenty-seven kids,

several of them eager students, with the other twenty or so intent on learning nothing more than how many times they can ask permission to use the bathroom in a single day without the teacher catching on.

Today is a typical day at South Bay. Seven kids are home on suspension for fighting. Two boys are sleeping, heads down on the six-foot-long tables that serve as communal desks here, their books unopened beside them. Tattoos and oversized baggies are in plentiful evidence among the student body, though all are on probation and barred from wearing gang-style attire, a violation of school rules and conditions of probation no one cares to enforce. It is not even a close thing—one thirteen-year-old baby face is wearing clothes that would swim on George Foreman, though no one calls him on it. On the wall, the following class schedule is posted:

> 10:00–10:30, class
> 10:30–11:00, physical education
> 11:00–11:30, lunch
> 11:30–1:30, movie

Videotaped movies—today's is *Malcolm X*—provide one of the few ways to engage the whole class in some kind of discussion, the teacher explains, though even that result is usually desultory at best.

"All they want to do is pass time, then go out and bang." The teacher sighs, ignoring the blank stares, the doodling, the snoozing children in her classroom. She has the exhausted look of someone who works the graveyard shift at a factory, though with less job satisfaction. "Do I think I'm really making a difference here?" she says. "No, not really."

South Bay CDC is Carla James's new school. The former honors student turned Tepa-13 gangbanger turned drive-by shooter and convicted juvenile felon has graduated from eight months in the counseling program at the Dorothy Kirby Center, and is back on the street, Home on Probation. She needs only a few more credits to receive her high school diploma, but only South Bay CDC will take her. It is a depressing place, more warehouse than school, but Carla doesn't seem to care.

"It doesn't matter to me," she says with her usual breezy diffidence. "I know where I'm headed, and that's all that counts. I'm on a new path."

Carla has come a long way, it seems. She is as personable and charismatic as ever, but gone is the tomboy dress and gangbanger attitude, replaced by casual clothes, styled hair, even a little makeup and nail polish, things the old Carla viewed with disdain. She is holding down a job, doing well in school, staying out of trouble. She swears she is no longer "kicking it" with her homeboys.

Her counselor at Dorothy Kirby, Mr. Shabazz, has pronounced Carla a rousing success for the juvenile justice system, writing a glowing report on her progress to Commissioner Polinsky, who then said it would be his pleasure to release Carla to go home.

She's been turned totally around, Shabazz crows after Carla departs his program. And the secret was pushing her into seeing herself and her actions clearly, forcing Carla to take responsibility for what she has done. Long and repeated counseling sessions with her mother brought the source of Carla's angry rebellion to the surface, Shabazz says—anger at her father's death, at her mother's remarriage, at the attention lavished on her younger brothers, at her mother's assumption that Carla could always take care of herself. Carla and her mother began to understand one another again, Shabazz says, and to see why she had deliberately gotten into so much trouble over the years. More importantly, Carla started to see she could break the old patterns, and be happier at the same time.

"Carla managed to make the transition she had to make, away from the gang lifestyle. With her it used to be, my barrio, my barrio, my barrio, like a mantra, it was all she lived for, and she was ready to kill or die for it," Shabazz says. "And it's true, once you are in a gang, you're in it for life, you can never fully leave it behind. But you can choose not to participate. You can choose to pursue other life goals, and that can be recognized and respected. You can make it clear that you still hold an allegiance to your neighborhood, that you know where you came from, but that you are moving on. She has done all that. She is not doing any of the activities that got her in trouble. She is staying home, going to school. She is going to make it. I have no doubt."

But despite Shabazz's optimism, once she is out of Kirby and back on the street, the transition is not so easy to maintain. To make it in a gang, to be a leader like Carla and to command respect, requires a strong-willed personality, particularly for a girl moving up in the macho hierarchy of street gangs. That willpower served Carla well at Dorothy Kirby, but it has its drawbacks on the street. She remains a natural leader, and the teenaged delinquent boys at South Bay follow her around like an entourage, part of it the attraction all boys have for a pretty girl, but part of it because she is Carla James, a heavy from Tepa-13, a former "shot-caller"—the name given to a gang's boss, a term both figurative and literal. And the old ways die hard: She has just been suspended from school for three days for yelling out her gang's name during a tense moment in class, provoking a fight among rival gang members.

Carla returns to school contrite after her three days off, determined, she says, to stay out of trouble—even as the gangbangers in her class moon over her and follow her around, hanging on her words. She says that they're not discussing anything bad, that she tells them what she has learned herself: that you don't have to fight or shoot in order to have respect. "That's all it takes to lead a normal life," she says. "That's all it takes to make me just like anybody else, realizing that simple little thing."

It's always hard to tell with Carla. She's so bright and personable and eager to please, her eyes steady when she says she has changed. But the fact is, these are the words the system wants to hear, and Carla knows this as well as anyone. Indeed, she candidly admits that, throughout her years in Juvenile Court, and even at Dorothy Kirby, she has always told people what they wanted to hear. She has always promised to change, to go straight, ever since she first got in trouble four years earlier. She has promised repeatedly to have her gang tattoos removed, but the giant Tepa-13 is still emblazoned across her belly, and the three dots on her right knuckles, signifying *mi vida loca*, my crazy life, are still in place.

"It's just so easy to get over on people," she explains. "At Kirby, I had it good with the staff, with the supervisor, with the director—they trusted me, and I could do whatever I wanted and never get in trouble. It's like I ran the place. If there was a problem with the other kids, I took care of it, I kept everyone in line, the girls and the guys. Some knucklehead would try to talk shit, I'd go in and take care of it. I made life easier for the staff."

She is on a break between classes, holed up in a small conference room, talking easily about why she graduated with honors from the Kirby Center. "I showed them a side of me that's like a normal person, which is what they wanted to see. It's like, I played by the rules, not because anyone had changed me, but because that was the smart thing to do in the situation. But I was always the same person. Locking you up, even at a place like Kirby, doesn't help you change. It makes you worse. If I changed, I did it because I wanted to, not because some program made me change."

Even so, Carla says, there have been changes in her life. Things are different now, and that's not just her saying what she knows people want to hear. The counseling sessions with her mother really helped, as did the group meetings with the other kids at Kirby. A lot of it was just growing up, she says. Hanging out, fighting, shooting, drinking—the same repetitious gang life—is less attractive to a girl about to turn eighteen than it was when she was fourteen and did her first drive-by. "Before, I'd do anything, I didn't care. I'd do shootings, drive-bys, I was doing so much work, my name was going up, if I had killed someone, I just wouldn't have cared. Now, I don't kick it anymore. I'm not into that. Let the youngsters do that, the next generation coming up. That's not me anymore. It's boring to me now. Look, I know what's going to happen. It's Friday night, and it'll be like every other. Hanging out, drinking, somebody will get in a fight, then somebody will start shooting. You get tired of the same old after a while, you know?"

It sounds so simple, but many of Carla's friends never grow bored with living on the edge of dying. They remain predators, destined for early deaths or lives spent in and out of prison, wilder, even, than the younger Carla. Once, she might have been willing to attack and even kill an enemy of her gang, but she never considered robbing a stranger, or sticking up a bank, or attempting a carjacking—to her, such crimes would have been immoral. The willingness of newer, younger gang members to commit such crimes has turned her off of gangbanging, she says. The new generation is too crazy even for her.

So now Carla is a month away from high school graduation. She has a job working in a shopping mall, wearing a silly hat and selling hot dogs on sticks. In addition to South Bay, she goes three days a week to a community college, and will start full-time after she gets her diploma. She's thinking about majoring in sociology, corrections, firefighting, or orthodontics ("I like to try different things," she says). She is living at home with her mother and, six months out of Dorothy Kirby, has had no problems other than the one suspension. Her old probation officer, Sharon Stegall, is back on her case, added incentive for Carla to stay straight.

As her eighteenth birthday approaches, odds are she will never be charged as a juvenile again, whether she stays straight or not. A Juvenile Court success: She's a kid who won't be back. Still, Carla's probation officer fears that, despite the girl's newfound maturity and restraint, she could be sucked back into her old life at any time. Sharon Stegall wants to believe Carla will make it and that Mr. Shabazz is right; she also knows Carla still sees her old gangbanger friends and still flirts with being a shot-caller, unwilling to give up the power and respect she has earned on the street. Carla hasn't completely removed herself from her old life, and being partway in is even more dangerous than doing it all the way.

"You're trying to lead two lives, Carla, I know it," Sharon tells her probationer during a visit to South Bay. "You've got all the confidence in the world in yourself, but you underestimate other people, you always think you're one up on them, and I'm afraid you'll end up dead because of it. Dead or in jail—and the next time, it's gonna be as an adult."

"No, I am through with it," she assures Sharon. "I'm staying clean. I'm thinking of the future." She gives her PO a gleaming smile. "You know me, Ms. Stegall."

"Yes, I do, Carla." Sharon sighs. "That's the problem. And maybe if we're lucky, that's the answer, too."

At the end of an essay on the future, Carla wrapped up her plans with an unintended irony—one that speaks volumes about Juvenile Court and the kids who come through it, because the sentiment is so surprisingly common, even among the most hardened offenders: "Los Angeles is getting really crazy, so if it gets any worse, I will then move far away or just out of state. Where, it's undecided still."

In person, she explains this sentiment in a more concrete way: "I don't want to die. Before, that didn't matter to me: I never thought about it. Now I do. If that means I've changed, I guess I have."

Then she dashes out the door with an apology thrown over one shoulder. "I don't want to be late for work," she calls, her footsteps receding down the hallway.

PART FOUR

Epilogue

"I think by age fifteen there is a small number of kids who, for whatever deprivations they have suffered, are cooked, as my grandmother would have said. They are gone. Whatever you do is not going to make a difference. . . . I think the solution is to pare down the money we spend on those kids . . . [and] invest in the vast majority of kids who come from the same environment and are right on the cusp. . . . People will say, You are stigmatizing the bad kids. Well, if you have 36 kids in a classroom and four are throwing chairs at the teacher, you have to excise them. Otherwise, all will be lost. This is war."

    JUDGE JUDITH SHEINDLIN, supervising judge, Manhattan Family Court, in the *New York Times*, December 30, 1994

Every 5 seconds of the school day, a student drops out.
Every 10 seconds a teenager becomes sexually active.
Every 26 seconds a baby is born to an unmarried mother.
Every 30 seconds a baby is born into poverty.
Every 59 seconds a baby is born to a teen mother.
Every 2 minutes a baby is born without prenatal care.
Every 4 minutes a child is arrested for a violent crime.
Every 7 minutes a child is arrested for a drug crime.
Every 2 hours a child is murdered.
Every 4 hours a child commits suicide.

    CHILDREN'S DEFENSE FUND, "A Child's Day"

12-13-94

Dear Sister Janet,

I hope when you receive this letter that it finds you in the best of health and in God's loving care. So how are you doing today? How is Ruth doing too? I hope you two are still touching hearts and putting smiles on the new minors' faces, just like you did to me when I was doing my time there. So how is Ed, is he still doing his writing classes there too?

Well, I'm doing fine up here in prison, very different from the other places I've been to since I've been locked up. But right now here in Wasco we are always on lock-down, it is very messed up here. There's really no program except for the one T.V. that's in the day room that we have to watch from our cells. But at least I won't be here long, I should leave any week . . . I saw my counselor already and he gave me my first eligible parole date, it is September the First, 2002. No later, no sooner.

I'm the youngest one here in Wasco. I'm only eighteen years old. Some of the guards here tell me: "Hey Kid, why don't you go back to CYA or Juvenile Hall, you're only eighteen." I guess they think it's funny, but when they checked my background and found out I got busted when I was sixteen years old and done about two years in Central Juvenile Hall and got kicked out of CYA, then they stopped making smart remarks to me.

Well in this letter I'm sending you a poem about my loved ones that have passed away. Show it to Ed and the rest. If you want to, go ahead and make yourselves some copies. I love and miss you all, from Blinky Clanton.[1]

Love Always,
Elias Elizondo

It's Not All In My Mind

My outside may make you think that my heart is made of stone . . .
Is it my baggy pants, my tattoos and the sharp look that I own?

I look just like every Clanton cholo around,
standing on the neighborhood's corner tall and thin . . .
If I were to show you my true feelings,
this is where I would begin.

Abandoned by a father, raised by my mother . . .
Tios, Tias, primos, primas,[2]
Familia always lying to each other.

Not much love would come from me . . .
Because if you take a good look, I'm hurting pretty badly.
I have stared down at my Abuelo[3] Alex's grave . . .
The flowers I've picked for him, I've saved.

Now I've buried my fourteen-year-old homeboy Payaso . . .
who took his last breath in my arms because of a cuetaso.[4]

My heart has screamed nothing but pain and agony . . .
Why did God take away my newborn primo, Baby Stevie?

One second I'm strolling with my homie Looney down the street . . .
The next second I hear bang, bang, bang only to find myself kneeling by him,
without his heartbeat.

I've missed three funerals since my incarceration, both of my abuelitas[5] and
one childhood friend . . .
Natural causes will always be here, but all this murder must end!!

We all know that our loved ones will come and go . . .
Oh Lord Jesus, please don't take any more until I parole.

Elias Elizondo, Wasco State Prison, December 13, 1994
15 Years to Life, Torcido:[6] 1992-93-94-??

CHAPTER 18

A Year Later, Another
Day in Court

JUDGE Roosevelt Dorn's bench is, as usual, piled high with files this
morning, another crammed docket, another typical day in a Los Angeles Juvenile Court that has lost ground in the year since Dorn took back his
bench at Thurgood Marshall. With the fervor of a minister, he regularly
pronounces the Juvenile Court he loves under siege and on the verge of
extinction, exhorting the disaffected professionals who work there to give
more of themselves, to make a difference, to resist the unraveling of this
place. He continually pleads with lawmakers to lift the shroud of confidentiality from his court, so the public can see beyond the well-publicized
failures of the system and glimpse how juvenile justice can work—and
why it is in need of rebuilding, not demolition.

His pleas, so far, have been in vain, and so he does what he can, jam-
ming more and more files onto his docket and those of the other two Inglewood courtrooms, an almost frenzied effort to help as many kids as he
can, as fast as he can. As long as he can.

The files themselves, piled so high on his bench and his clerk's desk,
make for an interesting and revealing study—not their contents, but their
actual physical size, shape, and weight. As telling a trend as any visible in
Juvenile Court can be discerned from such simple observation. Some of
the dog-eared manila folders are barely the width of an Oreo creme filling.

Others are so thick that if tossed onto a desktop, they would land with the same heavy, hollow thud of a Sunday paper hitting a concrete porch. The thickness of a file is crucial, the single most revealing thing about any Juvenile Court case because, unlike adult court, where each new crime generates a new file, juveniles get one folder for life, with each new offense piled in with the others. It's as if you kept the same report card from your first day of kindergarten through your last day of high school—your entire institutional life, all in one place.

One quick look at a file, even a brief heft without benefit of a glance inside, speaks volumes to an experienced judge or prosecutor or defender. Dorn can tell down to the fraction of an inch what the probable ending to a case will be, without ever having to read the contents. When a file is a sixteenth of an inch, it will almost certainly end in probation. A quarter to a half inch, add some time in the hall, maybe move the kid to a group home after release. An inch or so in thickness, and the likely sentence is one of the county's two dozen juvenile camps. And over two inches, the kid is probably a Sixteen Percenter, allowed too many bites of the apple, and now headed to the Youth Authority.

In the past year, the files have gotten thicker. More kids have been allowed to commit more offenses, and the time lag between arrest and a first appearance in court has blossomed, sometimes as long as eight or nine months, an effect so far removed from the cause that, to kids, the Juvenile Court appears to have no power at all. At the same time, the options available for dealing with juvenile offenders when they finally do appear in court have shriveled, thanks to harsh new laws and even harsher budget cuts.

Judge Dorn calls his calendar, the voice just as booming and rich as ever, gentle persuader soaked in molasses one moment, strident and intimidating the next, his biting words shaking insolence from young criminals—and torpor from disinterested attorneys—as if he were shaking dust from a rug. He hefts a thick file, then glances over his glasses at the defense table. A sixteen-year-old charged with burglary and auto theft—committed while he was on probation for cocaine sales and assault with a deadly weapon—has been escorted in for disposition. The judge looks the boy over, rifles the file one more time, then makes a snap decision to disregard a Probation Department recommendation that he go to the California Youth Authority prison system. Dorn chooses a far milder sentence of long-term probation camp instead—despite the boy's failure to be reformed by two previous camp sentences from other judges. It is a common

Dorn tactic, one that irks prosecutors without necessarily endearing him to defenders—kids get one across-the-board break the first time he sees them because, as he so often notes, being on probation to Judge Dorn is a whole new experience.

"You've received your break. Everyone gets one break in Judge Dorn's courtroom," he tells the boy, glancing at a report that shows the kid has led a double life as an inner-city gang member nicknamed "Lefty," while staying in school and earning good grades. "Now it's up to you. . . . You've been exceptionally lucky—lucky you haven't been killed with the kind of life you've been living. How many of your friends have you seen get killed?"

"A lot," Lefty answers truthfully. The two simple words, announced without sorrow or pity, say much about Lefty: He has witnessed so many kids in his neighborhood killed in drive-bys and jackings that he has come to see violent, premature ends as the natural way of things. Dorn knows this, and sees in it a reason for mercy, a child he might save. Others see only a hardened, calloused indifference to life, something to fear and lock away. Today, in this courtroom at least, it is Judge Dorn's vision that will prevail.

"A lot," Dorn repeats quietly. "Do you want to die in the streets?"

The kid has to think about it a second—not that he wants to die, but that it never occurred to him that he might have a choice in the matter. Hesitantly, Lefty says, "No."

"Then things have got to change."

The boy nods and agrees—though whether Dorn has planted a seed of hope in this kid, or if Lefty is merely telling the judge what he wants to hear, will not be known for months or years, if ever. Either he will leave camp and never appear in Juvenile Court again, or he will commit yet another crime, with only prison ahead of him, all other options exhausted. In the first scenario, sending him to camp will prove to be the best thing that ever happened to Lefty. But if he commits another, worse crime, he may find himself headed not to CYA, but to adult court and adult prison, in which case Dorn's decision will become Lefty's—and his next victim's— worst nightmare, mercy converted to curse. It is a gamble. Juvenile Court is always a gamble. Dorn is betting Lefty can be saved. He'd rather lose that wager, he says, than bet the other way, and never know if he could have turned the kid around. "That's what Juvenile Court is all about," he says. "These are our children. They deserve every chance we can give them."

"Yeah, well, it's not because he wants to be nice, or even because it's the best thing for this kid," whispers a deputy public defender sitting in the courtroom. "Dorn just likes to keep them all under his thumb. He can't do that with a kid in CYA, but he can with camp." This aside is intended as a criticism, but the truth is, Dorn heartily agrees with this assessment. Later on, he even laughs about it. "Better my thumb than prison, I daresay."

As usual, there is no time to agonize over any of this while court is in session. With a shuffle of papers and a scurrying of lawyers, before Lefty and the bailiff even make it through the back door to the holding tank, the roll call resumes. A fifteen-year-old girl with a teardrop tattooed in the corner of her left eye hears her name called out, stands, and says, "Here." She is at least six months pregnant, a huge, low belly on a tiny frame. She is charged with theft. The unmarried mother who bore her at age sixteen sits nearby in very tight black acid-washed jeans and jacket, the faded blue ink of crude gang tattoos still visible on her fingers and wrist, those three dots that signify "my crazy life," the gangster's shorthand for *I don't care if I live or die, so why should I give a shit about you?* This is the family he has to work with. Dorn sighs and rubs his eyes, and begins the process anew, looking for a way and a reason to save a lost child.

The job has gotten harder. In the year since Judge Dorn returned from his adult court exile, the system of juvenile justice in Los Angeles, in California, and nationwide has been shaken far more than at any time since the first juvenile court opened for business in Chicago at the turn of the century.

Juvenile crime overall leveled off or declined slightly in 1994 compared with years past, but no one is celebrating any victories. Juvenile violence and serious crimes are still climbing, and they remain far higher than a decade ago. With the population of older teenagers in America growing—just now entering the "prime crime" years between sixteen and nineteen—most experts have predicted new record highs in youth crime before the turn of the century, and continuing for years to come—a 150 percent increase by 2010, by Justice Department estimates. Any current declines, it seems, are merely a lull before the storm. These trends are exacerbated in Los Angeles County, where there are 150,000 *known* members of 900 criminal street gangs; there were only 30,000 gang members in 1982. (By way of comparison, there are 640,000 kids in the Los Angeles Unified School District.) Projections for the year 2000 put LA area gang membership at 250,000. Based on current trends, 90 percent of these kids can be expected to have been arrested at least once as juveniles; 75 percent arrested twice. Sixty percent will be dead or in prison by age twenty.[1]

These experts—esteemed academics and advisors to presidents— couldn't have been more wrong about the predicted growth in juvenile crime. It would never happen. Indeed, within a year, juvenile crime would, like crime in general, begin a decline that the experts refused to acknowledge for years, until the numbers became so stark that they could not be denied. Some of the nation's most esteemed (or, at least, most quoted) criminologists were warning of an approaching "super predator" apocalypse. But instead of the predicted 150 percent increase in youth crime by 2010, juvenile offenses would show double-digit declines by that year. Murders committed by children would dip to a third of what they were in 1994. The coming wave of young predators would be shown to be a myth of tragic proportions. One of the myth's chief purveyors, John J. DiIulio, Jr., a Princeton University star in the 1990s, would later recant his demographics-based predictions, explaining his hubris with a simple lesson: "Demography is not fate."[2]

But fear is a powerful motivator, and it has not mattered that this new "evidence" goading us to fear our children would soon be proved to be myth. The outrage of the present, fueled by false fears of the future, pro- pelled movements in a majority of states to adopt laws that limit or elimi- nate juvenile court jurisdiction over entire groups of children once guar- anteed treatment in juvenile court. In Pennsylvania, for one, new laws now require kids fifteen and older who commit violent crimes to be automat- ically tried as adults. Georgia one-upped by doing the same for kids four- teen and older. No fitness hearings are required, no debate about whether or not a child can be saved or whether there are special circumstances at work. Just put them in with the adults, no questions asked, subject to all the same sentences as any adult, including death in Pennsylvania. This ap- proach to juvenile justice mirrors new laws in Colorado, Arizona, Illinois, and other states, already in place or proposed for the near future.[3] Many others have lowered the fitness age. These new laws are wildly popular with elected officials and many voters, but they also make the late Justice Potter Stewart's dissent in the Gault decision thirty years ago all the more prescient. The inevitable outcome of making juvenile court a miniature version of adult court, he foresaw, is the end of treating children differently from adults. That single dirty phone call in 1964 is still slowly but surely putting the juvenile justice system out of business.

In California, the process of dismantling Juvenile Court is moving along at an equally brisk pace: In 1994, legislators in Sacramento changed the fitness law to eliminate any future Ronald Duncan cases. Now, many violent criminals fourteen or older can be sent to adult court after a fitness hearing, lowering the cutoff from age sixteen, and making it possible to sentence fourteen-year-old adolescents to life in prison (though the death penalty for juveniles remains out of reach in California). This new law is largely a panacea for public fears about juvenile crime—only a tiny fraction of 1 percent of juvenile offenders will be affected by the lower age threshold—but it also marks a critical philosophical turning point. California was one of the last states in the Union to have clung to the sixteen-year threshold. By the beginning of 1995, only the state of Hawaii still treated all kids under sixteen as juveniles in all cases. Jubilant supporters of lowering the fitness age suggested the change in California would make future attempts to get tough on juvenile offenders far easier. Indeed, additional legislation soon followed that makes it harder to sentence kids back into the juvenile system once they have been transferred to adult court, a process that was never easy to begin with, but which is now almost impossible.

The change will be unlikely to satisfy any faction in the juvenile court debate. Such reforms still keep the debate—and the system—stubbornly fixated on chronological age as the single most important factor in deciding who should be treated as a kid and who should be viewed as a legal adult. This will always produce unfair results on both ends—there will always be the cold killer too young to try as an adult; there will always be the heartbreaker who deserves a break but can't get one because of his birthday; there will always be the clever, older gangbanger who finds a young kid to manipulate into doing his dirty work for him—they'll just be younger now than before.

Beyond new laws that shrink the Juvenile Court's jurisdiction, the simple reality of diminishing budgets is devastating the system nationwide (and will continue to do so for decades). In Los Angeles, the Juvenile Court's best hope for stemming the rising tide of youth violence and crime—programs that prevent rather than react—are dying. The enormous budget crisis in LA County has spiraled out of control, requiring a sixty-seven-million-dollar cut to the Probation Department alone. Very quietly—without even telling the juvenile court judges what it was doing—the Probation Department has moved to save money by cutting sentences to camp from eight months to as little as twelve weeks. But the kids know. They are all happily copping to camp sentences now whenever they can. If they had any reason to fear a sentence to camp before, which few did, they now laugh it off. Some kids in the hall have started calling camp sentences "pit stops."

Meanwhile, Central Juvenile Hall has been unable to pay for repairs more than a year after earthquake damage crippled the facility, closing off several wings and even its main entrance. At the start of 1995, the abandoned portion of the structure is an eerie place, barren and disused by day. At night, with steam seeping from cracked subterranean pipes and drifting into the air through fissures in the earth, dozens of feral cats breed and prowl the grounds, looking for food.

Central Juvenile Hall, along with LA's two other detention halls, have a rated capacity to hold thirteen hundred kids. Most days they hold more than two thousand children in custody. The halls have responded to the crunch of kids and the escalating tensions and violence that result by issuing caustic pepper spray to their staff members, a measure long resisted but now embraced in the wake of the killing of the staff member at Dorothy Kirby. Now, several juveniles a week get doused with the paralyzing, painful "chemical restraint"—though it is not as severe as the military chemical agent used at CYA.

These problems are likely to worsen soon: One of these halls may have to be closed because of the budget cuts, along with several of the probation camps, which would force the system to shorten detention time for kids who commit crimes and who desperately need to be kept off the street. The policy of detaining all kids arrested for illegal possession of firearms, already spotty at best, may have to be relaxed or halted entirely to free up bed space. One prosecutor estimates four out of ten kids arrested with guns get a walk, despite the policy.

At the same time more juvenile offenders are being turned loose, the mechanism for supervising them on the streets—the probation officers, the ears and eyes of the Juvenile Court—are having their inadequate ranks further shorn by the budget shortfall. Already unworkable caseloads of two hundred kids to supervise will balloon into a thousand, possibly several thousand, the product of planned layoffs. These huge loads of probationers will then be monitored through something called the Probation Bank. Instead of actively working with and supervising these children, helping them to stay straight, probation officers will enter the names of their juvenile charges into computer banks that are connected to law enforcement computers. If any of the kids on the list get arrested or charged with a crime, a computer message will automatically be sent to the probation officer assigned to that kid, so that the PO will know there's a problem.

Juvenile probation in LA will come down to this for a majority of kids who commit crimes: The PO will watch a computer every day. Otherwise, the kids will be on their own, free to go on doing what they want.

This blow to the Juvenile Court is worsened further by another budget cut: a small but effective program that devotes fifty-eight probation officers to work with elementary and middle school kids before they join street gangs is on the chopping block, along with a companion program that puts POs directly in schools with their probationers.

The budget cuts—now, as in the past—target the juvenile programs designed to deal with minor offenders before they commit serious crimes, the very programs that common sense and every serious study of juvenile crime suggest should be beefed up. These are the programs, however inadequate, that target the repeat offenders, the Sixteen Percenters. Instead of strengthening these programs, the old priorities that have crippled Juvenile Court are being observed: Preserve the lockups, the Youth Authority, the detention programs for the most serious, hardened offenders least likely to be rehabilitated, and cancel efforts to turn around the young, impressionable first- and second-time offenders.

The budget cuts, then, are creating a Juvenile Court destined to fail even more often than before. That failure—in the form of repeat offenders—will increase the need for more lockups and more programs for the hardened, dangerous kids, which will in turn increase the pressure to try more children as adults because, the critics of Juvenile Court will argue, the system isn't working.

Most every one who works in the system—judges, defenders, even prosecutors—decry this cycle. Yet they can't seem to stop it.

Deputy District Attorney Peggy Beckstrand, for one, has given up trying. She has finally washed her hands of juvenile law. Her long-awaited transfer has come in, bringing her to an adult branch of the District Attorney's Office, where she is trying adult criminal cases—a much more satisfying pursuit, she says. "It wore me down, fighting every day to make a dysfunctional system work. I don't miss it a bit."

All the prosecutors that worked for her have moved on as well, each of them to more coveted assignments in adult court, replaced by a new troop of neophyte lawyers charged with making decisions that alter children's lives daily. The same sort of turnover has drained the experienced lawyers from the Public Defender's Office as well.

Deputy Probation Officer Sharon Stegall, meanwhile, is trying to start her own business and talks often of quitting the Probation Department, though those who know her well say she will never give up working with kids.

Sherry Gold, one of the top appointed lawyers at Thurgood Marshall Branch, has been looking for a job with a law firm that handles adult court appointments in the San Fernando Valley. She, too, has grown tired of laboring in a juvenile justice system that she fears is headed for extinction, though she is not yet sure she will quit.

"The kids I represented ten, fifteen years ago were so different. They were still kids. They knew right from wrong, more or less," Gold says over morning coffee at her favorite spot across from Thurgood Marshall. "Now they have no respect for life. They seem like they are brain-dead. You can't reach them. Sometimes I try to shock them a little. I say, 'Hey, don't look at me like I'm just some white bitch preaching to you. Why don't you go to school? Why do you hang out with a gang?' All I get is 'I dunno. I dunno.'

"They're a lost generation. And nothing we're doing now will change that. My husband hears me on the phone talking to these kids and says, 'Why are you wasting your breath? Don't you know you're saying the same things over and over, and it's not accomplishing anything?' I hate to say it, but I'm starting to see that he's right. I don't know how much longer I can do this."

Sister Janet Harris is not giving up any time soon. She is still chaplain at Central Juvenile Hall, still walking the units, looking for kids who need her. Of late, she has been trying to find some way to reopen Elias Elizondo's case, so far without luck. And she has found a fourteen-year-old boy in the hall with dozens of aliases, no family, no official existence, no future, no one in the system who is interested in him—and, by the way, he's a genius. Literally. She and several Jesuit volunteers working in the hall have taken the time to get to know this boy. They learned he had been raised since he was a toddler by street gang members, becoming a kind of homeless mascot passed around from crash pad to crash pad. He would go to school for the older gangbangers, assuming their identities, doing their homework, taking their tests, earning them A's and helping them appear to be fulfilling court orders to go to school. He has never taken a class under his own name, though he is always in school for one criminal or another. He devours books in a day. He has no values, other than those of a street criminal. The system has no idea what to do with him—it took fourteen years just to notice him. "They can't even figure out what his real name is, or his birthday," Janet says. "He's our latest project. We have to find a home for him somewhere. In another reality, this boy could be president."

In an office strewn with papers and computer printouts, Roy Sukoda is still working on his Sixteen Percent Study, creating a detailed profile of repeat offenders that is supposed to open a whole new direction for the Probation Department and the Juvenile Court, enabling it to target the kids in need of help before they commit serious offenses, thereby preventing juvenile crime, rather than merely reacting to it. The same study that shows the current Juvenile Court to be statistically irrelevant in stopping youth crime also provides a road map for making the system work far beyond anything imagined before. "We truly believe this is the best hope for the future," he says proudly. "This has the potential for saving a lot of kids we are not helping now."

But Sukoda's reports, for the time being, are destined to do little more than collect dust on someone's shelf, profound ideas with no constituency behind them. There is no money to make the enormous changes in the system implicitly called for by his study. Nor is there the political will to hammer through a policy that emphasizes preventing crime over punishing criminals, even though Sukoda's study shows that investing now in a new and better juvenile system would almost certainly save money and prevent crime ten years down the line. The only segment of the California budget that is growing now is the prison budget, a priority that is unlikely to change any time soon.

Los Angeles County District Attorney Gil Garcetti won passage of his most prized legislative proposal, a law that creates a statewide task force to reinvent the Juvenile Court in California. But it remains unclear what, if any, impact this task force will have. Already, the outlook is grim. It is off to a poor start, behind schedule and lacking funds to carry out its mandate of finding a way to make juvenile justice work. Even appointments to the task force were made late, and now the group is playing catch-up. There is also the "So what?" factor to deal with: Similar efforts in the past have yielded interesting reports that no one read or acted on. Another recent juvenile task force—created by a respected state watchdog agency called the Little Hoover Commission—spent a year hearing testimony and interviewing experts, then made a series of commonsense recommendations to fix the juvenile justice system in California. These recommendations boil down to three basic overriding proposals: Make prevention and programs for the youngest, earliest offenders the system's top priority, instead of the current balance that spends most of the time and money on older, hardened child criminals. Restore the flexibility and reasonableness the system lost in the wake of the Gault decision that transformed juvenile into a mini-adult court, with the resulting focus on litigating cases rather than dealing with children. And revamp the system to impose firm, quick, and predictable consequences on misbehavior instead of the current revolving door that allows a child to commit many crimes before facing any meaningful sanction.

Most professionals who labor within the system—and many of the kids who pass through it—agree with these straightforward recommendations. Yet the report has been ignored and even derided as unrealistic. The new state task force created at DA Garcetti's urging faces a similar fate—unless it leans less toward fixing the juvenile justice system, and more toward dismantling it. There is no shortage of support for that approach.

Judge Dorn, meanwhile, stays ensconced at the Thurgood Marshall Branch, and in the absence of any systemwide fix on the horizon, he remains intent upon creating his own program to save both juveniles and the court that serves them. If he cannot save the entire system, then he will remake it within the walls of his own courthouse, where no one can tell him what to do. If the Probation Department is cutting back elsewhere, Dorn makes special orders requiring them to work harder in his courtroom and with his kids. If the police departments give short shrift to juvenile crime, taking weeks to act on arrest warrants issued by the court, he orders police departments to serve Judge Dorn's warrants ahead of all others—and the kid he wants arrested is brought in within a few hours. If efforts to deal with delinquents are fragmented and bedeviled by interagency rivalries, he pressures schools and social service agencies and prosecutors and defenders to meet and find ways to work together.

And if no one else is interested in preventing crime by targeting incorrigible status offenders, then he does it alone. The parents keep flocking to him with their disobedient children, and though the laws says he cannot punish them with stays in Juvenile Hall, he and the other judges at Thurgood Marshall find ways to do it anyway. In chambers, Dorn keeps dealing informally with dozens of status offenders a week. "It is never recorded in court, but they are on Judge Dorn probation nevertheless," he gleefully tells a conference of cops, lawyers, and probation officers who work with kids.

The public defenders' latest cause for outrage stems from another Dorn policy: He has been taking kids who successfully graduate from camp and sending them to group homes and foster care if their mothers and fathers fail to take court-ordered parenting classes. The judge—and many a lawyer practicing in his court—see this as a tool for improving the home lives of delinquent children, the surest way possible of stopping a kid from becoming a repeat offender. But critics say Dorn's new ploy is illegal, and amounts to punishing kids for their parents' conduct. Kids end up asking, Why should I try hard and do what the courts and the camps ask, if I'm only going to be punished for something I can't even control?

"There will always be critics," Dorn scoffs. "They don't want anything to change. They don't care about these children's lives. They don't see that the Juvenile Court is a way to save lives. But I do. And I will never give up on saving children. Never. I will do what is necessary. That is why I am a judge.

"That is why I am here."

At a winter conference on youth gangs he helped sponsor, Dorn seizes the microphone and walks the stage with the same drama and urgency he uses in church on Sunday. He roundly criticizes many probation officers, juvenile lawyers, and some of his fellow judges for laziness, for failing to give the necessary effort to save kids—and his court—from destruction. He pleads with his audience of cops and counselors and lawyers and POs to support commonsense reforms of the system. He calls for an end to informal, unsupervised probation that does nothing but encourage kids to commit more crime. He begs for a systemwide expansion of his status offender program, with new laws that allow up to a year's detention for incorrigible kids if they fail to straighten up. Parents with kids out of control should not have to come from all over Los Angeles to his lonely courthouse because no one else will help them, he shouts, arms waving. He asks for a Juvenile Court open to the public, and a new law to make possession of a gun by a juvenile a felony, so he can have three years, rather than six months, to work with kids who carry deadly weapons.

"Our children are killing each other on the streets ninety miles an hour. . . . Yet we treat possession of a firearm as a misdemeanor. It is wrong. . . . Why can't we make commonsense changes? It makes sense, doesn't it? There should not be any question on this. But there is."

Dorn tells his gathering that Juvenile Court ought not be the unwanted, underfunded bottom of the barrel of our judicial system, but its highest priority. Our children—even our wayward and dangerous children—deserve the best, not the least, he says. He wants his audience to rediscover the essential optimism that spawned Juvenile Court in the first place—the notion that society ought to protect and attempt to save children, simply because they *are* children. As Dorn speaks, the judge slowly gives way to the preacher in him, his voice rising, both hands gripping the microphone.

Each time he pronounces a word beginning with the letter *P*, it sounds like a gunshot, so close are his lips to the mike. And this audience of cynical cops and probation officers and lawyers who have seen it all find themselves nodding as if they are Judge Dorn's congregation. Listening to him, they can almost believe again that what they do really *does* matter.

"There may be some individuals who believe this problem we have with our young people is not their problem. .... Let me tell you, half the kids I get are not from the inner city. They're from Santa Monica, Beverly Hills, Rolling Hills. ... They are all our children. They ARE OUR CHIL-DREN. Unless you believe that, you have no business in the position you're in. Unless you believe we can make a difference, change jobs. ... Unless we make a difference, you and I cannot be safe in our homes. If we do not make a difference, our society will never be the same."

Judge Dorn pauses then, breathing deeply, lowering his voice for effect. His audience is rapt now, he is preaching to the choir.

"Let me tell you," he almost whispers. "We can do it. And we must do it."

Judge Dorn's one-year anniversary back in Juvenile Court also marks one year since Elias Elizondo entered the writing class at Central Juvenile Hall. In that time, having had his minor crimes and gang membership ignored by the Juvenile Court for years, the system transferred him without hesitation or qualm to the adult court once his transgressions were deemed serious enough.

Now he finds himself in a state penitentiary. He is one of 120,000 inmates in California's $3-billion-a-year, twenty-eight-prison corrections system (bigger and more expensive than the U.S. federal prison system, the only state in the Union that can make that claim). By the time his earliest possible parole date comes around in 2002, the state prison population in California is expected to reach 350,000 inmates in eighty-one prisons with an annual cost of $6.8 billion, thanks to new sentencing laws—also adopted in the past year—that require extremely tough prison sentences for more juveniles and for all adult three-time losers.

After being moved several times around the system, Elias has been placed in the notorious Folsom State Penitentiary, one of the roughest prisons in the California penal system, a stronghold for the Mexican Mafia and other prison gangs. Because he was participating in a robbery attempt when a fellow gang member stabbed a man to death, Elias is being treated no differently by the prison system than if he plunged the knife into his victim himself. There will be no more school for Elias, no attempts to rehabilitate him. He will simply be warehoused with hardened criminals and gangsters, the youngest person on his cellblock, until he finishes his fifteen-years-to-life sentence. He will reach manhood in prison. He will spend most of his twenties there. Then he will return home to be someone's neighbor, someone's employee, someone's uncle, cousin, and father. He will have to find a life, and a way to avoid going back. And he will have to do it on his own.

Geri Vance's experience in the adult system has been vastly different. Though sentenced to state prison for attempted murder, Geri was accepted for housing at the California Youth Authority's Ventura School, the youth prison system's finest facility—a beach community paradise compared with some of the barren facilities in desert country that could have claimed him. His counselors at CYA, like those who worked with him at Central Juvenile Hall, feel he has enormous potential, despite the Juvenile Court's decision to give up on him. Ventura is the only CYA facility with a four-year college program. With luck, Geri says, he'll have a degree when he gets out. And his autobiography will be finished.

"Once it's written," he says, "then I can start my life over. With a new beginning."

After eight months, John Sloan, who avoided adult court for armed robbery thanks to Judge Dorn's refusal to enforce the state's tough fitness law, graduated from probation camp with honors. He has returned home to live with his parents, and is attending Los Angeles City College, earning good grades and pursuing a career in the arts. He is an extremely quiet and withdrawn teenager, reluctant to talk about his experience in the system, or much of anything else, introspective and difficult to read. He is eighteen now, legally an adult, though he remains on juvenile probation. He never sees his probation officer, however; the PO has placed him in a low-risk pool of offenders who need not check in unless there's a problem.

So far, there have been none, as far as the system can tell. And that, by definition, is success in Juvenile Court.

Despite the erroneous and incomplete picture painted of George Trevino at his sentencing hearing for the home invasion robbery, his ten-year sentence to adult prison still stands. When I bring his record of achievement and the potential witnesses on his behalf who work at Juvenile Hall to his court-appointed attorney's attention, the lawyer, William O'Donnell, is at first stunned by the news—"I had no idea," he says—and two days before the filing deadline expires, he goes to court to ask for a hearing to change George's sentence.

George's principal, his tutor, a volunteer at the hall, and Sister Janet all troop to court and wait in a sweltering, ninety-degree hallway in the Norwalk Branch of the Superior Court, where the air-conditioning only seems to work in the courtrooms and judges' chambers. George doesn't come, and isn't even aware of the hearing. "I didn't want to get the kid's hopes up," O'Donnell explains, a showing of little confidence not lost on the judge or prosecution.

Despite heartfelt testimony from George's supporters, the hearing is a muddled mess. O'Donnell, rumpled and disorganized and stating in open court that he hopes this will be his last criminal case ever, did not meet with his witnesses until the day of the hearing, and it shows. His presentation is disjointed; his witnesses come across as bleeding hearts blinded by fondness for George. It is never made clear just how misleading and erroneous the probation and CYA reports on George were. This is critical, because these reports helped guide the judge in sentencing George in the first place.

The prosecution offers no testimony to counter the glowing comments from Sister Janet and the others. He merely argues that George, whatever his accomplishments since his arrest, has proven himself to be dangerous, and that returning him to the juvenile system—and the possibility of a much earlier release from custody—would pose a threat to public safety.

"It's clear that whatever's wrong with him will not be taken care of in six months or one year or two years," the prosecutor says and, sadly, no one in the courtroom can truly dispute this, as it took years to make George what he is today. They can only disagree on who is to blame.

"I am not going to recall my sentence," Judge Philip Hickok says at the end. "I hope and pray Mr. Trevino has learned his lesson and will become a productive member of society. . . . The sentence will stand. I feel comfortable with what I've done."

Still, like Geri Vance, Judge Hickok's order allowed George to be housed at the Youth Authority, possibly for his entire sentence, since he can make parole before he hits the age-twenty-five ceiling at CYA. All he has to do is behave. He, too, hopes to earn a college degree while behind bars. He is not nearly so upbeat as Geri, though he has stopped refusing visits and letters from the people he cares about in life. The failed hearing on his sentence—and the fact that people cared enough to show up and speak out on his behalf—astonished him once he was told about it. "I just can't believe you would all do that," he tells Janet. He holds the memory close to him, something to cherish, this feeling that he matters to someone, though he still doubts he will ever amount to anything more than a criminal. And yet, a new, fragile optimism creeps briefly into his poetry:

> My life has come to
> an end, but if I turn
> around on the road
> again it will begin.
> It's up to me to decide
> For me to make a selection,
> I just hope I get guided
> in the right direction.

A few weeks before his transfer out of Central Juvenile Hall to CYA, George had been nominated as the facility's Outstanding Student of the Year. By the time the winner is picked—and George is named first runner-up—he is gone.

A few months later, there is a fight among inmates at the CYA facility where George is housed. He is identified as one of the culprits and transferred to adult prison. For good.

Ronald Duncan, kept by the juvenile system only because his birthday saved him by nine days, is in the California Youth Authority, where he will likely stay until age twenty-five. Even so, even though his vicious double murder was far more egregious than Elias's crimes, or George's, or Geri's, Ronald will probably get out before any of them. Only his record will be cleansed and sealed, as if those two murders never happened.

Ronald has never admitted responsibility for the murders. He doesn't have to. The calendar will set him free.

Andre, the gangbanger whose conduct and outlook on life was no different or worse than George's or Geri's or Elias's—but who was given a chance by the juvenile system to work with handicapped children and to turn his life around—has left the gang life and the streets behind. He has graduated high school and is going to community college while holding down a job as a clerk for Los Angeles County.

"A person can change," he says. "It takes guts—and you have to have someone out there willing to help you, to treat you like a person instead of a criminal, someone who believes in you, the way my teachers did—but you can do it."

Andre isn't sure yet what he would like to do in life. He is only now getting used to the notion that his horizons are bigger than the cramped barrio One-ways of Norwalk. There is one career he is interested in, though something he would never have considered just a few years ago, but which now seems appealing because it would enable him to help people, particularly kids like himself.

He thinks, just maybe, he'd like to be a cop.

Carla James also graduated from high school, then left the dismal confines of the South Bay school for good. As planned, she now attends college as a full-time student, and holds down two jobs as well, selling ice cream and hot dogs at a shopping mall. She and her mother are talking more instead of arguing, letting go the old tensions that once filled their home. Carla's little brother is in private school—she made sure he didn't follow in her gangster footsteps. And, after eight months on The Outs, she has stayed straight and clean. She has done so well that her probation officer, Sharon Stegall, is recommending that she be terminated from the Juvenile Court docket, her probation over, her record sealed.

"This was a kid who was always in it because she liked the thrill," Sharon says. "But I think she's realizing she has half a brain, and that she can accomplish anything she puts her mind to. I'm pretty sure she's going to channel those abilities into legal things from here on out. If not, though, if I'm wrong, well, she's just turned eighteen. Next time, she goes to adult."

"There won't be a next time," Carla says. "I know that, for sure. Not that I learned any big lesson from the system, or anything. But I'm older now. I know better."

Carla, it seems, offers a powerful lesson for the system—and a powerful reason to keep it alive. It is not so much that the Juvenile Court has the power to change kids like Carla. It doesn't, really, though few are articulate enough to make that as clear as Carla does. What the system can accomplish—and what transferring kids to adult court can never do—is to give Carla and others like her the time and opportunity and tools to consider other, more constructive paths in life than gangs and crime and violence. As often as not, kids will choose not to be criminals if given another option—not because they are compelled to do so, but because it makes sense to them.

Carla smiles that big, white smile of hers, eyes crinkling, expression confident and sure, agreeing with this assessment. As always with Carla, it's impossible to imagine this girl hurting someone, pointing a gun at someone, shooting at someone—though there is no doubt she has done all those things in the past, and worse. And even knowing that, it still doesn't seem possible.

"Yeah," Carla says without a trace of irony. "That's what everyone has always said about me. That's how come I always worked the system, rather than the system working me."

In the end, though, the result is the same. For all her talk of working the system, and of telling judges and counselors what they want to hear, Carla is straight now. She's on The Outs, and out of trouble. It doesn't matter why, only that it is so. And her mother has no doubt that the Juvenile Court saved Carla's life.

A year ago, these seven children found themselves before the Juvenile Court, kids accused of car theft, of murder, of violent assaults, of armed robbery, and of violating probation by skipping school and dressing like a gangster. Three of these kids had been hard-core gang members. Two were very poor, one was very wealthy, the others somewhere in between. The system of juvenile justice, where rehabilitation, not punishment, is— or was—the theoretical goal, was supposed to save them all, or to at least go down swinging.

It saved three. It proved itself impotent before the one remorseless killer among them. And the system gave up on the rest.

There is no easily identifiable reason for these divergent results. There is little logic to Juvenile Court's successes and failures. But for a bit of luck, a chance encounter with a caring judge or probation officer or volunteer— or, conversely, with a tired bureaucrat, an incompetent lawyer, or an inflexible DA—any one of the seven could have traded places with the others. That is the heartbreak of Juvenile Court, the wonder of it, and the scandal. Heartbreak, because every kid cannot be saved. Wonder, that this broken, battered, outgunned system saves even one child. Scandal, because it so seldom tries to do anything at all.

AFTERWORD

Twenty Years Later

1. BLINDERS

Not long after *No Matter How Loud I Shout* was published, I was surprised to receive an invitation to testify before the US Senate Subcommittee on Children, Youth, and Families in Washington, DC. The subject of the hearing was juvenile crime and reform, by which the senators meant charging, trying, and imprisoning yet more children as adults.

I found myself to be the only journalist in a room full of legal experts, angry crime victims, and scholars, including those who had predicted the approach of a tidal wave of juvenile super predators, who were the "stars" of this hearing. I was in the distinct minority in suggesting that the most effective response to juvenile crime — even a tidal wave of it — might not lie in shifting the lion's share of resources to programs targeting the worst of the worst. Instead, I told the senators about the solution commended to me by most of the cops, prosecutors, judges, and defense attorneys I met during my year in the life of juvenile court: that we should be intervening in a big way in the lives of children who are just embarking on criminal careers—well *before* they become the worst of the worst. We were missing an opportunity, I argued; I'd seen it happen day after day: the nation's juvenile courts were an engine for identifying new small-time offenders, thousands of them every week, who could be stopped from committing more crimes—who could be helped (or at least restrained) before it was too late, whose families and school careers could be revived. But we were doing nothing with them or their families. Instead, we waited for them to commit some truly heinous offense, waited for them to victimize someone terribly, waited for them to become the so-called predators everyone feared. Only then did we spend inordinate amounts of money to imprison them—at a yearly cost greater than tuition at our priciest colleges. The system's priorities were exactly backward: we had a perfectly good smoke alarm in place, but we ignored its warnings until the house burned down. Only then did we turn on the fire hoses.

The senators appeared mildly baffled by this digression from their discussion of the coming super predators who had to be locked away in adult prisons, and how we needed new, tougher, adult tools to battle this mythic foe. And that's when it hit me: based on their puzzled responses, it appeared that few, if any, of these senators had spent even a day—much less a year—watching the juvenile court at work. These men who were determined to fix the system, mostly by tearing it down, seemed to have no idea what it even looked like.

2. JUDGE DORN

None of the major reforms of the juvenile justice system contemplated during my year in juvenile court ever made the leap from hopeful memo to working reality.

The ambitious Sixteen Percent Solution project, with its aspirations of remaking juvenile court into an engine for prevention and early intervention, came to naught. There was no money and no political will to rebuild the system from the ground up with a solution that did not put adult prison sentences as its priority. After a small pilot study, the initiative ended for good.

Likewise, nothing came of former District Attorney Gil Garcetti's legislatively mandated study of juvenile justice, with its notion of creating a two-tiered system that channeled more offenders directly into adult court while throwing intensive social services at the most promising candidates for rehabilitation. Declining juvenile crime sucked the wind out of all such reform ideas, whether they emphasized prosecution or prevention.

And then there was Judge Roosevelt Dorn, who vowed to use truancy, running away, and other status offenses, along with an army of empowered parents, to remake the system one kid at time. Try as he might, Dorn could not muster support from his fellow judges to follow his example by opening their courtrooms to parents and wayward kids. Nor would they hammer probation officers into writing more reports and doing more investigations. Nor would they bend the law and run roughshod over prosecutors and defense attorneys to get their way. Dorn was the judge who would be king, but the problem with kings is that they rule alone.

Facing increasing resistance to his policies and his my-way-or-the-highway style, Dorn turned to politics. In 1997, he left the court for good and became mayor of the surrounding community of Inglewood, where his advocacy for kids and parents, and notoriety for doing things his way, made him a popular leader of the city for three terms.

Shocking his supporters—though not the critics of his autocratic approach—a public corruption scandal finally took Dorn down in 2010. The charges revolved around a half-million-dollar low-interest home loan he received from a program operated by the very city of Inglewood he led. Prosecutors leveled felony charges that could have sent Dorn to prison for four years. The judge-turned-mayor always maintained his innocence but ended up resigning his office and pleading guilty to a misdemeanor conflict-of-interest charge. This earned him two years probation and a lifetime ban on holding elected office.

No more would any child be offered a choice between the penitentiary, the cemetery, or Judge Dorn's tough love. His parting words were a shockingly ironic cop-out from a judge who so often imposed his will on others, and who so many times had demanded personal responsibility from the kids, parents, and lawyers who once stood before him: "There comes a time when even the innocent can be forced to take a plea," he said. "And that's what happened to me."

3. THE JUDGE WHO WON THE LOTTERY

One of the great obstacles to an effective Los Angeles Juvenile Court has been a chronic lack of continuity. Kids would be shuttled to court for a crucial hearing and find a strange lawyer, a different judge, or a new probation officer who didn't know their names, much less their histories. Files would be lost. Vital information would not be shared between the foster care world of dependency court and the criminal world of delinquency court. Kids like George Trevino who could have been saved instead slipped through the cracks—not just their cases but their very lives and fates mishandled and misjudged. And with the regular turnover of presiding juvenile judges who sought more prestigious (or less depressing) assignments, there was a persistent lack of continuity in leadership.

Until Judge Michael Nash came along.

Shortly after I finished *No Matter How Loud I Shout*, Nash took over as juvenile presiding judge. Instead of two years and out like most of his predecessors, Nash has stayed. And stayed. At the time of this writing, he has been presiding over Los Angeles's fractious juvenile court for most of the last twenty years.

"I came here," he tells me, "because I like the mission . . . putting families together instead of putting people away. That's the goal . . . But we can do better. We have to do better."

When the subject turns to the failings of Los Angeles County's immense foster care and child welfare bureaucracy, as problem-plagued today as it was twenty years ago, the laid-back California jurist with the sweep of silver hair suddenly disappears and the plain-talking native New Yorker within takes over, as Nash's voice rises with such choice phrases as "It's a stinking mess!" and "The blind leading the blind!"

As he speaks, Nash manages to locate the few square inches on his formidably cluttered desktop not obscured by journal articles, legal briefs, spreadsheets, or complaint letters (in addition to his other duties, the presiding judge is also the courthouse Dear Abby). He starts pounding on the little clearing with one fist, punctuating each word with a thud. Soon the entire mound of papers on his desk has begun to shudder and shimmy like a hillside during a 5.0 magnitude quake, until his pounding finally sends a framed photo of his daughter (one of a dozen on display) tumbling to the floor.

This is not theater. Nash just can't help himself, and this says something about the kind of operator he has been. Here's a sixty-five-year-old judge who has spent twenty years at the same often thankless, usually frustrating job—a job that has burned out some very good men and women—and yet he's still enthusiastically pounding the desk like a freshman debate team president. Only the clatter of his daughter's portrait brings him up short. He eyes the mess he's made, takes a calming breath, grins sheepishly, and assures me he's going to clean up his desk after our visit.

"Don't believe it," attorney Sherry Gold later observes. She, too, has not stopped working with kids. She's now with the LA County Alternate Public Defender and works in Nash's Mental Health Court, his innovation for delinquents with heavy-duty psychiatric diagnoses. She is Nash's friend, ally, nudge, and occasional combatant, and she credits him with some genuine improvements in the nation's largest juvenile court over the past twenty years. A tidy office is not one of them, she says, laughing. "He's totally dedicated. But that office has been like that as long as I've known him."

Nash tends to brush aside praise, allowing only that "I like to think I'll leave the court in a little better shape than I found it." And that, it turns out, may be his secret. Instead of pushing large-scale reforms of the juvenile justice system that never come to pass, instead of fomenting revolution and alienating everyone around him as Judge Dorn did, Nash has been an incrementalist. He sees a need, such as the poor treatment of mentally ill juveniles, recruits energetic allies such as Sherry Gold to help, and says, *Let's see if we can make this one thing better, this one area where the court fails. Just this one thing.*

Nash has made a career of "just this one thing," and he has an office wall filled with plaques and awards attesting to the results. Early in his tenure, he created "Adoption Saturday" to show off one of the more positive moments in the juvenile court workday: successful adoptions of the system's wards. Court staffers, lawyers, and judges volunteer their time on Saturdays throughout the year to help close out the 1,500 to 2,000 annual adoptions of Los Angeles's foster children, with the public invited to observe what had always been a secret proceeding. The program succeeded so wildly that more than two hundred other jurisdictions in all fifty states have adopted it, ultimately spawning a National Adoption Day.

In 2010, Nash started a similar showcase for a different juvenile court milestone: reunification, in which the public is invited to attend the final hearings in some of the six thousand annual cases that end with parents and children put back together as families—the foster kids who didn't have to be adopted because they went home.

"It doesn't get any better than that," Nash says.

Many of his initiatives have been adopted elsewhere, and Nash has served as both president and treasurer of the National Council of Juvenile and Family Court Judges. He pioneered juvenile drug courts to better deal with kids with addictions. He created a one-family-one-judge system to make sure fewer juveniles fall though the cracks by requiring that the same judge stick with a child throughout his or her years in the system. And he has improved the abysmal level of communication between the two sides of the juvenile court when it comes to "crossover kids"—those who move from dependency and foster care to delinquency and probation or detention. No more summarily dropping foster kids who commit crimes while under the care of the dependency court, Nash has insisted. George Trevino's fate might have been quite different if he had entered the system today. Or perhaps not; Nash, more than anyone, knows that his improvements, needed as they were, can do only so much, as they are erected atop a shaky and flawed foundation.

All this seems a bit unlikely for a man who started his legal career in 1974 as a tough prosecutor for the California Attorney General (having given up his childhood dream of a football career when he stopped growing at five-foot-five). Nash co-prosecuted the infamous Hillside Strangler serial murder case from 1981 to 1983—the longest criminal trial in US history. But a hint of the career to come was captured by a news photographer who snapped Nash's glum, exhausted expression after the guilty verdict came in, then asked why he wasn't celebrating with his colleagues. "What's to celebrate?" Nash recalls saying. "We're talking about human tragedy all the way through."

A few years later, after he had been appointed to the Superior Court bench and began hearing criminal cases in Hollywood, a defense lawyer approached him about a young woman with a chip on her shoulder and a drug and alcohol problem that contributed to her crimes. Nash had given her a long jail term, but her lawyer said he had found a program that might help her—the then new, now respected Phoenix House—if the judge would agree to free her. Nash said okay and put her on a very long probation, and the young woman turned her life around. Nash even wrote her a letter when she successfully completed her probation, saying she had done a great job and that he was proud of her.

Nash had always found incarcerating people a depressing necessity of his job. But this case, finding a way to help a young woman change her life, thrilled and inspired him. It led Nash to move to juvenile court not long after, believing he might find more opportunities there for such positive outcomes. He tried dependency cases at first, then became supervising dependency judge, then took over as presiding judge in 1995 and, except for a two-year hiatus, has been presiding ever since.

Now his duties are almost entirely administrative. These days he convenes committees, not courtrooms. He struggles to accomplish the court's work after budget cuts axed six of his twenty-eight delinquency judges.

He's also the unofficial shrink for the judges still on the job, who sometimes feel unable to go on, crushed by the weight of the hopelessness so many parents and, worse still, so many children carry into the courtroom. Nash tells them his own method of coping: just before you leave, go through your daily calendar and look for the one positive thing that happened that day.

"If that's the last thing you think about, you can come back the next morning," says Nash, who has announced he will retire in 2015. "On your worst day, you're going to do something good for someone. I guarantee it."

Every once in a while, someone will provide such a reminder for him, Nash says, and he'll remember anew why he does this work. Not long ago, he received a letter from the woman he sent to Phoenix House so many years before. She had been sober all this time, had a family up in Northern California, and worked as a drug court coordinator. One day she heard Nash's name mentioned by one of the judges she worked with and looked him up to confirm that this was the same person who had given her a second chance in life. She felt she owed all her achievements to him, and that the letter he wrote her to close her probation had inspired her. It was, she told him, her prized possession. Which is something, because Nash says the same about *her* letter to him.

Nash drove home from work that night, rushed into his house, and said to his wife, "Guess what."

"What?"

"I won the lottery today."

4. ELIAS

A handsome young couple approaches me. I'm at the Los Angeles Times Festival of Books on the leafy campus of the University of Southern California, and the dark-haired young man, dressed sharply in black, is grinning at me. It's plain that he knows me, and I realize I know him, too, though I cannot say how or why.

"It's Elias," he says at last. "Elias Elizondo."

So my soulful, angry, heartbreaking teen poet, now in his thirties, is back in the world after being sent from juvenile hall to adult prison. Elias is back.

And he looks great. I soon learn he *is* great, with a good job, a nice young woman on his arm and in his life, a plan for the future. He was able to take college classes in prison, earned a degree, and is continuing his education. I had not seen Elias in twenty years, and the transformation renders me speechless, the wounded boy I still remembered, now this confident man before me, whom society had given up on, sent to enter adulthood in a terrible and inhumane place of cages and desperation.

As we embrace before parting, I can't help but marvel at Elias, whose case I had deemed an abject failure of juvenile court. And so it was, for a young man who had so much to offer, so much potential, and who had been so deserving of a break that the system could not or would not offer. Yet he had the resilience and courage to triumph in the end, to finish his sentence, to come back, and to move forward. I look at him and think of all the other young men and women I met in that year in the life of juvenile court, all of them now in their thirties, and wonder how many of them have been able to persevere and build a life like Elias.

He walks off with his friend, and I watch them recede into the distance until I can no longer see Elias. I feel a fierce and humbling pride for his accomplishments, which came largely despite the juvenile court's efforts in his behalf, not because of them. It is as Judge Nash said: in that moment, I feel like I won the lottery.

But, of course, that's the real problem with juvenile court: lottery winners are all too rare.

—Edward Humes
Los Angeles
July 2014

NOTES

PROLOGUE

1. Numbers are for arrests of juveniles in Los Angeles County in 1994, as compiled by the California Department of Justice's Law Enforcement Information Center. These represent arrests only, not actual cases filed in Juvenile Court, or convictions. For example, out of 27,144 arrests of juveniles for felonies, nearly 22 percent were released without charges ever being filed in court—in part because of system overcrowding and backlog, in part because of evidentiary problems.

2. Richard Perez was eventually transferred to adult court and convicted of first-degree murder; he faces thirty years to life in prison.

3. From *Initial Referrals to Juvenile Probation in Los Angeles County, January–June 1990: A Cohort Follow-up*, by the Los Angeles County Probation Department; and from interviews with senior Probation Department officials.

CHAPTER 1

1. A complaint of misconduct against Beckstrand and one of her deputies was ultimately dismissed.

2. The Probation Department's study of repeat offenders, referred to by Juvenile Court insiders as the Sixteen Percent Solution, not only showed that many of its efforts are statistically futile, but also that those efforts are primarily aimed at the children least likely to benefit—the most hardened repeat offenders, rather than the neophytes who could still be turned from a life of crime.

Another 1994 study, *The Juvenile Crime Challenge: Making Prevention a Priority*, by a respected California state watchdog agency called the Little Hoover Commission, also criticized these skewed priorities: "Front-line workers decry their inability to cope with the minor juvenile delinquent because of the pressing demands on their time and resources by chronic, violent offenders. This situation is especially distressing since these worst-case juveniles not only soak up resources because of the high cost of their treatment but also are the least likely to be deterred from a life of crime regardless of the treatment options undertaken. Placing a high priority on 'front-end' programs is difficult without new funding but is critical to any successful crime prevention effort."

3. Figures are from the U.S. Justice Department's Office of Juvenile Justice and Delinquency Prevention's 1994 statistical report on the nation's juvenile courts (the report examines the calendar year 1992). A separate study of arrest rates contained in *Juvenile Offenders and Victims*, May 1995, also from the Justice Department, reaches similar conclusions and states: "The proportion of violent crimes committed by juveniles is disproportionately high compared with their share of the U.S. population, and the number of these crimes is growing." The report found that juveniles are responsible for one in five violent crimes, one in three burglaries, and nearly half of all arsons and auto thefts.

4. This figure includes the two sides of Juvenile Court in Los Angeles. The delinquency court, which handles children under the age of eighteen who commit crimes, has ten different courthouse locations, with twenty-eight bench officers (judges and court commissioners). The court handles about 30,000 new prosecutions a year, with about 35,000 kids under supervision as wards of the court at any one time, and conducting about 150,000 hearings a year. The dependency side of the court, which cares for and supervises abused and neglected children, removing them from (or reuniting them with) their biological parents, has twenty-one judges in one courthouse. It takes on about 14,000 new wards every year, with about 48,000 under supervision of the court at any one time. Source: Jim Shepard, Court Administrator, Juvenile Court Services. In some other California jurisdictions and in many other states, the dependency and delinquency functions are not separated, with the same judges handling both types of cases.

CHAPTER 2

1. The 1994 Little Hoover Commission report, *The Juvenile Crime Challenge: Making Prevention a Priority*, notes: "In 1977 status offenders (runaways, truants and incorrigible children) were taken out of the juvenile incarceration system with the goal of keeping them separate from hardened criminals. Once again, local services did not develop to take up the slack and today status offenders receive little of the attention they need until they topple over the brink into delinquency" (p. 59).

The report continues (p. 123): "Juveniles . . . are the critical linchpin in any effort to divert criminals from lifelong predatory careers. The earlier a person is reached with rehabilitation opportunities, the more likely change is to occur and the greater the rewards in crime cost avoidance. Despite this universally accepted credo, California (and the nation as a whole) has placed far more emphasis on dealing with the end product of crime than on prevention and early intervention measures."

2. Delays are a critical problem in Juvenile Court, because children do not respond well to sanctions and discipline unless they are imposed quickly. "The message that

individuals are responsible for the decisions they make and that illegal actions are accompanied by consequences is often lost in today's juvenile justice system. A child may face little more than a lecture for the first half-dozen offenses, tactics that are the hallmark of the adult system are employed to get the youth 'off the hook,' and long delays separate deed from outcome. The stark reality of the impact of the juveniles' actions on their victims and other members of society is also lost in a system that has little room for victim input" (ibid., page viii).

3. The author, in interviews with more than a dozen probation officers and their supervisors, found that overburdened caseloads make most efforts at juvenile supervision, in the words of deputy probation officer Sharon Stegall, "a joke." The problem is by no means unique to Los Angeles. According to the report *State/Local Juvenile Corrections in California—A Systems Perspective* (California Youth Authority, January 11, 1994): "Currently, large numbers of probationers on county caseloads go essentially unsupervised because available resources are no match for the multitude of cases. Minimum supervision/service and 'paper' caseloads predominate; and in general even 'supervised' probationers are rarely seen by a probation officer."

4. Again, the author found this grim outlook common among probation officers interviewed. The Little Hoover Commission report noted: "Front-line workers decry their inability to cope with the minor juvenile delinquent because of the pressing demands on their time and resources by chronic, violent offenders. This situation is especially distressing since these worst-case juveniles not only soak up resources because of the high cost of their treatment but also are the least likely to be deterred from a life of crime regardless of the treatment options undertaken" (p. vii).

CHAPTER 3

1. The focus of many, if not most, recent attempts to reform the juvenile justice system throughout the nation has revolved around making it easier to try kids as adults—a throwback to the days before juvenile court was even conceived, and a direct result of the burgeoning violent crime committed by kids, which the juvenile justice system seems ill equipped to handle. Thanks in part to Ronald Duncan's case, California changed state law so that that kids fourteen and older charged with serious and violent crimes could be shifted to adult court at prosecutors' behest. The law was passed in 1994 and took effect January 1, 1995. By the beginning of 1995, only one state in the nation—Hawaii—still tried all children under sixteen as juveniles.

2. Many studies of juvenile offenders have found common threads in the backgrounds of kids who commit crimes, and these threads tend to be the ones that common sense dictates should be there. The Probation Department's Sixteen Percent study, for example, found that repeat offenders more often tend to come from homes in which only one parent is present (in many cases, the father is never present in the home); from homes where child abuse and/or substance abuse is a problem; and where school attendance and performance is not a priority. Poverty is also a common factor, though not as high on the list. Kids from such homes are considered to be "at risk," meaning they should get increased attention from the system. Often, though, such children are low priorities for the system—until they commit serious crimes.

The importance of having supportive, nonabusive parents in lowering the risk of delinquent and criminal behavior was demonstrated by a fascinating and unusual study conducted by the High/Scope Educational Research Foundation in Michigan over a period of decades beginning in the 1960s (the results of which were reported in the *New York Times* on November 30, 1994). Two groups of toddlers were chosen at random from a poor neighborhood; in one group, the children were sent to a high-quality preschool program, and their parents attended parenting and violence-prevention classes. The control group received neither service. The children were reinterviewed at age twenty-seven. Researchers found that the group that received no preschool and no parenting classes was five times more likely to have serious arrest records.

The full results:

	Preschool/Parenting	No Preschool/No Parenting
Five or more arrests	7%	35%
Had received welfare	59%	80%
Had out-of-wedlock births	57%	83%
Income over $24,000	29%	7%
High school grad	71%	54%
Own a home	36%	13%

3. Plea bargains did not generally exist in the juvenile justice system until the Supreme Court's Gault decision that transformed Juvenile into a mirror image of adult court, where plea bargaining has long served as vital lubrication of the system. In the past, Juvenile Court sentences were determined solely by the judge's estimation of what a child needed. Now, the sentence is determined in large part by agreements between defense attorneys and prosecutors, over which judges have little or no control.

CHAPTER 4

1. Geri Vance provided this account of his childhood, in his writings and in interviews with the author. Court records confirm that he had a chaotic childhood, the fact that his mother was incarcerated for a time, and that he had been removed from his home. Specific details of his upbringing are based solely on Geri's recollections. The author could not locate either of his parents in order to obtain their account of events.

2. In the first five months of 1994, postponements were granted in more than fifteen thousand hearings in Juvenile Court. For 11 percent of these, the reason for the delay cited in the court's minute entries was "FTA"—failure to appear by the juvenile.

3. In an effort to differentiate juvenile proceedings from adult criminal hearings, the founders of the juvenile justice system in California and around the nation tried to create a different series of terms, supposedly to avoid the stigmatizing impact of words such as "defendant," "indictment," "conviction"—even the phrase "guilty as charged" is, technically, not supposed to be used. Using the term "delinquent" rather than "criminal" was supposed to eliminate most of the stigma; instead, the new term developed a stigma just as serious as, and virtually synonymous with, the one it replaced. Still, the system clings to its alternative terminology. Instead of the "defendant," the juvenile is referred to as a "minor." Instead of the DA filing criminal charges, prosecutors file a

"delinquency petition." Instead of a "bail hearing," juveniles get a "detention hearing." Instead of a "preliminary hearing" to determine probable cause, juveniles get a "William M." or an "Edsel P." hearing—names drawn from California court cases decided on appeal (William M. and Edsel P. are the names of minors, their last names reduced to initials in appellate pleadings to protect the confidentiality granted most juveniles, again to avoid stigma). Instead of pronouncing the child guilty, a judge finds "the petition is sustained." Instead of sentencing the child, a "disposition" is imposed.

The most important distinction is that juvenile offenses are part of the civil legal code, not the criminal code. This distinction is confused somewhat, however, because in California, like most states, the juvenile civil code is a mirror image of the adult penal statutes. As the Hoover Commission report, *The Juvenile Crime Challenge* (1994) notes on page 16, "Originally created to be a swift, confidential mechanism for getting youths treatment and services, the juvenile courts operate today much like adult criminal courts because of changes in law, court rulings and public attitudes."

In the wake of burgeoning serious juvenile crime and court decisions granting more rights to children, new laws have been passed that alter the original juvenile codes, shifting the emphasis away from rehabilitation and toward punishment and the protection of society, further blurring the distinctions between juvenile and adult systems. In contemporary juvenile courts, for example, children charged with serious and violent crimes are no longer entitled to confidentiality—the hearings are open to press and public—and many of these children can be transferred to adult court. As such, the alternative terminology used in the juvenile system is less an effective tool to avoid stigma, and more a vestigial organ, like an appendix, with no useful function. System insiders and the kids themselves view the terminology as little more than a lexicon of euphemisms for proceedings that no longer differ substantially from adult criminal matters. And in court, their usage has gradually relaxed—the attorneys talk of guilty pleas, the prosecutors of charges, the judges sometimes slip and sentence a child instead of disposing of him.

CHAPTER 5

1. Shabby treatment of witnesses is endemic in the juvenile system. The Hoover Commission report concludes: "The victim has no role in the courtroom and the confidentiality that cloaks the juvenile in large part keeps the victim in the dark about the case as it proceeds. The result, according to victims' rights organizations, is that citizens who are injured or who suffer damages from the juvenile are 're-injured' by the system and are denied a feeling of resolution. An opportunity is also lost to confront the juvenile with the real-life impact of his actions . . . In adult criminal cases they [victims] may provide input during sentencing hearings—not an option that is open to victims of juvenile crime" (*The Juvenile Crime Challenge*, 1994, p. 76).

2. The California legislature recently changed state law so graffiti on public property such as highway overpasses would be presumed to have been done without permission, eliminating the need to bring highway department officials into court to testify to the obvious. However, prosecutors decried this new law as a half-measure; the legislature ignored their request that the law be changed so that *private* property owners—the only ones who are at risk for retaliation should they testify—be spared from having to come to court to prove that gang graffiti was done without permission.

3. California Welfare and Institutions Code Section 707b states that children sixteen or older who commit one of the following crimes are presumed to be unfit to be
tried as a juvenile: murder, arson of an inhabited building, armed robbery, rape by force
or threat of harm, sodomy by force or threat of harm, lewd acts with children under
fourteen, oral copulation by force or threat of harm, genital or anal penetration by a
foreign object, kidnapping for ransom, kidnapping for purpose of robbery, kidnapping
with bodily harm, assault with intent to murder or attempted murder, assault with a
firearm, assault by any means of force intended to cause great bodily harm, discharge
of a firearm into an inhabited or occupied building, first-degree burglaries and violent
crimes committed against disabled and senior citizens, any felony committed with the
use of a gun, any felony in which the minor personally uses a variety of exotic weapons,
including explosives, nunchucks, billy clubs, dirks and daggers and dart guns, witness
intimidation, influencing testimony, selling a half ounce or more of PCP and several
other dangerous depressant drugs (but not cocaine, methamphetamine, or heroin), any
violent felony committed by a street gang member, escape from any juvenile facility
when great bodily harm is inflicted, torture, and aggravated mayhem. (A year after this
case was resolved, the law was changed to lower the fitness age to fourteen and over for
a shorter list of major crimes.)

4. Section 707 of the California Welfare and Institutions Code governs fitness hearings for juveniles (called waiver hearings or amenability hearings in other states). The
original statute—now called 707 (a)—presumed all kids *were fit* to be tried as juveniles.
It allowed judges to ship kids over sixteen to adult court if they were found to be unfit
under one or more of the five factors—criminal sophistication, potential for rehabilitation, previous delinquent history, success of previous attempts at rehabilitation, and the
gravity of the offense. The question judges had to resolve was whether or not kids were
amenable to treatment as juveniles. Under this test, most children subjected to fitness
hearings were retained in juvenile court.

In 1982, the California legislature—concerned that it was too difficult to try juveniles as adults—created 707 (b) and (c), which stated that juveniles over sixteen accused of serious, violent felonies were presumed to be *unfit* to be tried as juveniles,
exactly the opposite of 707 (a). Failure on any one of the five factors meant transfer to
adult court. For judges to find kids fit, they have to cite specific evidence that overturns
the presumption of unfitness for each of the five factors. Under this standard, most kids
subjected to fitness hearings are transferred to adult court—which was the legislature's
intention. Under 707 (a), now rarely used, the judge has broad discretion in making
this call. Under 707 (b) and (c), the primary decision-maker in the process is the district
attorney, who makes the call at the outset on whether or not to file a fitness motion.

5. "There is little doubt that the ruling was in error and not supported by the evidence," the DA's appellate section later wrote in a memo, stating further that a proper
appeal would be virtually guaranteed to overturn the decision. Records from other cases
at Thurgood Marshall and elsewhere in the system show that appellate courts have
consistently overturned similar decisions.

6. The memo from the DA's appellate division, while finding Dorn's ruling illegal,
explains why no appeal could be pursued. "Research indicates that the prosecution is
barred by double jeopardy from litigating a minor's fitness and transferring his case to
adult court once the minor's petition has been adjudicated. . . . It is crucial that trial
deputies make appropriate objections, indicate the intent to seek review and otherwise
follow code provisions."

CHAPTER 6

1. This figure represents an average, based upon the total number of transfers and the number of days Juvenile Courts are in session. In 1992, the last year for which figures are available, a total of 11,700 children were tried as adults nationwide, according to yearly estimates by the U.S. Justice Department's Office of Juvenile Justice and Delinquency Prevention.

2. In California, the Juvenile Court may be divided into two separate branches, the dependency court, which deals with adoptions, foster children, and abused and neglected children, and the delinquency court, which handles criminal matters and status offenses. Both sections of the court are part of the Superior Court, the principal trial-level court in California. Other jurisdictions—New York, for example—have a single, unified Family Court that handles both types of cases.

3. This account is based on probation reports that detail George's history, a psychological report by Dr. Michael P. Maloney, filed in both juvenile and adult courts, and on the author's interviews with George Trevino. The author was unable to locate George's aunt for an interview.

4. The dependency court eventually released full control of George to the aunt and terminated its jurisdiction over George when he was thirteen.

5. At George's trial in the Norwalk Branch of Los Angeles Superior Court, the prosecution alleged George was a ringleader with Villa; the defense argued he was naïve and had been used by older, hardened criminals. The evidence was unequivocal in showing that a second adult not present at the crime had conceived and planned the robbery, then involved George and Villa.

CHAPTER 7

1. Judge Dorn later explained to the author, as well as to Deputy District Attorney Peggy Beckstrand, that he would not have objected to the presence of the District Attorney's Office, but that inviting prosecutors would have required him to invite the public defender's staffers as well, and he viewed them as obstructions to his brand of reform. Dorn, however, invited both offices to attend subsequent meetings and to help carry out various reforms he wished to pursue, though the public defender's participation was minimal.

2. According to *State/Local Juvenile Corrections in California—A Systems Perspective* (California Youth Authority, January 11, 1994), ineffective probation programs like 654 are becoming increasingly predominant: "Currently, large numbers of probationers on county caseloads go essentially unsupervised because available resources are no match for the multitude of cases. Minimum supervision/service and 'paper' caseloads predominate; and in general even 'supervised' probationers are rarely seen by a probation officer."

3. Repeated efforts to change the law on juvenile gun possession have met with defeat in the California legislature, except for a recent law that makes carrying firearms on school campuses a felony. The failure to make unlawful possession of a firearm by a juvenile a serious offense is at odds with information on the impact firearms have had on juvenile crime. The U.S. Justice Department reports that, in 1976, 59 percent of juvenile homicide offenders killed with a gun; by 1991, the figure was 78 percent.

The department also reports that teen homicides using firearms have quadrupled since 1985.

Meanwhile, a Virginia survey of juvenile inmates found 20 percent reported owning assault rifles, and that youths were more than twice as likely as adults to have carried semiautomatic pistols at crime scenes.

A four-state Justice Department study found that 55 percent of confined juveniles owned a revolver before being locked up, 55 percent owned a semiautomatic handgun, and 51 percent owned a sawed-off shotgun.

A 1993 Harvard University School of Public Health survey of middle and high school youth nationwide, conducted by LH Research, found:

59 percent of students say they can get a gun if they want one.
39 percent know someone killed or wounded by gunfire.
35 percent believe self "somewhat" or "very likely" to die from guns.
15 percent carried a handgun in the last thirty days.
4 percent carried a handgun to school in the last academic year.
9 percent shot a gun at somebody.
13 percent had been seriously threatened with a firearm.
11 percent had been shot at.

A California State Department of Health Services study found that in 1994 a California youth is ten to fifteen times more likely to be murdered by a firearm than his or her counterpart in the 1950s and 1960s.

4. Dorn is not alone on this point. The confidentiality of Juvenile Court, once sacrosanct, has come under increasing fire from prosecutors, police agencies, victims' rights groups, and many judges, who have come to feel an open system might have more impact and be more responsive to public safety. The juvenile defense bar is fighting hard to preserve confidentiality, but in many jurisdictions, this is proving to be a losing battle. In California, the Little Hoover Commission recently recommended that confidentiality be greatly reduced in the system, opening all trials and sentencings for serious crimes involving kids over fourteen, and curtailing the right of such offenders to later have their records sealed. "The present laws are too broad and allow protective cover for too many youths who later continue a life of crime," the report states. "[Confidentiality] has weakened the credibility of the entire system."

CHAPTER 8

1. The account of this in-chambers meeting is based on the author's interviews with Peggy Beckstrand and Judge Roosevelt Dorn.

CHAPTER 9

1. This account of the DAs' meeting is based on the author's interviews with Peggy Beckstrand and Jim Hickey.
2. This is not a new proposal, nor is it one with narrow ideological appeal. No less staunch a child advocate than U.S. Attorney General Janet Reno proposed a similar

restructuring of the juvenile system when she was State Attorney for Dade County, Florida, where the Miami juvenile system was just as swamped as LA's. She wanted a juvenile system that dealt intensively with kids fourteen and under, where the most good could be done in altering a kid's descent into crime. Every older juvenile would go to a specially designed Youthful Offenders Unit of the adult court, where adult laws and punishments applied, though they would be coupled with special programs and intensive supervision designed for older delinquents. It was not an ideal solution, but given limited resources and the backwards priorities now rampant in the juvenile system, it provided the best possible solution to an intractable problem, Reno maintained. The proposal, deemed too radical at the time, has never been enacted.

Critics suggest a possible problem with this two-tiered approach is that it does little to prevent juvenile crime in the first place—it just shifts resources and punishments around the criminal justice system, and keeps juvenile criminals locked up longer with fewer efforts to rehabilitate them. There is no evidence that harsher sentences have decreased juvenile crime. Indeed, the crime rate among older juveniles has continued to soar even after laws were passed that place many of them in adult court.

3. In a speech before the U.S. Senate in 1992, Sen. John Glenn of Ohio cited a survey that listed the top school problems listed by principals in 1940: talking out of turn; chewing gum and making a noise; running in halls; cutting in line; dress code infractions; littering. In 1980, a similar survey of principals found their major concerns had shifted: drug abuse, alcohol abuse, pregnancy, suicide, rape, robbery, assault.

4. According to juvenile delinquency expert Peter W. Greenwood of the RAND Corporation, in testimony before California's Little Hoover Commission, the justice system has yet to find a satisfactory middle ground in dealing with child criminals. In his February 28, 1994, testimony, Greenwood said:

"Many juvenile killings appear to take place without any rational cause or purpose. It is this latter characteristic that has caused some observers to question the whole concept of rehabilitation upon which the juvenile justice system is presumably based. Another concern expressed by many observers is that, in the name of rehabilitation or protecting the interests of the minor, hardened young criminals are let off much more leniently than would be the case if they were treated as adults. . . . The most difficult aspect of any examination of the juvenile justice system is maintaining the perspective that the subjects being dealt with are both children and criminals at the same time, with all the limitations and vulnerabilities which the first label implies and all of the problems and risks implied by the second. Reconciling these competing demands is the most difficult task confronted by juvenile justice policy makers."

5. The need for such reform, coupled with the sort of firm treatment of serious offenders envisioned by the DA's two-tiered plan, has been championed by many juvenile advocates, including Attorney General Janet Reno. The Hoover Commission report urges similar changes: "The challenge is to have a system that functions well for both ends of the spectrum: one that takes strong intervention measures when they are most likely to be productive while at the same time protecting society when the chances of rehabilitation are dim. The present juvenile justice system falls short at both ends of the spectrum. . . . There is little time, attention or remedy for the novice juvenile delinquent" (*The Juvenile Crime Challenge*, September 1994, p. 69).

6. James Q. Wilson, professor of management and public policy at the University of California, Los Angeles, and a nationally recognized expert on crime and delinquency, wrote in the December 30, 1994, *New York Times:* "There are one million people in

prison. We are not going to change them. We have boys on the streets; we can't change them. So we have to push the intervention back to where we know it is possible to make a difference: in childhood. . . . The crucial turning point is the third grade. It is not an iron law. There are a few late bloomers who turn to crime in their teens. But if kids are going to do badly in school, third grade is where it starts . . . : The main goal in welfare reform ought to be saving the children, not necessarily making mothers work."

In the same issue of the *Times*, Judge Judith Sheindlin, supervising judge of the Manhattan Family Court, made a similar point in an essay: "I think by age fifteen there is a small number of kids who, for whatever depravations they have suffered, are cooked, as my grandmother would have said. They are gone. Whatever you do is not going to make a difference. . . . I think the solution is to pare down the money we spend on those kids . . . [and] invest in the vast majority of kids who come from the same environment and are right on the cusp. . . . People will say, You are stigmatizing the bad kids. Well, if you have 36 kids in a classroom and four are throwing chairs at the teacher, you have to excise them. Otherwise, all will be lost. This is war."

7. Sukoda's study confirms long-known principles, though his promises to be more detailed and far-reaching than its predecessors. In the 1972 landmark "Wolfgang Study" in Philadelphia, research showed that 18 percent of all juvenile delinquents accounted for 62 percent of all offenses. More recently, a widely publicized study in Orange County, California, just south of LA, found its hard-core repeat offenders were made up of 8 to 12 percent. Orange County is also attempting to use a profile of repeat offenders to identify them early in their delinquency careers, so far with mixed results.

8. By contrast, kids who get arrested who do not fit the 16 percent profile can be released with little or no supervision or court action, the study suggests. Statistically, most of them will never get in trouble again regardless of what the court does—even if the court does nothing. In time, in theory, juvenile crime should decline dramatically with this reordering of priorities. In Sukoda's vision, the role of Juvenile Court shrinks as prevention programs take hold, not because more kids are booted into the adult system, but because more kids are stopped from committing crimes in the first place.

9. From *The Juvenile Crime Challenge: Making Prevention a Priority* (California's Little Hoover Commission, September 1994, p. vii):

"Despite the universal belief among experts that the only hope of halting or diminishing juvenile crime is in taking appropriate steps before a youth is entrenched in a delinquency pattern, early-intervention programs have all but disappeared as fiscally strapped county and state departments have made selective budget cuts in the past decade. Front-line workers decry their inability to cope with the minor juvenile delinquent because of the pressing demands on their time and resources by chronic, violent offenders. This situation is especially distressing since these worst-case juveniles not only soak up resources because of the high cost of their treatment but also are the least likely to be deterred from a life of crime regardless of the treatment options undertaken. Placing a high priority on 'front-end' programs is difficult without new funding but is critical to any successful crime prevention effort."

Choosing which end of the system to emphasize is no small issue in a state like California, where the governor is committed to an accelerating prison population, where more per capita is spent on prisons than on public education, and an enormous $2.8 billion penal system sucks hundreds of millions of dollars from grade schools, state colleges, parks, recreation, medical care, everything that might keep kids from getting involved in crime. State universities and public schools, once the envy of the nation, have been severely cut while prison spending in California has grown to record levels every year.

The effectiveness of California's current order of priorities has long been in question, given the recidivism rates seen in juvenile penal institutions around the nation. In 1978, the National Advisory Commission on Criminal Justice Standards and Goals reached this conclusion about juvenile prisons in a report entitled *Correctional Institutions*: "Institutions do succeed in punishing but they don't deter. They protect the community temporarily, but the protection does not last. They relieve the community of responsibility by removing the young offender, but they make successful integration unlikely. They change the committed offender, but the change is more likely to be negative than positive." More recent studies of youth prison systems around the country confirm this viewpoint, showing recidivism rates ranging from 50 to 75 percent.

CHAPTER 10

1. Richard Dent, forty-four, was killed in the attack. Court records and police reports show that two other gang members actually tackled and held Dent, while another knifed him repeatedly—something Elias may not have even known until the police arrested him and told him someone had died. (Still, Elias should have figured out what was about to happen—the same knife-happy gang member who killed Dent had earlier that night dished out a serious but nonfatal stomach wound to someone else they stopped on the street to rob.) Legally, Elias was still guilty of murder because he participated in the fatal attack, but the DA agreed he deserved less time than those who did the actual killing, particularly as one of them, fourteen-year-old Jane Martin, remained in the juvenile system and would be released at age twenty-five, along with the fifteen-year-old getaway driver, whose participation in the crime was also greater than Elias's. The two boys most responsible for Dent's death were over sixteen and will receive twenty-five years to life in prison; a sixth gang member, a girl whose involvement was roughly identical to Elias's, agreed to testify for the prosecution under a grant of immunity and walked free. Such divergent outcomes are common in a justice system that makes chronological age the primary factor, satisfying neither the proponents of more punishment nor those who seek more attempts at rehabilitation.

2. In Los Angeles, only eight out of every thousand juveniles prosecuted as delinquents are charged with criminal homicide. The ratio is considerably smaller nationwide, just over two out of a thousand—which adds up to 2,700 juvenile murderers out of the 1.5 million kids prosecuted annually in juvenile courts around the country.

These lethal numbers are still shockingly high, of course—the United States is the world capital for teen killers, and LA accounts for nearly one out of ten of them. And the numbers have gotten worse, with the growth of juvenile violent crime rates in recent years (up 68 percent between 1988 and 1992, and 165 percent since 1985) far exceeding violent crime increases by adults. In the past decade, Juvenile Court has seen such an upsurge in acts of extreme violence by young males—and more recently, by young females—that few can doubt the urgent need for solutions.

Still, when all is said and done, murder remains a very small piece of the booming business conducted in Juvenile Court, and cases like Ronald Duncan's an even tinier part. In Los Angeles, fewer than 6 percent of juvenile murder cases involve kids under age sixteen—about fifteen to twenty cases a year. This represents about .05 percent of delinquency cases in LA—hardly a number on which to base wholesale reform of the system.

Proponents, however, argue that the numbers are high enough to warrant action even though the statistical impact may be small. In the past five years, an average of just under eighty-nine kids a year have been sent to the California Youth Authority by juvenile courts from throughout the state for murders committed when the offender was fourteen or fifteen. If the fitness law had been lower, these kids could have been tried in adult court, supporters of a lower fitness law say.

But there is a flaw in this argument: The proponents assume that such children *would* be tried in adult court if the fitness age was lowered, an unwarranted assumption, since juvenile judges still have the power to find kids fit even when the law allows transfer to adult court. During the same five-year period, an average of 152 kids a year who were sixteen or seventeen at the time they committed murder—and were therefore eligible for adult sentences under existing laws—were still treated as juveniles and committed to CYA by juvenile courts throughout California. It is reasonable to assume that an even higher percentage of younger juveniles would be found fit.

(Statistics and percentages for Los Angeles County are drawn from 1993 statistics maintained by the Los Angeles County District Attorney. National percentages are based on estimates in *Juvenile Court Statistics* 1991, by the U.S. Justice Department's Office of Juvenile Justice and Delinquency Prevention. The California Youth Authority provided statistics on the age of juveniles committed to CYA for homicide.)

CHAPTER 11

1. The crisis in money and manpower in probation is well documented, nationwide and in California, where the Little Hoover Commission reports: "Between 1983 and 1992, adult and juvenile probation caseloads increased 73 percent while the number of probation officers increased only 24 percent . . . [and] the probation department's share of county funds declined 9 percent."

2. California, with the highest juvenile incarceration rate of any state (in a nation with the highest rate among developed countries), has a 50 percent rate of return on the fifteen thousand youths it incarcerates in the California Youth Authority at any one time, according to the CYA. Other studies suggest a higher figure. A 1989 survey by the National Council on Crime and Delinquency found that 70 percent of CYA inmates were arrested for a new crime within 12 months of their release, while 61 percent ended up reincarcerated. Other juvenile prison systems report recidivism rates ranging as high as 75 percent in New York State. The effectiveness of juvenile incarceration has been challenged in recent years by studies that suggest probation and other "rehabilitative" programs have better performance with lower cost.

In "Reaffirming Rehabilitation in Juvenile Justice" (*Youth & Society*, September 1993), Dan Macallair, Center on Juvenile and Criminal Justice, writes: "During the 1980s, new evidence emerged suggesting that the demise of rehabilitation was premature. A growing number of studies indicates the rehabilitative intervention is effective in de-escalating criminal behavior. Various well-designed interventions reduce the severity and frequency of delinquency and alter the cycle that leads to adult crime. . . . Although rehabilitation does not eliminate recidivism, it is more effective than correctional institutions in reducing the rate and seriousness of criminal behavior."

3. Most California jurisdictions outside Los Angeles County do not have such extensive networks of county-run camps, and so they tend to rely to a greater degree on contracts with private programs and institutions. Supporters of the LA camp system say the program is both cost effective and successful at what it does—placing delinquents in stable, safe, rigorous environments with structure and traditional values. But critics—particularly in the Public Defender's Office—suggest that LA is missing out on some of the best and most innovative programs for juveniles around the country by sending so many kids to the county-run camps. They point to a highly successful and much-imitated program in Pennsylvania that takes in hardened offenders, educates them with a prep-school-quality program, and has a very low recidivism rate—all for about the same monthly cost as a stay in one of LA's camps. Yet, Los Angeles will not recommend sending any of its delinquents there.

An apparent conflict of interest does exist within the Probation Department, since POs must recommend a sentence most likely to benefit a delinquent, while the department has a vested interest in sending the most kids possible to its in-house camps, in order to preserve its budget. Sending kids to other programs would be like giving customers to a competing business. The Probation Department has a de facto policy against recommending (and paying for) private programs outside the Los Angeles area. As a result, in most cases, only kids with parents capable of paying for private rehabilitation programs such as the one in Pennsylvania can elude this policy.

4. The September 1994 report by the Little Hoover Commission on California's juvenile justice system makes this observation about CYA facilities: "Gang activity and individual aggression are able to flourish in crowded dormitory settings. . . . The safety of wards cannot be assured."

CYA statistics show in 1993, there were 277 assaults by wards on CYA staff (93 with weapons); 1,090 assaults by wards on other wards (140 with weapons); 97 staff injuries; 410 ward injuries. Pepper spray and a chemical warfare agent called CS are used to subdue and incapacitate kids in CYA—some 2,700 kids a year are sprayed with these "chemical restraints." In the five years leading up to and including 1993, seven kids in CYA have committed suicide.

In interviews with the author, teenagers who have been incarcerated at CYA stated that gang activity, violence, sexual assault, and, to a lesser extent, drug use flourish in the youth prison system. While some of the facilities have the feel of campuses, others are grim, high-security lockups. Waiting lists for substance abuse programs and other therapeutic and rehabilitative services tend to be extremely long—longer than many offenders' sentences. Most juvenile judges in Los Angeles—as well as caseworkers in the CYA system—view CYA as a last resort for youths who have little hope of straightening out, a dire alternative that compares favorably only to adult prison.

5. Los Angeles County Juvenile Court makes this admission an average of five times each workday, 1,200 times a year. Out of the 8,664 juveniles housed at CYA at the end of 1993, 42 percent came from LA—a tragically high rate of failure, given that LA County is home to only 30 percent of the state's children.

6. CYA figures are as of January 1994. Male domination of juvenile crime of all sorts—serious and minor—is also pronounced, though not as overwhelmingly. Eighty-two percent of the nation's 1.5 million juvenile offenders in 1992 were boys, according to the *Sourcebook of Criminal Justice Statistics*—1992 (Bureau of Justice Statistics, U.S. Department of Justice).

364 EDWARD HUMES

CHAPTER 12

1. The intake problem in Los Angeles grew worse shortly after Keesha's arrest, when earthquake damage to Central Juvenile Hall destroyed its ability to perform the intake function. Los Padrinos had to take over, doubling its intake load, accepting new detainees, then shipping some of them later on for housing at Central—a logistical nightmare of delays and misplaced children. Eighteen months after the January 1994 earthquake, Central intake was still down.

2. When prosecutors file petitions in Juvenile Court, they are either detained, which requires that the kid be locked up, then tried relatively quickly, or nondetained, which allows the child to remain at home, with a much longer amount of time allowed before the case is brought to trial. In this case, the boy was arrested on a nondetained petition. In order to put him in Juvenile Hall, Judge Dorn had to make a legal finding that there had been a change in circumstances in the boy's life that required his incarceration for his own protection and the safety of the community. Dorn found that his truancy was the change in circumstances, but as his lawyer pointed out, that was no change at all—he had not been going to school before his arrest, either. Once again, it seemed to be a case of Dorn doing the right thing—taking steps to get a truant kid back in school—rather than the precisely legal thing.

3. From the author's interviews with Deputy District Attorneys Tom Higgins and Peggy Beckstrand.

CHAPTER 13

1. National statistics compiled by the U.S. Justice Department show that while white youth make up the majority of delinquents, African-American youth have delinquency rates more than twice as great. For every thousand youth at risk for referral to a Juvenile Court, 41.7 whites are actually found to be delinquent; the rate for African-Americans is 107.8. (For this study, the Justice Department includes Hispanics with whites, so separate figures are not available.)

In Los Angeles, racial and ethnic disparities are even more pronounced, with the Juvenile Court population dominated by Hispanics. The Sixteen Percent study that examined six months' worth of first-time offenders found that 16 percent of them were white (white juveniles made up about 27 percent of the total juvenile population in LA County at the time), blacks accounted for 24 percent of first-time offenders (and about 12 percent of the juvenile population), and Hispanics accounted for 56 percent of the first-time offenders (and just under 50 percent of the juvenile population).

2. The account of the in-chambers discussion is based upon the author's interviews with James Cooper and Peggy Beckstrand.

CHAPTER 14

1. One of the best measures of how hard a judge is working is how often he orders continuances on his own motions, rather than at the behest of defense or prosecution. Systemwide, for the first five months of 1994, about 20 percent of all continuances in Los Angeles Juvenile Court were on the court's own motion. Workaholic Judge Dorn's

percentage was under 15. But 81 percent of delays in Judge Luke's courtroom were at his own behest, a continuance rate unrivaled by his peers.

Trials are another good measure. During the same five months, Judge Dorn had 545 trials scheduled, and managed to reach verdicts in 39 percent of them, a startlingly high rate, especially because his trial workload is much higher than the average judge. Systemwide, the rate of bringing trials to a conclusion hovered near 33 percent, with the balance continued to a future date. Judge Luke, with 111 fewer trials scheduled than Judge Dorn, only managed to conclude 17 percent of them during that five-month period, and all but a handful of those were through quick plea bargains rather than full-blown trials.

2. Judge Luke later transferred to adult Civil Court.

CHAPTER 15

1. "The presumption that sending juveniles to adult court is a tougher response to crime is not necessarily borne out. The reality of the current system . . . is that youths sent to adult court 1) sometimes are not convicted at all because a jury cannot bring themselves to find someone so young guilty; 2) sometimes are put on felony probation when the juvenile court would have incarcerated them; 3) may benefit from a plea bargain designed to avoid the cost or uncertainty of a trial; 4) may be sentenced to a determinate period and earn half-off credit for good behavior in the adult system when they would have spent a greater time incarcerated in the California Youth Authority" (*The Juvenile Crime Challenge: Making Prevention a Priority*, California's Little Hoover Commission, September 1994, p. 83).

CHAPTER 16

1. Crime rates have declined slightly in the last two years—leveling off at a perilously high level after years of growth—but most experts in 1994 believe this is a temporary lull in a storm that will rage for decades. Based on recent acceleration in juvenile crime rates, and factoring in the growth in the nation's juvenile population that census data show will occur, Shay Belchik, administrator of the Justice Department's Office of Juvenile Justice and Delinquency Prevention, made this prediction in a recent report: "By the year 2010 the number of juvenile arrests for a violent crime will more than double and the number of juvenile arrests for murder will increase nearly 150%."

Other experts make similar assessments. James Alan Fox, dean of the College of Criminal Justice at Northeastern University, said at the 1995 conference of the American Association for the Advancement of Science: "The really bad news is that the worst is yet to come. I believe we are on the verge of a crime wave that will last out the century. Unless we act today, I truly believe we will have a blood bath when all these kids group up. . . . There are 40 million children in this country right now under the age of 10. By the year 2005, the number of teenagers in the U.S. will increase by 23 percent, which will undoubtedly increase the levels of violence."

All of these predictions will turn out to be wrong—hugely wrong. Juvenile crime will drop sharply and stay well below early 1990s levels for the next two decades. But the false predictions and ensuing drumbeat to dismantle juvenile court protections would lead to more and younger children tried and sentenced as adults nationwide. These "reforms" would remain in place long after their rationale was shown to be a mistake.

2. Statistics are from *Juvenile Court Statistics 1992*, and *Juvenile Offenders and Victims: A Focus on Violence, 1995*, both by the U.S. Justice Department's Office of Juvenile Justice and Delinquency Prevention; and the *Bureau of Justice Statistics Sourcebook*. The same funnel holds true for the state of California (247,000 arrests in 1992, with only 64,000—26 percent—resulting in actual consequences) and Los Angeles (50,000 referrals to the Probation Department, but only 13,000—26 percent—sentenced to formal probation, foster care, or detention).

CHAPTER 17

1. Ronald's lawyer, James Cooper, spent much of the disposition hearing trying to undo the damaging psychiatric report that he initially requested. He said the daily beatings occurred only while Ronald was in second grade, when his behavior was particularly bad; that it was never actually proven that Ronald possessed cocaine at school; that the fire-setting involved igniting some gasoline on a pond and had done no damage; and that Ronald had joined a gang in Juvenile Hall only for protection against other inmates who had threatened him.

EPILOGUE

1. Blinky is Elias's gang name; Clanton Street Locos is the name of his street gang.
2. Uncles, aunts, cousins (male), cousins (female).
3. Grandfather.
4. According to Elias, this is Spanish slang for a gang conflict.
5. Grandmothers.
6. Busted, locked up.

CHAPTER 18

1. Statistics provided by the Los Angeles Police Department and the Los Angeles School Police Department.
2. "When Youth Violence Spurred 'Superpredator' Fear," *New York Times*, April 6, 2014. DiIulio briefly served as a senior advisor on faith-based initiatives to President George W. Bush, but resigned after finding the administration too dominated by staffers he famously referred to as "Mayberry Machiavellis" and joined the faculty of the University of Pennsylvania.
3. The charges are almost always provoked by a particularly outrageous case. In Illinois, for example, hundreds of kids will be tried as adults because an eleven-year-old and a twelve-year-old in Chicago dangled five-year-old Eric Morse from a fourteenth-floor window, then dropped him to his death, for refusing to steal candy for them.

INDEX